THE
WAR INDUSTRIES
BOARD

THE
WAR INDUSTRIES
BOARD

Business–Government Relations during World War I

ROBERT D. CUFF

The Johns Hopkins University Press

Baltimore and London

The publication of this book has been aided by a grant from the Social Science Research Council of Canada, using funds provided by the Canada Council.

Manufactured in the United States of America

The Johns Hopkins University Press, Baltimore, Maryland 21218
The Johns Hopkins University Press Ltd., London

Library of Congress Catalog Card Number 72-4022
ISBN 0-8018-1360-3

Library of Congress Cataloging in Publication data will be found on the last printed page of this book.

FOR MARY LOU

CONTENTS

PREFACE

Although I have made the evolution and operation of the War Industries Board the empirical and narrative focus of this book, I have not attempted a definitive study of that agency. My purpose is rather to analyze some broader historical problems for which aspects of the WIB's history provide illustrative material. The ultimate goal is to develop and explore interpretations of the political economy of war, not to detail an institutional life. The WIB is examined in terms of three interrelated problems central to industrial mobilization during the war: (1) the motives, methods, and values of businessmen in government; (2) the nature of business-government relations; and (3) the structure and impact of an emergency state bureaucracy. A partial account of only one segment of Wilsonian war government offers an admittedly narrow base for generalization, but nevertheless it is my hope that readers will find here some insights into the broader dimensions of America's political economy during the Great War.

I have incurred many debts in the course of writing this book. Robert A. Lively stimulated my initial interest in the subject and guided me through its Ph.D. stage at Princeton University. His intellectual insights and practical injunctions are as valuable to me now as they were then. My former colleagues at the University of Rochester provided a remarkably exciting intellectual environment in which to rethink and revise the dissertation. Louis Galambos proffered not one but two critiques of the entire book in manuscript form, coupling his incisive suggestions with a warm encouragement I have very much appreciated. Melvin Urofsky also contributed much to the study by conversation, by reading the entire manuscript, and by his own scholarship. My colleagues at York have in conversation triggered fruitful lines of thought. Comments by Gabriel Kolko have been particularly provocative and helpful. All these people, in company with the scholars cited in the notes, have shaped and improved my work. Needless to say, I alone am responsible for its shortcomings.

A Woodrow Wilson dissertation fellowship funded the initial research; the subsequent generosity of Princeton University and the University of Rochester helped me carry it forward. This crucial financial assistance allowed me to visit a number of libraries and archives and to benefit from their resourceful and friendly staffs. Sarah Jackson and John Taylor of the National Archives and William Mobley of the Library of Congress have put me especially in their debt. I would also like to thank John Eisenberg, who searched through the papers of Kenneth D. McKeller in the Memphis Public Library several years ago.

I am grateful for the permission granted by the Yale University Library to use quotations from the Edward M. House Papers, by the University of Missouri Library to use quotations from the George N. Peek Papers, by the Princeton University Library to use quotations from the Bernard M. Baruch Papers, and by Mrs. Katherine Graham to use quotations from the Eugene Meyer, Jr., Oral History. The editors of the *Business History Review*, the *Canadian Annual Historical Association Report*, the *Princeton University Library Chronicle* and the *Review of Politics* have graciously allowed me to draw upon material which first appeared in their journals. And Thomas Nelson & Sons (Canada) Ltd. and the Macmillan Company have kindly consented to let me draw upon my work in *War and Society in North America*, edited by J. L. Granatstein and Robert D. Cuff, copyright 1971; and *Building the Organizational Society*, edited by Jerry Israel, copyright 1972.

The book has been published with the help of a grant from the Social Science Research Council of Canada, using funds provided by the Canada Council. And I have received thoughtful editorial direction throughout from the staff of The Johns Hopkins University Press.

Finally, I should like to thank Mary Lou, my wife. She has been part of this study from the beginning. Her support and encouragement have been vitally important to its completion. And even now, three children and a book later, she retains the patience, understanding, and good humor which made it possible to begin. The book is dedicated to her.

INTRODUCTION

The Great War produced an unparalleled expansion of the state in the United States, as it did in every country under arms. An administrative army marched into Washington before a military force sailed overseas. Networks of agencies spanned the nation and cut deeply downward through the country's social structure. State agencies organized and administered social and economic functions normally left to private, uncoordinated decision-making. The Committee on Public Information, the Food and Fuel Administrations, the Allied Purchasing Commission, the United States Railroad Administration, the War Finance Corporation, and other wartime experiments produced the greatest concentration of public bureaucratic power to that point in American history.

This book is about the origins, evolution, and operation of one segment of this emergent administrative state—the War Industries Board, the major civilian agency for industrial mobilization. Established as a subordinate part of the Council of National Defense at the end of July 1917, almost four months after America entered the war, it was the outgrowth of a number of earlier, less satisfactory arrangements. The original members of the board were Frank A. Scott, a Cleveland manufacturer, chairman; Bernard M. Baruch, a Wall Street speculator, commissioner of raw materials; Robert S. Lovett, chairman of the Union Pacific Railroad, commissioner of priorities; Robert S. Brookings, retired millionaire and former president of Washington University in St. Louis, commissioner of finished products; Hugh A. Frayne, an American Federation of Labor organizer, commissioner of labor; and Colonel Palmer E. Pierce from the army and Rear Admiral F. F. Fletcher from the navy. The WIB's duties were defined as follows:

The Board will act as a clearing house for the war industry needs of the Government, determine the most effective ways of meeting them and the best means

1

and methods of increasing production, including the creation or extension of industries demanded by the emergency, the sequence and relative urgency of the needs of the different Government services, and consider price factors, and in the first instance the industrial and labor aspects of the problems involved and the general questions affecting the purchase of commodities.[1]

The WIB traveled a rocky road in subsequent months. The presence of the two military representatives implies a promise of cooperation from the services, and indicates further how the board had to operate in a "twilight zone" between public and private institutions, depending greatly on goodwill from both sides. Its effectiveness also had to depend on the degree of harmony achieved among its various functional units such as priorities, finished products, and so on. Without synchronization of its internal operations, it could hardly act as an agency for national economic coordination. Its status as a subordinate and advisory agency of the Council of National Defense compounded these early difficulties.

From the summer of 1917 to the spring of 1918 the board was engaged primarily in a struggle for survival. Lacking full cooperation from the military services and full coordination of its own operations, it floundered badly and found it impossible to fulfill its July mandate. It reached safety in the spring of 1918 only because of the strength of its semi-autonomous divisions and President Wilson's decision to strengthen it. As part of his response to pressure from all sides to improve the administration of the war program, Wilson elevated Bernard Baruch to the chairmanship of the WIB on March 4, 1918, and personally defined Baruch's duties as well as those of the board. The president did not actually call for a drastic change in administrative procedures, but he did concentrate final authority in Baruch's hands for all the board's operations except price fixing, a subject which fell to a separate Price Fixing Committee under Robert Brookings (with Baruch as ex officio member).

Although this action virtually divorced the board from its parent body, the Council of National Defense, and made it an administrative agency reporting directly to the president, the formal act of separation did not occur until passage of the Overman act, legislation which gave the president the right to reorganize his administration at will. This act became law on May 20, 1918, and on May 24, Baruch suggested that to facilitate the WIB's ability to compete for appropriations, the president should issue an executive order making the board a separate administrative agency. Wilson signed a statement to this effect and the WIB at last became officially free from the CND, and with a new-found vitality which stayed with it till the end of the war.

[1] Richard H. Hippelheuser, ed., *American Industry in the War: A Report of the War Industries Board, March 1921* (New York: Prentice-Hall, 1941), p. 21.

One of the central purposes of this book is to reexamine the motives, methods, and values of the businessmen in government most directly associated with the evolution and operation of the WIB. While I admit to a revisionist perspective on this subject, my intention is not to debase the dollar-a-year men of the war, or to give credence to the "merchants of death" cry of the 1930s. On the contrary, I have found the key WIB administrators remarkable men in many ways—in their foresight, their broad vision, their aggressiveness, and their managerial expertise. Men like Scott, Baruch, Lovett, and Brookings exhibited very different styles in their march to high office and were divided over many issues along the way, but it is more useful for the purpose of introduction to stress the elements they held in common, especially with respect to their ideology and methods of organization. No single individual exhibited all the features described below, but all of them shared a sufficient number to permit their characterization as a group.

The major business administrators in the WIB aimed to create the kind of institutional order that would both effectively mobilize the nation's resources for war and protect the industrial economy's basic structure and character for peace. In the course of this work they displayed a uniform sensitivity to the interdependent nature of a society and economy at war; they were more aware of the system's requirements than many military officials and federal politicians, or even the business specialists along the periphery of their own organization and the various industrial representatives who negotiated with them in Washington.

To obtain their dual goal the WIB men intervened on a variety of fronts, including the national economy, the state, society at large, and international politics. In all cases, individuals and groups had to be either persuaded or forced to cooperate in producing those conditions conducive to a smoothly functioning political economy. Thus within industry itself individualism and competition had to give way to associationalism and cooperation. The greater the degree of organization in any single industry, the easier the task of coordinating the industrial structure as a whole. And just as a strategy of systematization and stabilization required coordination of industry, so it also demanded a correlation between the country's industrial structure and other segments of the mobilization program, especially the chaotic emergency state system. The traditional military departments occupied a critical segment in this administrative group, although emergency agencies like the United States Railroad Administration and Shipping Board also required serious attention. Likewise, pressures from the state's political components—Congress and the courts—had to be adjusted to industry's requirements and the demands of war. The WIB's business administrators had to move very warily as far as Congress and the general public were concerned, lest traditional public hostility to intimate business-government relations interfere with the integrated system they were struggling to create. As a group of middlemen between American industry and Congress, the business administrators demanded administrative centralization and great power for themselves so as to be better able to secure their positions as champions and protectors of America's economic structure. Only insofar as they maintained control could they ensure that those hostile to or ignorant of industry's broad needs would not obstruct their quest for institutional order.

The international dimension of the war, which is not treated in this study, provided a fourth challenge to the search for institutional coordination. The demands upon American industry came from abroad as well as from home, and Allied needs had to be somehow balanced against public and private requirements in the United States. Since neither the WIB men nor their colleagues in industry could ignore the fact that peace would transform wartime allies into postwar competitors, international cooperation for war had also to be balanced against protective advantages for the peace. The widespread belief on both sides of the Atlantic that the armistice would inaugurate a fierce battle for markets doubled the determination of businessmen in the WIB to correlate the short-run demands of war with the long-run interests of American industry's position in the postwar world.

In their drive for order, the WIB men pursued two methods of organization which were both complementary and contradictory at the same time. The first was institutional, the second rested on a system of shared values. The administration's business advisors sought a formal, rational authority for their work which could be embodied in a properly bureaucratic organization. This would give them the statutory and administrative means for economic control and the kind of coercive power required to force holdouts into line. Since some amount of formal, institutional authority was obviously necessary, if only to protect an informal cooperative system against minority disruption, the question for business mobilizers was one only of degree. Their chief challenge in this respect lay in the fact that while the institutional method was administratively attractive, it was also politically dangerous. For inherent in its very logic was a trend toward central bureaucracy, independent state power, and public planning which by implication admitted the failure of privately led, capitalist organization to perform adequately in a national crisis. This development, in turn, supported those who proposed strict state control of business for war and peace. Businessmen in government were willing to modify substantially the role of the state in a war economy, but they were not about to change the fundamental nature of the political economy itself. Indeed, one of their central ideological aims throughout the war was to prove what private corporate leadership could achieve in conjunction with a friendly, business-dominated state agency. Any trend toward an independent bureaucratic power for the state ultimately conflicted with this goal.

The other method which the business administrators embraced, and which they found far more congenial, rested on a system of shared values. WIB officials brought to their side men and associations committed to a similar ideology: the cooperative ethic in industry, systematic coordination, business-government cooperation, and so on. To recruit trustworthy and sympathetic individuals and business groups held out the promise of maximum administrative reach with a minimum of formal, public organization. Here ideology and necessity coincided to a great degree, for an emergency state bureaucracy had inevitably to rely heavily on private groups in public adminstration. Still, it was the logical result of this method that the WIB men tended to move in an antibureaucratic direction—toward a series of haphazard, informal, personal agreements among men of goodwill, among whom the gentleman's code carried more weight than the administrative sanctions of the state. Not only did this method conflict with the bureaucratic imperatives of modern war, but it also threatened to reduce its proponents to little more than the prisoners of their various clienteles. Under those circumstances how could the WIB possibly coordinate and protect America's industrial structure?

Each method then held threats as well as promises and the WIB men moved uneasily between them, sometimes veering toward the one, sometimes toward the other, depending upon the issues and stakes involved. In some ways, theirs was a rear-guard battle against the very logic of war administration as they tried to sustain a system founded upon ideology in a situation tending toward strict bureaucratic control. In another sense, however, they led unwilling groups within the economy and the state out of a disorganized, individualistic past into a more integrated, disciplined future. Businessmen in government groped for some middle way which would combine the traditional virtues of the free enterprise system as they understood it with the national planning required by war. The outcome, as might be expected, was a bundle of paradoxes and contradictions which cannot be described as either free enterprise or public planning.

Woodrow Wilson shared many of the assumptions held by his business advisors. With his great talent for intellectual synthesis the president had already helped fashion an ideology of liberalism which subsumed both the idea of friendly cooperation between business and government and an ambiguity toward the role of the state. Moreover, the institutional manifestation of this ideological paradigm was already evident in a general way in the banking and antitrust reforms of his first term. In the debate over both the Federal Reserve system and the Federal Trade Commission Wilson had clearly tried to balance the powerful, competing political and business interests who represented their struggle for power in the rhetorical slogans of centralization versus decentralization and public regulation versus private control. The institutional result in the case of the Federal Reserve was an administrative arrangement wherein a central, state agency loosely coordinated private decision-making in the banking community. And to take charge of the Federal Reserve Board and Federal Trade Commission Wilson chose administrators who could live with this kind of institutional and ideological compromise. Similarly, during the war, Wilson chose for his top administrative posts men who not only were loyal to him personally but also shared his values and principles and sympathized with his quest to adapt nineteenth century values to a modern industrial economy in the crisis of twentieth century war.

The kinds of answers which Wilson and WIB administrators gave to administrative questions have an intrinsic interest, but they are also significant as reflections of the broader theme of business-government relations in these years. The ways in which business volunteers solved specific methodological questions interacted as both cause and effect in business-government relationships. In conceptualizing the WIB experience from this perspective I have leaned heavily upon the work of students of business behavior in the prewar period. Robert Wiebe has provided insights into the multitude of issue-oriented interest groups that composed the business community on the eve of the war; William Appleman Williams and James Weinstein have illustrated the popularity of corporatist ideas among business ideologues; Samuel Hays has revealed the antidemocratic impulse behind business-sponsored administrative reform; and Gabriel Kolko has shown how business support for an expanding federal bureaucracy can reflect the structural needs of fragmented sectors of the national economy.[2] Of course, as important and useful as these models are, no one of them can comprehend the total range of business-government relationships during the war. For one thing, the historical context shifted dramatically under the forces of modern war and revolutionary crisis. The very structure of the state altered sharply as emergency agencies like the WIB assumed unprecedented significance in the industrial economy. Since the war was an occasion for radical readjustments it is not historically accurate simply to extrapolate from models of business-government relations derived from a nation at peace. At the same time, to study business-government relations in the crucible of war affords a kind of comparative perspective from which to assess the strengths and weaknesses of various approaches to a study of business-government relations for periods of either war or peace, or both.

There is one strain in recent comments about the war experience with which this book is at variance and which deserves special mention. It is the tendency of some first to conceptualize the political economy of the war years as a fully integrated institutional order and then to make it a paradigm for future histori-

[2] Robert H. Wiebe, *Businessmen and Reform: A Study of the Progressive Movement* (Cambridge, Mass.: Harvard University Press, 1962); William Appleman Williams, *The Contours of American History* (Chicago: Quadrangle, 1966); James Weinstein, *The Corporate Ideal in the Liberal State* (Boston: Beacon, 1968); Samuel P. Hays, "The Politics of Reform in Municipal Government in the Progressive Era," *Pacific Northwest Quarterly* 55 (October 1964): 157–69; Gabriel Kolko, *The Triumph of Conservatism: A Reinterpretation of American History, 1900–1916* (New York: Free Press, 1963).

cal development. Fostered in part by an excessive present-mindedness, this tendency is evident in a variety of superior studies including Paul A. C. Koistinen's recent article on the "industrial-military complex," William E. Leuchtenburg's pioneering probe of the interconnections between the war and New Deal activity, Gabriel Kolko's *The Triumph of Conservatism*, James Weinstein's *The Corporate Ideal in the Liberal State*, and Melvin Urofsky's *Big Steel and the Wilson Administration*.[3] One of the overarching theses of this book is that fuller attention to the details of industrial mobilization, treated primarily in the context of the war years, requires that serious qualifications be made about the thoroughness and permanency of structural integration between business and government before, during, and after World War I. Insofar as the WIB experience is any guide, the keynotes of business-government relations during the war are complexity, hesitancy, and ambiguity. It suggests that the historical significance of the war years lies less in the strengths of the kind of trends implied by "industrial-military complex," "political capitalism," and "corporate liberalism," and more in their comparative weakness. It also offers grounds for arguing that treating the war period as essentially a paradigm for future historical development, either in the New Deal or in the years after World War II, both diminishes the uniqueness and exaggerates the modernity of America's response to the crisis of World War I. To treat the war period as simply an epilogue for business-government relations in the Progressive period or as solely a prologue for subsequent developments in liberal reform or the political economy of the warfare state diverts our attention from the very aspects of the experience which can change our perspective on the nature of the historical changes which preceded and flowed from the war.

The organizational dimension of mobilization is one facet of wartime change that has not received the attention it deserves. Wars in the twentieth century have required a total preparedness which means, as Hans Speier puts it, "large scale planning with an inflated bureaucratic organization its inevitable concomitant."[4] With this perspective in mind, I have attempted to analyze the structure and function of the WIB as a modern, large scale organization. Studies of bureaucracy in the social sciences have directed me to a number of important subjects including the role of informal groups, the distribution of authority in external and internal relationships, and the symbolic functions inherent in

[3] Paul A. C. Koistinen, " 'The Industrial-Military Complex' in Historical Perspective: World War I," *Business History Review* 41 (Winter 1967): 378–403; William E. Leuchtenburg, "The New Deal and the Analogue of War," in John Braeman, Robert H. Bremner, and Everett Walters, eds., *Change and Continuity in Twentieth-Century America* (New York: Harper & Row, 1966), pp. 81–143; Melvin I. Urofsky, *Big Steel and the Wilson Administration* (Columbus: Ohio State University Press, 1969).

[4] Hans Speier, *Social Order and the Risks of War* (Cambridge, Mass.: M.I.T. Press, 1964), p. 261.

administrative systems. Furthermore, I have adopted several points of view about organizations from this literature which ought to be made explicit. Chief among them are a skepticism about the potential for centralized control in any large organization and an appreciation for the critical implications of decentralized administration in the distribution of functional power. My bias here is toward the limitations on central decision-makers rather than upon their freedom of action. One of the objects of the study is to show how often the processes of industrial mobilization originated and transpired outside the control and sometimes even the knowledge of major office-holders. Consequently, less attention is given to central figures like Woodrow Wilson or Bernard Baruch than would have been the case had the book been written from the point of view of the presidency or the chairman's office of the WIB.[5]

HISTORICAL SETTING

While useful for gaining some perspective on problems and themes, this overly schematic outline must be supplemented by an understanding of the historical setting in which the WIB men designed their organizational experiments in business-government relations. After all, they did not operate in a vacuum. The institutional structure of prewar America partially determined the outcome of their quest for concentration and control, just as specific historical circumstances partially defined their ideas and actions.

In the decades before World War I, the United States made a decisive leap into what one social scientist has called "the organizational society," and several

[5] The following is a brief sampling of studies on organization and bureaucracy I consulted: Michael Crozier, *The Bureaucratic Phenomenon* (Chicago: University of Chicago Press, 1964); Anthony Downs, *Inside Bureaucracy* (Boston: Little, Brown, 1967); Harry Eckstein, "Group Theory and the Comparative Study of Pressure Groups," and "The Determinants of Pressure Group Politics," both in Harry Eckstein and David E. Apter, eds., *Comparative Politics: A Reader* (Glencoe, Ill.: Free Press, 1965), pp. 389–97, 408–21; Robert K. Merton *et al.*, eds., *Reader in Bureaucracy* (Glencoe, Ill.: Free Press, 1952); Robert Presthus, *The Organizational Society: An Analysis and a Theory* (New York: Vintage, 1962); Fred W. Riggs, *The Ecology of Public Administration* (London: Asia Publishing House, 1961); Philip Selznick, *TVA and the Grass Roots: A Study in the Sociology of Formal Organization* (New York: Harper & Row, 1966); Herbert A. Simon, *Administrative Behavior* (New York: Macmillan, 1963); Herbert A. Simon, Donald W. Smithburg, and Victor A. Thompson, *Public Administration* (New York: Knopf, 1961); Victor A. Thompson, *The Regulatory Process in OPA Rationing* (New York: Columbia University Press, 1950), and *Modern Organization* (New York: Knopf, 1961); James D. Thompson and William J. McEwen, "Organizational Goals and Environment: Goal Setting as an Interaction Process," *American Sociological Review* 23 (February 1958): 23–31; and Gordon Tullock, *The Politics of Bureaucracy* (Washington, D.C.: Public Affairs Press, 1965).

features of this organizational revolution had significant implications for the business mobilizers of World War I.[6] First was the striking disparity which existed in the pace and level of bureaucratic development between the private and public sectors of American society. Big business outdistanced all others in organizational achievement, and provided the major model for bureaucratic developments among most other economic, political, and social groups, including the state itself. Even while they battled corporate power, farmers, skilled laborers, and middle class professionals adopted some of its characteristic strategems. A federal government which numbered only 256,000 civil servants by the turn of the century could hardly compete with the bureaucratic power available in private hands, and it was commonplace for government officials to cooperate with private interest groups in designing and mounting public programs throughout the period.[7] In the conservation movement, for example, federal specialists fell into a natural alliance with corporate interests and professional associations in their early campaigns for rational resource development.[8] The war system which America developed after 1914 would emerge out of a similar interaction among government officials and business and professional groups, with the latter providing the bulk of the administrative resources.

An entire class of organizational personnel appeared during the bureaucratic explosion of these years, and as Robert Wiebe has recently shown, its members placed a premium on such bureaucratic values as specialization, stabilization, rationalization, and administrative continuity.[9] Giant business enterprise held the largest fund of private talent, but corporate law firms, professional associations, and academia spawned their own pools of upper-class managers. Naturally, the experience of this class was essential for the organizational challenge of a war mobilization. It is a mark of the crisis of 1917-1918 that specialized elites from a variety of institutions and associations banded together to build the emergency war machine.

The private planning experience, the pools of administrative talent, and the patterns of private-public cooperation available in the prewar years all had obvious advantages for the business mobilizers of 1917. And yet, the nature of America's organizational revolution resulted in enormous obstacles to their work as well. First and most obvious is the fact that the bureaucratic trends symbolized by the growth of national business corporations by no means swept the

[6] Presthus, *The Organizational Society*.

[7] *Ibid.*, p. 82. Fred W. Riggs touches on the ideological roots of private-public cooperation in American public administration in *The Ecology of Public Administration*, p. 45.

[8] Samuel P. Hays, *Conservation and the Gospel of Efficiency: The Progressive Conservation Movement 1890-1920* (New York: Atheneum, 1969), chaps. 3 and 7.

[9] Robert H. Wiebe, *The Search for Order, 1877-1920* (New York: Hill and Wang, 1967), especially chaps. 5, 6, and 7.

field clear of opposition before America entered the war. Indeed, the pitched battles which the spokesmen for individualism, competition, decentralization, and popular control fought with the champions of corporate, bureaucratic trends gave a distinctive tone to America's entry into the twentieth century. The kinds of compromises that resulted from the pulls of decentralization and regionalism can be seen very well in organizations like the American Federation of Labor and the United States Chamber of Commerce, which were federated rather than centralized structures. Even within the economy, where the most successful national organizations were located, the older entrepreneurial spirit retained pockets of support. Although under attack through the Progressive era both within and without the business community, it still dominated such industries as lumber, coal, and cotton textiles. Moreover, Gabriel Kolko has argued that even among industries such as steel and farm machinery, where corporate enterprise had advanced toward oligopoly, competition still challenged market stability, and throughout the Progressive period major sectors of the industrial economy were characterized by large firms losing market control. Older habits also persisted in the nation's military institutions as competitive rivalries fractured the army bureaus, and the two services pursued independent policies despite repeated attempts at administrative coordination. Here then were significant long-range structural influences on the nature of either private or public industrial planning for war.[10]

And what of the relationship between business and military institutions? No mechanisms existed to bind these two orders together for war. Businessmen were generally unfamiliar with this sector of the state, and military officials had been traditionally alienated from the ethos of a civilian, business-dominated society. The fact that American business reaped huge profits from Allied munitions orders after 1915 reduced still further the incentive among American industrialists to develop a systematic relationship with such an impoverished customer.[11]

Short-range political conditions in the prewar years compounded these broader institutional factors to contribute further obstacles to wartime coordina-

[10] Kolko, *Triumph of Conservatism*, chap. 2; Paul Y. Hammond, *Organizing for Defense: The American Military Establishment in the Twentieth Century* (Princeton, N.J.: Princeton University Press, 1961), chap. 2.

[11] Samuel P. Huntington, *The Soldier and the State: The Theory and Politics of Civil-Military Relations* (Cambridge, Mass.: Harvard University Press, Belknap Press, 1957), pp. 222–30. Alfred Chandler and Louis Galambos argue that prewar America was particularly deficient in strong coordinating mechanisms among its major national organizations. Not until the 1930s could the state assume this function with real effect. See Alfred D. Chandler, Jr., and Louis Galambos, "The Development of Large-Scale Economic Organizations in Modern America," *Journal of Economic History* 30 (March 1970): 201–17.

tion and control. Among them we should emphasize the general American policy of neutrality and the ambiguous state of business-government relations under the Wilson administration. The slogan "He kept us out of war" helped to carry the Democratic party to victory in 1916, and opposition to preparedness remained strong in Congress after that. The president himself discouraged war planning in 1915-1916 lest it jeopardize his role as neutral peacemaker. Furthermore, the great division of American opinion on the question of intervention made it politically dangerous to encourage the institutional cooperation among civilian and military groups required of prewar planning. Similarly, the kind of suspicion over close business-government cooperation concentrated in the Bryanite wing of the president's own party also set political limits on the extent and pace of institutional coordination in these years. Wilson's acceptance of a wide range of business proposals after the recession of 1914 helped clear the air between American business and the chief executive, but the progressive bloc in Congress remained hostile to giant enterprise. Furthermore, Josephus Daniels, secretary of the navy, gave the populist-progressive impulse of southern democracy a strong voice in the Wilson cabinet. His bitter battle with the steel industry over navy prices in 1915 and 1916, for instance, boded ill for easy cooperation between that industry and Washington during the spring of 1917.[12]

Creating an institutional synthesis for war out of the organizational and political materials of prewar America was an enormous undertaking, for there were many individuals and groups within its industrial, military, and political institutions who by no means shared the enthusiasm of the WIB men for the centralizing, nationalizing, integrating trends of modern technology and war. Yet the attempt had to be made, and it should not surprise us to find the initial response originating with that class of private bureaucrats so closely associated with the organizational revolution of the late nineteenth century. War for them was less a duty than an opportunity. While some of their class marched off to General Leonard Wood's summer camps in 1915, and others responded to pleas for a volunteer naval reserve from Assistant Secretary of the Navy Franklin Roosevelt, still others began to ponder the mechanics of mobilization.[13] How

---

[12] See Arthur S. Link, *Woodrow Wilson and the Progressive Era, 1910-1917* (New York: Harper & Bros., 1954) for the best survey of that subject. For the details of Daniels's clash with the steel industry, see Melvin I. Urofsky, "Josephus Daniels and the Armor Trust," *North Carolina Historical Review* 45 (Summer 1968): 237-63.

[13] Secretary of War Newton D. Baker later characterized these preparedness enthusiasts as "the better informed people." See Baker to Captain Thomas E. Frothingham, January 26, 1927, Frank A. Scott Papers, Princeton University Library, Princeton, N.J. For the upper-class tone of the preparedness movement, see Ralph Barton Perry, *The Plattsburg Movement: A Chapter of America's Participation in the World War* (New York: Dutton, 1921), pp. 26-28, 37-39, and "A Plattsburg of the Sea," *The Outlook* 113 (May 10, 1916): 51; Hermann Hagedorn, *Leonard Wood*, 2 vols. (New York: Harper &

should industry be organized and prepared for maximum war production? What place would scientific research have in industrial mobilization? How could business and military institutions be adequately interrelated? These are the kinds of questions which generated America's first significant experiment in prewar institutional coordination, the Council of National Defense and Advisory Commission of August 1916. By examining its origins and character we tap the deepest roots of that organizational response to war which would ultimately produce the WIB of World War I.

Bros., 1931), vol. 2, chap. 7; Cedric C. Cummins, *Indiana Public Opinion and the World War 1914-1917* (Indianapolis: Indiana Historical Bureau, 1945), pp. 76-78, 176-79; and Randolph Bourne, *Untimely Papers*, ed. James Oppenheim (New York: B. W. Huebsch, 1919), pp. 25-26, 142-43.

CHAPTER 1

THE FORMATION OF THE COUNCIL OF
NATIONAL DEFENSE AND ADVISORY COMMISSION

War pressed hard upon Franklin Martin in August 1914, as he sped across Europe to retrieve the daughter of a Chicago friend stranded in Munich. The grimness of battle was evident on all sides: the marching German soldiers in Frankfurt; the Belgian prisoners of war in Koblenz; the trenches near Cologne; the English cruisers in the North Sea. Just weeks before, Martin had been in London with his friend Franklin F. Simpson attending the Clinical Congress of Surgeons of North America, and even then war had been ominous. At the conclusion of the conference Martin and Simpson spent time calming the fears of the eleven hundred American doctors and their families who were apprehensive about finding return passage to the United States. They reconfirmed tickets, extended reservations, and persuaded Thomas Cook and Sons to underwrite credit for those whose stays had outrun their bank accounts. It pleased both men to learn that Herbert Hoover, the famous engineer, would accept the American embassy's invitation to set up a formal program to assist American tourists in Europe.[1]

Martin could breathe easier after accomplishing his rescue mission, but the guns of August made an indelible impression on him, as they did on Frank Simpson. Martin did not share the uncompromising Allied sentiment of his friend, but he agreed wholeheartedly that once back in the United States the two of them would have to work to "arouse the doctors to prepare for what will soon be our war."[2]

Simpson and Martin were well suited for this task. They were highly respected members of the medical profession as practising gynecologists, and they possessed marked ability and enthusiasm for organizational work. In more

[1] Franklin H. Martin, *The Joy of Living: An Autobiography*, 2 vols. (Garden City, N.Y.: Doubleday, Doran, 1933), vol. 2, chaps. 1–3.

[2] *Ibid.*, p. 39.

general terms, they were members of that class of private bureaucrats spawned by the organizational revolution which swept through America in the late nineteenth and early twentieth centuries. As a young practitioner, Martin had launched the South Side Medico-Social Club in Chicago in 1883, and thirty years later helped found the American College of Surgeons. Similarly, Simpson had organized the American Gynecological Club and had also served as president of the Gynecological Society. Both men were deeply committed to the professionalization of medical practice. Simpson and Martin not only wanted to prepare the doctors of America for war; they also hoped the profession would receive the recognition it deserved in the event of mobilization. Patriotism and professionalism fused in their minds; the status of medicine could be enhanced as it fulfilled what the two men believed was its patriotic duty.

How could this be achieved? They agreed at once that the movement should include all medical men regardless of their specialty. The two gynecologists therefore asked the presidents of all the representative medical associations to participate in planning and to join the proposed crusade. In April 1916 a "Committee of American Physicians for Medical Preparedness" was formed. Simpson was chosen secretary and Martin was elected to the executive committee. An advisory committee was selected from the medical societies in each state to assist in surveying the medical resources of the country. The two men visited the War Department to develop some liaison with the military services, and Martin, as secretary general of the American College of Surgeons, offered that organization's services to the medical corps. The preparedness committee officially launched its campaign on April 20, 1916.[3]

George Ellery Hale was as anxious as Simpson and Martin to move his profession toward preparedness in 1915. Respected as much for the skill with which he organized scientific institutions as for his contributions as an astronomer, Hale had actively promoted the National Academy of Sciences in the prewar years as the recognized spokesman for the nation's scientists. Like Simpson, Hale was an inveterate Allied sympathizer, convinced that the United States should and would enter the war, and eager to secure a prominent position for science and scientists in the inevitable mobilization. He believed the academy was "under strong obligations to offer its services to the President [of the United States] in event of war with Mexico or Germany."[4] In April 1916 he even refused to fill his usual position as the academy's foreign secretary unless he was free to express these views. Once this condition was accepted, Hale presented a resolution offering the academy's services to the country. He himself headed the academy's preparedness committee and pressed its plans for a National Research

[3]*Ibid.*, chap. 4.

[4]Quoted in Helen Wright, *Explorer of the Universe: A Biography of George Ellery Hale* (New York: Dutton, 1966), p. 286.

Council which would coordinate the country's entire scientific effort. "I really believe," Hale wrote a friend in May 1916, "this is the greatest chance we ever had to advance research in America."[5] Combining a loyalty to the Allies with an intense allegiance to the scientific profession and a strong belief in his own ideas for reform within it, Hale shared the personal, professional, and national goals of Simpson and Martin as they worked to prepare America for war.

When Secretary of the Navy Josephus Daniels announced the formation of the Naval Consulting Board in July 1915, he did not realize he was opening the way for members of yet another professional group to join the ranks of preparedness specialists. Daniels had good reasons for his move, but assisting engineering societies in their drive for status was not one of them. The U-boat menace had burst into public view that spring with the sinking of the *Lusitania*, and in July President Wilson requested plans for an adequate program of national defense. The NCB was part of Daniels's response. The board might also silence the big navy advocates who had been harassing Daniels for so long, and even motivate Congress to increase its naval appropriations.

Daniels derived the actual inspiration for the idea from an interview with Thomas A. Edison that appeared in the *New York Times* on May 30, 1915. "Edison's Plan for Preparedness" made an appeal for preparedness from a thoroughly antiwar position. Edison, the popular folk hero-prophet, promised the advantages of preparedness without the costs usually associated with it. In an age of mechanized warfare, he explained, America required only a small number of trained specialists to develop military art through laboratory research, and to prepare the country's industry for massive armament production through an inventory of present resources. Edison's plan was cheap and simple: it obviated the need for heavy taxation or a large standing army. America's scientific genius alone could overcome any challenge. Edison avowed that "no engine of destruction or defense" could withstand "the ingenuity of desperate men." "If any foreign power should seriously consider an attack upon this country," he proclaimed, "a hundred men of special training quickly would be at work here upon new means of repelling the invaders. I would be at it myself."[6]

Secretary Daniels took Edison at his word. He wrote the scientist two weeks later to ask for his cooperation in establishing "a department of invention and development" in the navy which could evaluate suggestions made by either military or civilian inventors.[7] The secretary pointed out that the project would

---

[5] *Ibid.*, p. 288. Also see Daniel J. Kevles, "George Ellery Hale, the First World War, and the Advancement of Science in America," *Isis* 50 (Winter 1968): 427–37.

[6] Quoted in Edward Marshall, "Edison's Plan for Preparedness," *New York Times Magazine*, May 30, 1915, p. 6.

[7] Daniels to Edison, July 7, 1915, reprinted in Lloyd N. Scott, *Naval Consulting Board of the United States* (Washington, D.C.: Government Printing Office, 1920), p. 286. See

have a much better chance of popular and congressional approval if Edison headed the board of scientific experts. The "electrical wizard" accepted the invitation and Daniels and Edison proceeded to the task of staffing their new board.[8]

Daniels immediately turned to private organizations to administer his governmental board in what was to become typical practice in mobilization during the war. The best ideas about mobilization and the best executive talent to implement them would come from private sources. At Edison's suggestion, Daniels asked each of the eleven largest engineering societies to select two of their members to serve on the board. This was an advantageous arrangement for Daniels and his department, for the board's membership symbolized the popular, nonpartisan, and democratic nature of the undertaking and appeared to give the navy the facilities of all these groups and the 36,000 engineers that composed them, a formidable adjunct to the cause of naval preparedness.

Composed of engineers and inventors of the Edison stripe, the board divided itself into a series of committees covering a wide range of technological problems and proceeded through 1916 to promote Edison's suggestion of a naval research laboratory. The board also began to develop antisubmarine devices and to screen suggestions from private inventors, a task that proved to be its most significant function throughout the war. More important, however, is the role the Naval Consulting Board played in the origins of the Council of National Defense and Advisory Commission. Neither Daniels nor most of the board members themselves had foreseen this development, which can be credited largely to the ideas and initiative of Howard E. Coffin, president of the Society of Automotive Engineers.[9]

The nomination of Coffin to the NCB was destined to take the board along paths far different than Secretary Daniels had intended. Forty-two years old in 1915, a graduate in engineering from the University of Michigan, and vice-president of the Hudson Motor Car Company of Detroit, Coffin had already

---

also *New York Times*, October 7, 1915, p. 4; E. David Cronon, ed., *The Cabinet Diaries of Josephus Daniels* (Lincoln: University of Nebraska Press, 1963), p. 102; *New York World*, July 15, 16, 1915. The *World* reported that naval officers were "delighted" to have a board of experts that would support navy expansion; *New York World*, July 15, 1915, p. 3. See also Joseph L. Morrison, *Josephus Daniels, the Small-d Democrat* (Chapel Hill: University of North Carolina Press, 1966), p. 72.

[8]*New York World*, July 14, 1915, p. 1. Also see Matthew Josephson, *Edison* (New York: McGraw-Hill, 1959), pp. 447–52.

[9]Scott, *Naval Consulting Board*, chap. 1; Thomas Parke Hughes, "Early Government Research and Development: The Naval Consulting Board during World War I," paper delivered at the annual meeting of the Organization of American Historians, Dallas, Texas, April 18, 1968, pp. 6–15; L. H. Baekeland, "The Naval Consulting Board of the United States," *Metallurgical and Chemical Engineering* 13 (December 15, 1915): 943–46; *New York World*, October 8, 1915, pp. 1 and 3.

demonstrated as president of the Society of Automobile Engineers in 1910 the executive ability and dynamism he would bring to the consulting board. He had transformed the SAE from a small, lethargic, insolvent group to a superbly organized body, three times larger, and affluent enough to hire a full-time general manager. Coffin had worked this miracle through a campaign to standardize automobile parts. Speaking and organizing on behalf of such manufacturers as Hudson he sought to liberate each of them from the captivity of a single supplier who alone could make parts to his unique specifications. A system of interchangeable parts would lower the price of supplies and free the manufacturer from this dependency on a single supplier. Standardization was a form of self-defense and self-preservation for the auto industry, Coffin argued, and the economic crisis which the industry had suffered in 1909 reinforced his argument. The large companies which manufactured their own parts did not share these problems and remained aloof, but small companies responded enthusiastically to Coffin's appeals.[10]

The auto engineer applied the same zeal, organizational ability, and goals to his efforts as a preparedness enthusiast and member of the NCB. From the moment he was elected, Coffin set out to shape the board in the SAE image. Dashing off lengthy notes to Thomas Robins, a representative of the Inventor's Guild and board secretary, Coffin urged him to take, "a very strong grip on the reins" and to wield the "big stick" when necessary. "Organization is absolutely essential for practical results and no organization can be had if the individuals of our Board are permitted to carry on independent negotiations pertaining to the work in hand." Coffin asked Robins to speak with the executive manager of the SAE to learn the secrets of successful management.[11]

At Coffin's suggestion, the board divided into subcommittees with each member assigned to those committees on which he was most qualified to serve. This technique, which he had employed at the SAE, decentralized authority and function so as to give each committee the greatest freedom to set and achieve its goals. Each NCB committee would be limited only by the ambition and ingenuity of its chairman. Coffin was elected chairman of the Committee on Production, Organization, Manufacture and Standardization, which nicely sum-

---

[10] George V. Thompson, "Intercompany Technical Standardization in the Early American Automobile Industry," *Journal of Economic History* 14 (Winter 1954): 1–20; John B. Rae, *The American Automobile: A Brief History* (Chicago: University of Chicago Press, 1965), p. 40; Society of Automobile Engineers, *S.A.E. Bulletin* 8 (July 1915): 284–85, and 8 (August 1915): 309.

[11] Coffin to Robins, November 13, 1915, Record Group 61, Records of the War Industries Board (hereafter cited as RG 61), Federal Records Center, Suitland Md., File 21A–A4, box 1503, 2 letters. See also Coffin to Robins, October 11, 15, 1915; November 4, 6, 8, 13, 1915, all *ibid*. See also Coffin to Coker Clarkson, November 13, 1915, and Robins to Coffin, November 5, 1915, both *ibid*.

marized his interests, and his committee embarked on activities which soon warranted a new name, the Committee on Industrial Preparedness.

Coffin transferred his organizational principles and business values to the NCB. He now extended to all American manufacturing his concept of standardization and his protective instinct for small business. Just as firms in the car industry had to cooperate to avoid economic distress, so too all American manufacturers had to stress standardization to avert wartime disruption. American industry had to think as a unit; it had to develop the kind of defensive strategies which could ease the eventual transition from war to peace. With these broad goals in mind, Coffin sought to make the NCB a powerful voice not only in the Navy Department, but also in the general debate over the economics of national defense. As Coffin proudly admitted some time later, his activity on the NCB "far exceeded the limits of the advisory function for which the Board was originally created."[12]

Even before the board's first meeting, Coffin began laying the groundwork for a nation-wide campaign of industrial preparedness. Edison had already suggested an inventory of the country's industrial resources and Coffin intended to supplement this with a proposal to place annual educational munitions orders with all manufacturers. This would acquaint them with the techniques of munitions production, stimulate closer contact between industry and the military services, and generally ease the process of conversion. As a first step Coffin told Robins to learn if the "Morgan and Schwab interests" or the military departments had tried to classify production capacity and thus avoid duplication in their proposed work. There was at first some thought of appointing two or three leading manufacturers in each state to coordinate industries, but in the end Coffin's committee turned once again to the engineering societies for both money and personnel.[13]

Coffin himself was most enthusiastic about using the engineering groups in his campaign, for like Simpson, Martin, and Hale, he was enamored of his profession and saw in preparation for war an opportunity to win it greater public recognition. Coffin was a self-conscious member of what he believed to be a technical elite in American society. He considered the engineers who composed this group as the experts who should rationalize, standardize, and manage industry—both in peace and war. In phrases redolent of Veblen, Coffin proclaimed that engineers were "the creative influence in every line of American industry." They were "the driving power behind all scientific, manufacturing and

[12] Howard E. Coffin, "The Automobile Engineer and Preparedness," *S.A.E. Bulletin* 10 (July 1916): 467.

[13] Coffin to Robins, November 8, 1915, and Robins to Pierre Jay, December 30, 1915, both in RG 61, File 21A–A4, box 1503.

commerical development in every business."[14] The problems the country faced in preparing for war were industrial problems, he explained to a meeting of the SAE, and they "must be handled by those men skilled in quantity manufacturing and in the organization of the great industries,"—the engineers.[15] He referred with admiration to the part engineers had played in Germany's mobilization. In company with other efficiency-minded businessmen and social reformers, Coffin envied German methods and the prestige that he believed engineers and their ideas enjoyed. When Coffin suggested to Daniels that his colleagues be placed in charge of his campaign, he argued that they represented "those very channels through which Germany had accomplished her wonderful mobilization of industry."[16]

Coffin, of course, was only expressing a widely shared feeling among the leadership of the engineering societies. The beginning of the twentieth century was a time of rapid growth for them, and despite persistent internal feuding, their cooperation and unity increased. Like Coffin, the engineering leaders sensed how participation in preparedness could increase cohesion and self-consciousness, and generally enhance the profession's reputation. Close cooperation with conservation programs under the Roosevelt administration had already provided the major societies with an education in national affairs. Indeed, their proposal for a grand survey of national resources in 1908 provided a good precedent for the next tactic in Coffin's general strategy.[17]

Just as Martin and Simpson would later do with the medical societies, Robins and Coffin met on January 4, 1916, with the presidents of the five largest engineering societies and gained their cooperation in a nation-wide industrial inventory. One member from each society in each state would sit on a five-man board with the state members of the five societies serving as their

[14]Howard E. Coffin, "Extract of report made to Secretary of the Navy at his request March 26, 1916," Record Group 40, Records of the Department of Commerce, National Archives, Washington, D.C. (cited hereafter as RG 40), File no. 67009/43.

[15]Coffin, "The Automobile Engineer and Preparedness," p. 473.

[16]Coffin to Daniels, January 9, 1916, RG 61, File 21A–A4, box 1502.

[17]For a discussion of the engineering profession in the Progressive era, see Edwin T. Layton, "The American Engineering Profession and the Idea of Social Responsibility" (Ph.D. diss., University of California, Los Angeles, 1956); and Monte A. Calvert, *The Mechanical Engineer in America, 1830-1910* (Baltimore, Md.: Johns Hopkins Press, 1967), pp. 219-24. Good examples of the status aspirations of the engineering profession are contained in F. Austin Lidbury, "The American Electrochemical Society in its External Relations," *Metallurgical and Chemical Engineering* 13 (May 1915): 277-79; "The Status of the Engineer: A Symposium," *Proceedings of the American Institute of Electrical Engineers* 341 (1915); Samuel P. Hays, *Conservation and the Gospel of Efficiency: The Progressive Conservation Movement 1890-1920* (New York: Atheneum, 1969), pp. 123-24, 129-30.

volunteer assistants. Two weeks later a letter written by Coffin and signed by President Wilson asked the societies to nominate their state representatives for the approval of Secretary Daniels. The *New York Times* remarked that the plan partially fulfilled "the dream of military and naval officers in this country who were impressed for a long time prior to the European conflict with the advantage of the German system of making industrial resources capable of immediate mobilization in the event of hostilities."[18] The vision of a rationalized German society was never far from the minds of American preparedness groups.

Coffin accepted the offer of John L. Carty, chief engineer of the American Telephone and Telegraph Company and president of the American Society of Electrical Engineers, to lend him one of the company's bright young executives, Walter S. Gifford, to manage the committee's head office in New York. This thirty-two-year-old, Harvard-trained statistician had already demonstrated his interest in preparedness by attending General Leonard Wood's officer training camp for businessmen in 1915. And since poring over columns of figures was far more congenial than hiking twenty miles a day in the woods of northern New York, Gifford accepted his new position with alacrity.[19]

With a statistician-manager in hand, Coffin searched next for a propagandist. In one of his frequent lectures to Robins on the principles of sound business practice, Coffin had explained that "the importance of publicity in any business or in any undertaking cannot be overestimated."[20] In Grosvenor B. Clarkson, Coffin found a public relations man who certainly shared this view. Born in Des Moines, Iowa, in 1862, the son of a former chairman of the Republican National Committee, Clarkson had pursued a varied career as newspaper reporter, cowpuncher, special agent in the U.S. General Land Office, Republican speech writer, and New York-based public relations man. He had done some work for the automobile industry, no doubt gaining that account through his brother Coker, the celebrated executive manager of the SAE. Clarkson was constantly

[18] *New York Times*, January 17, 1916, p. 3. See also "Linking Up American Industries for Defense," *New York Times Magazine*, February 6, 1916, pp. 11–12. For the mechanics of the process, see Minutes of the Naval Consulting Board, February 9, 1916, in Record Group 80, Records of the Navy Department, Naval Consulting Board, National Archives, Washington, D.C. (hereafter cited as *NCB Minutes*), box 30; Daniels to Wilson, January 12, 1916, Woodrow Wilson Papers, Library of Congress, Washington, D.C. (hereafter cited as *Wilson Papers*); Howard Coffin, "The Council of National Defense," lecture delivered at the Army Industrial College, Washington, D.C., September 14, 1932, in *Army Industrial College* 9: 14.

[19] U.S. Congress, House, Select Committee on Expenditures in the War Department, *Expenditures in the War Department, Hearings . . .*, serial 3, 66th Cong., 1st sess., 1920 (hereafter cited as Graham Committee, *Hearings*), p. 878; James B. Morrow, "This Breakfast Made History," *Nation's Business* 5 (May 1917): 28–30; William Hard, "America Prepares," *New Republic* 10 (March 31, 1917): 253–55.

[20] Coffin to Robins, January 10, 1916, *NCB Minutes*, box 35.

concerned with his own prestige in the campaign organization, and he promoted industrial preparedness with a zeal equalled only by the devotion he showed for his own advancement. Clarkson lacked the technical orientation of Coffin and Gifford, but he had an undeniable flair for flamboyant public relations. His contacts with the media offices in New York helped him mount a press campaign more impressive than the inventory itself. Partly owing to the general patriotic enthusiasm among various professional organizations in the Northeast, the Associated and United Press Services together with the Associated Advertising Clubs of the World gave Clarkson their support, and he received equally sympathetic assistance from the *Review of Reviews, Scientific American*, and the *New York Times*.[21]

Throughout the spring and summer of 1916, while the state committees of engineers distributed their industrial inventory forms, Coffin, Clarkson, Gifford, and others from the head office outlined the broader principles of industrial preparedness. The general goal, they explained, embraced three basic steps. First, a nation-wide industrial inventory would analyze the country's capacity for munitions production and develop plans to increase it. Second, various manufacturers would be taught to produce those munitions for which the inventory had shown their equipment was best fitted. They could do this by accepting small, annual educational orders which would give them sufficient familiarity to switch smoothly into mass production. Third, to prevent a wholesale and indiscriminate movement of labor from the factory into the military services, skilled workers would be enrolled in an "Industrial Reserve" which exempted them from the draft. The numbers of men involved would also be revealed from the inventory.[22]

[21] Grosvenor B. Clarkson, *Industrial America in the World War: The Strategy behind the Line, 1917-1918* (Boston: Houghton Mifflin, 1923), pp. 13-14; Clarkson to Coffin, January 27, 1916, and Clarkson to Robins, February 14, 1916, both in RG 61, File 21A-A4, box 1502; Clarkson to Newton D. Baker, May 18, 1918, Newton D. Baker Papers, Manuscript Division, Library of Congress, Washington, D.C. (hereafter cited as *Baker Papers*). For a sampling of preparedness enthusiasm in *Scientific American*, see "National Defense," 114 (January 1, 1916): 6; "The Navy We Need,"114 (January 8, 1916): 54; and "Industrial Preparedness for Peace," 114 (March 25, 1916): 320.

[22] Howard E. Coffin, "Teaching the Manufacturer of United States Munitions," *American Machinist* 45 (October 12, 1916): 617; Walter S. Gifford, "Realizing Industrial Preparedness: An Inventory of Our Resources," *Scientific American* 114 (June 3, 1916): 576, 598-99; Spencer Miller, "Organizing for Industrial Preparedness," *Transactions of the American Society of Mechanical Engineers*, 38 (1916): 47-54; *New York Times*, March 27, 1916, p. 4; "Extract of report made to Secretary of the Navy at his request March 26, 1916," RG 40, File no. 67009/43. Clarkson summarizes his work in "The First Educational News Campaign in America for Industrial Preparedness," a report submitted to Coffin on November 15, 1916, in Record Group 62, Records of the Council of National Defense, Federal Records Center, Suitland, Md. (hereafter cited as

If a nation at peace ought to be prepared for war, the next question for Coffin the engineer was how this could be done at the least cost. Coffin's answer was as attractive as Edison's. Industrial preparedness did not require large expenditures of time, money, or lives. The campaign financed itself through voluntary contributions from the participating engineers (Coffin gave $20,000), the inventory required only goodwill to be workable, and the educational orders would never exceed $1,000, a small price to pay for trouble-free wartime conversion. Once America entered the war, over 80 percent of her manufacturing capacity would be engaged in military production, argued Coffin. Such a wholesale transformation obviously had to be carefully planned. American manufacturers had experienced difficulties filling Allied munitions orders even under peacetime conditions, for lack of standardized specifications. Without some kind of widespread education and tooling up process, production under wartime conditions would be chaotic, and industry would emerge seriously harmed, probably permanently damaged. The preparedness committee repeatedly contrasted the disorder of British and French mobilization with the smooth transition of an idealized scientific Germany. "In England and France the plants were closed down and manufacturing organizations built up during a long period of years were broken up. In both countries a large percentage of the skilled labor went to the front."[23] A wide distribution of educational orders, an industrial reserve, and a general application of the concept of standardization could avoid this in the United States. Such a program would have "the greatest possible stabilizing influence upon our economic system."[24]

The committee tried to heighten its appeal to the self-interest of the American manufacturer by arguing that industrial preparedness would stifle growing pressure for government ownership of munitions plants. If private manufacturers proved their willingness to support the military with goods and services, the federal government would not feel compelled to assume the task itself, and industry would escape yet another "serious disarrangement of the economic system."[25] Furthermore, the widespread distribution of educational orders would counter the argument that a few manufacturers would monopolize private munitions production. Spreading munitions orders throughout the country, sup-

---

RG 62), File 2A–A4, box 80. See also Coffin to Daniels, March 24 and 26, 1916, in RG 61, File 21A–A4, box 1502.

[23] Coffin, "The Automobile Engineer and Preparedness," p. 462. Also see the speech of W. L. Saunders, chairman of the board of the Ingersoll-Rand Company, president of the American Institute of Mining Engineers, and a member of the Coffin committee, in *Metallurgical and Chemical Engineering* 14 (March 1, 1916): 259–60.

[24] Coffin, "The Automobile Engineer and Preparedness," p. 468.

[25] Walter S. Gifford, "Realizing Industrial Preparedness," draft of an article in RG 61, File 11A–A1, box 1143.

plemented by measures to control profits, could end "the boogaboo of the Munitions lobby," as Coffin phrased it.[26] "A great many people object to preparedness," explained Thomas Robins to the NCB, "because they feel that the purchase of war supplies would fill the pockets of a few unholy manufacturers who are supposed to incite war in order to create business. This plan would divide that business among their own friends and neighbors in all parts of the country."[27]

Throughout their discussion, the campaigners identified private interest with public need, trying all the while to break down the traditional distinction made between private and public institutions. To prevent economic dislocation and to anticipate probable government munitions requirements was advantageous to both government and industry. Were industry not prepared for war, the government and the public would ultimately suffer, for only a healthy industry could provide the country's military requirements. Thus on the one hand self-interest and the patriotic duty of industry to prepare for war were compatible; on the other hand, the national interest demanded that government do all it could to put industry on an efficient footing. This fusion of private and public purposes remained a fundamental strand of business ideology throughout the war.

Coffin and the preparedness committee hoped that labor and the general public would support the concept of industrial planning, but their main concern was winning over American businessmen. Coffin depended on their sympathetic response not only to make possible the industrial inventory and the placement of annual educational orders, but also to demonstrate to the Wilson administration that the project warranted complete support. Assent from manufacturers could prove the political advantage in backing the campaign, while the administration's enthusiastic endorsement might make manufacturers more willing to comply. Coffin tried to persuade President Wilson, through Secretary Daniels, to address a letter "To the Business Men of America," soliciting their cooperation. "The confidential industrial inventory you are asked to supply," Coffin's letter explained, "is intended for the exclusive benefit of the War and Navy Departments, and will be used in organizing the industrial resources for the public service in national defense."[28] He attempted, too, to enlist the aid of the United States Chamber of Commerce. Aware that the chamber was going to vote heavily in favor of industrial preparedness, Coffin asked the chamber's directors to urge all their members to cooperate with him immediately. "In short," wrote

[26] Coffin to Daniels, March 9, 1916, RG 61, File 21A–A4, box 1502.

[27] *NCB Minutes*, February 9, 1916. See also Coffin to Senator George Chamberlain, March 30, 1916, RG 61, File 21A–A4, box 1502.

[28] Coffin to Daniels, April 14, 1916, RG 61, File 21A–A4, box 1502; and Wilson to Daniels, April 17, 1916, Josephus Daniels Papers, Manuscript Division, Library of Congress, Washington, D.C. (hereafter cited as the *Daniels Papers*).

Coffin, "we know perfectly well that the chambers are in favor of this work and stand ready to push it along, but it is only through some quick and decisive action that any practical support can be given during the period covered by our inventory."[29] For some reason the chamber's directors remained unpersuaded, but the referendum passed in July gave overwhelming approval to "educative arrangements with private manufacturers for the production of war material in time of peace."[30]

Public support among manufacturers was required in order to conclude the first step of the preparedness campaign, the industrial inventory. An appeal to yet another constituency was necessary to ensure the second step, the distribution of educational munitions orders, for this proposal was best implemented by congressional legislation. While making further pleas to the chamber's leadership to use its influence, Coffin also made contact with Senator George E. Chamberlain, a Democrat from Oregon and chairman of the Senate Committee on Military Affairs, who was waging his own preparedness battle. Coffin rehearsed the present difficulties that American manufacturers were experiencing with foreign munitions orders and argued for an amendment to the Hay Bill that would permit the War and Navy departments to place educational munitions orders. Every other nation except the United States, Coffin claimed, would soon be able to mass produce armaments "at a moment's notice."[31] Coffin also won Secretaries Daniels and Baker to his side and Chamberlain finally inserted a measure which opened the way for Coffin's plan. Section 120 of the National Defense Act, passed on June 3, 1916, gave the president the power, exercised through his department heads, to place obligatory orders directly with any manufacturers who produced or could produce war material. It also authorized the secretary of war to make complete lists of all private plants equipped to manufacture arms and ammunition as well as those plants that could be converted to munitions production. Finally it empowered the president "in his discretion" to appoint "a nonpartisan Board on Mobilization of Industries Essential for Military Preparedness" to "organize and coordinate" this work.[32]

[29] Coffin to Basil Miles, May 15, 1916, RG 61, File 21A–A4, box 1502.

[30] Chamber of Commerce of the United States of America, Fifth Annual Meeting, Board of Directors, *Annual Report* (Washington, D.C., 1917), pp. 15–16. See also "How Business Men Stand on National Defense" (n.p., n.d.), a pamphlet in the library of the Chamber of Commerce of the United States of America, Washington, D.C.; and "Business Men for Preparedness," *The Outlook* 113 (June 14, 1916): 333–34.

[31] Coffin to Chamberlain, May 5, 1916, RG 61, File 21A–A4, box 1502. See also Coffin to Chamberlain, April 19, and May 17, 1916, both *ibid*.

[32] U.S., *Statutes at Large*, vol. 39, part 1, 213–14. See Coffin to Daniels and Baker, May 5, 1916, and Daniels to Coffin, May 6, 1916, and Baker to Coffin, May 10, 1916, all in RG 61, File 21A–A4, box 1502.

As it turned out, Section 120 provided Coffin with his only major success. This legislation formally enacted two of the three steps of his program, and provided an agency to continue it when and if the Industrial Preparedness Committee disbanded. Coffin hardly exaggerated when he wrote his state chairmen that "such legislation is, we believe, due entirely to the work of the engineers and of this committee of the Naval Consulting Board."[33]

The general preparedness campaign achieved far less. It ground to a halt in late summer. Inventory forms trickled into the head office after August and some state committees maintained their momentum, but by that time the campaign was officially at an end and could no longer be sustained. The committee had not been as successful with all of its constituencies as it had been with the government. Manufacturers who apparently had the most to gain from the plan were not universally sympathetic, and public opinion was not entirely convinced of future American entry into the war. The engineering committees themselves shared the prevailing peace sentiment of their sections of the country. The situation in the state of Washington was symptomatic. The chairman of the engineering committee reported:

The Washington Board commenced its labors with enthusiasm which it still retains, but experience does not indicate that the same degree of enthusiasm permeates society as a whole nor the technical professions in particular. The Board is frankly disappointed in the result of its work; the canvass of the state has not been complete. Voluntary service has not proven a success; the lethargy and procrastination of the manufacturers has been irritating and the deliberateness of the Field Aides embarrassing.[34]

On a more general level the industrial preparedness campaign reflected the broad contours of the president's own preparedness policy. In the summer of 1915, when the NCB originated, Wilson had only begun to formulate a program of national defense; by the fall he had become a convert to preparedness. He made preparedness the key issue of his annual message in December; and in January 1916 he undertook a speaking tour on behalf of his defense proposals. Six months later, however, in that zig-zag pattern characteristic of presidential politics, the Democratic convention echoed to the cheers for Wilson as the man who had kept America out of war. And as the Democrats campaigned as the party of peace it was neither prudent nor convincing for preparedness specialists like Howard Coffin to trumpet the president's support. As the peace crusade

[33] Coffin to the chairmen of the state boards, July 7, 1916, RG 61, File 21A–A4, box 734.

[34] A. O. Powell (chairman for the state of Washington committee) to Coffin, September 14, 1916, RG 61, File 21A–A4, box 1502. See the report of June 28, 1916, of the New York State campaign for the description of a more successful experience, *ibid.*

mounted, Coffin diverted his attention to the more pressing and practical proposal for a Council of National Defense. The idea of an industrial inventory lingered on into the spring of 1917, but it was never again put into operation, despite the authorization of Section 120.

In the last analysis, the campaign offered little of practical value. Inventories were ultimately taken of approximately thirty thousand plants, but they did not prepare industry for war. In the words of the final report of the War Industries Board, the survey was made "at a time when the nature of the problem and the character of the data needed were not clearly determined, and does not appear to have been useful in practice as might have been expected."[35] The Kernan committee cited this information in its report of December 1916, against government munitions production, and the inventories themselves were later transferred to the statistical section of the Council of National Defense, but only to gather dust.[36] Responding to an enthusiastic description of the campaign that Clarkson prepared later in the war, Walter Gifford wrote: "I doubt if we can rightly claim for that any more than a start at educating the people and the government as to the problem of industrial preparedness. Our program, to be carried out, would have taken several years. It was prevented by our entrance into the war."[37] Even Clarkson ultimately recognized that the campaign did more to spread general preparedness sentiment than to provide an inventory of industrial America.[38] Moreover, the "industrial reserve" never did achieve legislative status and the drain of skilled labor into the military services remained a constant source of irritation to manufacturers throughout the war.

The preparedness committee was a weak, jerry-built association of independent engineering groups struggling valiantly in an inhospitable public environment. Even at its most effective it could not guarantee cooperation of the nation's major business interests. Veblen's hope for engineering control of the production means was still a dream, a utopia for visionaries like Howard Coffin. In 1915, America's major corporations could afford to treat business dreamers with skepticism. Only after America entered the war would Coffin's theories and business self-interest begin to converge in any significant way.

[35] U.S. Congress, Senate, Special Committee to Investigate the Munitions Industry, *Munitions Industry. Final Report of the Chairman of the United States War Industries Board to the President of the United States, February, 1919*, 74th Cong., 1st sess., 1935 (Senate Committee print no. 3), p. 19.

[36] For a brief discussion of the Kernan committee report, see Paul A. C. Koistinen, "The 'Industrial-Military Complex' in Historical Perspective: World War I," *Business History Review* 41 (Winter 1967): 383–84. Also see U.S. Council of National Defense, *First Annual Report 1917*, p. 53; and Maxwell Laheman to Dr. Ayres, November 12, 1917, RG 61, File 11A–A1, box 1143.

[37] Gifford to Clarkson, June 14, 1918, RG 62, File 2–A1, box 31.

[38] Graham Committee, *Hearings*, p. 336.

The *American Machinist* was more optimistic, however. Speculating on the campaign in the summer of 1916, the engineering magazine concluded that it was worthy of support for two reasons. First, it would familiarize the military services with American manufacturers, and second, it would "make manufacturers generally feel that a closer connection exists between them and the Government at Washington. . . ."[39] Here the journal touched on the most significant principle of Coffin's work. Standardization and an industrial inventory were important ends in themselves, but they were also part of a broader design of business-government relations envisioned by Coffin from the very beginning. Coffin emphasized throughout his work that the NCB members were businessmen as well as engineers and that their dual roles as engineer-entrepreneurs made them the logical people to enlighten public officials as to the needs and capabilities of a wide variety of industry. Likewise, through industrial preparedness "the business end of the institution [corporation] " could be "brought more closely in touch with governmental affairs and with governmental methods of business." Coffin concluded that "the benefits of this closer business contact will accrue to both government and the manufacturer."[40] In fact, the preparedness campaign contributed most in the realm of personnel and ideology. Its practical impact on business-government relations was slight indeed, but it did bring men like Coffin and Gifford into public life, and it did introduce important principles in the early debate over how best to mobilize the American economy for war.

Howard Coffin made the most important single contribution to the prewar discussion of industrial preparedness, but he was not the only individual influential in shaping government policy in this area. Hollis Godfrey started from a somewhat different perspective and experience from that of Coffin, but he too concluded that military success lay ultimately in the mobilization of a nation's economic resources. His interests paralleled the work of the Industrial Preparedness Committee, and Godfrey played an important role in the legislative infighting that preceded the creation of the Council of National Defense and Advisory Commission.

Godfrey was born in Lynn, Massachusetts, in 1874 and educated at Tufts, MIT, and Harvard. He spent time as a free-lance consulting engineer and chief of the Bureau of Gas in Philadelphia before becoming president of the Drexel Institute of Philadelphia in 1913.[41] As a member of that little band of scientific

---

[39] "Progress of the Industrial Inventory," *American Machinist* 45 (August 17, 1916): 303.

[40] Coffin, "The Automobile Engineer and Preparedness," p. 468.

[41] See the biographical sketch in RG 62, File 2-A2, box 64. See also Graham Committee, *Hearings*, p. 881; and Samuel Haber, *Efficiency and Uplift: Scientific Management in the Progressive Era 1890-1920* (Chicago: University of Chicago Press, 1964), pp. 108-9.

management enthusiasts who had gathered around Frederick Winslow Taylor and begun applying the stop watch to American life, Godfrey embraced the principles of the efficiency movement with all the conviction of a true believer. Like Howard Coffin he assumed that the values that guided him in his private world could be applied with great success to the public task of industrial preparedness. Also like Coffin, he was filled with the occupational nationalism which carried the engineering profession into the vanguard of industrial preparedness.

A trip to Europe in 1906 to study the problem of urban public health persuaded Godfrey that war between Britain and Germany was inevitable, and upon his return home he began agitating on behalf of military and economic preparedness, writing books and articles which reflected his preoccupation with the coming war. *The Man Who Ended War*, a science fiction tale for children published in 1907, embraced his assumption of British-German rivalry, and as with his other children's novels the book glorified New England character, Yankee ingenuity, and scientific discovery. Its hero stumbled upon a process that disintegrated metal on contact, and operating from his own submarine he systematically destroyed the British and German fleets, forcing the warring nations both to sue for peace and to agree to total disarmament. Anglo-German rivalry also figured in *Jack Collerton's Engine*, written in 1910. But in this work Godfrey's Allied prejudices surfaced, for American inventiveness rescued the British War Department by producing a superior airplane engine.[42]

But if Godfrey's European trip had given him a premonition of war, it had also introduced him to one way America could prepare for it—by forming a Council of National Defense. Godfrey derived the prototype for such a body from the Council of Imperial Defense currently under discussion among British government officials. He added a special twist by placing it in the context of scientific management. "I . . . came back in 1906," he recalled later, "believing here was a great means for obtaining the knowledge necessary to pour out on industry, and that the Government needed the thing." Until 1916, he contented himself with writing articles and gathering further information about the project. In the spring of that year he determined to become more actively involved, and as a good Taylorite decided "the best thing I could do . . . was to develop the idea of management again and create it or use it through a council and to organize a body that should make for service ahead of time and who could teach

---

[42] Graham Committee, *Hearings*, pp. 880–82. Godfrey's boys' stories include *The Man Who Ended War* (Boston: Little, Brown, 1908); *Jack Collerton's Engine* (Boston: Little, Brown, 1910); *For the Norton Name* (Boston: Little, Brown, 1909); and *Dave Morrell's Battery* (Boston: Little, Brown, 1912). A sample of Godfrey's technical thought can be found in "Application of Engineering Methods to the Problems of the Executive, Director and Trustee," *Transactions of the American Society of Mechanical Engineers*, 37 (1915): 633–51.

the country what they had to know in industry . . . in order to get the product and service at a minimum of cost and time."[43] Godfrey moved in two directions at once: to gather the kind of information the council should disseminate, and to establish the agency itself. The first of these activities brought him into touch with Coffin's work.

In prewar America, interest in preparedness of any variety inevitably led to General Leonard Wood, commander of the Eastern Department of the Army, patron saint of the Plattsburg summer training camps for business and professional men, and official drillmaster for the preparedness crusade. Godfrey went to the general to be officially confirmed and was delighted to hear his plan adjudged a "splendid idea."[44] Wood solicited money for Godfrey and gave him letters of introduction to Secretary of War Garrison and other Washington officials. Garrison in turn gave his blessing to the scheme, as did Secretary of Commerce William Redfield, who shared Godfrey's admiration for the wonders of scientific management.[45]

Godfrey struck nearly everyone who met him more than briefly as slightly mad, and his eccentricities sometimes did indeed triumph over his common sense. Throughout the spring and summer of 1916 he seemed to regard himself as an undercover agent on a dangerous mission of the utmost secrecy. When Secretary Redfield eagerly apprised Coffin's committee of his project, Godfrey was genuinely alarmed at the security breach and calmed down only after Secretary Garrison assured him that it was proper to acknowledge his purposes to Coffin. William Saunders of Coffin's committee considered the two lines of work complementary, not identical. "We begin where he leaves off. He finds out the sources of a product which may be useful in war and we take that product as it is and record and coordinate it."[46] Thus reassured, Godfrey went on his way, gathering a statistical index of the kinds of personnel and materials the country would require in war. He was assisted in this by the businessmen for whom he

---

[43] Graham Committee, *Hearings*, p. 881.

[44] Leonard Wood, diary, May 27, 1915, in Leonard Wood Papers, Manuscript Division, Library of Congress, Washington, D.C. (hereafter cited as the *Wood Papers*).

[45] Wood to Godfrey, June 4, 1915; to Lindley Garrison, August 25, 1915; to Benjamin Strong, Jr., February 2, 1916; to E. C. Converse, February 2, 1916; to Henry L. Higginson, March 18, 1916; all in the *Wood Papers*, box 82. See also Lindley Garrison to Grosvenor E. Clarkson, March 24, 1921, in the Bernard M. Baruch Papers, Princeton University Library, Princeton, N.J. (hereafter cited as the *Baruch Papers*); William C. Redfield, *With Congress and Cabinet* (New York: Doubleday, Page, 1924), pp. 73–74; *Congressional Record*, 65th Cong., 1st sess., 1917, vol. 55, part 5, p. 5037.

[46] Saunders to Redfield, January 20, 1916, RG 40, File no. 67009/73; Redfield to Saunders, January 17, 1916; Saunders to Redfield, January 20, 1916; Godfrey to Redfield, January 20, 1916; all *ibid.*; and Wood to Garrison, August 25, 1916, *Wood Papers*.

had served as management consultant, by some faculty members at the Drexel Institute, and by Dr. Henry E. Crampton, a Columbia University zoologist and curator at the American Museum of Natural History.[47]

There were significant differences in the approaches of Coffin and Godfrey to the problems of industrial mobilization. Coffin tried to build a mass base, sought publicity, aimed to standardize and protect industry, and interested himself in a wide range of institutional problems. Godfrey, on the other hand, prized anonymity, shunned publicity and was not so much interested in protecting industry as in discovering the personnel and vital raw materials the country had available with which to fight a war. But the similarities are more important. Both men were trying to determine the economic demands of modern warfare and to develop communication between business and government. Both saw the task as a problem in engineering, to be solved by members of the engineering profession like themselves. Scientific management and standardization were merely two variations on the same theme of applying scientific principles to public life—highly trained experts engineering industry for war. Although both Coffin and Godfrey had to frequent the halls of Congress in the process, they believed they did so for professional rather than political reasons. As engineers they adhered to an ideology that in theory valued nonpartisanship and in practice preferred the neutral application of scientific principles by highly trained experts.

Bernard M. Baruch provides a sharp contrast. From the time he first interested himself in industrial preparedness before the war until he stepped down as chairman of the War Industries Board in December 1918, Baruch was acutely aware of the broadly political nature of industrial mobilization and the power relationships which lurked within it. No man was more sensitive to the ill-defined and emotional nature of business-government relations which underlay mobilization during the war. This tall, courtly, middle-aged southerner had already gained a taste for partisan politics as he moved rapidly to the front ranks of the Democratic party after a remarkable career in speculation on Wall Street. The son of a warm, idealistic doctor, Baruch had long regarded his career on Wall Street with a certain ambivalence, if not guilt, and in a tentative and then determined search for a more emotionally satisfying role he gravitated increasingly to public life. Woodrow Wilson and the Democratic party offered one attractive alternative after 1912, the preparedness movement another after 1914, and by 1915 Baruch was devoting his not inconsiderable talents and money to both with the ingenuity and self-confidence that had fueled his rise on Wall Street. He was equally successful, as his career during and after the war attests.

[47]For some of the administrative fallout from Crampton's work, see boxes 1 and 2 of the Henry E. Crampton Papers, Columbia University, New York, N.Y.

Certain characteristics facilitated Baruch's association with President Wilson. Baruch was born in the South, and despite his family's early migration to New York City he identified strongly with it throughout his long life. For Baruch the South was the memory of a happy childhood. This background gave him not only an understanding of key men in the Democratic party, but also a sense of the conservative principles which infused an important segment of it. Moreover, his background could not help but enhance his relationship with a president who always remained a southerner at heart. Politically, Baruch was an ardent, loyal Democrat, at least after 1912; personally he was willing to serve the party; and financially he was willing to spend for it. Equally important was the fact that to Wilson, Baruch was a friend in what at times seemed an enemy camp. Running with the Wall Street crowd might have barred him from Democratic councils—indeed some people never forgave Baruch this part of his background—had not Wilson had good reason to ignore it. Shaken by business criticism during the recession of 1914, the president had begun a systematic effort to prove himself the friend of business enterprise, and he greeted warmly Baruch's own efforts to create an atmosphere of good feeling between the administration and the generally Republican Wall Streeters.[48]

Added to the personal and partisan motives that drew Wilson and Baruch together was the mounting preparedness agitation and the haunting possibility that America might one day enter the war. Should this occur it would be essential for the administration to have trusted businessmen who could direct economic mobilization and oversee the understandings between business and government which would inevitably come with it.

Baruch donated money in support of preparedness to the usual organizations—the National Security League, the Navy League, the United States *Army & Navy Journal*, and General Wood's student camps. He also subscribed to the Anglo-French loan of October 1915, and did so, he wrote, "not because I thought I wanted it but to help it along."[49] That same month New York Mayor John P. Mitchel appointed him to the city's "Committee of 1,000," a body formed by the preparedness-minded mayor to publicize the cause. Baruch also

[48] Bernard M. Baruch, *Baruch: My Own Story* (New York: Henry Holt, 1957); and *Baruch: The Public Years* (New York: Holt, Rinehart & Winston, 1960), pp. 1-17; Margaret L. Coit, *Mr. Baruch* (Boston: Houghton Mifflin, 1957), chaps. 1-5. There are many references in the secondary literature to Wilson's campaign to win businessmen to his administration, especially after 1914. See Arthur S. Link, *Woodrow Wilson and the Progressive Era, 1910-1917* (New York: Harper Brothers, 1963), pp. 75-80, 228-29; and Link, *Wilson: The New Freedom* (Princeton, N.J.: Princeton University Press, 1956), pp. 446-57, 469-71; Robert H. Wiebe, *Businessmen and Reform: A Study of the Progressive Movement* (Cambridge, Mass.: Harvard University Press, 1962), pp. 141-42; and Melvin I. Urofsky, *Big Steel and the Wilson Administration* (Columbus: Ohio State University Press, 1969), pp. 55-83.

[49] Baruch to W. H. Crocker, October 18, 1915, Baruch journals, *Baruch Papers*.

lobbied vigorously in his own areas of influence: in South Carolina, where he had an estate, and on Wall Street. He urged his contacts in South Carolina to have the governor form a committee to support expansion of the army and navy and to have the mayor of Charleston or its leading citizens establish a committee like the "Committee of 1,000" to lead a preparedness crusade. In New York he organized a delegation from the financial district to march in the citizen's preparedness parade held in May 1916. Baruch wrote afterwards: "The Parade went off with great success and everybody seemed very well satisfied."[50]

As early as June 1915, in one of his frequent talks with General Wood, Baruch offered to organize a commission of businessmen to aid the government in purchasing supplies and arranging transportation.[51] Three months later he presented an outline of his plan to President Wilson himself. Baruch spoke vaguely of German industrial preparedness and proposed a "Business Men's Commission" to outline the necessary procedure. The NCB provided a precedent, he argued, and could be expanded informally into his commission without awaiting congressional action. The *New York Times* believed American businessmen would respond favorably to the idea. "An invitation from the President, it is thought, would be followed by a response from industrial and financial leaders throughout the country who would be willing to co-operate in adjusting financial and industrial affairs to a war footing."[52] Baruch emerged confident and optimistic from his first trip to the White House, certain the president would comply with "many or all" of his suggestions.[53]

Some weeks later Baruch wrote Colonel House about his plan to develop a more effective relationship between the military services and American industry. Baruch proposed that a "Defense, Munition, or some other name, Committee" would be "a practical organization on which shall be mobilized the industries which would supply the Army and Navy with all the things which go to equip, feed, transport and take care of them." Only corporation executives possessed the experience necessary to supply and equip an army, and to have them act on a committee "would be of enormous benefit to the Army and Navy in efficiency and economy of time and materials."[54] Furthermore, the army and navy would

[50] Baruch to P. Hamilton, May 25, 1916, Baruch journals, *Baruch Papers*. These journals are thick with evidence of Baruch's preparedness activities. It seems redundant to cite individual letters.

[51] Leonard Wood, diary, June 3, 1916, *Wood Papers*. See also diary entries for September 7 and 9, 1916, and November 4 and 6, 1916; and Wood to Baruch, June 29, 1915, October 12 and 26, 1915, and Baruch to Wood, July 4 and 14, 1915, and August 30, 1915, all in the *Wood Papers*, boxes 81 and 86.

[52] *New York Times*, September 9, 1915, p. 12. The summary of Baruch's proposal is drawn from this source.

[53] Baruch to W. H. Crocker, October 7, 1915, Baruch journals, *Baruch Papers*.

[54] Baruch to House, October 23, 1915, *ibid.*

greatly increase their public prestige through association with eminent business-men. General Wood had undoubtedly lamented to Baruch about the gulf then separating the military establishment from American society, especially from the business community. Baruch intended to close it.

Baruch's communications with Wood and others made it clear that he was ready and willing to help organize such a commission. "Although I am not looking for work," he informed House in 1916, "I would be glad to open the way for such an organization, or even if it were found necessary, to help continue its work."[55] His great desire for a public post made Baruch avoid acquiring any stocks which might compromise his future. He transferred an allotment of shares of the Midvale Steel & Ordnance Company to friends, and scrupulously shunned munitions issues. Such investments "might open me to criticism on the part of many small and suspicious people and might affect the great cause I have been working [on] for so long."[56] Of course Baruch recognized the need for a munitions industry and believed that those who invested in it were good businessmen and true patriots.

In the spring of 1916 Baruch was still urging the president to follow his suggestions for industrial preparedness, coupling this with advice on how to win business confidence in a presidential election year. Following the strategy of courtiers over the centuries, he counseled that responsibility for the "unfortunate" state of business-government relations lay not with the president, but with those around him. Baruch suggested several remedies. He himself was trying to dissipate this suspicion in New York City, and with the president's personal support he could do much more. He suggested, rather audaciously, that those against whom business prejudices were directed should resign and stop infecting the entire administration with their own unpopularity. Foremost among them was Secretary Daniels who, as already noted, had recently locked horns with the steel industry over the price of navy supplies. Daniels should be dropped from the cabinet, Baruch told the president, and replaced by a leading businessman such as John D. Ryan of the Anaconda Copper Company. Indeed Baruch was ready to carry out the unpleasant assignment of informing Daniels of his dismissal, and then to find a place for him in private life, a remarkable proposal with which Wilson could hardly have been in sympathy. The process of industrial mobilization itself could also be used to win business confidence. Baruch coupled his proposed commission with other schemes such as a tariff board and antidumping legislation to prove that the president's heart was in the right place. Baruch repeated his suggestion that Wilson proceed "with the

---

[55] Baruch to House, April 24, 1916, *ibid.*

[56] Baruch to R. R. Lydon, October 14, 1915, *ibid.* Baruch refused shares in Midvale Steel, passing his options to his friends. Baruch to Guaranty Trust Company, Ambrose Monell, and Baruch Brothers, October 14, 1915, all *ibid.*

immediate appointment of business men on the industrial mobilization committee."[57] Wilson replied: "I am eager to make the appointments . . . but am not
yet authorized to do so by legislation. The Army appropriation Bill, which
carries the provision, was passed by the House on June twenty-sixth but has yet
to be acted upon by the Senate."[58]

The president had consistently supported preparedness enthusiasts like
Coffin, Godfrey, and Baruch since at least the summer of 1915. And he had
already outlined a number of concessions to them in his annual message to
Congress in December of that year. Congress, he charged, "should have very
much at heart . . . the creation of the right instrumentalities by which to mobilize our economic resources in any time of national necessity." Wilson believed
he could "take for granted" that congressional authority was not necessary "to
call into sympathetic consultation with the directing officers of the Army and
Navy men of recognized leadership and ability from among our citizens" who
could make recommendations on the coordination of transportation facilities,
the cooperation among manufacturers, and "the solution of particular problems
of defense." He hoped too that if an advisory body on defense were constituted,
Congress would be willing to appropriate adequate funds.[59] In subsequent
months the president kept the administration abreast but not ahead of the
preparedness specialists like Martin, Hale, Coffin, and Godfrey. He gave his
blessing to Martin and Simpson's marching doctors; he endorsed publicly Hale's
National Research Council; he backed Coffin's campaign; and in the spring of
1916 he included in the administration's appropriation bill the proposal which
would ultimately create the Council of National Defense.

When the Council of National Defense entered the legislative lists it became
at once the focal point for all individuals and groups working for industrial and
scientific preparedness. The activities of Martin, Hale, and others began to converge. Coffin decided to hold up his inventory until the council was formed, and
Secretary Baker and army officials decided to halt formation of the Board on
Mobilization of Industries Essential for Military Preparedness, which had been
authorized under Section 120 of the National Defense Act passed in June. For

[57] Baruch to Wilson, June 23, 1916, *ibid.*; diary of Edward M. House, June 23 and Novem-
ber 19, 1916, in the Edward M. House papers, Yale University Library, New Haven,
Conn. (hereafter cited as the *House Papers*); Baruch to Wilson, August 17, 1916, and
Wilson to Baruch, August 19, 1916, both in the *Wilson Papers*.

[58] Wilson to Baruch, June 28, 1916, *Wilson Papers*.

[59] Ray Stannard Baker and William E. Dodd, eds., *The Public Papers of Woodrow Wilson*, 6
vols. (New York: Harper Brothers, 1925–1927), 3:425–26. For other references to the
themes of social coordination and private-public consultation, see *ibid.*, 4:100, 101,
116, 371.

its part, the administration hoped that once a council was formed it could coordinate their disparate efforts to the advantage of country and party.[60]

The CND was, of course, hardly a new idea in 1916. Both the army and navy had recommended the formation of an agency of that name well before the start of the Wilson administration, even though they were fundamentally divided on its purpose. The navy envisioned a body that would coordinate military and naval strategy and establish a national defense policy for both services. Army reformers wanted an agency that would shield the War Department from the vagaries of pork barrel politics. Neither service envisioned a role in industrial mobilization for such a council. Except for General Wood, who was peculiarly sensitive to every preparedness stimulus, both services were remarkably backward in this area. Only as the older idea of a CND passed through the crucible of specialized preparedness after 1914 did it gain its new dimension as a broad and comprehensive instrument for national economic mobilization. A number of factors caused this transformation, but none was more important than the influence exerted by the preparedness specialists.[61]

Hollis Godfrey had thought about a CND since his return from Europe in 1906. Proposals introduced in Congress in 1910 and 1912 aroused his interest and he shared the disappointment of military officers when the measures failed to come to a vote. Meanwhile he was bent on incorporating his theories of scientific management into a new scheme. He seemed to have in mind a central body that could gather, classify, and disseminate data essential to wartime mobilization. An indefatigable lobbyist, he used his natural enthusiasm to overcome the doubts his listeners must have had about his vague proposals. Among those with whom he discussed his work, and from whom he gained personal endorsements, were General Wood, Secretaries of War Garrison and Baker, Senators Chamberlain and Lodge, Secretary Redfield, Colonel House, and the president himself. "This is admirable; this is extraordinary, this composite work," Godfrey reported the president as saying. "It is exactly the putting of this theory of education into government. I am heartily for it."[62]

[60]Coffin to Major Palmer E. Pierce, August 14, 1916, Record Group 165, Records of the War College Division of the General Staff (hereafter cited as RG 165), box 402, Doc. no. 9432-23; and Chief of Staff to the Adjutant General, August 10, 1916, *ibid.*

[61]Paul Y. Hammond, *Organizing for Defense: The American Military Establishment in the Twentieth Century* (Princeton, N.J.: Princeton University Press, 1961), pp. 64-84; Warner R. Schelling, "Civil-Naval Policies in World War I," *World Politics* 7 (July 1955): 572-91; Samuel P. Huntington, *The Soldier and the State: The Theory and Politics of Civil-Military Relations* (Cambridge, Mass.: Harvard University Press, Belknap Press, 1957), pp. 260-63. A good example of Leonard Wood's views on industrial preparedness can be found in *S.A.E. Bulletin* 9 (January 1916): 202-3.

[62]Graham Committee, *Hearings*, p. 883. See also Baker to Captain Thomas G. Frothingham, January 26, 1927, *Baker Papers*; and Godfrey to House, July 19, 1919, *House Papers*.

Whomever Godfrey overlooked was very likely to encounter Alfred P. Dennis, a University of Wisconsin history professor and CND enthusiast. Dennis also made the rounds in Washington in 1915 and 1916 and talked to a number of people, including Frank Polk of the State Department and Secretary Baker, who personally scrutinized his plan. His most enthusiastic admirer within the administration was the ambitious assistant secretary of the navy, Franklin D. Roosevelt, who in 1915 took Dennis's idea to Wilson. He had to report back, however, that the president "does not want to 'rattle the sword' when Germany seems anxious to meet us more than half way."[63]

It was a different story by the spring of 1916. Germany no longer seemed eager to pacify the United States and the demand for a CND became part of a growing pressure for military preparedness. The administration took up the question in March. Secretary Baker gathered all suggestions—from Baruch, Godfrey, Dennis, and others—and asked General Crowder, judge advocate of the army, to put together a comprehensive memorandum that he could use as the basis for discussion among Secretary Daniels, the president, and himself.[64]

As Crowder understood the secretary's aim, the council's broad function was to make investigations and recommendations in eight general problem areas: railroad building, highway location, the availability of military supplies, liaison with producers of government requirements, increased war production, sea transportation, and scientific and industrial research. The council would be "representative of the leading thought in the forces which it seeks to coordinate," and would include "men eminent in the financial, industrial and scientific world as well as experts in military and naval matters." Crowder did not foresee the council having "any large measure of power." Its effectiveness would depend upon the "convincing correctness" of its advice, or more realistically, upon the willingness of executive departments to accept it. The members of Crowder's "Council for the National Security and Welfare" included the secretary of the navy, the secretary of war, the secretary of agriculture, the secretary of commerce, the secretary of labor, the chief of staff of the army, the chief of ordnance of the navy, the governor of the Federal Reserve Board, and seven additional specialists.[65]

Crowder did not include the secretary of state partly out of conviction as an army man, and partly out of conviction that the council would play no part in

[63] Quoted in Frank Freidel, *Franklin D. Roosevelt: The Apprenticeship* (Boston: Little, Brown, 1952), p. 255.

[64] Baker to Daniels, March 27, 1916, *Daniels Papers*. Baker sounded out Baruch in May. Baker to Baruch and Wilson, May 9, 1916, *Baker Papers*; and Baruch to Baker, May 10, 1916, Baruch journals, *Baruch Papers*.

[65] Enoch H. Crowder, "Informal Memorandum for the Secretary of War," March 25, 1916, *Daniels Papers*.

the determination of national defense policy. It was to be strictly limited to domestic concerns and denied executive authority in any area. The navy, on the other hand, also partly out of habit, but also because it wanted an agency to treat with military policy, later sought to include the secretary of state and was backed in this by Hollis Godfrey. Crowder and Secretary Baker ultimately prevailed, however, and with the State Department's full agreement eliminated the secretary of state.[66]

In subsequent discussions Crowder's council suffered major alterations in personnel, structure, and name. First, Baker removed the military officers from the council, for he believed it inappropriate to place subordinates on the same board as their superiors. In any case, the council was not to discuss military policy. The governor of the Federal Reserve Board was also removed and replaced by the secretary of the interior. Baker also shaped a distinct body known as an Advisory Commission out of the seven specialists Crowder had placed on the council; it was better to separate those with official responsibility from volunteers, Baker believed. A draft bill creating the council specified that the seven specialists should, in addition to supervising investigations into the eight areas already mentioned, establish those "relations which will render possible in time of need the immediate concentration and utilization of the industrial resources of the nation."[67] Revealing the hand of Howard Coffin, the draft also empowered the Advisory Commission to organize subordinate committees to assist its investigations.[68] This action would permit the AC the same kind of unofficial administrative expansion which had marked the NCB and its preparedness committee.

Daniels and Baker were anxious to avoid the name "Council of National Defense" which, because of its history, had connotations very different from what they had in mind for the present agency. Simply stated, the agency in Crowder's draft was designed to function only in peace, not war. That it possessed neither adequate administrative resources nor sufficient authority for wartime conditions became abundantly clear soon after its formation. "Council of Executive Information," which Daniels and Baker favored, caught its intended role much more accurately. But "Council of National Defense" proved inescapable. In July Senator Chamberlain replaced the administration proposal with the older concept of a council engaged in matters of defense policy and with the old

[66] Frank L. Polk to Grosvenor B. Clarkson, March 24, 1921, *Baruch Papers*; and "Remarks of Secretary Baker . . . November 10, 1919," in Course at General Staff College 1919–1920, RG 165, box 240.

[67] From the draft of a bill "To provide for the creation of a Council for the Coordination of Industries and Resources for the National Security and Welfare, and for other purposes," attached to Baker to Daniels, May 1, 1916, *Daniels Papers*.

[68] Coffin to Daniels, April 11, 1916, RG 61, File 21A–A4, box 1502.

name attached. The secretary of state found his place once again, along with a number of senior military officers. Civilian personnel were eliminated; the specialists, now six in number, were integrated into the parent body, and the appropriation reduced from $200,000 to $10,000. Most significantly of all, the Advisory Commission would now be appointed by the advice and consent of the Senate and not by executive order. It was a bold challenge and offered a premonition of the tension which would characterize congressional-executive relations during the war. In this case the administration successfully restored all the original elements of its bill except the name. It was a considerable victory, but the misnomer remained with the council, and this title was to give all but its closest sponsors a fundamental misconception about its nature.[69]

Staffing the Advisory Commission began in June 1916, after the measure was introduced into Congress as section 2 of the army appropriation bill. Godfrey and Crampton submitted a list of names from their personnel index and its composition illustrates Godfrey's conception of national defense as a problem in industrial engineering and scientific management. Of the fourteen men listed, nine were engineers or scientists. Godfrey then singled out seven who "could do most for the country." These were Howard Coffin; Robert S. Perry, president of the Kalbfleisch Chemical Company; George D. Dixon, president of the Pennsylvania Railroad; E. H. Simmons, vice-president of the Simmons Hardware Company; Robert S. Brookings, a retired St. Louis businessman; Simon Flexner, director of the Rockefeller Institute of Medical Research; and Mr. Van Rensselaer Lansingh, president of a Chicago commercial firm, whom Godfrey placed in a class by himself. With the exception of Crampton, Lansingh had "the best mind in the country in the collection and use of statistical data and in the organization of science as applied to industry."[70] Godfrey wanted him made director of the commission. Colonel House forwarded the list to Baker on July 3, 1916, advising that the names of its authors be added. Actually Godfrey's list came too late for consideration in the first recommendations to the president, but Baker promised to use Godfrey's selections as alternates. Some of the names were identical in any case.[71]

The canvassing of names continued apace. Baruch prodded the president to staff the commission with outstanding businessmen; Clarkson told his friend William McAdoo, the treasury secretary, that Coffin's brilliance should be recog-

---

[69] Professor Dennis had drawn up the substitute bill. See Baker to Wilson, May 9 and July 8, 1916, *Wilson Papers*; *Congressional Record*, 64th Cong., 1st sess., vol. 53, 1916, part 9, pp. 8620, 8628, and part 12, pp. 11564–65.

[70] Godfrey to House, June 27, 1916, *House Papers*. Also see Godfrey to House, July 1, 1916, *ibid.*

[71] Godfrey to House, July 2, 1916, House to Baker, July 3, 1916, Baker to House, July 5, 1916, all in the *House Papers*; and Godfrey to Baker, July 6, 1916, and Baker to Daniels, July 8, 1916, both in the *Daniels Papers*.

nized and McAdoo found that Baker agreed; Coffin suggested that Herbert Hoover should direct food and sanitation efforts; and the president discussed candidates informally at cabinet meetings.[72]

The army appropriation bill passed Congress on August 29, 1916, and on September 18 the cabinet members who constituted the council met in Secretary Baker's office to make their final recommendations. They had decided that the Advisory Commission should represent transportation, labor, general industry, finance, mining, merchandise, and medical science. To fulfill this objective they submitted these names: Daniel Willard, president of the Baltimore and Ohio Railroad; Samuel Gompers, president of the American Federation of Labor; Howard Coffin; Bernard Baruch; John Ryan; Julius Rosenwald, president of Sears Roebuck; and Franklin Martin. An earlier version submitted to the president had included all these names except Martin's. William H. Welch, president of the National Academy of Sciences and a good friend of Hale's, had been chosen to represent both medicine and pure science, but persistent lobbying by Frank Simpson and the fact that Welch was visiting Europe in September—he and Hale had gone to observe the mobilization of science in Europe at first hand—eliminated him from the second list. The president had only one reservation. Apparently John Ryan had recently shown his Republican colors, so Wilson turned him down and appointed Hollis Godfrey instead. The appointments were announced on October 11.[73]

The CND now had its Advisory Commission and with the later addition of Clarkson and Gifford of Coffin's staff it gained a secretary and director. Coffin had persuaded Clarkson to handle the council's publicity immediately upon its formation, and it was Clarkson's statement with only minor stylistic alterations that the president issued on October 11. Clarkson was reluctant at first to accept the position of secretary because of the lack of a "decent compensation,"[74] but

---

[72] Baruch to Wilson, August 17, 1916, *Wilson Papers*; Clarkson to McAdoo, July 24, 1916, RG 61, File 21A–A4, box 1502; McAdoo to Baker, September 14, 1916, and Baker to McAdoo, September 16, 1916, both in the William Gibbs McAdoo Papers, Manuscript Division, Library of Congress, Washington, D.C.; Coffin to Daniels, September 16, 1916, RG 61, File 21A–A4, box 1502; David F. Houston, *Eight Years With Wilson's Cabinet, 1913 to 1920*, 2 vols. (Garden City, N.Y.: Doubleday, Page, 1926), 1:183. Also see Chief of Staff to Adjutant General, June 7, 1916; W. S. Graves to Chief, War College Division, June 8, 1916; and H. L. Scott, Chief of Staff to Adjutant General, June 17, 1916, all in RG 165, box 402.

[73] Baker to Daniels, September 13, 1916, *Daniels Papers*; Baker to Wilson, September 18, 1916, House to Wilson, September 29, 1916, Wilson to Baker, October 10, 1916, and Baker to Wilson, October 14, 1916, all in the *Wilson Papers*.

[74] Clarkson to McAdoo, September 8, 1916, RG 61, File 21A–A4, box 1505; Clarkson to Coffin, September 7, 1916, and Clarkson to McAdoo, September 8, 11, and 14, 1916, all *ibid.*; Clarkson to Coffin, October 16, 1916, *ibid.*, box 1506; and Clarkson to Daniels, September 26, 1916, *Daniels Papers*.

in March 1917, he finally relented and stayed with it until he succeeded Gifford as director late in the war. Coffin had written to Daniels as early as mid-September to say that Gifford's company would probably comply with a request for his services. "The Council will, in its dealings, come directly in contact with the best brains in every line of the country's activities," warned Coffin, "and it is essential that the secretarial or directing agency of the Council be of the highest possible class."[75] At the council's meeting in December 1916, Gifford was made temporary director for twelve weeks, at the end of which time he assumed the post permanently.[76]

The CND and AC obviously meant different things to different people. That was inherent in the diverse forces that shaped them. They were interpreted in part as a recognition of the importance of science in modern America. From Secretary Daniels's call to Thomas Edison, through the proposed appointment of Dr. Welch, to the advent of Hollis Godfrey to the commission, emphasis had been placed on the value of science in preparing the nation for war. Closely allied to this was the application of science to industrial problems which so fascinated Godfrey and the Taylorites. The engineering community was immensely gratified: the entire industrial preparedness campaign had demonstrated the profession at its best. The appointments of Godfrey and Coffin capped its success. "An impartial review of the facts," observed the *American Machinist* on behalf of the engineers, "shows that there have been more of these recognitions during the last three years than ever before in the history of the United States."[77] "The personnel of the Council's advisory members," ran a draft for the president's public statement prepared by Clarkson, "marks the entrance of the non-partisan engineer and professional man into American governmental affairs on a scale wider than ever before."[78] The Advisory Commission also symbolized the Administration's effort to draw business groups to its side, and Baruch quite rightly linked it to Wilson's other probusiness strategies. The council and commission, trumpeted the presidential statement, would open up "a new and direct channel of communication and cooperation between business and scientific men and all departments of the Government."[79]

The motives that inspired the preparedness specialists were complex, but in all of them personal, professional, and patriotic values converged. The professional identification was especially prominent in Martin, Simpson, Hale, God-

[75] Coffin to Daniels, September 16, 1916, *Daniels Papers*.

[76] Minutes of the Advisory Commission, December 7, 1916, in RG 62, File 1B–1, box 25.

[77] "Council of National Defense," *American Machinist* 45 (September 21, 1916): 521.

[78] From a memorandum, "Statement by the President," attached to Baker to Wilson, September 25, 1916, *Wilson Papers*.

[79] *Ibid.*

frey, and Coffin. Coffin shrewdly played upon the desire for status among engineering societies; and medical, scientific, and engineering leaders saw how an active role in preparedness could augment their power and prestige. Considerations of power and prestige also motivated the individuals themselves; certainly they help explain Baruch's participation. Coffin and Hale were trying to prove the validity of certain of their own values: standardization, scientific management, and organized research. Their missionary zeal suggests that their identification was so great that to affirm these values was in a sense to affirm themselves.

While the council and commission symbolized the need to draw the nation's resources together for war, the choice of resources and groups, as well as the individuals considered most representative, was made largely from among those people already active in some variety of preparedness. The administration acted within guidelines set by the preparedness specialists in the private sphere. For the most part it merely gave belated recognition to activity already under way, activity that would continue as usual, but under the auspices of the CND and AC. With the benefit of hindsight we can see that in creating the CND and AC the Wilson administration employed what would become a fundamental principle of the national war mobilization: the development of national policy through the public institutional recognition of private individuals and private interest groups. At this point in its historical development the state remained particularly dependent upon outside talent and administrative mechanisms to fulfill the demands of modern warfare. Unable to generate and administer its own plans, it had to rely upon what was available elsewhere.

Although the private specialists would ultimately provide an invaluable pool of talent and techniques for war management, they were probably more useful to Wilson in 1916 as bridges to pro-preparedness opinion. Certainly his advisors wanted to capitalize on the administration's connections with technical groups. Colonel House argued, for example, that Coffin's and Godfrey's surveys "will be a complete surprise to the American people when the full facts are known and will reflect credit upon your Administration."[80] In July 1916, when George Hale, eager for the president's endorsement, threatened to reveal his ideas about the mobilization of science to the Republican National Committee, House urged Wilson to give the astronomer his endorsement and to couple it with public approval of all private efforts for technical preparedness.[81] No doubt Wilson also hoped his appointment of the AC and CND just before the election would help to blunt Republican charges that the Democrats had studiously neglected questions of national defense.

[80]House to Wilson, July 6, 1916, *ibid.*

[81]See proposed press release announcing Wilson's support, dated July 28, 1916, *ibid.* See also Hale to House, July 21, 1916, and House to Wilson, July 22, 1916, both *ibid.*; and Wright, *Explorer of the Universe*, p. 288.

It is especially noteworthy, finally, that the individuals who championed the prewar impulse for institutional coordination stood apart from the dominant centers of power in American social and economic life. The huge industrial bureaucracies that stood astride the American economy had not yet allied themselves with these organizational entrepreneurs. United States Steel, Standard Oil, International Nickel, and other business corporations were busily engaged in the lucrative European munitions trade, and while they had no reason to oppose the efforts of Coffin, Baruch, and others, they felt no immediate reason to support them. They possessed their own developing political and economic contacts with European governments and the American military services. Until America actually entered the war they had no need to merge their preparedness activities with the work of those professionals now moving into public life. It would become one of the central tasks of Baruch, Coffin, Willard, and the other members of the AC and CND to convince big business executives to cooperate with them in designing a system to coordinate business, government, and military institutions in preparation for American entry into the war to end all wars.

CHAPTER 2

TOWARD A GENERAL MUNITIONS BOARD,
DECEMBER 1916 TO APRIL 1917

The origins of the Council of National Defense and Advisory Commission, at once broad, variegated, and diffuse, left a tenacious legacy of imprecision. No one could predict their future roles. If President Wilson were successful in his diplomatic initiatives at this point the war might soon end and the entire experiment would come to an immediate close. The commissioners who trooped into Secretary Baker's office on December 6, 1916, for the first joint meeting of the AC and CND were enthusiastic but uncertain. They had met at a dinner given by Julius Rosenwald at the Willard Hotel the night before, and were now eager to assess their future colleagues on the council. As they arranged themselves around the broad mahogany table in Baker's office they wondered exactly why they had been summoned to Washington.

There was no doubt they had entered an organizational vacuum insofar as central planning and coordinating units were concerned. Several weeks would pass before they heard more than the echoes of their own voices. Yet their particular position was not without its compensations. The very absence of formalized patterns and complicated structures afforded them a wide field for creative action. They stood at the fluid beginnings of an organizational process where the opportunity for achievement matched the burden of individual initiative.[1]

[1] U.S. Congress, Senate, *Digest of the Proceedings of the Council of National Defense during the World War*, by Franklin H. Martin, 73rd Cong., 2nd sess., 1934, doc. no. 193, pp. 53–57. Both Willard and Baruch expressed some reservations over their appointments. Willard to A. W. Thompson, October 14, 1916, and to Major Charles Hine, October 16, 1916, both in Record Group 62, Records of the Council of National Defense, Federal Records Center, Suitland, Md. (hereafter cited as RG 62), File 1–A1, box 1; and Edward M. House, diary, October 12, 1916, in Edward M. House Papers, Yale University, New Haven (cited hereafter as *House Diary*). Secretary Baker touched on the council's uncertain future in his year-end report for 1916: "It may well be that

In the most general terms, the commissioners had necessarily to confront the challenge of building bridges between the state and the nation's economy and society. They had to forge channels of communication with those who controlled the kind of economic power and expert knowledge required in modern war. Simultaneously they had to link these interests to relevant sections of the state, especially to the military departments. Left essentially to their own ingenuity in this task, most commissioners simply pursued the activities that they had first entered into upon coming to Washington. Formation of the CND and AC by no means integrated the pockets of specialized preparedness. Nor did their inception offer the private planners meaningful independent power. Their fate rested largely upon the voluntary cooperation of individuals and groups who shared their enthusiasm for general preparedness.

The absence of consensus on what course the CND and AC should follow contributed to the lack of integration and central control. Informal speculation before the December meeting had only highlighted the confusion. Hollis Godfrey sent Baker a preliminary report in November which, in the patois of the management consultant, outlined a long-range mobilization program to occupy the council for the next five years. Godfrey recommended an extensive campaign to inculcate patriotism among the American people and an effort to gather comprehensive information on national resources. For the short run, he urged the council to set up its administrative offices (on scientific principles, of course), and direct the preparedness activities of Martin, Coffin, and himself until an investigation showed the need for new directions.[2] Secretary Daniels agreed with much of Godfrey's report but found it too theoretical and vague on civilian-military relations. "I do not think," Daniels wrote Baker, "that Professor Godfrey himself has thoroughly grasped the wide range and scope of the matter, nor the essential principles which underly [sic] its real work. It seems to me that the biggest thing this Council will do will be to find the ways and means of carrying out the military plans for the defense of the country."[3]

The December 6 meeting did not provide direction. Speeches by Secretary Baker, President Wilson, and others were inspiring but inconclusive. Taking the

---

some part of the work of the council having a purely military usefulness will not be needed." He believed, however, that "the general effect of such a plan in operation will be to produce more healthful and harmonious relations between the Government and business." Quoted in Daniel R. Beaver, *Newton D. Baker and the American War Effort, 1917-1919* (Lincoln: University of Nebraska Press, 1966), p. 54.

[2] "Preliminary Report on the Council and Advisory Commission of National Defense," enclosed with Baker to Daniels, November 21, 1916, Josephus Daniels Papers, Library of Congress, Washington, D.C. (cited hereafter as *Daniels Papers*). Also see *House Diary*, November 23, 1916; and Baker to Godfrey, January 17, 1917, RG 62, File 2-A1, box 34.

[3] Draft of a letter, Daniels to Baker, n.d., *Daniels Papers*.

line of least resistance, the commissioners decided simply to continue the independent preparedness work that had brought them together. Reflecting the country's general peacetime mood, the commissioners did not think they would complete their projects until September 1, 1917.[4]

While the president searched for peace abroad, the council and commission drifted along with little sense of a national defense policy, or even a sense of how they might manage their own limited activities. The second set of meetings in January produced only a small advance. Hollis Godfrey, who dominated the commission's initial deliberations, became temporary chairman and presented his charts on "Governmental Media," much to the irritation and boredom of the other members. Secretary Baker raised the question of publicizing their enterprise, and the commissioners enquired whether as civilians they could obtain military information. They later agreed on a list of six subject areas for immediate attention including such topics as an industrial reserve, which was unfinished business from the industrial preparedness campaign, methods of determining costs and profits on war contracts, information on mineral resources, and the proper response to a growing number of suggestions from private citizens.[5]

The members of the AC were annoyed with the desultory nature of their deliberations. In their collective judgment the commission and council were heading straight for disaster. Ambitious, independent, and strong-willed, the commissioners would have been restive in any subordinate position, but the amorphous nature of their present situation severely aggravated this discontent. The commissioners' belief that the American public would hold them responsible for any errors or omissions in the country's mobilization program fueled their apprehension. But what, exactly, were they supposed to do? Baruch wrote a friend: "The position of the Commission is rather a curious one; the only thing definite about the law is that we serve without compensation."[6] Were they supposed to administer as well as recommend? Could they gain access to privileged information? What was their power under the law?[7]

The winter of 1916–1917 was not an auspicious time to find answers to these questions. The president had recently dispatched peace notes to all the belligerents, and the cool response they elicited, coupled with the blacklist practices pursued by the British, made him more genuinely neutral during these

---

[4] U.S. Congress, Senate, *Digest of the Proceedings of the Council of National Defense during the World War*, p. 66.

[5] *Ibid.*, chapter 10.

[6] Baruch to W. H. Crocker, March 10, 1917, Baruch journal, in the Bernard M. Baruch Papers, Princeton University, Princeton, N.J. (cited hereafter as *Baruch Papers*).

[7] Baruch drew up a critical letter in early January. Daniel Willard agreed with the contents but cautioned against sending it to the council at that time. Baruch to Godfrey, January 10, 1917; to Willard, January 24, 1917; to Gifford, January 27, 1917; and to Rosenwald, January 27, 1917, all in the Baruch journal, *Baruch Papers*.

months than at any time since the start of the war. Not even the German declaration of unlimited submarine warfare on January 31, or the break in German-American diplomatic relations on February 3, improved the Advisory Commission's position. The administration was simply not ready to direct its energies to defense planning.

The president's decision of February 3 did, however, trigger a countrywide flood of patriotic service offers, including promises by manufacturers to turn over their plants to the government in the event of war. The council called a special meeting on February 12 to respond to this public expression of goodwill. Secretary Lane, the council's most outspoken preparedness enthusiast, proposed that the government call a series of conferences with the leading businessmen in every industry designated fundamental to the country's defense and ask them to cooperate with the council in an orderly fashion through one man or a small committee. The AC members could administer the arrangements.[8]

The commissioners responded enthusiastically to the idea, for it offered a long-awaited step toward mobilization and it finally assigned them a very definite and congenial role. The commission subsequently expanded the proposal to apply to a broad spectrum of American life and divided itself into seven permanent committees, with each member chairing the one on his specialty. These were: medicine, including general sanitation, organized under Martin; labor, including conservation of health and welfare, under Gompers; transportation and communication, under Willard; science and research, including engineering and education, under Godfrey; raw materials, minerals and metals, under Baruch; munitions and manufacturing, including standardization and industrial relations, under Coffin; and supplies, including food and clothing, under Rosenwald. These committees were responsible for having their respective constituencies pick a liaison committee for advice and assistance.[9]

The commissioners had already begun to act on their special interests— Baruch was investigating raw materials, Willard was studying the railroad situation, and Martin was organizing his doctors—and in one sense the Lane resolution and subsequent commission expansion merely confirmed this policy. Still, we should not underestimate their very positive effects. First, they helped to legitimize the commissioners' private efforts. Public authority now touched private schemes more directly. The commissioners partook of the magic of the state and thereby increased their credibility with the groups they sought to convert to prewar planning. Private visions were now more easily transformed

[8] Minutes of the Council of National Defense and joint meetings of the council and Advisory Commission (hereafter cited as *CND Minutes*), February 12, 1917, RG 62, File 2–B1, box 104; *New York Times*, February 10, 1917, p. 2.

[9] Minutes of the Advisory Commission, February 12, 1917 (hereafter cited as *AC Minutes*), in RG 62, File 1B–1, box 25; *CND Minutes*, February 13, 1917.

into public policies. Second, the events of early February enhanced the commissioners' transition from voluntary advisors to executive administrators. As they enlarged their private staffs in subsequent weeks, what at one point seemed a transitory function assumed the attributes of permanency. The actions of February 12 hastened administrative growth and augmented the state resources available to the AC.

Such achievements were not had without a price, however. Decentralized activity gently accelerated and more groups were recruited into the mobilization process between December 1916 and April 1917; but while individual units grew stronger, central coordination lagged.

Efforts by the commission to reach the industrial economy can illustrate some of these general observations. Certainly no other activity was more important during these months, and no other activity better portrays the ideas and methods of the mobilizers at work.

Howard Coffin, unyielding engineer to the end, was still fascinated with the "national mechanism" he had fashioned from the engineering profession and hoped to extend it in new directions. He argued:

We cannot afford to discard this present machine, which has worked conscientiously in the traces for more than a year. . . . These men, upon whom must devolve the accomplishment under any well-conceived and continuing plan of action, collectively represent an expert opinion nowhere else in existence.[10]

Moreover, he adhered to his belief that industrial mobilization should enlist the maximum number of businessmen. To engage numerous manufacturers in war production would mean prosperity in every corner of the nation as well as widespread public confidence in the program itself. Coffin's experience in a consumer industry had taught him that mass appeal was an essential ingredient of any successful program, including the mobilization of industry. Perhaps, too, his past differences with the large manufacturers in the Society of Automobile Engineers fed his determination to see that small producers also gained access to any production bonanza. Coffin's fascination with his technical elite, however, partially blinded him to economic and administrative realities. He failed to distinguish clearly enough between his hopes for the engineers and the actual distribution of power in America's industrial system. He proposed to place far more responsibility on the engineering profession than it was designed to bear. Nor did he really foresee the tremendous administrative innovation required by a meaningful war preparedness.

Walter Gifford also came from a consumer industry and appreciated Coffin's emphasis on a broad, popular base. Both men perceived America as a national

[10] Coffin to Gifford, January 19, 1917, RG 62, File 2–A3, box 78.

market to be opened up and organized for government much as it would be developed for AT&T or Hudson Motors. Both men shared the managerial ethos of modern business enterprise and aimed at a formal, institutionalized, predictable system. Where they differed was over the source of its organization. Gifford showed greater realism in favoring extensive use of industrial and commercial trade associations. Both Godfrey and Rosenwald backed Gifford on this point. Gifford wanted "to get all in an industry together in a room and say, 'Gentlemen, we cannot deal with each and every one of you. We need to have the advice of your particular industry to go on. We must know what your industry thinks its difficulties and problems are. We would like to have you appoint a committee of, say, three representatives who will consult with us and give us the best advice available.'"[11] The qualities of popular participation and systematic organization were present, but interest in geographical distribution and the engineering profession had disappeared from Gifford's conception.

Gifford possessed a good sense of organizational requirements, better than either Coffin or Baruch, and it is interesting to speculate why he did not become equally prominent in the mobilization hierarchy. Part of the explanation lies in his close identification with an agency, the CND, which by its very nature could have only a small part in the mechanics of industrial organization. Gifford found himself organizationally stranded when other agencies, such as the War Industries Board, surpassed the council in strength and power. Equally important in limiting Gifford's wartime career was his textbookish approach to war organization. He tried to apply too literally the lessons he had learned at the Harvard Business School and AT&T. The very chaos of war undermined the best principles of business management and made Gifford, like Coffin, somewhat more of a theoretician than a sharp, practical operator.

Bernard Baruch, on the other hand, never wasted time with theory. His conception of how best to reach private industry was thoroughly appropriate to an independent Wall Street speculator, and to wartime chaos. Baruch's strengths meshed perfectly with the peculiar administrative setting of World War I. From a mercurial world of colorful individuals and quick, well-placed phone calls, where fortunes could be won and lost in a day, and the qualities of a poker player were more valuable than the intricacies of a sound organization chart, Baruch conceived mobilization primarily in terms of powerful personalities and only secondarily in terms of broad-based institutions. His interests in mining enterprises reinforced this orientation. Knowing the right man in the right place with the right information was and is an obvious requisite of any operation, business

[11] Walter Gifford, "The Council of National Defense," a lecture delivered to the Army Industrial College, Washington, D.C., June 1925, in Record Group 61, Records of the War Industries Board, Federal Records Center, Suitland, Md. (hereafter cited as RG 61), File 21A-A1, box 1; Godfrey to Coffin and Willard, January 5, 1917, RG 62, File 2-A3, boxes 78 and 1.

or otherwise, but it was much more a fundamental law of survival for Baruch than for either Coffin or Gifford. Hudson Motors and AT&T required interdependency, teamwork, long-range planning, stability and public acceptance; Baruch's Wall Street expected, and Baruch's own temperament ensured, individuality, sudden intuitive changes of mind, and independence from public sanctions.

It is one of the more notable ironies of Baruch's wartime career that he should emerge in the twenties and thirties as the foremost spokesman of mobilizing a democracy for war, for he held a far more elitist conception of mobilization than any of the early war administrators. He wanted the commission simply to contact the "leading man or men" in each trade. Not only could the commission acquire the requisite information this way, but it "would also have the personal help and assistance of these leading men to rely upon for quick and economic action."[12] When Walter Gifford asked Baruch how he could obtain information on copper, lead, zinc, and steel production, Baruch told him to write John D. Ryan of the Anaconda Copper Company, Daniel Guggenheim, president of the gigantic Guggenheim mining interests, and Elbert H. Gary, chairman of the board of United States Steel and public spokesman for the entire steel industry. "These men, in my opinion," wrote Baruch, "either are equipped to do this work well or can make you suggestions that are well worthy of consideration and adoption."[13] Baruch's informality emerged most clearly in his comments regarding the steel industry. Write Gary, he explained, and "ask him to consult with the people in the trade, if he so desires, or do it in any way that he would deem more efficient and let you know."[14]

Tension developed immediately between Gifford and Baruch on this point. Writing Gifford two weeks later, Baruch remarked rather testily that, "in view of the fact that the matter was referred to me, do you not think that you should carry out the line of enquiry suggested by me, otherwise I might be in the position of not having done what I was asked to do."[15]

At their February 12 meeting, the council and commission actually adopted the kind of procedures Gifford favored. The leaders of each industry would come together to organize their trade and select a small committee to represent them. The council envisaged an industry-wide organization founded upon thoroughly democratic procedures involving the participation of all trade members. Furthermore, the government indicated its intention to assume the task of

---

[12] Baruch to Gifford, January 16, 1917, Baruch journal, *Baruch Papers.* The Advisory Commission adopted Baruch's suggestion when it first met on December 6, 1916. See the *AC Minutes*, December 6 and 7, 1916.

[13] Baruch to Gifford, January 12, 1917, Baruch journal, *Baruch Papers.*

[14] *Ibid.*

[15] Baruch to Gifford, January 29, 1917, *ibid.*

organizing the unorganized. The council directed Gifford to inform Baruch and Rosenwald of important industries that needed Washington's helping hand, and they would inform Gifford of individuals he could write to get the program under way. In the AC's subsequent meeting that day each commissioner agreed to conform with the procedures approved by the council and inaugurate their conferences with industry. Gifford immediately entered lengthy talks with representatives of the United States Chamber of Commerce and the Department of Commerce to compile a list of all industrial and commercial organizations. He intended to coordinate all the committees subsequently elected and to create administrative mechanisms in those industries yet unorganized. Had this plan actually materialized, Gifford would have emerged in the front ranks of the war mobilizers.[16]

As a champion of regularized procedures, Gifford was destined for disappointment. The decision to subdivide the AC into seven special subsections and to make each commissioner master of his own domain ruled out the possibility of organizational coherence. The commissioners simply proceeded according to their own ideas and opportunities. Moreover, the thoroughness and symmetry of Gifford's scheme required a great deal of time to develop. Disorganized industries would not produce effective trade committees overnight. The sheer press of events rendered Baruch's approach the most practical. After April 6 there would be hardly enough time even for quick phone calls.

But there was another reason why Gifford fell from the front rank of mobilizers. Unlike the raw materials commissioner, Gifford directed his attention to secondary centers of economic power. In this respect he shared Howard Coffin's penchant for missing the point. Even if Gifford had accomplished his scheme before April 6, his series of trade organizations would still have depended ultimately on the willingness of giant business corporations to cooperate. Establishing an effective liaison with an organization like the United States Chamber of Commerce had several real advantages, but it could not in itself actually mobilize key sectors of the national economy. Baruch proved more perceptive. He cultivated good relations with corporate executives themselves, with those who possessed the most direct access to economic control. His ability to attach himself to the major centers of power in the industrial economy propelled him to the forefront of industrial mobilization. For this reason alone Baruch's committee on raw materials and metals was destined to become the most significant subcommittee of the CND and AC. In fact, Baruch's organiza-

[16] *CND Minutes*, February 12, 1917; *AC Minutes*, February 12 and 15, 1917; "Report of the Director," *CND Minutes*, February 28, 1917; U.S. Congress, Senate, Committee on Military Affairs, *Hearings, Investigation of the War Department*, 65th Cong., 2nd sess., 1917–1918 (hereafter cited as Chamberlain Committee, *Hearings*), part 3, p. 1853; E. E. Pratt (chief, Bureau of Foreign and Domestic Commerce) to Gifford, March 12, 1917, RG 62, File 2–A1, box 32.

tion ultimately became more central than any other in the general issue of business-government relations, and in the specific chain of events surrounding the formation and evolution of the War Industries Board.

Howard Coffin was a significant force in this early period, of course, but he too proved less important than Baruch for the development of business-government relations under the WIB. His committee on munitions, manufacturing, standardization, and industrial relations created tentative links between the AC, the business world, and the military departments, and Coffin recruited a number of important business experts to Washington before April 1917. But the engineer's personal interests carried him toward aviation production, and in mid-April the president appointed him head of the Aircraft Production Board. Coffin thus associated himself with a totally underdeveloped sector of the economy—aircraft production. He had virtually to create constituencies on either side, among businessmen and with military officials unfamiliar with the requirements of aircraft manufacturing. Furthermore, Coffin remained mesmerized by the panacea of standardization. "If I heard Coffin talking in his sleep," remarked a Washington official during the war, "I wouldn't take the trouble to go over and listen because I would know exactly what he would be saying. 'Standardize! Standardize! Standardize!' That's his motto, his slogan, his creed."[17] All these factors set limits on how far Coffin could move toward the center of decision-making in industrial mobilization.

The strengths and weaknesses of Coffin's passions are revealed in the brief rise and fall of the Munitions Standards Board. In his obsessive quest for standardized munitions production, the auto engineer proposed the creation of an "expert body" which could criticize existing munitions specifications, make the necessary adjustments for mass production, and generally extend the theories of his industrial preparedness campaign. As a result of this suggestion, the MSB was formed on March 3. Its members included W. H. VanderVoort of the Root and VanderVoort Engineering Company, manufacturers of special machine tools; E. A. Deeds of the Dayton Engineering Laboratories; Frank A. Scott of Warner and Swasey Company, manufacturers of machine tools and optical instruments; Francis Pratt of the General Electric Company; Samuel Vauclain of the Baldwin Locomotive Works; and John E. Otterson of the Winchester Arms Company. Aside from Coffin's partiality for engineers, the major criterion for selecting these men was their familiarity with munitions production. All of them had been filling Allied orders for the past two years and were now intimately connected with the process, aware of the state of this new and rapidly growing industry. Their own companies had already discussed conversion with army and navy ordnance officers and they were in a good position to prepare their own plants

---

[17]Quoted in Edwin Wildman, "Howard Coffin and the Air War in the Air," *Forum* 59 (March 1918): 260.

for orders, as well as to recommend the kinds of tooling changes that other less experienced companies would have to make. Samuel Vauclain, the hard working, irascible vice-president of the Baldwin Locomotive Works, had travelled twice to Russia in 1914 to procure locomotive orders, and by March 1917 had extended that company's war production to rifles, manufacturing four thousand a day for the British government.[18]

In one respect, of course, the MSB was an extension of Howard Coffin's work of the past year and a half. Coffin explained to the board members on March 21 that he wanted the MSB to become that channel between the munitions industry and the military departments he had been trying to build since 1915. As usual, Coffin was sensitive to the grand possibilities which lay before a government agency if it seized every opportunity to grasp power. "It seems to me there are two main values of this Board," he explained. "One is, to put it simply, the getting of arguments out of the way now in time of peace, instead of trying to avoid them and having to fight them out in time of war. The other is to get Congressional influence, and the value of getting men who represent big business affairs intimately in touch with the inside conditions, down here."[19]

The military officers present indicated their willingness to cooperate in the project even while they bemoaned the legal restrictions and financial penury that prevented them from resolving the problem the way they would have liked. They looked forward to any power or appropriations the MSB could gain for them. Admiral Earle commented that his bureau of ordnance suffered from a shortage of draftsmen and clerks, but his hands were tied since no additional people could be employed without specific congressional appropriations. General Babbitt of the army ordnance department nodded in agreement.[20]

To enter any meeting in Washington in 1917 was to walk in a volunteer and come out a committee chairman, and the first meeting of the MSB proved no exception. The board divided into six committees: J. E. Otterson took charge of small arms and small arms ammunition; W. H. VanderVoort, naval artillery and ammunition; Francis Pratt, gauges, specifications, gigs, and fixtures; E. A. Deeds, time fuses and detonators; and Frank Scott, scientific instruments, including optical and range-finding apparatus. Each man was instructed to engage his own set of experts, as the members of the NCB and AC had done before them, and to

---

[18] *CND Minutes*, February 17 and March 3, 1917; *AC Minutes*, February 24 and March 3, 1917; "Statement of Samuel Vauclain," *Baruch Papers*; U.S. Congress, *Hearings before the Commission Appointed under the Authority of Public Resolution no. 98*, Res. 251, 71st Cong., 2nd sess., 1931, part 1, pp. 288–309.

[19] Minutes of a meeting of the Munitions Standards Board (hereafter cited as *MSB Minutes*), March 21, 1917, in the Frank A. Scott Papers, Princeton University, Princeton, N.J., box 1.

[20] *Ibid.* Also see *New York Times*, March 16 and 22, 1917, pp. 7 and 2.

decide on the changes needed to inaugurate mass production of munitions for American use.[21]

By bringing men like Vauclain and Pratt to Washington, Coffin certainly extended the interconnections between industry and the military, and since each of these individuals took on responsibility to recruit his friends, Coffin had also multiplied the potential personnel for industrial preparedness many times over. Additionally, the MSB subcommittees began to develop their individual programs and to that extent improved the chances for effective munitions production.[22]

What the MSB experiment tells us about the organizational evolution of the WIB, however, follows not from the MSB's achievements, but from its limitations. First, the MSB was based on a fairly narrow concern. Although standardized munitions production was a worthy goal and an important contribution to any successful industrial mobilization, more pressing problems awaited solution before the country could mobilize all its resources. Without full mobilization, even standardized munitions production appeared a relatively minor if not wholly academic question. Second, the MSB essentially aligned itself with only one small segment of the government, the ordnance department, a factor which also limited its role on the broader questions of economic preparedness. Third, the board itself never developed any unity. Coffin exercised no control over his body of experts. They ventured forth independently, just as Coffin had done on the NCB. The individual subcommittees may have thrived, but the MSB disappeared as a functioning agency by the end of March. Finally, Howard Coffin's mania for standardization isolated him further from the mainstream of policy development. Not content with small triumphs at home, he turned next to propose uniform production standards for the world. On April 26 Coffin urged the CND to consider creation of a commission on international munitions standards as well as an interchange of technical commissions among foreign countries and the United States.[23] Baker ultimately vetoed this proposal.[24]

---

[21] *CND Minutes*, March 24, 1917.

[22] The members of the MSB lobbied on behalf of the Kernan report (against government munitions manufacturing), offered their services to private manufacturers and the military bureaus, and organized information and personnel from private munitions firms. J. E. Otterson's committee had representatives from twelve leading armaments manufacturers, including Remington Arms Company, Smith & Wesson, and Colt Firearms. See Scott to Moline Forging & Manufacturing Company, April 6, 1917, RG 61, File 1–A1, box 17; J. E. Otterson to Chester C. Bolton, April 11, 1917, *ibid.*, box 23; Francis C. Pratt to Scott, April 2, 6, and 8, 1917, all *ibid.*, box 10.

[23] *AC Minutes*, April 26, 1917; *CND Minutes*, April 28, 1917; Coffin to House, April 5, 1917, Edward M. House Papers, Yale University, New Haven.

[24] *AC Minutes*, June 1, 1917.

Walter Gifford and Howard Coffin were not the only mobilizers to fall behind Bernard Baruch in the drive for influence and power. Julius Rosenwald's committee on supplies also dealt with industry; it contributed a large number of industrial committees to the early preparedness program; and it touched directly the development of the WIB. Yet it, too, never kept pace with Baruch's operation. As with Coffin and the MSB, the committee on supplies made the mistake of focusing its energies on a single segment of the military and federal bureaucracy. The supplies committee became intimately associated with the army's quartermaster department and although it thoroughly dominated activities there, this connection necessarily limited the total range of its influence. Baruch, on the other hand, never offered the regular departments any opportunity to define or absorb his committee. His allegiance was to his business clientele first, and to the military departments second. While this bias generated antipathy from some military officials, it gained Baruch the favor of a broad cross section of American industrialists.

An equally important factor in accounting for Rosenwald's secondary role was that the kinds of commodities the committee dealt with often put it in direct competition with Herbert Hoover's Food Administration; and while the Rosenwald committee was able to maintain its primacy in the early stages, it eventually succumbed to Hoover's more powerful and effective agency. Rosenwald's voice was simply not heard very often in meetings of top level government officials. After his initial participation in the AC's work, Rosenwald assigned major responsibility to his assistant, Charles Eisenman of Cleveland, and then moved to the sidelines. The charges of corruption levelled at Eisenman later in the war, coupled with a congressional investigation into the committee's relationship with the quartermaster department, further undermined the supplies committee.[25]

As his competitors moved off into administrative cul-de-sacs, Baruch made his committee on raw materials one of the most impressive satellites of personnel and power in the organizational galaxy of wartime Washington. And with good reason. Although Baruch had been appointed to the commission "because of his ability as a financier and his valuable connections with matters of finance," the president's rejection of John Ryan had left the commission without a "representative of the mining, engineering and producing interests of the country," and Baruch moved eagerly to fill that post.[26] His own previous interests in mining

---

[25] President Wilson felt it necessary to write Rosenwald later in the war: "I have realized that you must have felt recently that you and your associates were a bit thrown out of function, but I hope you realize that if that is true, it is largely because of the excellence of the work you did and the fact that it has come to a full fruitage." Wilson to Rosenwald, March 7, 1918, Woodrow Wilson Papers, Library of Congress, Washington, D.C. (hereafter cited as *Wilson Papers*).

[26] Baker to Wilson, September 18, 1916, *ibid.*

and raw material ventures gave the switch some justification, and his drive for power gave it some urgency. By virtue of this strategic move, Baruch attached himself to one of the most dynamic and vital sectors of an emerging war economy. The booming American munitions industry had already afforded business firms some experience crucial to his raw materials committee. The lengthy conferences which Baruch held with Leland L. Summers at his South Carolina estate soon after his AC nomination are symbolic of the growing connection which would occur between Baruch and the private munitions industry. Baruch thereby secured the services of one of the most knowledgeable of munitions experts to guide his private strategy. Summers was an engineer-entrepreneur, acquainted with metallurgical and chemical processes, familiar through travel with the European munitions market, and recently in command of Allied heavy gun and shell purchases at the J. P. Morgan Company.[27]

It was one of Baruch's great talents to surround himself with men like Summers from private industry who understood the technical side of economic mobilization and could thus compensate for the deficiencies in his own knowledge. Baruch was a stock speculator, not a mining engineer or industrial developer. An acquaintance recalled:

Baruch was a very personal operator. He wasn't a technician in any sense. He wasn't used to dealing with engineering problems. He was good at getting men, backing them, testing them, and keeping his equanimity.[28]

In retrospect, the far-ranging interests and aggressiveness of Baruch and his men made his rise to a position of eminence seem inevitable. But this was in the future. From December 1916 to April 1917, Baruch was only beginning to reach his particular clientele—the business elite of the world of raw materials. Among those to whom he wrote in March were Coleman DuPont, president of the DuPont Powder Company; John P. Wood, president of the National Association of Wool Manufacturers; Ambrose Monell, president of the International Nickel Company; Elbert H. Gary, president of the American Iron and Steel Institute; and Arthur V. Davis, president of the American Aluminum Company. By the

[27]Diary of Chandler P. Anderson, January 25 and March 22, 1918, in the Chandler P. Anderson Papers, Manuscript Division, Library of Congress, Washington, D.C.; "Statement of L. L. Summers," *Baruch Papers*; Bernard Baruch, *Baruch: The Public Years* (New York: Holt, Rinehart and Winston, 1960), pp. 75–76. Baruch may have lured Summers to Washington by topping his $30,000–$35,000 salary at Morgan's.

[28]Eugene Meyer, Jr., Memoir, Oral History Collection, Columbia University, New York (hereafter cited as *Meyer Memoir*). For an amplification of this point, see Robert D. Cuff, "Bernard Baruch: Symbol and Myth in Industrial Mobilization," *Business History Review* 43 (Summer 1969): 119–29. As early as April 1917, Baruch's wartime operation was costing him $375.00 per month in rent alone. See correspondence attached to Gifford to Pierce, April 21, 1917, RG 61, File 21A–A1, box 20.

end of the month Baruch had formed committees in the leather, rubber, steel, wool, copper, and oil industries, and he reported that committees were being formed on zinc, coal, spruce wood, sulphuric acid, alloys, tin, brass, and tar products. Trade jealousies hindered the work in several industries, but Baruch claimed that he had generally encountered "a unanimous disposition among all classes of businessmen to join in the work."[29] He informed the AC that he was also negotiating with raw material producers for lower prices on government supplies, and making studies of the production of cans, tin plate, and minerals of military importance. He urged the commission to consider transportation conditions, the development of rubber and nitrate soda supplies, and raw material prices. A month later he indicated that more than twenty committees were under discussion. By June he listed 33 committees in his jurisdiction involving approximately 170 eminent businessmen.[30]

In testimony before the Graham committee in 1920, Baruch claimed he had written every committee member.[31] In truth, the situation was somewhat more complex. In some cases, Baruch did get in touch with all the members of a particular committee. But in many others he thought it sufficient to make contact with the industry's leading spokesman and let him designate any associates. Baruch asked Judge Elbert Gary to form a committee on steel and steel products, but left the task of mobilizing personnel for the entire industry to the judge. That the committee on steel eventually spawned eleven subcommittees was the result of Gary and the American Iron and Steel Institute, not Baruch. To fill the complement of three on the aluminum committee, Baruch readily accepted the suggestions of its chairman, Arthur V. Davis.[32] Moreover, Baruch

[29] AC Minutes, March 23, 1917; Baruch to Coleman DuPont, March 6, 1917, RG 61, File 21A-A1, box 20; Baruch to John P. Wood, March 19, 1917, and to Ambrose Monell, March 10, 1917, both in Baruch journal, Baruch Papers; Elbert H. Gary to Baruch, March 16, 1917, Daniels Papers; Arthur V. Davis to Baruch, April 4, 1917, RG 61, File 21B-A4, box 171. See also Baruch to H. B. Endicott, March 10, 1917, Baruch journal, Baruch Papers; Baruch to George S. Davidson and to E. L. Doheny, March 30, 1917, and to J. W. Van Dyke, March 31, 1917, all ibid. Baruch later claimed that, "In many instances there was great difficulty in getting them to serve, because they would rather not have served, for many reasons." U.S. Congress, House, Select Committee on Expenditures in the War Department, Expenditures in the War Department, Hearings... , 66th Cong., 1st sess., 1920 (hereafter cited as Graham committee, Hearings), serial 1, p. 1795.

[30] Baruch to Gifford, April 20, 1917, RG 62, File 2A-8, box 86; CND Minutes, April 21, 1917; Baruch to Frank Scott, April 20, 1917, RG 61, File 21A-A1, box 19; "Sub-Committees of the Committee on Raw Materials, Minerals and Metals," list no. 4, June 1917, ibid.

[31] Graham Committee, Hearings, serial 1, p. 1795.

[32] Gary to Newton D. Baker, March 29, 1917, Daniels Papers; Davis to Baruch, April 4, 1917, RG 61, File 21B-A4, box 171.

did not personally know all the businessmen he did write. This is not to deny his claim that no man "had a much better idea of . . . the men in the organizations of the various industries than I had, because I used to make it my business to know who they were and what they were doing,"[33] but only to point out that he could not be expected to know every important businessman in the whole field of raw materials. He frequently sought the advice of personal acquaintances and welcomed the suggestions of the man who was already his contact in an industry. In searching for a committee on raw rubber, he wrote a contact, "I am told that the Rubber Association of America is the proper authority with whom to take up this matter. I would like to know the individual there who would have a driving force."[34]

Baruch employed a mixture of recruitment techniques. But at no time did he meet with an entire industry or encourage it to elect a small committee, as Gifford and the council had suggested. Baruch adhered to his original premise of dealing exclusively with the two or three most powerful men in the industry and leaving the rest in their hands. "The plan was one of decentralization," he recalled later, "so that, as long as we got cooperation, we left the interior organization and control of the particular industry to the leaders of that industry as represented by these committees."[35]

The cooperative committees, as they were called, inaugurated during peacetime when the chief goal appeared to be the collection of information, were conceived as strictly advisory groups, similar to the AC itself. They were to serve as information centers, collating data from industry studies which the commissioners could assimilate in making recommendations to the council. When Baruch suggested that Gifford write Gary of U.S. Steel, he outlined the kinds of things the commission should know about that industry.

. . . What the steel and allied manufacturers of this country can do in case of necessity for the defense of the country as well as supplying both Army and Navy, Railroads and whatever may be necessary for the defense and maintenance of the country. Some idea of the location of the various plants, their capacities, how much they could supply, or, instead of giving the location of each plant, a general locality. How much they can still increase their capacities and in what time. What arms or ammunition the steel manufacturers or their allied or owned companies now make, if they do not make, what length of time would be necessary to convert their plants into the manufacture of armor, arms and artil-

---

[33] Graham Committee, *Hearings*, serial 1, p. 1807.

[34] Baruch to Raymond B. Price, March 6, 1917, RG 61, File 21A–A1, box 20. Price responded with a list of names. Price to Baruch, March 19, 1917, RG 62, File 2–A1, box 49.

[35] Bernard M. Baruch, "Address on Economic Mobilization before Corps of Cadets, West Point, May 4, 1929," Public Papers of Bernard Baruch, vol. 1., *Baruch Papers.*

lery; what ingredients or metals they do not own or are not produced in this country by others that would be necessary for their purposes. Whether it is possible to develop production of these necessary ingredients.[36]

And finally, the commission should discover the average age of steel employees and how many men could be replaced by women workers.

Little of substance was really accomplished in steel or any other industry before America entered the war. Baruch wrote directly for information to executives at DuPont, International Nickel, New Jersey Zinc, and other firms. He also requested that Gifford get from all government departments lists of foreign imports required by the military services and he would "endeavor to complete the data by getting the men and firms who deal in those articles and endeavor to form committees through whom the Government can deal."[37] But the committees themselves were just in the process of formation before April; they were not yet coherent units.

With typical energy and ambition, the raw materials commissioner decided in mid-March of 1917 to have the price of copper reduced on government supplies, and wrote both Secretary Baker and Secretary Daniels to discover the amounts they might need along with the favored delivery dates.

I wish you would take this matter up immediately as I believe that it would result in establishing a precedent in the naming of prices for all raw material which would result in large savings to the Government and which perhaps might affect contracts already given out and which might be most potent in causing coordination between business and the Government which I understand was one of the underlying reasons for the President's desire in forming the Council and its Commission.[38]

Both Daniels and Baker were gratified to learn of the possibility of obtaining their copper requirements at reduced prices and indicated their need of 45.5 million pounds, 20 million pounds to the navy, and 25.5 million pounds to the army.[39] Baruch now had to make good on his promise.

He sought out Eugene Meyer, Jr., in New York to get an idea of the kind of price he could expect to pay. Meyer, a director of the Utah Copper Company then controlled by the Guggenheim mining empire, was already experienced in engineering price agreements among competitors, and acquainted with Baruch from stock deals on Wall Street. Well before they met on Fifth Avenue on a Sunday afternoon, Meyer had concluded that the present copper price of 36 cents

[36] Baruch to Gifford, January 12, 1917, Baruch journal, *Baruch Papers.*

[37] Baruch to Gifford, March 12, 1917, *ibid.*

[38] Baruch to Daniels, March 13, 1917, *ibid.*

[39] Daniels to Baruch, March 16, 1917, *Daniels Papers.*

was undesirable and dangerous. As Meyer and Baruch talked, they agreed that the ultimate goal at this point was more psychological than economic, however. They would have their triumph in public relations, not economics. Meyer and Baruch wanted to stabilize the copper market, but they were even more eager to show the American people that big business was not driving the country to war in search of profits. Meyer believed the producers could be persuaded to agree to sell at the average selling price of the last ten years, which would be 16 2/3¢ per pound. "My God," said Baruch, "I never expected to get it at a price like that."[40]

Daniel Guggenheim, doyen of the copper trade, lived close by at the St. Regis Hotel and held an open house at 5:00 o'clock every Sunday afternoon, so Meyer and Baruch went over to explain their proposition. Meyer took the position that he was "talking from the point of view of the industry, and what it should do for the common good."[41] Guggenheim was intrigued with the proposal, but he had first to discuss it with his brothers and with the people at Anaconda, Phelps Dodge, Calumet, and Hecla, the four big selling groups in the industry. Baruch received word on Monday morning: the producers had agreed. On March 20, Baruch wired the good news to Daniels and Baker.[42]

As Meyer recalled later, it was "really a feather in Baruch's cap."[43] The press wrote up the producers' patriotic gesture, as Baruch and Meyer had hoped, and Baruch became the man of the hour. Encouraged by this coup, he set out to arrange similar agreements with the aluminum, lead, zinc, and steel industries. Baruch knew that early successes like this one "helped to ease my way into official Washington, and to win the confidence of my associates and the President."[44]

The copper incident did not involve a regular cooperative committee, but it did foreshadow a number of their later developments and it does highlight

---

[40] *Meyer Memoir. Engineering and Mining Journal* argued that "the copper market will be better for everybody if a decline to 20–25¢ comes soon"; "The Copper Producers Gift to the Government," *Engineering and Mining Journal* 103 (March 31, 1917), 547. Colonel House had also been thinking of asking industrial leaders to give some public display of their patriotism. See *House Diary*, February 7, 1917.

[41] *Meyer Memoir.* See also Baruch, *The Public Years*, pp. 39–40, and Baruch, *My Own Story* (New York: Henry Holt, 1957), pp. 194–95.

[42] Baruch to John D. Ryan, March 19, 1917, and to Daniels, March 20, 1917, both in Baruch journal, *Baruch Papers.*

[43] *Meyer Memoir.*

[44] Baruch, *The Public Years*, p. 40. See also Franklin D. Roosevelt to Baruch, March 22, 1917, *Baruch Papers*; Baruch to Baker, March 24, 1917, RG 61, File 21B–A4, box 171; *New York Times*, March 21, 25, and 27, 1917; and Lewis Kennedy Morse, "The Price-Fixing of Copper," *Quarterly Journal of Economics* 23 (November 1918): 71–106 for an overview of copper price fixing.

essential features of early business-government relations under the AC. The copper deal was an exercise in business connections. Baruch's personal acquaintances provided him the necessary entrée. Baruch had known Meyer previously and had had a long association with the Guggenheims. They had made his father their family doctor and had asked the young Baruch to run a number of financial errands for them.[45] The copper industry had good reason to ingratiate itself with the Wilson administration and with the American public in general, but still, the role which personal friendships played ought not to be overlooked. The interests of Baruch and the copper producers coincided at this point. And as it evolved, the entire committee network depended less on formal regulation than on gentlemens' agreements among colleagues, friends, and sympathetic government officials.

In confining his enquiry to a large, low-cost producer, Baruch set the pattern for all committee actions to follow. It was far more possible for large firms than for small ones to offer lower prices, to arrange shipment at short notice, and to encourage others to enter agreements by means of their trade leadership. The general familiarity which large producers had with such values as stability, industry-wide cooperation, price maintenance, and long-range planning also made them more sympathetic to the efforts of the government's business advisors. Large producers dominated all subsequent arrangements. The success of Baruch's strategy depended in large part on the extent of monopolistic or oligopolistic control in an industry, or the degree to which a more competitive trade had developed organizational techniques of cooperation and control.

The curious amalgam of patriotism and self-interest that distinguished the copper agreement would characterize business-government relations in the future, just as it had characterized preparedness activity in the past. Some members of the industry were convinced that prices should come down, and Meyer sensed that whatever opposition remained in the trade might quickly dissipate if the move were cast in a patriotic mold with the unofficial sanction of the federal government. Meyer considered the agreement "the beginning of a little more reasonable price-fixing than this anarchy which prevailed before this arrangement."[46] A patriotic gesture might also avoid the public obloquy usually associated with private collusion. Although nothing bound the parties in the future, the copper agreement set a precedent which could possibly curb the price spiral and ward off the need for strict federal controls in the event of war. Baruch had demonstrated in this agreement his tactic of cultivating an image in business of selflessness as a way to ward off radical antibusiness attacks.

Baruch and the advisory commissioners fashioned their own spheres of influence as best they could, but their agency still languished on the sidelines. The

---

[45] Baruch, *My Own Story*, pp. 71–72; Margaret L. Coit, *Mr. Baruch* (Boston: Houghton Mifflin, 1957), pp. 117–23.

[46] *Meyer Memoir.*

military departments were officially charged with the big tasks of mobilization—raising and equipping the army and navy—while Congress was responsible for determining the flow of funds to support them. For information the AC depended upon the first-hand accounts of Americans recently returned from Europe; for action, on its own initiative. Council and commission meetings increased to two or three a week but they accomplished little of practical value. The commission remained severely circumscribed by lack of authority, an uncertain mandate, and official indifference. "It is altogether likely that the Commission will fall far short, in accomplishment, of what the public will expect, regardless of what its accomplishments may be," Daniel Willard commented in early March, "but that, I suppose, is true to a greater or lesser extent concerning all positions in the public service, and generally I think in a service of any kind or character."[47]

By the end of March, relations between the AC and its parent council had reached their lowest point. Regardless of the formation of the MSB and the actions they were taking in their independent spheres of influence, the members of the AC felt acutely the absence of leadership and direction in the fledgling mobilization program. No single agency combined the scope, desire, or power to bring about central coordination and an aggressive departure from a policy of drift. On March 23, Daniel Willard, the commission's permanent chairman, read a letter to the council which he and the other commissioners hoped would spur the department heads to greater activity. The report called for an army of one million men, a navy at full strength and fully equipped, the protection of all strategic sites, and "some definite and comprehensive" policy of coordinating local defense efforts with the federal government.[48] It only hinted at the commission's bitterness at being shut out of the real areas of Washington decision-making. A second report submitted a week later broadened the scope of the attack and demanded action on ocean transport, railroad transportation, and airplane and munitions production. Furthermore, the commission recommended that, to ensure the coordination of Allied and American needs, "the time has arrived when we should give serious consideration to the establishment by this Government of what might be called a Bureau of Production and Distribution, something in fact analogous to the Ministry of Munitions in England." To supplement this bureau, a priorities committee should also be formed to "pass upon

---

[47]Willard to Charles R. Neill, March 9, 1917, RG 62, File 1–A1, box 1. Willard's skepticism about public life was matched by a deep commitment to his private business career. He wrote, "I would not give up my position as President of the Baltimore & Ohio Railroad Company for any office in the gift of the Government." Willard to Roland E. Stevens, March 9, 1917, *ibid.*

[48]This letter, written by Daniel Willard on the AC's behalf, can be found in RG 62, File 2–A9, box 89. See also *AC Minutes*, March 23, 1917, and *CND Minutes*, March 24, 1917; *House Diary*, March 25, 1917; and Chamberlain Committee, *Hearings*, part 6, pp. 2253–69.

the relative importance of all work to be done by our manufacturing plants."
And finally, recognition should be given at once to the fact that "many activities
such as ordinarily go on in time of peace will have to be discontinued or very
largely curtailed during a state of war."[49]

These reports were direct and critical judgments of the capabilities of the
military services as presently constituted to handle the whole problem of industrial mobilization. According to the AC, the bureau of production and distribution would "take charge in a general way of all purchases for all departments of
the Government," in effect relieving the military departments of all responsibility
in the matter.[50]

From their very first days in Washington, the business members of the
commission had been disturbed about the situation within the War Department.
Military thinkers and civilian secretaries of war had long made the department
the object of reform. But it had managed to defy innovation and concentration
with a fiercely obstinate tradition and individualism. Elihu Root's general staff
system was more effective on paper than in practice, and the semiautonomous
supply bureaus practiced for war by fighting each other. The army's purchasing
functions had escaped the grasp of a single hand and lay scattered throughout
the department bureaus. The quartermaster and ordnance departments did
most of the buying, and the Rosenwald and Baruch committees directed most of
their attention to them. Other bureaus, like the office of the surgeon-general and
the office of the chief signal officer, were also involved, and they absorbed
the attention of Martin and Coffin. The decentralized, disconnected army supply
organization made it impossible for the AC to coordinate and centralize its
efforts. Nor were means available to terminate the fierce competition between
the army and navy. Furthermore, the planners in both departments were uncertain as to what supplies full-scale mobilization might require. To someone like
Howard Coffin, who had spent two years trying to design long-range conversion
plans, the apparent unwillingness or inability of the military departments to
compile estimates of future needs was disheartening to say the least. Julius
Rosenwald and Bernard Baruch, who had caught a glimpse of the chaos as they
endeavored to arrange purchases of raw materials, food stuffs, and clothing,
shared Coffin's alarm. Baruch asked Daniels and Baker to have their two departments cooperate, and Coffin wanted the AC to consider how to coordinate army
purchasing. At last the three commissioners were empowered to form a special
investigating committee, and thus was launched a continuing battle by businessmen to reform the regular military supply structure.[51]

[49] Willard to Baker, March 31, 1917, Newton D. Baker Papers, Library of Congress,
Washington, D.C.

[50] *Ibid.* Secretary Lane was also pressuring the council for greater preparedness; *CND
Minutes*, March 31, 1917.

[51] *AC Minutes*, March 23, 1917; Baruch to Daniels, March 21, 1917, Selected Correspondence, *Baruch Papers*; Gifford to Baruch, March 22, 1917, RG 61, File 21A–A4, box

The commissioners' radical proposals demanded the immediate overthrow of traditional military prerogatives without even a hint of compromise. Born more of frustration than rational calculation, such recommendations were far in advance of sentiment within either the administration or among the public at large. So remote were they from the realm of possibility in March 1917, that we might better regard them as a dramatic, protective gesture by the commission to avoid future recriminations over failure to prepare America for war. A munitions ministry was only a dream at this stage, destined to evaporate before the realities of politics and power. Sentiment for it lingered on among the business-commissioners, however, and the dream reappeared with the same allure in the winter of 1917-1918, when the mobilization program again seemed to have come to a standstill.

The commissioners' program did not fully appreciate the handicaps under which the military departments struggled, hedged in as they were by peacetime statutes on appropriation allocations, by presidential declarations against war planning, and by lack of personnel. The Washington general staff had less than 20 officers to direct the American war effort, and only 11 of these were attached to its planning section, the War College Division. The army had not stood still, though, as the AC report would lead us to believe. In mid-February, for example, the War College submitted a scheme to raise a "National Army" of four million men and laid down a theoretical structure for the nation's draft system. The War Department bureaus, meanwhile, pursued their own preparedness measures. They had prompted a survey of the country's capacity for munitions production as early as November 1915; the ordnance department discussed orders with large manufacturers; and the War College cooperated with Coffin's plans for educational munitions contracts. Moreover, on March 26, 1917, Baker approved the idea of a "steering committee" of bureau chiefs to coordinate their purchasing program.[52] Colonel House was a strong preparedness advocate and sympathetic to the discontent among business advisors in March. But even he felt they were too harsh in their criticism of military officials. "There is something ... to be said for them," he wrote, "and that is an active business man coming in touch with governmental affairs for the first time is apt to misjudge

---

1210. Coffin and Baruch also took their complaints to Colonel House, *House Diary*, March 25 and April 6, 1917.

[52] Tasker C. Bliss to the Chief, War College Division, November 11, 1915; "Mobilization of Industries and Utilization of the Commercial and Industrial Resources of the Country for War Purposes in Emergency" (doc. no. 8125-45); William Crozier to Chief, War College Division, March 24, 1916; and W. M. Black to Chief, War College Division, March 24, 1916, all in Record Group 165, Records of the War College Division of the General Staff, National Archives, Washington, D.C. (cited hereafter as RG 165), box 240; and "Memorandum for the Chief of Staff," from Joseph E. Kuhn, March 31, 1917, RG 165, box 259. Also see Edward M. Coffman, *The War to End All Wars: The American Experience in World War I* (New York: Oxford University Press, 1968), pp. 23-24, 29, 32-33, 51-53.

conditions and want to hurry things beyond prudence."[53] Moreover, as the administration's business advisors frequently learned throughout the war, the army was not deaf to the cries for innovation. Given sufficient pressures, it could respond well enough at times to diffuse radical civilian challenges. It did precisely this at the end of March, on Secretary Baker's initiative.

For an antimilitarist, Newton D. Baker identified remarkably fast with the prerogatives of military institutions. He became secretary of war in March 1916, and tenaciously fought off encroachments on his departmental preserves. His experience as city solicitor and mayor of Cleveland planted in him a great faith in local government and a parallel bias against federal power. Baker was fully convinced that America could respond to wartime demands with a minimum of change in her traditional institutions. The corollaries of this assumption included a fear of major organizational innovation, a distaste for emergency government, and a deep suspicion of increased state power. Once changes were admitted as necessary, Baker preferred to expand old procedures rather than design new ones. For Baker, organizational adaptation in the context of American war government meant greater efficiency for a chain of command which on the civilian side ran through the subordinate parts of the CND, and which on the army side ran through the subordinate parts of the general staff system, and which culminated finally in his double office as secretary of war and chairman of the CND. To head off the AC challenge and strengthen his own position within the military-CND structure, Baker set up a General Munitions Board in early April and tapped Frank A. Scott to direct it.[54]

Scott is one of the forgotten figures of industrial mobilization during the Great War. He was born in Cleveland in 1873, received his education there, and joined its business community as an official of the Cleveland Chamber of Commerce and as president of the Warner and Swasey Company after 1909. A trip to Europe on business before 1914 convinced Scott of the inevitability of Anglo-German conflict and he directed Warner and Swasey to gear up munitions production, having munitions supplies on English docks when the war broke out. Scott satisfied his preparedness instincts by establishing contacts with the army ordnance department and by joining Coffin's campaign in 1915 as a representative of the Ohio branch of the American Society of Mechanical Engineers. In March 1917, he received two invitations to come to Washington, one from the

---

[53] *House Diary*, March 25, 1917.

[54] Daniel R. Beaver, "Newton D. Baker and the Genesis of the War Industries Board, 1917-1918," *Journal of American History* 52 (June 1965): 44-45; and Beaver, *Newton D. Baker and the American War Effort, 1917-1919* (Lincoln: University of Nebraska Press, 1966), pp. 1-8, 51-52, 217. Baker recalled, with some bitterness, after the war: "Every time a new need arose, or some new functions, a new board was created, until we had a wilderness of boards. Nobody knew who they were." "Remarks of Secretary Baker at First Meeting of the Inter-Departmental Board, Council of National Defense, November 10, 1919," RG 165, box 240.

ordnance department to join the reserves, the other from Secretary Baker to join the MSB. Baker had known Scott in Cleveland and could now appreciate the industrialist's high regard for military institutions. From the time his father had suggested he study the Civil War as a hobby, Scott had devoured military lore with a passion and developed a deep admiration for the military profession in the process. Scott deferred to Baker's request and was thereupon elected chairman of the MSB on March 21, beginning a wartime career in Washington which brought him to the chairmanship of the General Munitions Board in April 1917, and of the War Industries Board the following July.[55]

From the outset, Scott displayed a deference to military sensibilities which became his trademark in Washington. Unlike those businessmen attached to the AC, Scott did not seek to redistribute power among the military services and emergency civilian organizations. He came to Washington to help preserve military authority, not undermine it. His vision of industrial mobilization gave the dominant role to the military services. "We have no thought, whatever," he told the military officers at the first MSB meeting, "of paralleling the system which you have already built up, with another system."[56] Scott believed the AC's munitions ministry was the penultimate threat to traditional military roles. He envisaged himself as directing a holding action for the services until they could adapt sufficiently well to direct mobilization without leaning on emergency civilian agencies. All this, of course, stands in marked contrast with Baruch and the AC, who hoped to integrate the military services into a larger corporate system administered by a civilian, business-dominated organization.[57]

Discussions over some kind of coordinating agency in the latter part of March brought these differences to a head, and as it turned out immediate events favored Scott's predispositions. As we have said, something as drastic as a munitions ministry was far too premature. Baruch and like-minded men could not expect to break through traditional authority and institutions at this point, with the United States still out of the war.[58] Scott's approach was more attuned to

---

[55] Address to the Epworth Men's Club, November 30, 1914, Frank A. Scott Papers, Princeton University, Princeton, N.J. (cited hereafter as *Scott Papers*); *Cleveland Plain Dealer*, July 10, 1916, a clipping in *ibid.*; "Statement of Frank A. Scott," *Baruch Papers*; Scott to Colonel Irving J. Carr, April 17, 1928, and Colonel C. B. Babbitt to Scott, February 21, 1917, both *Scott Papers*; Frank A. Scott, "Industrial Mobilization for a Great War," lecture delivered to the Army War College, December 16, 1926, bound with ten others as part of the *Scott Papers*, and cited hereafter as *Scott Lectures*; Graham Committee, *Hearings*, Serial 3, p. 987.

[56] *MSB Minutes*, March 21, 1917.

[57] "Statement of Frank A. Scott," *Baruch Papers*; Frank A. Scott, "Industrial Mobilization for a Great War," October 29, 1926, and "Organization of the War Industries Board," both in *Scott Lectures*; Graham Committee, *Hearings*, Serial 3, p. 994.

[58] The reaction of Secretary of the Treasury McAdoo to Baruch's early campaigns for centralization is interesting on this point. "We are doing all that can be done in this direction. Some of your proposals, I think, will have to await an actual state of war, as

current political realities, realities which were clearly evident in the organizational structure of the GMB.

Reacting to Baker and Scott's initiatives, the commission and council ultimately settled on a "purchasing board" along lines congenial to Scott and the services. Under this new scheme each army and navy bureau would have a representative, along with Baruch, Coffin, Rosenwald, and Martin of the AC. The board would broadly coordinate military purchasing—the activities of the army, navy, and AC—without actually buying or letting contracts. These duties would remain with the departments. The new board was strictly an advisory body, subordinate to Secretary Baker and the CND, not unlike the AC itself.

Certainly this was not the kind of strong measure the commissioners favored. The twenty-three man membership was unwieldy, the diffusion of purchasing power persisted within even the military departments, the body was subordinate to the council, and existed only at the sufferance of the military establishment. Even the council noted that such an arrangement could be only a beginning "which may prove inadequate for the larger needs which may develop if war is declared," and recommended an increase in army and navy staff in accordance with Scott's strategy.[59]

Frank Scott was elected chairman of the new body. The enabling resolution made it abundantly clear that this agency was in no way to handle actual purchasing, but nonetheless Scott wanted to disabuse Congress and the services of any notion that a strong, new, centralized authority had been created in Washington. So he changed its designation from purchasing board to munitions board.[60] Since it could never be more than an advisory body in any case, Scott avoided a misnomer and thus headed off any criticism from the army and navy upon whose acceptance, after all, the board ultimately depended. The General Munitions Board held its first meeting on April 3—just three days before America entered the war.

Four months had now elapsed since the first meeting of the AC and CND. In the meantime, the business commissioners had extended a primitive network of links to both the private economy and the military services. Howard Coffin played an important role in this process, particularly through formation of the

---

I do not believe it would be possible to induce Congress to take such drastic action unless we were actually engaged in hostilities with a foreign power." McAdoo to Baruch, February 9, 1917, General Correspondence, *Baruch Papers.*

[59]*CND Minutes*, March 31, 1917. See the GMB's membership list, "General Munitions Board" (n.d.), *Scott Papers.*

[60]Graham Committee, *Hearings*, Serial 3, p. 989; Gifford to Scott, March 31, 1917, RG 62, File 2–A1, box 45. Scott consulted with Gifford regarding the change of name. See Gifford to Scott, March 21, 1927, *Scott Papers.* Scott even circulated his scheme among the procurement officers to ensure their cooperation. See Scott to Gifford, March 17, 1927, *Scott Papers.*

MSB committees. Bernard Baruch had also encouraged closer relations between the services and the raw materials industry as exemplified by his negotiations with the army, navy, and copper interests. At this particular stage in policy formulation, however, Frank Scott emerged as the most influential business advisor of all. Because traditional mores and traditional constitutional arrangements held fast, the military services retained their statutory and functional prerogatives in industrial mobilization. Because of his past acquaintance with Baker and his proper appreciation of the secretary's importance, Scott worked well within this particular administrative structure.

Though President Wilson took no direct hand in the infighting that swirled around the CND committee structure, his stand on general policy questions helped set the parameters of prewar administrative struggles. Neither his break with Germany on February 3, 1917, nor his request to arm American merchant ships some three weeks later signalled presidential support for the kind of preparedness advocated by AC members. Insofar as he considered administrative questions at all, Wilson stood by his regular departments. He did not intend to displace his service secretaries as his chief advisors on military and industrial mobilization. The CND, after all, centered upon his Cabinet officials. Expert volunteers remained subordinate, although it is true that as a matter of practical administration they did perform increasingly important executive functions on a daily basis. Colonel House had asked permission after the break with Germany to inaugurate plans for an administrative "war machine," but the president had refused to cooperate. "He feared I would displace certain members of his Cabinet," House recalled some months later, "and he did not wish that done without first trying to work out a satisfactory organization with them."[61]

Only after America became deeply immersed in the maelstrom of war itself would the president moderate his caution toward governmental innovation. Only then would influence swing more positively to men anxious to break down the walls of traditional government on behalf of a new kind of war system.

[61] *House Diary*, July 4, 1917.

CHAPTER 3

THE COOPERATIVE COMMITTEES OF INDUSTRY,
APRIL TO JULY 1917

The twists and turns of American prewar diplomacy came to an end on April 2, 1917. On that day Woodrow Wilson asked a hushed Congress for a declaration of war. After sketching his idealistic aims for the United States and her people he concluded: "To such a task we can dedicate our lives and our fortunes, everything that we are and everything that we have, with the pride of those who know that the day has come when America is privileged to spend her blood and her might for principles that gave her birth and happiness and peace which she has treasured. God helping her, she can do no other."[1] Four days later America was at war.

The challenges that now confronted the Wilson administration were enormous. Manpower, shipping, credit, trade, munitions—a whole range of problems came crashing in on an administrative structure ill-equipped to meet them. The growth of public organizations over the previous two years contributed no more than a launching pad for subsequent innovation. An emergency crisis was upon the United States, but the obstacles to a systematic response remained.

Uncertainty about the specific nature of the nation's contribution to the Allied cause was an especially inhibiting factor in the early weeks. Wilson had pledged material aid in his war message, and the British and French representatives who crossed the Atlantic in late April to press for ships, food, credits, and manpower also gained promises of American troops for France. A month later over nine and a half million men registered for the draft. The selection process began on July 20, and the first recruits reached cantonments in September. To feed, house, equip, and transport any substantial number of these men was an extraordinary task under even the best conditions. When military requirements reflected the vagaries of international politics, however, estimates which were

[1] Ray Stannard Baker, *Woodrow Wilson, Life and Letters*, 8 vols. (Garden City, N.Y.: Doubleday, Page, 1927, and Doubleday, Doran, 1927–1939), 6:514.

wholly adequate one month could be woefully short the next. Such fluctuations held disastrous consequences for mobilization planning.

Inaccurate, shifting assessments was only one of several factors which impeded business-government cooperation in the spring of 1917. It was difficult enough for business advisors to lure American businessmen from a relatively established and highly profitable Allied munitions market; unreliable information on government requirements made the task even harder. Could business advisors expect business to cooperate enthusiastically with a purchaser who never knew his own mind? How could civilian mobilizers stabilize demand and supply relationships when demand altered weekly, even daily? Competition among the military bureaus fed the confusion. Business mobilizers wondered how they could modify the entrepreneurial habits of decentralized military bureaus so as to bring them into a system of coordination and control which would fit the economy as a whole. Every partial answer raised another question. Even if the requisite military information and cooperation were forthcoming, would the attorney general and Congress be receptive to the kind of cooperative alliances in industry which Baruch and the others had in mind? How could an impulse aimed at the integration of business and the state skirt the traditional values of separation between private and public interest?

Matters were complicated further by the rapid expansion of the state bureaucracy after April. A host of private bureaucrats now followed Coffin, Godfrey, Baruch, and the rest to the organizational frontiers of wartime Washington. The fledgling war organization was not nearly large or strong enough to contain the sudden deluge of emergency activity. Individuals and interest groups simply planted themselves in the capital and wrestled with whatever puzzle intrigued them. Throughout the spring, little interconnection existed between the formal public agencies of industrial mobilization on the one hand and the spontaneous, private actions of interested individuals on the other. Early mobilization became simply a disjointed collection of independent feudalities.

In sum, the obstacles to business-government cooperation, to institutional synthesis, were enormous. An extraordinary effort was required to grapple with them. Organizational pioneers like Coffin and Baruch recognized this imperative well in advance of many groups in either the state or the economy. They recognized the need, and they believed they possessed the method. Filled with hope and confidence, business synthesizers elected to build a voluntary system of business-government relations. Founded on the rock of corporate capitalism and a loose coalition of like-minded men, it was to be equally removed from either the social model of laissez-faire or the left wing goal of state control.

At the heart of this springtime experiment stood the cooperative committees of industry which Baruch and the others had been forming since the beginning of the year in their drive to rationalize the American war economy. Baruch realized before April that various committees of big businessmen could contribute something far more important to the war effort than information, and acquire far more than an advisory role. Those negotiations with the copper producers had suggested as much; events after April 6, 1917, confirmed it. Supplying information had now to give way to initiating action; long-range planning to short-run execution; advisory position to executive status. Until this point, Walter Gifford had entertained some hope of inaugurating his more complicated, extensive scheme, but intense wartime pressures made ad hoc negotiations with industrial leaders all the more practical. Gifford continued to lobby for rationalized procedures, but in the meantime, the creation of cooperative committees moved ahead.

Baruch had always believed that successful businessmen were best qualified to mobilize the economy and he eagerly encouraged his committeemen to grasp more power and influence. He himself tried to open military doors and he also asked the committeemen to make their availability known to the appropriate officials.[2] A number of industries responded favorably to Baruch's appeals. He reported in May that the zinc committee had contracted for twenty-five million pounds of zinc "at practically two-thirds of the market price"; that the steel committee had contracted for "several hundred thousand tons of ship plates for Navy at great concessions"; that the aluminum committee had saved the government ten and one half cents per pound on all purchases; and that the oil committee had accepted contracts to supply the navy.[3] While the extent of financial sacrifice involved in these transactions may be debatable, there is no doubt that Baruch and his committees were securing a critical role in the war program. "While these committees were formed to mobilize the industries and act only in an advisory capacity," commented Baruch, "experience has shown that they have been of great and immediate value to the government in perfecting early deliveries and the making of lower-than-market prices."[4]

Negotiations with the copper industry illustrate, though, that the success of future efforts by Baruch and the other commissioners depended entirely on the willingness of the military bureaus to use the committees, and on the willingness

[2]Baruch to Daniels, May 3, 1917, Josephus Daniels Papers, Library of Congress, Washington, D.C.; Baruch to Clinton Crane, April 16, 1917, Record Group 61, Records of the War Industries Board, Federal Records Center, Suitland, Md. (cited hereafter as RG 61), File 21A–A4, box 259; Baruch to Robert F. Downman, May 5, 1917, RG 61, File 10A–A2, box 1031.

[3]Baruch to (no name), May 12, 1917, RG 61, File 21A–A1, box 20. The committees also began surveys of industrial capacity and forwarded their analyses to Baruch. See Clinton H. Crane to Baruch, April 16, 1917, RG 61, File 21A– A4, box 787; the weekly reports of Edgar Palmer, chairman of the zinc committee, in RG 61, File 21A–A1, box 20; the work of Dr. William H. Nichols of the committee on chemicals in RG 61, File 21B–A6, boxes 7 and 180; and Arthur V. Davis of the aluminum committee, "Survey of Aluminum Situation," in RG 61, File 21B–A4, box 171.

[4]Baruch to Gifford, May 17, 1917, RG 61, File 21A–A1, box 20.

of businessmen to cooperate with commission requests. On the one hand, Baruch had to convince military officials that they could obtain fast, efficient, dependable deliveries through his office; on the other, he had to convince businessmen that both self-interest and patriotism demanded their cooperation. Nor would it be suitable for the military departments and business committees merely to negotiate with one another without reference to the central commissioner. That might secure the requisite material, but it would hamper general coordination and undercut the sphere of power that Baruch was trying to establish. He had to make himself and his personal organization the linchpin between his clientele and the military services.

Ideally, each trade committee would funnel information on prices and capacity through the central office and receive government specifications and requirements in turn from that central office. The central committee would be in close and continuous contact with both sides, ultimately able to exercise full control over the system of supply and able to move at will to break any bottlenecks in the flow of goods. To enhance the system's operation, each trade group would speak with complete authority for its trade. It would become, in the metaphor of John P. Morron, president of the Atlas-Portland Cement Company and chairman of the committee on cement, a "turnstile"[5] between industry and government, deciding who operated the turnstile, when it turned, what passed through it, and the price of admission. Likewise, the military services would have to develop a single point of contact from which the committee chairman and the commissioners could receive knowledgeable, authoritative information regarding public needs.

The work of the raw materials committee, the committee on supplies, and indeed of all the others, diverged widely from this ideal. First, there was a widespread lack of coordination among military bureaus and business groups. As early as the first week of May, Judge Gary complained of confusion. "It has seemed to me," he observed, "there is danger of having too many different people or committees assuming responsibility for the same subject. If we do not proceed in an orderly way it will not be long before the whole business is so confused as to interfere with reasonable success."[6] Walter Gifford recommended that all committees operate through his office (a move which Baruch could not greet with enthusiasm), and some talked of making the Council of National Defense a more effective supervisor.[7] But strict control proved elusive. Neither

[5]Morron to John Hancock (paymaster general of the navy), June 19, 1917, RG 61, File 21A–A1, box 312.

[6]Gary to Baruch, May 4, 1917, RG 61, File 21A–A4, box 169.

[7]Minutes of the Council of National Defense and joint meetings of the council and Advisory Commission, in Record Group 62, Records of the Council of National Defense, Federal Records Center, Suitland, Md. (cited hereafter as RG 62), May 24 and 31 and June

the council and its Advisory Commission nor the military services could weave all the strands into a finished piece. Businessmen moved in and out of Washington without reference either to the chief commissioner or the cooperative committee which ostensibly represented them. Some committee chairmen set up emergency headquarters in Washington; others conducted negotiations solely from their home offices. The committee on cotton goods, for example, met daily in New York, and took offices there as its work load increased. The committee sometimes dealt through Eisenman of Rosenwald's committee on supplies, at other times directly with the military bureaus. "I do not know what happened in Washington," recalled its chairman, Spencer Turner, "and we really did not care."[8]

Perhaps the most burdensome and irritating problem was the military's inability to forecast potential requirements. This is not surprising, since official planners had given little thought to the whole problem of industrial mobilization, and a host of questions remained unanswered, including such a basic issue as the nature of America's war contribution. But the instability, whatever its cause, harassed business planners and strained the relationship with the military, a relationship which was already delicate by virtue of its very novelty. Business advisors did what they could. According to Leland Summers, the raw materials committee

endeavored in every way to have both the Army and the Navy formulate their programmes and advise as to the materials they would require. Where we could not get any action from them, we proceeded as best we could to warn the industries that large requirements might be expected and endeavored to have the industries prepare to supply these materials. . . . Many of these industries had representatives who had been abroad, and almost all the industries had done business with the Allied purchasing departments, and in most instances understood the necessity even more than the Army or Navy officials.[9]

In the course of their work the subcommittees expanded their functions to include the search for low government prices, for methods to increase production, and for agreements to allocate government contacts. But these were secondary to their main aim of stabilizing industrial markets. Baruch's appeals aside, the trade committees had their own reason to reach a modus vivendi with military purchasing bureaus, and that was to protect themselves from unpredict-

---

8, 1917, File 2B-1, box 104. The Advisory Commission agreed on June 1, 1917, not to form any more committees until the council had thrashed out the issue. Minutes of the Advisory Commission, June 1, 1917, RG 62, File 1B-1, box 25. By that time, of course, public criticism had begun to mount. See chapter 4 below.

[8] "Statement of Spencer Turner," Bernard M. Baruch Papers, Princeton University, Princeton, N.J. (cited hereafter as *Baruch Papers*).

[9] "Statement of L. L. Summers," *ibid.*

able demands. The cotton goods committee persuaded army, navy, and marine corps officials to end their competition in cotton goods and consult the committee before entering the market. The navy continued the rhetoric of free bidding, but actually arranged its bids with the committee before their public announcement.[10] Businessmen and military officials were soon found together in all variety of friendly agreements, their interdependency so great at some points that public and private interests could no longer be separated.[11] It is a tribute to the great success Rosenwald's committee had in cutting the public-private tension in the quartermaster's department that it ran afoul of congressional investigations later in the year.

Individual successes, however, could not remove the unstable, uncertain, and fractionalized nature of the early committee system, and it is this side of the experience which needs to be emphasized if we are to understand the evolving business drive for centralized control. The raw materials committee, the committee on supplies, the Advisory Commission, the General Munitions Board, and the military bureaus all claimed a directional authority in the mobilization program; no single agency could commit the government to systematic policies in prices, precedence of orders, antitrust action, or general overall requirements. Many of the agreements won by committee chairmen, then, were merely the best defensive tactic available in a chaotic administrative environment.

The whole committee network, as well as Baruch's place in it, rested on the insubstantial basis of voluntarism. Baruch could compel neither businessmen nor the military services to cooperate with him. At one point he sought an agreement with the steel industry similar to the copper arrangement and traveled to New York to consult Elbert Gary. He encountered only uncompromising hostility, and had to return to Washington with nothing but a grudge against the steel industry which he harbored to the end of the war.[12] Baruch possessed less power to bargain with the cooperative committee chairmen than they had with their respective industries. As a member of the AC he possessed no sanctions whatsoever, whereas the committee chairmen could at least threaten to take advantage of their trade dominance.

But frequently they, too, could merely threaten. Official authority also eluded them, and private economic power was not always sufficient. They too

---

[10] "Statement of Spencer Turner," *ibid.*

[11] One student of war contracts puts it this way: "Somewhere in this jungle of intermediating agencies of an unofficial or advisory character the center of gravity of contracting responsibility disappeared for the time being. . . . Wherever it lay, it was equally remote either from the parental council on the one hand as it was from the legally liable bureau chiefs in the War Department on the other." J. Franklin Crowell, *Government War Contracts* (New York: Oxford University Press, 1920), pp. 53–54.

[12] The origins and consequence of this bad feeling are traced in detail in Robert D. Cuff and Melvin I. Urofsky, "The Steel Industry and Price-Fixing during World War I," *Business History Review* 44 (Autumn 1970): 291–306.

had to resort to group pressure, moral suasion, patriotic sentiment, and cultivation of business self-interest. After the war, when Spencer Turner described the operation of the cotton goods committee, he emphasized that "the cooperation within the industry was not brought about overnight and without a great deal of opposition."[13] Some producers protested against "the apparently unwarranted assumption of authority" by the cotton committee; others were not enthusiastic about meeting amicably with former competitors. Still others were reluctant to cooperate "because they knew that they might, probably would, be criticized for selling their own goods to the Government."[14] Lincoln Cromwell tried to solve some of these problems in knit goods by selecting for his committee men with the greatest prestige in the trade. "There were three or four who were not needed for any work, but they were needed for their influence. They had influence with a lot of mills." Only by having these kinds of representatives could the committee gain legitimacy before the entire industry. Furthermore, Cromwell found it necessary to grant wide latitude to his committeemen, permit them to choose their own assistants, and handle their respective specialties without interference. The gaps in communication and control evident between the AC and the committee network also appeared among segments of the cooperative committees themselves. It took Cromwell six months to secure the cooperation of most mills, and it was more than a year before the more recalcitrant gave in. Some mills shunned government contracts because they would mean government inspection ("some inspector would come to the mill and hold them up," explained Cromwell, "and he would have to be fixed"), or slow payment, or sudden contract cancellation at the war's end. Others balked because in the knit goods industry "Government contracts had been a scandal for twenty years." Cromwell had to promise these mill owners freedom from the kind of sordid graft which had marked business between the military services and certain knit good manufacturers in the prewar years.[15]

The available evidence suggests that businessmen did not clamor for government orders through the cooperative committees. Edgar Palmer, president of the New Jersey Zinc Company and chairman of the zinc committee, sent letters to twenty-nine producers in the spring requesting offerings to the government. Eleven submitted figures, eight declined, six did not bother to reply, three reported their plants closed, and one proved willing to offer the metal but not at the committee's prices.[16] Clinton Crane, chairman of the lead committee and president of the St. Joseph Lead Company, got in touch with eleven hundred producers in June, but received replies from only forty, of which by no means

[13] "Statement of Spencer Turner," *Baruch Papers.*

[14] *Ibid.*

[15] "Statement of Lincoln Cromwell," *ibid.*

[16] "Zinc Committee of the Advisory Commission of the Council of National Defense, Report to May 19th, 1917." RG 61, File 21A–A1, box 20.

all agreed to contribute at the committee's suggested price.[17] Baruch noted in his diary: "Lead Committee sent out letters advising producers to send in quotas and telling them that Pres. has authority and can and will have to execute changes unless done voluntarily."[18]

Not only did the committee chairmen lack sufficient power to bring all producers into government contracts, they were also frequently unable to prevent other producers from underselling the committee offering. This of course endangered whatever stability the committee agreement offered. Baruch could not force military officers to accept committee bids or prevent them from going outside his committee to businessmen who were willing to evade the agreement. Purchasing officers could hardly be blamed for this, however, since the peacetime statutes dictated open, competitive bids. The paymaster general of the navy noted in his report for 1918: "In certain cases, there have been attempts made by members of industry to discipline other members who have quoted prices below the price agreed upon by the industry as the right price to be charged the Government."[19] Many committee chairmen only wished they had been more successful in these attempts during the spring of 1917.

The suggestion that the cooperative committees possessed extraordinary power had a hollow ring for Robert H. Downman, chairman of the lumber committee. From April 1917, when he came to Washington, until his departure in January 1918, Downman was plagued by his inability to discipline the lumber trade. The Department of Agriculture's Forest Service had mentioned his name to Baruch as a likely candidate to take charge of lumber under the raw materials committee, and at the request of Baruch's group Downman left New Orleans for Washington in mid-April. He was an eminent figure in the lumber trade, commonly known as the "Cypress King," and a popular president of the National Lumber Manufacturers Association. He hoped this latter post would open to him the role of impartial arbiter among the great number of trade groups that criss-crossed the lumber industry. Downman had to thread his way through an organizational mosaic unlike anything encountered in the highly concentrated fields like steel or aluminum. He picked the twelve men on his committee with due regard for the geographical divisions of the industry, but he by no means satisfied all groups; criticism swirled about his administration from the beginning. To ward off the critics, the committee claimed that as a government agency it did not choose its own members and had no power to add members.[20]

[17] Eugene Meyer, Jr., to Baruch, July 11, 1917, RG 61, File 21A–A4, box 784.

[18] Baruch diary, June 4, 1917, *Baruch Papers*.

[19] U.S. Department of the Navy, *Annual Report of the Paymaster General of the Navy for the Fiscal Year 1918*, p. 37.

[20] H. S. Graves to O. F. Wiser, April 11, 1917, and Frederick Allen to Downman, April 14, 1917, both in RG 61, File 10A–A2, box 1031; Downman to Frank R. Gadd (assistant to the president of the National Hardwood Manufacturers Association), April 26,

Downman brought some of his staff and colleagues from the Manufacturers Association and arranged to take over the Washington quarters of the Southern Pine Association. But the committee remained understaffed, and cramped for lack of office space. It borrowed personnel from the Forest Service, depended on the national association for financial expenses, and expected the Pine Association to continue to pay the rent.[21] The committee worked "nights and Sundays, lacking desk room or seclusion from visitors, using high priced time for clerical work, borrowing or paying for inadequate stenographic service, and generally working at every disadvantage in an attempt to keep up work comparable to that of a large business."[22] "It is of course a shame that we have to work here under these conditions," said C. H. Worcester, a director of the national association and one of Downman's aides, "and we are making petitions to everybody interested in trying to get it changed."[23]

Downman faced overwhelming demands throughout the spring and summer of 1917. The Emergency Fleet Corporation, the army and navy, and the Aircraft Production Board were just a few of the agencies that clamored for lumber. The committee had no time to gather statistics and collate information, but it acted nevertheless and by the end of May had secured a large order of yellow pine for the Italian government; had arranged prices between lumber manufacturers and the Aircraft Production Board and Emergency Construction Committee; and had apportioned supplies to various army camps for cantonment construction.[24]

Downman worked in a constant state of crisis. His complaints, explanations, and recommendations were always urgent and always extensive. "Timber is not a

1917, RG 61, File 10A-A2, box 1037; C. H. Worcester (a lumber company president and member of Downman's staff) to Hoke Smith, May 28, 1917, RG 61, File 10A-A1, box 1029. The lumber committee corresponded with at least eighteen trade associations: Michigan Hardwood Manufacturers Association, American Oak Manufacturers Association, Northern Hardwood and Hemlock Association, National Lumber Manufacturers Association, National Association of Box Manufacturers, The Hardwood Manufacturers Association of the United States, National Hardwood Lumber Association, Southern Cypress Manufacturers Association, Virginia-North Carolina Association, Northern Pine Association, California Redwood Association, Southern Pine Association, West Coast Lumbermens Association, Western Pine Manufacturers Association, Montana Lumber Manufacturers Association, West Alabama Pine Manufacturers Association, Western Carolina Lumber and Timber Association, and Gum Lumber Manufacturers Association; RG 61, File 10A-A2, boxes 1036 and 1037.

[21] C. H. Worcester to R. B. Goodman, May 28, 1917, RG 61, File 10A-A2, box 1037.

[22] Downman to Baruch and Allen, May 25, 1917, RG 61, File 10A-A2, box 1032.

[23] C. H. Worcester to R. B. Goodman, May 28, 1917, RG 61, File 10A-A2, box 1037.

[24] "Report for Week April 30-May 5," RG 61, File 21A-A4, box 945; Baruch to Downman, May 22, 1917, and related correspondence, RG 61, File 10A-A2, box 1032; C. H. Worcester to J. C. Knox, May 23, 1917, RG 61, File 10A-A2, box 1031; Downman to Baruch, May 9, 1917, RG 61, File 21A-A3, box 27; Downman to Baruch, June 2, 1917, RG 61, File 21A-A3, box 28; "Notes from Washington," American Lumberman 2193 (May 26, 1917): 42.

staple product like steel, cement or alcohol," he remonstrated to Baruch in a typical brief.

It has infinite variation in dimension, species and grade; demanding thorough technical familiarity in its use and purchase. It is heavy and bulky; therefore purchase in large quantity involves knowledge of transportation. . . . Lumbering is a disorganized industry. . . . The purchasing must be highly complicated. . . . All of this is realized, but imperfectly comprehended, by the purchasing agencies of the government who need immediately between one and two billion feet of lumber. They frankly admit not only inability to purchase intelligently, but also inability to make practical specifications. Therefore, this subcommittee is called on first of all to go over and revise the lumber requirements of every structure, vessel, or article. . . . The subcommittee is then expected to find and price all these classes of lumber. . . . In short it must conduct heart to heart negotiations with the countless elements of a disorganized industry extending from coast to coast, including over 20,000 manufacturers and as many jobbers. Finally as actual purchasing begins, delayed to the eleventh hour and with contractors frantic for material, we are expected to have all these threads in our hands so as to advise on pricing and buying any quantity, for any job, so it may be shipped without a moment's delay, without fail, and without trade complaint. Meanwhile we are expected to entertain and inform every visitor or delegation who comes to Washington interested in either lumber, ship building, or contracting, and all letters on the subject received by the purchasing agencies are referred to us for reply.[25]

The situation required far greater centralization and control in the lumber committee. Throughout his Washington travail, Downman continued to call for central planning and concentrated authority. Voluntary means were insufficient to contain the expanding conflict and confusion. "If no one has authority now to let us serve efficiently to help get this lumber, there should be a conference of those in position to create such authority," he told Baruch. "Else we should be relived [sic] of responsibility and criticism."[26] After only a month in Washington he warned that "the situation grows more critical daily and a national scandal approaches in the danger that our soldiers will be unsheltered and our fleet unbuilt."[27]

Downman wanted "some central agency" to cooperate with so as to systematize his operations.[28] The committee foundered on the rock of fragmented power. No one in Washington possessed sufficient authority to help Downman concentrate his purchasing functions. The War Department provided

[25] Downman to Baruch and Allen, May 25, 1917, RG 61, File 10A–A2, box 1032.

[26] Downman to Baruch, May 25, 1917, *ibid.*

[27] Downman to Baruch and Allen, May 25, 1917, *ibid.*

[28] Downman to Colonel F. G. Hodgson, May 9, 1917, RG 61, File 21A–A3, box 27.

the greatest problem with its endlessly expanding program of cantonment construction. Angry and frustrated, Downman at one point demanded that Baruch discover if the army intended "to mobilize the industry for the emergency, or to shop indefinitely in search of the lowest price on each item."[29] Downman could not fashion a coherent organization if the army purchasing officers refused to operate through it. No time should be lost in designing a coherent plan of cantonment construction and a clear-cut policy for purchasing the material, he wrote in June.[30]

There were frustrations with the trade as well. Many producers objected to Downman's experiment in economic coordination. Some were irritated by the very thought of taking directions from a committee based in Washington; others criticized the goal of stabilized markets at reasonable prices. The values of a mature corporate capitalism faced a hostile audience in this intensely competitive, divided industry. "I am sorry to say," Downman informed a trade paper, "that it looks like the lumbermen are getting in bad again in Washington on account of their foolishness, being perfectly willing to cut each others' throats if they can get an order for a few cars of lumber."[31]

To lessen confusion within the industry and to acquire more regularized control, the lumber committee set up a number of emergency bureaus to correspond roughly with the industry's main geographic divisions. Downman inaugurated the plan in June by encouraging the Southern Pine Association to create a board from its members and others which could then clear all government lumber supplies in the area. He sought the secretary of war's approval and called on all manufacturers to negotiate only through the bureau. Other such boards followed, each run by the area trade association. The bureau invited all mills in the region to list their stocks at reasonable prices. Orders would then be distributed among the mills as they came in, according to their ability to obtain transportation. The bureaus intended to use their influence with the railroads and their ability to provide car service as a bargaining tool to force producers to operate through the bureau.[32] Downman was drawn to the bureau idea because it offered one chance at least to achieve continuous, predictable, long-range supply planning. Hopefully the bureaus could obtain "firm but low prices" and sound

[29] Dowman to Baruch, June 2, 1917, RG 61, File 21A–A3, box 28.

[30] "Sub-Committee on Lumber, Report for the Week June 2nd-9th, 1917," RG 61, File 21A–A3, box 26.

[31] Downman to *Southern Lumberman*, June 15, 1917, RG 61, File 10A–A1, box 1029. See the reference to complaints by local contractors in South Carolina in R. G. Rhett to Frank A. Scott, June 8, 1917, RG 61, File 21A–A3, box 27.

[32] Downman to F. H. Farwell, June 16, 1917, RG 61, File 10A–A1, box 1028; Downman to the General Munitions Board, June 15, 1917, RG 61, File 10A–A2, box 1032; Downman to Baruch, July 7, 1917, RG 62, File 2–A1, box 50; Downman to Baruch *et al.*, July 18, 1917, RG 61, File 2A–A4, box 839.

information, and diminish the influence of the middlemen and irresponsible companies which promised, but could not deliver low-priced goods.[33]

If the plan were to work at all, it had to have the full cooperation of the military purchasing departments, which was by no means a foregone conclusion. The utopian solution would have been for the departments to concentrate and systematize their own internal operations to match Downman's move on industry's side; at the very least they would have to use the bureaus in a consistent manner to provide the system with a sturdy foundation. The departments followed neither course. As a result, the emergency bureaus found themselves in a difficult position. "Their constituents see greater advantage through withdrawing and going after the business with their sales agents," and the lumber committee could not keep them in line.[34] The Fir Emergency Lumber Committee in Tacoma, Washington, informed Downman in late June 1917 that while it had successfully won an agreement from the coast mills to furnish lumber for wooden ships, government orders had still not arrived and the mill owners were beginning to feel tempted by the local market. If word did not come soon, the agreements would evaporate.[35] In mid-July, Downman suggested that the heads of all departments instruct their subordinates to give the lumber committee sufficient warning on all projects so that it might recommend a price and a source of supply. At the very least, they could refrain from independent, competitive buying until the committee had ascertained if such actions threatened supply quotas arranged for other purposes.[36]

The committee was slowly building a more effective organization through the summer, but in fact, its operations proved little smoother in subsequent months. The military bureaus were willing "to utilize the work of the Committee insofar as it has standardized prices or accomplished other good by mobilizing the industry, but on the other hand to ignore the machinery and deal in a conflicting manner whenever the whim seizes a purchasing agent."[37] One of Downman's staff complained in August that "some of the departments purchase through the arrangement made by the Lumber Committee, others on the old peace plan of proposal and bid, and still other purchases are being made arbitrarily."[38] Nor did the industry wholly acquiesce. "Misunderstandings are con-

[33]See, for example, Downman to Baruch *et al.*, July 18, 1917, RG 61, File 2A-A4, box 839.

[34]*Ibid.* Independent bureau action was a constant source of complaint for Downman. He bemoaned it in almost every brief he wrote.

[35]George S. Long to Downman, June 28, 1917, RG 61, File 10A-A2, box 1031.

[36]Downman to Baruch *et al.*, July 18, 1917, RG 61, File 21A-A4, box 839.

[37]*Ibid.*

[38]Edwin E. Meyers to Southern Hardwood Emergency Bureau, August 18, 1917, RG 61, File 21A-A3, box 27.

tinually coming up," observed a member of the committee, "and complaints filed with members of Congress and with the Council of National Defense and this Committee because of the opinion on the part of many that these emergency bureaus are purely association organizations."[39]

The officer in charge of the District Engineers Office in Mobile, Alabama, recited some typical charges: the bureau fixed inflated prices, awarded contracts arbitrarily, levied commissions, coerced independent mills, and generally discriminated against small owners by its emphasis on large orders and rapid deliveries.[40] Downman found these kinds of objections incomprehensible. He was hurt and exasperated, and greeted such an assault as "a thoughtless stab in the back."[41] Ignoring the practical effects of many bureau operations and the dangers inherent in their organization, Downman responded that they did not actually fix prices but only submitted them for the approval of the GMB or the interested military representative; that in war there was no room for either independence from government-sponsored organizations, or an attitude of noncooperation; that any charges made for administering the bureaus were reasonable; and that many small plants received orders only because they had joined a bureau and could thereby share in pooled orders. Replying to the accusation that the bureaus were strictly trade association monopolies, Downman claimed that "this cry originates and goes up from the numerous wholesalers of lumber who seek to make a middleman's profit on sales to the Government." In the end, Downman could only plead for sympathy and understanding. "It is impossible in a large enterprise of this kind to satisfy every one [sic] and avoid complaints from those who think they have not had their share. It seems to us that a man with just a medium scope of vision should be able to see this."[42]

Even the emergency bureaus wrangled with the Washington committee. Some would not accept its authority without the right of appeal. The executive committee of the Hemlock Manufacturers Emergency Bureau informed Baruch that although they were willing to cooperate with the lumber committee, they did not consider themselves "subsidiary to and under [its] unconditional direction."[43] Downman never freed himself from the divisiveness and conflict which characterized the lumber industry in the prewar years.

---

[39] Frank G. Wisner to J. E. Rhodes, August 18, 1917, RG 61, File 10A–A1, box 1029. See the complaint of a Mississippi law firm on behalf of a client who charged he was barred from bidding on government contracts because he refused to join the Southern Pine Association; McBeath & Miller to R. S. Kellog, June 28, 1917, ibid.

[40] W. L. Guthrie to Chief of Engineers, August 20, 1917, RG 61, File 21A–A4, box 836.

[41] Downman to War Industries Board, September 14, 1917, ibid.

[42] Ibid.

[43] Executive Committee, Hemlock Manufacturers Emergency Bureau to Baruch, September 26, 1917, RG 61, File 21A–A4, box 835.

By August 1917, he was thoroughly disillusioned. He wrote to the president of the California Redwood Association: "I feel quite sure that if you will stay in Washington for a little time and become active on this committee, you will realize what a hard job we have had and about come to the conclusion that patriotism, in most cases, is nothing much more than a thin veneer."[44] "Our work has been a constant catch as catch can process," he wrote two months later,

meeting over night emergencies, guessing probable wants, and through it all struggling to preserve our organization in the face of lack of cooperation at times from most of the Government departments and open antagonism from others. The principal troubles have arisen from aggressive individuals with a lack of perspective, and a tendency to view their own particular scope of action as paramount.[45]

Needless to say, not all business volunteers suffered like Downman. Spencer Turner's committee on cotton goods experienced fairly smooth sailing by the summer of 1917 in both its internal operations and its relationship with government purchasing agents.[46] Leroy Clark, president of a New York wire and cable firm in charge of purchases in those products, enjoyed the full support of both the industry and interested purchasing agents.[47]

Although not all committee chairmen complained of decentralization, non-cooperation, or lack of decisive authority, every committee chairman experienced all of these conditions some of the time. And all could subscribe to Downman's recommendations: more effective organization, more cooperation from industry and the military services and other war boards, more legal authority, and greater centralization and control. At bottom, Downman and the others sought greater power—power to discipline the industry, to compel cooperation from the various purchasers, and to construct an efficient, predictable, coherent mobilization system. Charles Brooker, president of the American Brass Company and chairman of the brass committee, reflected this sentiment in a letter to Baruch:

Now it seems to me if there is any reason for having a committee such as you appointed, who with their experience and judgement in these matters, is to be of

---

[44] Downman to Captain E. A. Selfridge, Jr., August 16, 1917, RG 61, File 10A–A2, box 1037.

[45] Downman to War Industries Board, October 17, 1917, attached to Baruch to Frank A. Scott, October 19, 1917, RG 61, File 21A–A4, box 835.

[46] "Statement of Spencer Turner," *Baruch Papers.*

[47] "Statement of Leroy Clark," *ibid.*

any use, that they should know what the purpose of the Government is in these very matters which, it is fair to believe, would naturally come under their juris-diction. . . . I know that a business-like way of handling the matter—having con-fidence in the Committee, or relieving them from any possible connection with it—would be much to the advantage of everyone concerned.[48]

Opposition from military purchasing agents and the absence of that corporate chain-of-command mentality characteristic of their private business dismayed many business volunteers and made some of them very uncomfortable in their new environment. Moreover, without legally constituted authority, busi-ness volunteers remained vulnerable to legal suits from both the attorney gen-eral's office and private manufacturers who objected to committee plans for pooling contracts and prorating production. The feeling was strong among com-mitteemen that adequate authority should be forthcoming or they should be relieved of responsibility. One chairman recalled: "It was really an almost impos-sible situation that was carried along for months at some risk legally and under the greatest possible pressure."[49]

This reaction among committeemen to the mobilization procedures held significant implications for the evolution of the War Industries Board. It placed important business volunteers in the vanguard of those Washington advisors who recommended creation of an agency with a mandate sufficiently broad and an authority sufficiently strong to establish effective control and direction over the mobilization process. Committee chairmen wanted to substitute uncoordinated efforts with a continuous plan, and fragmented authority with concentrated power. More aware than most Americans and most government officials of the economic chaos and disorganization which the country had to surmount before it could efficiently meet the demands of modern war, business volunteers were moving to modify drastically the principles of laissez-faire. They were far more willing than the public officials they served to scuttle these values. Business volunteers like Downman, Turner, Brooker, and Baruch sought to break up that alliance of individualists within the military services, the political system, and their respective industries who chose short-term gains over long-term systematization.

---

[48] Brooker to Baruch, May 4, 1917, RG 61, File 21A–A4, box 259. We might note here that this kind of comment by Brooker, Downman, and others tends to support a comment made by Randolph Bourne at the time to the effect that "from members of this class a certain insuperable indignation arises if the change from private enterprise to State service involves any real loss of power and personal privilege." Randolph Bourne, *Untimely Papers*, ed. James Oppenheim (New York: B. W. Huebsch, 1919), p. 154.

[49] "Statement of Spencer Turner," *Baruch Papers*.

These big business administrators did not call for a centralizing agency or upon concentrated power in order to demobilize themselves, however. On the contrary, they lobbied for the creation of a greater governmental power so they could acquire a large share for themselves. For them, centralized public power meant the opportunity to provide private arrangements with the sanction of public law; to give their private views some public standing; to carry their writ beyond the boundaries set by voluntarism and goodwill. When Downman pleaded for central authority, he did so to augment the chances of survival for his own system. When Clinton Crane informed Baruch that he should locate responsibility for settling the precedence of orders in lead supplies, he naturally suggested that the matter "be left to the Chairman of your Lead Committee, with the instruction that he is to go just as far as possible in arranging that all lead which is to be used for Government purposes be purchased at the Government's price."[50]

Significant too is the mutuality of interest that existed between Baruch and his committeemen in their search for more power and control in wartime Washington. Baruch wanted a more secure legal base as well as sanctions he could use against recalcitrant businessmen like Judge Gary, who did not always yield to his exhortations. Seeking to free himself from dependency on the military departments, he also wanted more public power to toughen the fibers of his own organization and to bind its disconnected parts into an organic whole. In this sense, authority for one (Baruch) meant authority for all. Thus when Baruch lobbied for centralization of the government supply program, he envisaged a system which would make the work of the volunteer committees more, rather than less, vital. It was no use, for instance, if concentrated authority developed only within the military services, where businessmen could not get at it, and to which they would be subordinate. Power needed to be concentrated, but it had to be in civilian, preferably business hands. Baruch sought increased public authority for those leading businessmen he trusted to mobilize their respective industries. He sought increased public power for himself to place all segments of the mobilizations process, including his business friends, within a larger cooperative system.

Baruch's own power and credibility within the administration depended largely on his ability to deliver his clientele and the goods they produced, so it is not surprising that he should regard their recommendations with great tenderness. His own predilections were reinforced, shaped, or qualified in turn as he assessed the information, suggestions, rumors, and complaints they passed on to him. His demands throughout these months reflected the sentiments of the private businessmen with whom he was so closely associated. Anything that made their work more effective helped the war effort and increased his prestige

[50] Crane to Baruch, May 30, 1917, RG 61, File 21B–A3, box 168.

as well. This is the context in which Baruch labored to link the two tiers of industrial mobilization in 1917 and 1918.

Many aspects of the committees' operations were not evident to the American public, or even to some of the participants themselves. And even when the implications were recognized, they could not always be admitted. Business volunteers felt compelled to resort to fiction to make reality more palatable to a curious Congress and public. Where did the public interest rest in this morass of conflicting mandates and competing jurisdictions? Where did responsibility lie? Who in fact made government contracts? For the reputation of themselves and the businessmen they had called to Washington, chief civilian mobilizers like Gifford, Scott, and Baruch found it tempting to find clear lines of control where confusion existed; to find responsibility where nonresponsibility was the rule.

Under congressional questioning after the war, Gifford found himself defending and explaining a system of industrial mobilization he had always opposed. The CND and AC exercised "complete control" over the cooperative committees, he informed one congressional inquiry, "But as a practical matter, if you will remember the crowded time we were going through then it was necessary to delegate as far as possible the carrying on of the functions of these committees. . . . " Gifford, who had secured committee control in one sentence, lost it in the next. Direct supervision was exercised, "but not exercised from minute to minute but from week to week and month to month."[51] The yawning void between theory and practice caught even the most honest of men.

Frank Scott emphasized that the GMB endeavored to see "that those committees did not extend their operations beyond the limits fixed by the Council of National Defense." Had the GMB been successful in this, Scott would have been unable to claim for the GMB as much as he did in postwar years. The committees "had no power," Scott recalled later. ". . . They were extralegal bodies, and their usefullness depended entirely upon their willingness to give what advice they could and rest the matter there."[52] In 1917, however, the value of the committees lay not in their advice, but in their action, and the success of their actions depended on the extent of their power.

Baruch waxed most eloquent of all in explaining the subordinate position occupied by his business committees in the spring and summer of 1917. The various steel committees "were the servants, I might say—that is not exactly the word—but they were the instruments by which the director of steel's orders could be carried out."[53] During the spring, Baruch praised the cooperative com-

---

[51]U.S. Congress, House, Select Committee on Expenditures in the War Department, *Expenditures in the War Department, Hearings. . .* , 66th Cong., 1st sess., 1920, serial 3, p. 875.

[52]*Ibid.*, p. 995.

[53]*Ibid.*, serial 1, p. 1796.

mittees for their ability to obtain early deliveries at low prices, but in 1920 he labored hard "to make it plain that the committees of the industry in no way dictated policy, in no way did they control any prices."[54]

In the spring and summer of 1917 the cooperative committees of industry proved a dynamic element in a process that lacked general leadership and central direction. Business volunteers found it difficult to admit to congressional inquiries that looked for and expected the worst, the extent to which economic mobilization was indeed out of public control in the early days, in fact, was out of control altogether in some areas. They could not admit the extent to which economic mobilization proceeded simply on the trust and faith that businessmen in government placed in those of their colleagues in industry who were willing to cooperate with them in coordinating the American economy for war.

Business advisors projected confidence in public, but they worried a great deal in private. For if public inquiries ultimately penetrated their facade then politically imposed controls would probably prove inevitable. Their strategy was therefore clear. They had to press for the centralized power they required to shape a context conducive to the cooperative method of industrial mobilization, maintaining all the while public confidence in the legitimacy of the system they were trying to build.

[54] *Ibid.*, p. 1798.

CHAPTER 4

TOWARD A WAR INDUSTRIES BOARD, APRIL TO JULY 1917

Where could business advisors find that powerful, coordinating center from which to bind American mobilization into an integrated whole? The answer seemed as remote in the spring of 1917 as it had two years before. A kaleidoscope of committees and departments jostled for position and power, and businessmen and government officials, civilian and military officers groped for certainty in an environment of bewildering flux. Designs for an emergency bureaucracy sufficiently integrated and powerful to impose the steady rhythm of routine had not even reached the drawing boards. The Council of National Defense was the focal point for early mobilization but specific functions fell to the alphabetical agencies that appeared in profusion that spring and summer—the Emergency Fleet Corporation, the Aircraft Production Board, the Committee on Public Information, the Food and Fuel Administrations, and more. Authority and power were decentralized and disconnected: independent-minded army bureaus flouted the general staff; raw material producers and manufacturers avoided the cooperative committees; and a department with an efficient procurement office like the navy purchased everything it could get its hands on.

Voluntary goodwill could clearly not substitute for a centralized administrative process. Continuing experience with the cooperative committees would prove this time and time again in the spring and summer months. If the spirit of voluntary cooperation were to thrive at all it required support from centralized decision-making administered through a coordinating public agency. As it stood, however, business advisors did not even have the authority to guarantee their cooperative friends immunity from antitrust prosecutions. How then could they ensure cooperation from the military services, the regular government departments, other war boards, and indifferent business groups? Simply stated, businessmen in government could advertise their coordinating functions, but they could compel no one to use them. They could plead, pressure, and cajole, but

without the tools of coercion they had ultimately to wait for a gradual convergence between their private vision and the self-interest of their various
constituencies.

Business advisors divided among themselves over where they might find that
administrative center they longed for, with Frank Scott and Bernard Baruch the
chief protagonists in this drama within a drama. Both Scott and Baruch showed
a basic commitment to the corporate capitalist system. They accepted as virtues
close continuing business-government cooperation, market stability, and long-
range planning. They even agreed on the desirability of specific policy changes.
But in the end, they parted company over the place of military institutions in
economic mobilization. Baruch aimed to break down military authority; Scott
rushed to support it. Scott protected military sensibilities; Baruch cared more
about complaints from his business clientele. For Scott, stronger and more effective military institutions held the key to industrial mobilization. For Baruch,
only an administrative agency under his personal control could shape the state
apparatus to support the structural requirements of corporate planning in wartime.

As we shall see, Baruch displayed extraordinary persistence and ingenuity
on behalf of his policies in the spring and summer. But his views had little
practical effect. Ironically, it was the very public hostility which Baruch sought
to deflect from his cooperative committees that was to break in on the councils
of government in July, precipitating creation of the War Industries Board. Indeed, the events surrounding the board's formation offer a classic instance of
that clash between the forces of institutional cooperation, systematization, and
centralization, and the traditional impulse to separate private and public interests, to encourage economic competition, and to open up the decision-making
process to all comers.

The task of reconciling these divergent forces and creating a unified war
effort fell most directly upon the president himself. Throughout the spring and
summer he pursued a cautious course in forging the administrative tools of
industrial mobilization. A commitment to his regular departments and a personal
reluctance to relinquish decision-making authority, as well as practical political
considerations, figured in his calculations. Suspicions of enhanced state power
and close business-government relations prevalent in Congress required special
attention. Southern and western Progressives fought a bitter battle over the
food and fuel bill in the summer of 1917, for example, and raised embarrassing
questions about the cooperative committees of industry championed by Baruch
and other business volunteers. Circumstances and convictions combined to have
Wilson restrain his business advisors throughout this early period. Debates among
his advisors and among the public over such issues as prices, scarce materials, and
priorities often reached the breaking point before the president intervened. And

his interventions, when they did come, were designed as much to promote public confidence in his general war program as to satisfy the specific requests of his advisors and administrative subordinates.

THE GENERAL MUNITIONS BOARD AND PRIORITIES

The General Munitions Board (GMB) could not coordinate the diverse parts of the nascent war machine no matter how valiantly Frank Scott strove to prove otherwise. It was essentially an adjunct to the War Department, arranging supplies and prices for the ordnance department. The GMB's subcommittees served the military bureaus in munitions supplies very much as Baruch's and Rosenwald's committees served them in minerals, metals, food, and clothing. The board was more an instrument of the services than a tool that civilian mobilizers could use to put the military in harness with the civilian sectors of the mobilization program. The tone of the first meeting was symptomatic of the board's deferential status and of Frank Scott's belief that military institutions would prove fully capable of meeting war's economic challenges. Scott felt certain that no new department would be required to direct industrial mobilization. With the proper assistance, existing agencies could respond adequately to the crisis.[1] Such a stance enabled Joseph E. Kuhn, chief of the army's War College Division, to report to the chief of staff at the end of May: "So far, no friction or trouble has developed and entire harmony exists between the supply bureaus and the General Munitions Board." As "a valuable auxiliary" in the department's "usual operations," the GMB would hardly be expected to threaten military prerogatives.[2] It must be remembered, however, that many factors limited Scott's options in these early stages and much can be said for a civilian who could convince military officials that coordination conferred benefits on both sides.

Nor did the GMB simply languish. It encouraged munitions production, it initiated an extensive construction program for military cantonments through its

[1] Minutes of a meeting of the General Munitions Board (cited hereafter as *GMB Minutes*), April 3, 1917, in Record Group 62, Records of the Council of National Defense, Federal Records Center, Suitland, Md. (cited hereafter as RG 62), File 5–B1, box 290. Coffin was more ambiguous at the meeting. The GMB would strengthen current activities, he said; still, "precedents and practice in many ways must go by the board. New things must be done in a new way." *Ibid.*

[2] Joseph E. Kuhn, chief of the War College Division, to the Chief of Staff, May 23, 1917, in Record Group 165, Records of the War College Division of the General Staff, National Archives, Washington, D.C., box 402. This praise lavished upon the GMB was in response to the suggestion of the American ambassador in London that the United States government create a department of munitions. Kuhn believed in expanding the GMB's authority when and if that were necessary. "It is believed that this will come by process of evolution, rather than of revolution." *Ibid.*

emergency construction committee, and it tried generally to coordinate purchase programs, to devise a method of fixing prices for government supplies, and to develop a system of priorities in placing and filling military orders.[3] The sheer administrative demands of the war itself would have expanded the functions of the GMB regardless of the predilections of its sponsors. Take priorities, for example. Upon America's entry into the war, munitions producers and business volunteers pressed the munitions board to establish precedence for government orders.[4] Frank Scott was reluctant to do more than advise in such cases, pointing out that the board had no legal right to decide these questions no matter how strongly it felt.[5] But Howard Coffin, who sat in on the early meetings, refused to remain passive and on April 25 he introduced a resolution to broaden the board's scope in all areas. Specifically he aimed at giving the board full power over priority in both deliveries and finished products. The board and the AC adopted Coffin's resolution and passed it on to the CND for final action.[6] The GMB took the matter up again on the twenty-sixth and passed a resolution defining an official policy for priorities. It asked the AC to urge upon the council the necessity of establishing the relative importance of the following: supplies required by the army; supplies required by the navy; supplies for belligerents friendly to the United States; and construction of one thousand standard-

---

[3]The GMB possessed fourteen subcommittees by early May—the six original MSB committees plus committees on machine guns, armored cars, army vehicles, emergency construction, priorities, accountancy, storage facilities, and legal problems. See "The General Munitions Board, and Various Sub-Committees and Functions," RG 62, File 5-C1, box 293. Samples of the negotiations and general administrative activities of these committees can be found in *ibid.*, boxes 294-97. The origins and development of the legal department can be traced in the testimony of Robert J. Bulkley, its head, in U.S. Congress, House, Select Committee on Expenditures in the War Department, *Expenditures in the War Department, Hearings . . .*, 66th Cong., 1st sess., 1920, serial 1, pp. 1038-56.

[4]Bethlehem Steel made a request on April 6, 1917. See *GMB Minutes*, April 6, 1917. Coffin warned military officials at the first meeting: "It is possible for the whole industrial machine to be wrecked without proper and efficient coordination"; *GMB Minutes*, April 3, 1917. See also his support for a "system of priority" before the Naval Consulting Board, April 28, 1917, Record Group 80, General Records of the Department of the Navy, National Archives, Washington, D.C., correspondence file 1915-1922, box 35. One domestic steel buyer had demanded the government set steel delivery dates even before America entered the war; see J. S. Record (president, Minneapolis Steel and Machinery Company) to Daniels, March 23, 1917, in Record Group 61, Records of the War Industries Board, Federal Records Center, Suitland, Md. (hereafter cited as RG 61), File 1-A1, box 16.

[5]*GMB Minutes*, April 18, 1917.

[6]*Ibid.*, April 25, 1917. The Advisory Commission adopted it on the twenty-sixth; see Minutes of the Advisory Commission (cited hereafter as *AC Minutes*) in RG 62, File 1B-1, box 25, April 26, 1917.

ized freight carriers.[7] In reply, the council decided on April 28, 1917, that as between the army and navy, priority should be given to those naval needs that could be completed within a year. As to supplies for belligerents, the council suggested that this could be determined by a representative of the country involved and the heads of the departments concerned. It recommended further that the wooden ship program be pressed forward in advance of all else "not immediately and vitally necessary."[8] This announcement was a definite advance over no policy at all, but the situation remained far from satisfactory. The problem of Allied needs vis-à-vis American government needs had escaped the board's jurisdiction altogether; and with regard to the third point, it was still necessary to decide what was not more or less "immediately and vitally necessary" than wooden ships. Moreover, even though the board had jurisdiction over priority between the army and navy with a broad principle to guide it, its sphere of action remained rigidly circumscribed.

To escape these confines the board suggested in early May 1917, that the council should authorize creation of a priority committee with power to establish precedence "between the general demands for material within our own country."[9] This would supplement its ability to establish priority between the army and navy. The council at first deferred action on this request on the grounds that the president was considering plans "of the same general nature,"[10] but on May 11 it responded and in effect recognized the existence of a priorities committee within the GMB. According to the memorandum drawn up by Walter Gifford, the priorities committee would determine priority of delivery in accordance with the general policy of government outlined on April 28. With regard to conflicting Allied and government needs, the committee would present the head of the interested department with any helpful facts.[11] As implied at that time, however, the committee had no power to determine priority among civilian needs in which the army and navy were not involved. Nor did it have any authority to act in a conflict between the needs of the Allies and the civilian population.

At the same time as the GMB was trying to devise a priority policy in manufacturing, Daniel Willard was urging creation of a committee to establish priority in transportation. In fact, the entire question of priority in manufac-

[7] *GMB Minutes*, April 27, 1917.

[8] Minutes of the Council of National Defense and joint meetings of the council and Advisory Commission, RG 62, File 2–B1, box 104 (cited hereafter as *CND Minutes*), April 28, 1917.

[9] *GMB Minutes*, May 3, 1917.

[10] *CND Minutes*, May 5, 1917.

[11] Gifford to the CND, May 11, 1917, RG 62, File 5–C1, box 295.

turing was intimately bound up with transportation, particularly the railroad problem, and the two remained intertwined throughout the war. The council decided that pending development of a plan the president then had under consideration, a temporary committee should be appointed consisting of representatives from the Departments of Agriculture, Interior and Commerce, and from the GMB, to consult with the Advisory Commission's transportation committee in the determination of priority of shipments.[12]

On May 18 the CND brought these two committees closer by suggesting that the representatives of the Departments of Agriculture, Interior, and Commerce on the temporary committee sit with the priorities committee of the GMB whenever necessary "to pass upon matters of priority other than those pertaining to the Army and Navy."[13] This was a substantial expansion of the committee's jurisdiction, for it could now deal with questions of priority affecting civilian needs even when the army and navy were not involved. It was still barred, however, from deciding questions between the Allies and the civilian population. On May 29 the GMB decided that in future it would proceed in its priority decisions according to schedules as announced first by cabinet officers, and second by the various government departments.[14] Guidelines, in other words, would still come from outside the priorities committee and the GMB.

The GMB made Major General J. B. Aleshire chairman of the new committee, and its membership and jurisdiction expanded during his tenure. In addition to the department representatives already detailed to it, a member of the Federal Trade Commission was appointed to give "a certain authority of law governing investigations, etc.," which it did not have at that time.[15] The navy also appointed a representative.[16] The committee then designed a tentative classification of priority requests comprising three categories: Class A for projects of military necessity; Class B for projects of national necessity other than Class A; Class C for all other work. This was soon expanded by dividing the classes into "immediate necessity," "future necessity," and "all other work," and by differ-

[12]*CND Minutes*, May 5, 1917. See also Joseph P. Cotton to Gifford, May 7, 1917, David F. Houston to Gifford, May 8, 1917, and William C. Redfield to Gifford, May 8, 1917, all in RG 62, File 5-C1, box 295.

[13]*CND Minutes*, May 18, 1917.

[14]*GMB Minutes*, May 29, 1917. For a brief summary of the "constitutional" history of the priority committee to May 29, 1917, see "The General Munitions Board, and Various Sub-Committees and Functions," RG 62, File 5-C1, box 293.

[15]Aleshire to Chester C. Bolton (GMB secretary and a friend of Baker's from Cleveland), May 25, 1917, RG 62, File 5-C1, box 295. The commission appointed Joseph E. Davies on June 5. See C. C. Bolton to T. M. Robertson, June 7, 1917, *ibid.*

[16]Daniels assigned Rear Admiral A. V. Zane, Ret., to the post. Daniels to Scott, May 30, 1917, *ibid.*

entiating between military needs and national needs within these categories, with the former having priority. By the end of June the committee was handling 30 to 40 cases a day.[17]

Grave deficiencies remained, however, and business advisors found the pace of change wanting in several respects. For one thing, these policy decisions had yet to become fully operational. The army and navy continued to demand precedence for their respective orders and to deal directly with manufacturers rather than through the GMB. In early July, for example, one firm reported it had received requests for expediting the same machinery from a department of the army, a department of the navy, a naval inspector, and the priority committee.[18] What request should it act upon? Only if all the military bureaus recognized the priority committee as supreme in this field could a definitive answer be given, and this was simply not possible in July 1917. The committee's jurisdiction was still too restricted. It lacked authority to decide between Allied and civilian needs, and conflicts between the army, navy, and foreign governments. Finally, it possessed neither the administrative staff nor the necessary sanctions to enforce even the decisions it was able to make.

The president of the Pressed Steel Car Company of Pittsburgh made a typical plea in June for "a centralized Board with adequate power" to end "the present deranged condition in business." Steel supplies reached his plant in haphazard fashion, a condition which he believed could be remedied only by some "scientific method of allottment [sic]" and "a Board clothed with sufficient powers" to ensure all industries their normal requirements.[19] Baruch found this suggestion very much to the point, for he too believed that until a central purchasing agency and priority committee were established, complaints would arise in every industry. "The less necessary will have to give way to the more necessary," he wrote Wilson, "and in steel as in other things, an allotment of the production must be made to those who can make the greatest use of it for the winning of the war and the benefit of the general community. No competition for any product should be permitted to interfere with this purpose. . . ."[20]

Demand for steel increased drastically in the summer of 1917 and pressure sharpened for some kind of allotment procedures. The National Implement and

---

[17] Aleshire to GMB, June 16, 1917, and "Instructions," June 28, 1917, both *ibid.*; and an undated, unsigned memorandum on the history of the priority committee, RG 61, File 7–B3, box 846.

[18] Chester C. Bolton to Scott, July 12, 1917, RG 62, File 5–C1, box 295.

[19] F. W. Hoffstot to Wilson, June 14, 1917, Woodrow Wilson Papers, Library of Congress, Washington, D.C. (cited hereafter as *Wilson Papers*). The counsel for the National Association of Steel Furniture Manufacturers requested the CND to undertake a complete survey of steel consumption; see Ralph R. Lounsberry to Gifford, June 16, 1917, RG 62, File 2–A1, box 45.

[20] Baruch to Wilson, June 19, 1917, RG 62, File 2–A1, box 45.

Vehicle Association sent lobbyists to Washington with priority requests in iron and steel products, and James B. Bonner of United States Steel, which produced about half the country's steel supply, appeared before the priorities committee seeking its cooperation in establishing a priority system. Within the administration, Herbert Hoover and Daniel Willard called for more effective administration in this area and Baruch suggested that as a stopgap the army and navy immediately appoint someone to take charge of their ordering.[21]

It should be noted at this point that business advisors consistently led in the campaign to rationalize and systematize priorities policy. Sometimes they expressed simply their own view of the situation; at other times they reflected a broader business opinion, an opinion generated by mounting war pressures. In any case, business advisors responded to their perception of the wartime requirements of America's corporate capitalist economy. They searched for a coherent priorities policy along with the kind of authoritative agency which could adequately administer it.

In the absence of such a strong body, the CND obtained a central place in early economic mobilization, and in so doing ensured the regular departments a prominent role for their secretaries who sat on the council's executive. The long hand of Secretary Baker and the War Department was especially evident in the presence of General Aleshire as chairman of the GMB's priority committee. The perspective required for industrial mobilization did not reside in the regular departments, of course; and no agency which did not place the War Department in a subordinate position within a larger system could ever appease a man like Baruch. All Baruch could do in 1917, however, was to struggle along as best he could, to press his cause at every turn, and to continue to hope for a sudden break in policy.

In the meantime, business criticism of priorities policy spilled over into other areas of the administration's mobilization program, for priorities were inextricably linked to problems of purchasing and price fixing. Little progress could be expected unless all three topics received simultaneous consideration.

THE PROBLEM OF PRICES

Inflationary pressures were severe in the spring and early summer months of 1917. From June 1915 to July 1917, the general price level rose 85 percent,

[21]"Request for Priority of Materials and Transportation Necessary for the Manufacture and Distribution of Agricultural Machinery," June 25, 1917, in the George N. Peek Papers, Western Historical Manuscript Collection, University of Missouri Library, Columbia, Mo. In support of this action, see "The Raw Materials Situation," *Implement Age* 64 (June 16, 1917): 6; and "To Prevent a Shortage of Farm Implements," *Hardware Age* 100 (July 26, 1917): 50–51. Also see the history of the priority committee, unsigned and

which was more than half as much again as the advance in the seventeen-year-period 1897-1914.[22] Taking the average weighted prices of 1,366 commodities for June 1913 as 100, the level had increased to 144 by December 1916, and to 156 by March 1917. The prices for such commodities as basic raw materials related directly to the war effort took astronomical leaps. Clothing jumped 30 per cent from March to July 1917, and chemicals 21 per cent.[23]

Again, business advisors initiated the search for stable policy. The AC recommended action to head off further price increases before America entered the war, and Baruch suggested soon after that he be allowed to take up the subject with government officials.[24] Baruch was especially vocal on this point, largely because his particular clientele figured prominently in all price discussion and he was anxious to protect their interests. Taking up his favorite position between business and government, Baruch sought cooperation from both sides, urging government officials to be lenient in their search for low prices, and urging businessmen voluntarily to meet the government half way so as to stave off drastic controls. As early as March 31 Baruch confided to Willard: "The question of price has become a very serious matter and unless judiciously handled may result in losing that which is most potent of all success—enthusiasm."[25] He informed the GMB in mid-April that he was reluctant to try to get more copper "until at a meeting of the Council of National Defence, or whatever the proper body may be, there is determined a general policy regarding prices."[26] A decrease in general economic activity was inevitable unless specific business queries were answered, he warned. "How will a fair price be determined? If this price is lower than the prevailing market price. . . will the burden

---

undated, in RG 61, File 7–B3, box 846. The Pierce Arrow Company requested help in obtaining materials to manufacture Allied trucks, but the priority committee could do nothing. See "Memorandum for: Mr. F. A. Scott," July 18, 1917, RG 61, File 7–B3, box 846. Also see Hoover to Wilson, July 5, 1917, *Wilson Papers*; *AC Minutes*, July 9, 1917; and Baruch to Baker, July 13, 1917, Josephus Daniels Papers, Library of Congress, Washington, D.C. (cited hereafter as *Daniels Papers*).

[22] Wesley C. Mitchell, "Prices and Reconstruction," *American Economic Review, Supplement* 10 (March 1920): 137.

[23] Richard H. Hippleheuser, ed., *American Industry in the War, a Report of the War Industries Board, March 1921* (New York: Prentice-Hall, 1941), p. 74. Also see Charles O. Hardy, *Wartime Control of Prices* (Washington, D.C.: The Brookings Institution, 1940), pp. 28, 112–14, 124.

[24] *AC Minutes*, April 4 and 6, 1917; Baruch to Daniels, April 13, 1917, *Daniels Papers.* Also see *CND Minutes*, April 7, 1917. Charles Eisenman of Rosenwald's committee also pleaded for fixed prices; see *GMB Minutes*, April 7 and 9, 1917.

[25] Baruch to Willard, March 31, 1917, RG 62, File 2–A8, box 86.

[26] Baruch to Chester C. Bolton (GMB secretary), April 14, 1917, RG 61, File 21B–A5, box 176.

fall on all alike? . . . The fears of the people are being aroused through uncertainty and the feeling that some general principle will be arbitrarily fixed without due allowance being made for the special conditions existing in each and every trade."[27] "A proper decision of the price policy," he wrote Wilson in May, would "set loose the great machinery of the Government, and clarify the situation tremendously."[28]

Key businessmen agreed that patriotic arrangements like the March copper deal offered no system of price control. Aside from the fact that those kinds of prices did not encourage production,[29] the method provided no systematic, continuous policy for the long haul. Nor did it offer any stable administrative structure to administer price agreements, or to formulate policy guidelines in the future. Concentrated decision-making offered the only hope for consistent policy in any area of the mobilization program.

Frank Scott's GMB did receive Baker's permission to determine a "fair and just price" for "munitions and related supplies" when called upon by a department head.[30] But this touched only one aspect of the many-sided price question; the concentration of authority was minimal; and only a limited number of products were involved. Two days after receiving this directive, Scott decided to discuss various commodity prices with Baker and let him know that the GMB felt he should limit prices on "cotton, iron, wood, steel, coal, coke, etc."[31]

As a result of prodding by Baruch and others, the CND voted to form a committee under Scott to consider the subject. Composed of representatives of

[27]Baruch to Gifford, April 19, 1917, RG 62, File 2–A8, box 86. *Engineering and Mining Journal* asked the same questions in "The Matter of Prices," 103 (April 14, 1917): 683. Also see E. David Cronon, ed., *The Cabinet Diaries of Josephus Daniels* (Lincoln: University of Nebraska Press, 1963), p. 137 (hereafter cited as *Daniels Diary*).

[28]Baruch to Wilson, May 15, 1917, RG 61, File 21A–A4, box 1147. Baruch urged his men to bring pressure to bear on the GMB for permission to fix prices. See Baruch to Summers, May 10, 1917, RG 61, File 21A–A4, box 784. Also see Baruch to Gifford, May 10, 1917, RG 62, File 2–A8, box 86, containing a lengthy demand for centralization and increased power in mobilization. Baruch wrote Baker on May 16: "A price policy must be determined immediately, and a conference with you should be had at once to settle exactly what price must be paid to the producers of copper, lead, zinc, steel, and other raw materials going into munitions." Baruch to Baker, May 16, 1917, RG 61, File 21A–A4, box 463.

[29]Howard Coffin informed the NCB: "There has been a tendency on the part of many of the industries to come in here and quote prices which in their patriotic desire to do something for the country . . . have been unsound from an economic point of view." Minutes of the Naval Consulting Board, April 28, 1917, in Record Group 80, Records of the Navy Department, Naval Consulting Board, National Archives, Washington, D.C. Also see *New York Times*, April 26 and June 11, 1917, pp. 17 and 10.

[30]Baker to GMB, April 16, 1917, RG 62, File 5–C1. This was in response to the GMB request in *GMB Minutes*, April 16, 1917.

[31]*GMB Minutes*, April 18, 1917.

the Departments of Commerce, Agriculture, and Interior, the Federal Trade Commission, and others Scott might select, the committee was directed to consult with Baruch on the questions he had raised.[32] The special price committee, as it was called, set forth its recommendations on May 3, 1917. It was "highly essential," the committee contended, "that some sufficient method of price regulation be attained immediately, in the more important items. . . ." This could be achieved through some agency established by the CND or by continuing the special price committee as a committee of the GMB. With such an agency, "sufficient price regulation" could be obtained "through immediately seeking the cooperation of the great owning and operating interests" of the country. If cooperation was not forthcoming voluntarily then it would have to be obtained by threats of embargo or restrictions on the use of certain articles by either patriotic pleas or arbitrary government action. According to the committee, the mainspring of successful price fixing was a central agency cooperating with the nation's big business interests. The problem of price should be solved where possible by amicable agreements between major corporations and the state, an approach which would lie at the heart of WIB price fixing later in the war.

The committee also submitted eight guidelines for government action. Among them were recommendations that prices be sufficiently high to help high cost producers and thereby augment production; that the prices be the same for both the United States and its Allies; and that any sudden changes be avoided. An announcement to this effect, the committee concluded, would "greatly clear the atmosphere."[33]

In essence, this report was an attempt by the price committee to assure businessmen that they need not fear any radical price fixing moves. At the same time, it did include a suggestion that was bound to meet business opposition. This was the matter of making prices identical to both the Allies and the government. John Morron, president of the Atlas Cement Company and chairman of the cement committee, for example, had warned against this policy. The whole operation would be a "fiasco." "Every one of us," he wrote, thinking of those producers who had been filling government requirements at reduced prices, "has made sacrifices in money voluntarily, because of his love of country and desire to help, but we do not feel that this same feeling extends to the Allies." If this were tried, even the United States government would fail to obtain adequate materials ("except under duress").[34] It was only fair to segregate government and Allied needs and name different prices for them. Clinton Crane, president of the St. Joseph's Lead Company and chairman of the committee on lead, had also

---

[32] *CND Minutes*, April 21 and 23, 1917; *AC Minutes*, April 23, 1917.

[33] Scott to Franklin K. Lane, May 3, 1917, RG 62, File 2–A8, box 86.

[34] Morron to Willard, April 18, 1917, RG 62, File 1–A1, box 12.

expressed his dissent. To adhere to this policy, he argued, "would seriously disorganize this Nation's requirements for industrial and commercial uses."[35] There were at least two things at stake here. For one thing the producers were aghast at the thought of taking reduced profits on Allied munitions' contracts. For another, American businessmen could hardly forget that the Allies were economic competitors, and war cooperation notwithstanding, they worried about being bested in economic agreements.

Baruch and Willard had shared the sentiments of Morron and Crane, and had assured them that nothing would be done to "discourage our own manufacturers, or make them think that they are being imposed upon." However, from their perspective as government officials, they could see the political and military reasons for identical prices. But if this were done, the prices thus named would have to be equitable. "I would not consider it at all fair to expect the manufacturers to name the same prices to the Allies that they are now naming to the United States Government," Willard had replied. "I assume that a compromise price could be named, however, which would be the same to both purchasers and at the same time be fair to the seller."[36] It was no doubt with this kind of adjustment in mind that the committee made its recommendations on this point.

The idea of controlling skyrocketing prices began to gain business support toward the summer. H. G. Dalton, president of the Picklands Mather Steel Company of Cleveland and a member of the American Iron and Steel Institute, wrote Scott, that "many business men . . . would welcome some plan that would put a brake on runaway business and the resultant high prices." The important question was how to do it. Both Dalton and Scott looked for conferences between the cooperative committee chairmen and the price committee. Selected from the most important committees, the conferees would be "confined to men known to be practicable [sic] and yet men of broad views and high ideals so that if they can be interested in the movement, their influence will carry weight not only in their several branches of trade but with the country as well." Dalton wanted an end to "the daily pyramiding of prices and speculation" but he did not want pervasive government control.[37] Cooperation among leading industrialists in conjunction with a government agency would do the job. The point was to obtain that government agency.

[35] Crane to Baruch, April 16, 1917, RG 61, File 21A–A4, box 787.

[36] Willard to Morron, April 18, 1917, RG 62, File 1–A1, box 12.

[37] Dalton to Scott, May 11, 1917, RG 61, File 21A–A3, box 34. Clinton Crane told Baruch that demands were so great that "if the market is left to itself, I do not know to what height the price will rise." This would prove difficult with labor and small producers. Presumably labor would demand wage hikes and small producers would refuse to take part in government contracts at below-market prices. Crane to Baruch, May 21, 1917, RG 61, File 21A–A4, box 789.

The price committee drafted a public announcement that summarized its recent recommendations. Government purchases would be made at "fair and just market prices to be based on producing conditions in any given industry." There would be no attempt "to fix arbitrarily a uniformly low level of prices." On the contrary, the idea was to eliminate hoarding and speculation, lower inflated quotations thereby, and thus eliminate any reason for a blanket price fixing program. The government would have authority to fix guaranteed minimum prices on staple products, to encourage production and to fix maximum prices on products to prevent market manipulation, but this would aid, not threaten, normal business.[38]

Despite all the flurry by Baruch, Scott, and their special price committee, Wilson could not be moved to action. Baker reported that the president would not make any announcement until he had had more opportunity to consider the matter. The CND and its subcommittees agreed to honor this request and take no further action on the price question.[39] In the meantime, Baruch urged his clientele to make their deliveries and leave the price question for future discussion.[40]

PURCHASES

Price policy remained the most contentious issue between business and government throughout the war, but business advisors proved no less anxious about the administration's purchasing program. We have already seen that members of the cooperative committees consistently sought greater coordination and centralization of this function, and Baruch took advantage of their dissatisfaction to pressure the CND into action. It was at Baruch's request, for instance, that both Summers and Downman sent letters to the council outlining the desperate confusion among the committees and the military bureaus.[41] On April 24 and again on April 25, after a preliminary attempt at securing clothing and food for the

[38] "Announcement to the Public," attached to Baker to Gifford, May 16, 1917, RG 62, File 2-A8, box 86.

[39] CND Minutes, May 18, 1917.

[40] Baruch to John D. Ryan, May 17, 1917, RG 61, File 21A-A4, box 463; Baruch to Scott, May 18, 1917, ibid, box 465. Such a procedure was highly unsatisfactory of course. Some companies were reluctant to ship unless a price was fixed; GMB Minutes, June 25, 1917. Baruch urged government buyers not to stall in hopes of getting lower prices. "I would rather pay too much now and get these pressing materials, even if I thought I was paying too high a price," he wrote Daniels, "than to wait and perhaps not get them in time." Baruch to Daniels, June 14, 1917, Daniels Papers.

[41] These letters can be found in CND Minutes, May 18, 1917. Baruch thanked Downman afterward and wrote: "Your contribution at this time is perhaps more helpful than you thought." Baruch to Downman, May 10, 1917, RG 61, File 10A-A2, box 1031.

army, Charles Eisenman informed the GMB that only clearance through "a central department" could guarantee supplies.[42] Howard Coffin called for a "Central Bureau of Securement" to process all requirements, and Baruch recommended that any future agencies should be separated from the CND and afforded adequate authority.[43] "The larger the Committee," he wrote Scott, "the less its efficiency. The smaller the Committee and more final the power given it, the greater its efficiency."[44]

The movement toward a more centralized purchasing system received an unexpected impetus in early May when the J. P. Morgan Company stopped Allied purchasing in response to the government's decision to displace it as financial agent for the Allies. When this information became public knowledge, rumor spread quickly that a department of munitions was in the offing with a cabinet officer at its head and Edward R. Stettinius, director of the Morgan Company's export department, in charge of purchases. Speculation in a similar vein occurred in the wake of a Washington meeting in mid-May between government officials and members of the British and French war missions.[45]

The interconnection between Allied purchases and American credit brought Secretary of the Treasury McAdoo into the debate over the organization of purchasing at this point. The administration had decided to establish a central agency to handle Allied purchases and McAdoo wanted to extend its jurisdiction as part of the arrangement for making credits available. Since it would be necessary to coordinate Allied purchases with the government's needs, why not amalgamate the two functions in one agency? This position made McAdoo and Baruch natural allies in the fight for centralized purchasing. As early as May 8, at a meeting with Daniels and Baker to discuss a "Commission to buy everything," McAdoo made it clear that he favored Baruch to head a centralized purchasing agency. "Baker liked [Baruch]," Daniels wrote in his diary, "but said country regarded him as [a] daring speculator on Wall Street." As for purchasing, "Baker thought [the] Council of National Defence could do it very well."[46] In subsequent weeks McAdoo tenaciously pushed his case with the president, arguing that the coordination of Allied and government purchasing was "vital" to successful cooperation between the United States and foreign governments.[47]

---

[42] *GMB Minutes*, April 24 and 25, 1917.

[43] *NCB Minutes*, April 28, 1917; Baruch to Scott, May 4, 1917, Washington correspondence, Bernard M. Baruch Papers, Princeton University, Princeton, N.J. (cited hereafter as *Baruch Papers*).

[44] Baruch to Scott, May 4, 1917, *Baruch Papers*.

[45] *New York Times*, May 3, 4, and 12, 1917, pp. 17, 1, and 1, respectively.

[46] *Daniels Diary*, p. 148.

[47] McAdoo to Wilson, May 16, 1917, William Gibbs McAdoo Papers, Library of Congress, Washington, D.C. (cited hereafter as *McAdoo Papers*).

Under persistent pressure from key advisors, President Wilson initiated conferences at the end of May and in early June to thrash out the issues of purchasing, priorities, and price policy, but they had no practical results. When Baruch, McAdoo, Baker, Daniels, and Hoover met with Wilson on May 28 they found it fairly easy to agree on such principles as making identical prices to the Allies and the United States government and fixing prices high enough to encourage production. But exactly when and how to fix them was unclear. The president complicated matters further by making known his wish to have private domestic buyers share in government prices.[48]

Baker and Baruch might disagree on the organizational dimension of mobilization, but they shared basic assumptions about price fixing: it should rest on cooperative, informal agreements between large producers and state agencies so as to avoid governmental control, and it should embrace the principle of uniform prices so as to avoid the complex administrative demands of a cost plus system. As discussions proceeded, it became clear that these assumptions were basic to the ideology of all leading Wilsonians except Josephus Daniels, whose populist heritage had implanted an abiding suspicion of giant enterprise.

Baruch was preeminently the spokesman for business at these May and June meetings, anxious to educate the politicians to big business sentiment. He lobbied against any abrupt move toward a program of arbitrarily fixed, low prices, recommending instead a flexible policy which would leave the way open to continue the gentlemen's agreements characteristic of price fixing to date.[49] In an attempt to achieve price stability without strict federal control, he proposed formation of a "Cost of Production and Adjudication of Fixing of Prices" committee to handle all price negotiations. To have the committee composed of public-minded men could hopefully head off any "nasty investigation that might come after the war." Baruch envisaged no great authority for the agency and assumed its decisions would be accepted by both producers and government departments. Nor did he seem to consider it a permanent fixture. He suggested that "after the adjudication of a few items, the work of the committee would grow less and less, because the industries would fall in line very quickly on the basis established by its decisions."[50] Baruch apparently did not foresee a far-

---

[48]*Daniels Diary*, p. 158. The preliminaries to this meeting are recorded in Baker to Baruch, May 25, 1917, RG 61, File 21A-A4, box 1146; and Baker to Wilson, May 28, 1917, *Wilson Papers.*

[49]"Baruch Memorandum," May 28, 1917, enclosed with Baker to Wilson, May 28, 1917, *Wilson Papers.*

[50]Among the men Baruch proposed for his price adjudicating commission were Robert Lovett, president of the Union Pacific Railroad; John Mitchell, as a labor representative; and former President Taft as chairman. Baruch to Wilson, June 4, 1917, *Wilson Papers.* Throughout this period Baruch received advice from his business friends which shaped his recommendations. Eugene Meyer, Jr., warned him, for instance, that "to

reaching program of price control at this point. In later years he would neglect to describe how the pressures of circumstance brought on more elaborate price fixing schemes than he had envisaged in the early days. But in May 1917, it is clear, he drew his model from the kinds of informal agreements his cooperative committees then practised.

While the administration worried over prices through May and June, Secretary Baker waged a successful counterattack against Baruch's and McAdoo's search for unitary purchasing controls. He argued at the all-purpose conference of May 28 that no one man could command the purchasing function. It was far beyond the reach of a single individual. Moreover, "no matter how patriotic, disinterested and wise in his determinations, the conflicts of interest will be such as to engender about him complaints and doubts which he cannot withstand."[51] One might think that this latter objection was essentially a diversionary tactic aimed at heading off Baruch's appointment. But, in fact, Baker seemed genuinely convinced that the American public would never accept a business czar. Whether he was merely using this political calculation to supplement his objections on organizational and personal grounds is, of course, a moot point. In any case, when he recommended Frank Scott for chairman of a new coordinating agency some weeks later, he thought that once the organization was launched Scott too would have to step down to appease public suspicion.[52] In place of a single administrator, Baker would constitute a board to which experts (like Baruch) could be summoned as specific cases arose. The permanent membership would include three or four members from the General Munitions Board and Rosenwald's supply committee, and representatives from the State and Treasury Departments. The latter would coordinate Allied and domestic purchasing. This was essentially a reshuffling of two committees under Baker's jurisdiction, with the treasury added to appease McAdoo. Apparently Baker was so thoroughly alienated from Baruch and his men that he refused to include them in his projected reorganization.[53]

Baker's concern with the conflict of interest problem, his fear of centralized power, and his desire for institutional continuity all influenced him to oppose a centralized civilian purchasing agency. The fear that Bernard Baruch might chair

---

reduce the prices [of copper] radically would, in my opinion, unquestionably reduce the production." Eugene Meyer, Jr., to Baruch, May 2, 1917, RG 61, File 21B–A8, box 176. Baruch sent the same kind of advice to Wilson through House on July 2, 1917. See "Baruch's Memorandum," enclosed with House to Wilson, July 2, 1917, *ibid.*

[51] Baker to Wilson, May 28, 1917, Newton D. Baker Papers, Manuscript Division, Library of Congress (hereafter cited as *Baker Papers*).

[52] Baker to Wilson, June 27, 1917, *ibid.*

[53] Baker to Wilson, May 28, 1917, *ibid.*

the new post strengthened this opposition. Colonel House shared his concern. Although House personally liked Baruch and believed him fully competent for the job, he refused to believe the country would tolerate "a Hebrew Wall Street speculator given so much power."[54]

On June 13, 1917, Baker forwarded to Wilson on the council's behalf the outline for a War Industries Board that was very close to the final form adopted in late July. Designed to replace the GMB, the proposed board consisted of a civilian chairman, army and navy representatives, and an allied purchasing agent. Its membership also included a chief of raw materials, a chief of priority, and a chief of finished products, with special members to be added as the need arose. The plan was far more inclusive than Baker's previous position, and it is possible its design had been influenced by discussions Baker had had with council members. But it remained peculiarly his own. He still conceived the agency as subordinate to the CND and as part of an overall structure quite distinct from the conceptions of either Baruch or McAdoo.[55]

Baruch argued that simply to readjust the old machinery could not suffice when that machinery was fundamentally unsound. He concluded, "We have not the authority yet anywhere, that will make an organization that will be effective without further legislation. The longer that the matter is delayed, the worse the tangle and the longer it will take to unsnarl it."[56]

By the end of June the prospect of a new purchasing commission seemed very close at hand and advice centered on personnel as well as structure. The CND discussed both problems in these weeks. Baker named Frank Scott as chairman in the list he sent the president on June 27, arguing that Scott was in a good position to use the administrative experience he had gained at the GMB. In addition to Scott, Baker suggested Robert S. Brookings, Harry A. Garfield, and Hugh M. Frayne. He lost his enthusiasm, however, when he learned that the majority of his candidates were Republicans.[57] As Daniels noted in his diary, it was "difficult to find men to fill [the] bill."[58]

Throughout these weeks McAdoo remained committed to an Allied-domestic purchasing commission composed of Baruch and businessmen like H. B.

[54] Edward M. House, Diary, in Edward M. House Papers, Yale University, New Haven (cited hereafter as *House Diary*), May 27, 1917. House believed, however, that Wilson was fully on Baruch's side in the matter. *Ibid.*, May 28 and 31, 1917.

[55] Baker to Wilson, June 13, 1917, *Baker Papers.*

[56] Baruch to Daniels, June 14, 1917, *Daniels Papers.* Daniels said he would refer Baruch's advice to Wilson. Daniels to Baruch, June 14, 1917, *ibid.*

[57] Baker to Wilson, June 27 and 30, 1917, both in *Baker Papers.*

[58] *Daniels Diary*, p. 168. See the *Daniels Diary*, pp. 172–173, for evidence of President Wilson's search for suitable Democrats.

Endicott, a progressive shoe manufacturer, or Henry Ford, "or some man equally efficient and able."[59] Baruch shared McAdoo's organizational conception but favored John D. Ryan and Frederick Allen as administrative colleagues. These men had had a great deal of experience as "enormous buyers of raw materials" and he felt he could work far more harmoniously with them than with Endicott and Ford.[60] Allen, a former buyer for the Simmons Hardware Company and presently employed with Lee, Higginson and Company of Boston, had already joined Baruch's Washington staff.

As of early July, the AC had not been consulted or involved in proposals for a War Industries Board. Talk of a reorganization was rife in the press by this time, though, and the AC now moved to assert itself and its principles of organization. On July 9, Willard read a statement to the council which focused on seven issues: sources of supply, production management, shipping, priority, prices, sanitation and safety, and the drastic need for "central authority and decisive information."[61]

Only at this point in his attempt to allay commission criticism did Baker reveal his WIB proposal. The commissioners were stunned. Not only had they not been consulted, which was offense enough, but the proposal itself fell far short of the centralized agency they favored. Baruch, Godfrey, and Rosenwald all objected, and both Godfrey and Baruch relayed their misgivings to House, urging him to speak to Wilson. House shared the commissioners' skepticism about the present war organization and advertised their dissatisfaction to Wilson. But House surmised that a "little personal direction"[62] on Wilson's part would calm the emotional storm. He underestimated the depth of the commission's disappointment and overlooked the substantial nature of their objections. The commission had compromised itself once with Baker and the War Department in the origins of the GMB. It had no intention of being rebuffed again. Furthermore, its business members were very sensitive to the rising tide of public criticism over their cooperative committees and anxious that any reorganization afford their men ample protection from accusations of corruption and graft. According to press reports, the resignation of the AC's business members was imminent.[63]

[59]McAdoo to Wilson, July 10, 1917. *McAdoo Papers.* McAdoo brought Wilson's attention to Allen once again on July 18; see McAdoo to Wilson, July 18, 1917, *ibid.*

[60]Baruch to Oscar T. Crosby, July 13, 1917, *ibid.*

[61]*AC Minutes*, July 8, 1917; *CND Minutes*, July 9 and 10, 1917; and *Daniels Diary*, pp. 175–76.

[62]House to Wilson, July 13, 1917, *Wilson Papers*; *House Diary*, July 11 and 12, 1917; and *Daniels Diary*, p. 176.

[63]*Detroit Free Press*, July 10, 1917, a clipping in RG 61, File 21A–A1, box 3.

THE ROLE OF CONGRESSIONAL CRITICISM

The War Industries Board evolved out of a number of forces that converged in the summer of 1917. These included the evident weaknesses in the coordinating functions of the GMB and CND; mounting pressures over such issues as priorities, prices, and purchasing; persistent lobbying from businessmen in government; and the inexorable demands of continuous mobilization. There is one factor, however, which requires special attention, and that is the impact of public censure of the cooperative committees of industry on government policy. There are at least three reasons to give this factor extended treatment. First, it illuminates that ongoing battle between those who championed a centralizing emergency war organization resting upon close business-government cooperation and those who favored a more decentralized approach that maintained strict separation of public and private responsibilities. Second, it shows how President Wilson strove to appease the critics of concentrated executive power and institutional integration without sacrificing the cooperative system his business advisors were struggling to create. Throughout the spring, Wilson watched pressure build across a whole range of issues until his intervention was absolutely essential if the bottlenecks were to be broken. He then intervened with his mandate for a WIB, a mandate that displayed the degree of ambiguity appropriate for a response keyed to such a diversity of interests.

The third aspect growing out of public censure of business-government relations which requires attention relates to the functions of the WIB. Implicit in the board from the very beginning was a charge to arrest public suspicions over business-government relations. As we shall see, Wilson obviously intended the WIB to act as a buffer between private and public, business and governmental institutions. He designed it specifically to reassure Congress and the American people that private industrial power was accountable to public authority in the mobilization program. The WIB would help to legitimize the breaches in traditional orthodoxies made by Baruch and the rest. Providing protection for unorthodox institutional arrangements was of course the other side of pacifying public anxiety, and this two-sided symbolic function lay at the heart of the WIB's administrative activity to the end of the war.

Sentiment hostile to Baruch and the system-builders had been evident in Congress as early as May, when the AC was singled out for attack.[64] The commission's freedom from congressional accountability rankled, and the activities of a number of cooperative committees raised many questions about the relationship among business volunteers, the administration and the military services. Many Congressmen were less enthusiastic than Baruch over the kinds of agreements he reached with raw material producers, and unconvinced about business

[64]*New York Times*, May 18, 1917, p. 8; *Daniels Diary*, pp. 153, 157.

patriotism. "The Attorney-General should put every one of those fellows in jail between now and Saturday night who keep the price up," charged Speaker Champ Clark at one point.[65] The public furor over the conduct of the CND's coal committee in late June exacerbated Clark's hostility. The coal committee called 400 operators together in Washington to agree to a price on coal, an action which was unusual only in its inclusiveness. When Franklin Fort of the Federal Trade Commission learned of the conference he hurriedly informed its sponsors that the FTC was just then investigating the industry for illegal price fixing at the president's own request. The CND men could not control the coal representatives, however. Anxious to take advantage of the current impulse to stabilize the trade, they agreed among themselves not to charge above three dollars per ton pending the FTC investigation. On the basis of this agreement, one which Secretary Lane praised publicly as the epitome of sound business-government cooperation, the press carried the story that three dollars per ton had received official sanction as a reasonable price.[66]

This caused an uproar within the administration. The president was angry that a subcommittee of the CND had preempted his study and wrote Baker: ". . . Unconsciously we are working at cross purposes."[67] Moreover, he was convinced that three dollars was clearly too high a price. Indeed it was the very price that had motivated Department of Justice officials to bring antitrust charges.

Responding to the president's indignation, Baker publicly rejected the agreement. He claimed that the CND had neither fixed the price of coal nor sanctioned the coal committee's action. In fact, wrote Baker, the council "has no legal power, and claims no legal power, either to fix the price of coal or fix a maximum price for coal, or any other product."[68] As a subordinate committee of the CND, in other words, the coal committee did not have the right even to consider price questions. It was an excessive reaction motivated by the administration's awareness of the picture the coal agreement presented to the public:

---

[65] *New York Times*, May 25, 1917, p. 13.

[66] *New York Times*, June 27, 28, July 1, 1917; Baker to Wilson, June 30, 1917, *Baker Papers*. Secretary Lane nearly resigned from the cabinet in the subsequent blowup. Anne W. Lane and Louise H. Wall, eds., *The Letters of Franklin K. Lane, Personal and Political* (Boston: Houghton Mifflin, 1922), p. 103. Also see J. Leonard Bates, *The Origins of Teapot Dome: Progressives, Parties and Petroleum, 1909-1921* (Urbana: University of Illinois Press, 1963), pp. 101-3.

[67] Wilson to Baker, June 29, 1917, *Baker Papers*. Also see *Daniels Diary*, June 29 and 30, pp. 169-70; Ray Stannard Baker, *Woodrow Wilson, Life and Letters*, 8 vols. (Garden City, N.Y.: Doubleday, Page, 1927 and Doubleday, Doran, 1927-1939), 7:138; and Daniel R. Beaver, *Newton D. Baker and the American War Effort, 1917-1919* (Lincoln: University of Nebraska Press, 1966), pp. 64-66.

[68] Baker's long letter to Walter Gifford is reproduced in the *New York Times*, July 1, 1917, pp. 1 and 2. The original can be found in RG 62, File 2-A1, box 55.

operators were, it seemed, determining their own exorbitant prices under government auspices.[69] The whole episode smacked more of collusion than patriotism. President Wilson wrote Fort: "I think that if the conference could have been confined to the objects stated in the first part of one of the resolutions I read, namely, to the means which would most tend to increase production and facilitate distribution of the product, it would have been wholly admirable. Whenever such conferences go beyond that and deal with matters of price, they open themselves to public misconstruction."[70]

It was in this kind of highly charged political atmosphere that the Senate Committee on Agriculture and Forestry inserted an amendment in the food and fuel bill as section 3, which made it illegal for a government agent or employee, including an advisory one, to contract for supplies in which he was in any way interested. While the confusion occasioned by the price of coal had proved only an embarrassment to the administration, section 3 threatened its entire scheme of business-government relations. It was aimed directly at destroying the informal network of advisory committees.

The impulse for section 3 came from a small number of Southern Democrats and Republican progressives. Senator James A. Reed of Missouri, for example, assailed Arthur V. Davis for acting simultaneously as chairman of the Advisory Commission's aluminum committee and president of the Aluminum Company of America. "Practically all the big trusts and monopolies" had mobilized under the CND, claimed Reed in a Senate speech on July 2, 1917, "making contracts for their own use, enrichment, and benefit."[71] Mississippi's Democratic Senator James K. Vardaman read his colleagues an editorial from the *Washington Post* which urged the administration to end a system which "lends itself to favoritism, overcharge and graft."[72]

The administration's business advisors were naturally chagrined at the attack, worried lest the men whom they had assembled on the various committees refused to serve. Julius Rosenwald regarded the challenge of section 3 as "stupid, shortsighted, nonsensical, and foolish,"[73] and urged Wilson to intervene. "It is vital," he warned, "that the cooperation which has already been

---

[69] Walter Gifford was certainly confused, for Baker's policy statement implied that the cooperative committees could no longer mobilize industries. If they were "purely advisory" as Baker stressed, then "it means a complete change of policy on the part of the entire organization and would throw back on to the military organizations the necessity for all initiative . . . ." Gifford to Baker, July 2, 1917, *Baker Papers.* Baker later assured Gifford that that was not really the case. *GMB Minutes,* July 3, 1917.

[70] Wilson to Fort, July 2, 1917, *Wilson Papers.*

[71] *Congressional Record,* 65th Cong., 1st sess., 1917, vol. 55, part 5, p. 4596.

[72] *Ibid.,* pp. 4593–94.

[73] *Ibid.,* pp. 4655–57.

established should be maintained and, furthermore, it is of greatest importance that confidence exist between government and industry and that suspicion, which has existed on the part of both, be eliminated."[74]

Wilson showed the special value he placed on the cooperative committees and the general accord between business and government they represented by the alacrity and persistence with which he intervened to ward off the challenge of section 3. He lined himself squarely behind the businessmen on the cooperative committees and moved to quell the rebellion, personally interceding to get the amendment defeated and to reassure business volunteers that he welcomed them in Washington. He defended them against charges of conflict of interest and collusion and argued that in matters of price, committeemen could not obtain excessive prices even if they wanted to. "If anything in the law should make it necessary to dispense with their services," Wilson wrote Kenneth McKellar (D., Tenn.), one of the dissidents, "the Government would be seriously and perhaps fatally embarrassed, inasmuch as we must in the circumstances have the cooperation, and the active cooperation, of the men who are in actual control of the great business enterprises of the country. I should find myself hampered in a degree which I think you cannot realize if I were deprived of the opportunity to use these gentlemen as they are willing to be used."[75] Wilson pleaded for flexibility and trust for, unlike the critics, he seems never to have doubted the probity of the committeemen or the basic soundness of the system of business-government relations they had devised.

Creation of the WIB lay at the heart of Wilson's strategy to defeat section 3 and to mitigate public criticism of his business volunteers. If the Senators would just trust him for a little while then he could so order the administration as to settle their objections once and for all. Yet in pressing his case he seemed to grant that perhaps the committees had arrogated excessive functions to themselves. He argued, for example, that under the reorganization then in process "such persons as the amendment refers to are being put very distinctly in the relation *which was originally intended*. They are, that is, to assist the Council by information and cooperation but are in no way to be connected with either the initiation or the conclusion of contracts."[76]

[74] Rosenwald to Wilson, July 2, 1917, Albert S. Burleson Papers, Manuscript Division, Library of Congress, Washington, D.C.

[75] Wilson to McKellar, July 9, 1917, *Wilson Papers*. This debate can be followed in greater detail in Robert D. Cuff, "Woodrow Wilson and Business-Government Relations during World War I," *Review of Politics* 31 (July 1969): 385–407, especially pp. 390–97. Both Secretary Baker and Secretary Lane also spoke out publicly on behalf of the business committees in the course of debate. See *New York Times*, July 13, and October 9, 1917, pp. 12 and 17, respectively; and Baker to Baruch, October 10, 1917, RG 61, File 21A–A1, box 20.

[76] Wilson to McKellar, July 9, 1917, *Wilson Papers* (italics added).

What bothered Baruch and Rosenwald, however, was the simple fact that the kind of reorganization which Baker, at least, had in mind would not satisfy the general aim of inserting "a disinterested governing board between the business experts and the making of contracts."[77] Baruch believed that Baker's plan as it stood "would only enrage as it looks like an endeavor to fool the people."[78] If the administration could not defend and explain the present relations between business and government, why not abandon the scheme altogether? Like other business advisors, Baruch was angry and dismayed at the critics who impugned the motives of American businessmen and the organization based upon their informal, voluntary cooperation.

Within the Senate itself Atlee Pomerene (D., Ohio) intervened with a substitute for section 3 which he hoped would eliminate the possibility of scandal in the present organization. His measure barred any government agent from soliciting contracts in which he had any personal interest, but allowed him to recommend a contract if he first disclosed in writing any interest he had in it. In no case, however, could such an agent actually award the contract.[79] Senator McKellar, for one, strenuously objected. He quite rightly pointed out that in a certain sense Pomerene's amendment merely condoned the very actions that he hoped to end. By declaring their interests, businessmen could recommend contracts be awarded to themselves. Surely this was just legal legerdemain, for who could fail to know that Arthur Davis was president of the Aluminum Company of America?[80] Most of the Senate was satisfied with the compromise, though, and passed it on July 18, 1917, by a vote of 53 to 17. The nays opposed it because of its weakness; many of the yeas supported it as the lesser of two unnecessary evils.[81]

The president was ultimately unsuccessful in prohibiting the passage of the Senate amendment (section 3 became law with the passage of the food and fuel bill on August 10), but he pressed on with the task of constructing a new

[77] Baker to Wilson, July 14, 1917, *Baker Papers*. It is not clear from this letter whether Baker himself regarded the central function of the new board in this light, or whether he was simply interpreting the perception of the business advisors.

[78] Diary of Bernard M. Baruch, July 13, 1917, *Baruch Papers*.

[79] W. C. Saeger to Pomerene, July 19, 1917, RG 61, File 2D-A1, box 21; *Congressional Record*, 65th Cong., 1st sess., 1917, vol. 55, part 5, p. 5218, and pp. 5047-52, for a copy of Pomerene's original amendment and the changes of wording made in it.

[80] *Congressional Record*, 65th Cong., 1st sess., vol. 55, part 5, pp. 5048-49.

[81] The following Senators were recorded in opposition to section 3: Borah (R., Idaho), Broussard (D., La.), Cummins (R., Iowa), Gore (D., Oklahoma), Gronna (R., North Dakota), Hardwick (D., Ga.), Johnson (R. Prog., Cal.), Kenyon (R., Iowa), La Follette (R., Wis.), McKellar (D., Tenn.), McNary (D., Ore.), Nelson (R., Minn.), Morris (R., Neb.), Ramsdell (D., La.), Shields (D., Tenn.), Sutherland (R., W. Va.), Trammell (D.,

mobilization agency. Just the day before the Senate acted on its substitute he outlined the kind of agency he wanted to Secretary Baker.

Baker had envisaged a kind of two-tiered agency in his early drafts, with the chairman, the military representatives, and the Allied purchasing agent on the first plateau and the three chiefs of raw materials, priorities, and finished products on the second. The second-level business advisors would be subordinate to the chairman and his colleagues, and without full-fledged official status. The president accepted much of Baker's basic structure but modified it in several respects. In doing so it is evident that his overriding concern was to legitimize the place of businessmen in government and to retain the extensive network of business-government contacts they had created. He placed the three business advisors firmly within the board's executive and added a labor representative. He also replaced the Allied purchasing agent with "an executive agency" composed of the three business advisors in company with Herbert Hoover. "It seems to me," he wrote Baker, "that in this way we shall get rid of what might be in danger of being a complicated piece of machinery without in any way interfering with the independence and energies of the three active officials mentioned."[82]

The president then explained, significantly, that "there would then be a free field for these three officials to use the various committees now associated with the Council of National Defense for the fullest information and for any kind of assistance which they can properly render, and it would be within their choice, of course, to employ assistants or lieutenants as systematically as seemed necessary."[83] Making the business advisors members of the central agency would remove any ambiguity about their status once and for all. They could then deal with private businessmen as extensively as they wished. In this way the president continued his efforts to save the committee system. The final statement accompanying the public announcement of the WIB on July 28 contains the clearest expression of this hope. The purpose of the Board's creation, it read,

is to expedite the work of the Government, to furnish needed assistance to the Departments engaged in making war purchases, to devolve clearly and definitely the important tasks indicated upon representatives of the Government not interested in commercial and industrial activities with which they will be called upon to deal, and to make clear that there is total disassociation of the industrial committees from the actual arrangement of purchases on behalf of the Government. It will lodge responsibility for effective action as definitely as is possible

---

Fla.). Senator Reed, after voting first in the affirmative, changed his vote to the negative.

[82]Wilson to Baker, July 17, 1917, *Baker Papers.*

[83]*Ibid.*

under existing law. It does not minimize or dispense with the splendid service which representatives of industry and labor have so unselfishly placed at the disposal of the Government.[84]

Although a crisis in business-government relations was a major force in determining the functions and structure of the WIB, other factors also influenced the board's organization and goals. The WIB was a partial recognition of the demand by business advisors for a more effective coordinating and policy-making body. President Wilson called upon the board to act as "a clearing house" for government requirements to "determine the most effective ways of meeting them, and the best means of increasing production, including the creation or extension of industries demanded by the emergency, the sequence and relative urgency of the needs of the different government services, and [to] consider price factors, and, in the first instance, the industrial and labor aspects of problems involved and the general questions affecting the purchase of commodities."[85] Obviously the WIB offered more to business planners than the GMB. The kind of appointments to the board's executive also helped. Bernard Baruch's influence would continue to be felt as chief of raw materials, and Robert A. Brookings, a retired millionaire and the new commissioner of finished products, promised added support for Baruch's point of view. The designation of Hugh A. Frayne, an American Federation of Labor organizer from New York, as commissioner of labor also enlarged the potential scope of the board in yet another direction.

Despite its advance over past experiments, however, the WIB could not escape the dominating influence of Secretary Baker and the War Department. Not only did the services gain two representatives to protect their interests in the new agency, but Frank Scott became WIB chairman and the board remained under the thumb of the CND. When the new agency was unveiled on July 28, 1917, Secretary Baker could take great satisfaction at the outcome: the president's plan did go some distance toward centralizing the direction of industrial activity, but purchasing control stayed with the War Department and the formal focus of industrial mobilization remained in the CND. The new agency was dependent ultimately upon the willingness of the army and navy to cooperate. Baker viewed the board's future optimistically. "I think, from such observation as I have been able to make of the new members," he informed Wilson, "that the Board is going to be a very strong and effective body, and that in a very little while its harmony will be complete."[86]

[84] *CND Minutes*, July 28, 1917.

[85] *Ibid.*

[86] Baker to Wilson, August 1, 1917, *Baker Papers*.

McAdoo, on the other hand, felt only regret, for the WIB structure by no means compared with the "single-headed Purchasing Commission" he had advocated since early spring. Whereas a commission responsible for both government and Allied purchases would have had "the prestige and power to do great work," a foreign mission separate from the WIB proper would be "a sort of sideshow . . . commanding small respect and having little power or influence."[87] Though the treasury secretary and the administration's business advisors might admit the WIB was an improvement over the GMB, they had no illusions about its ability to provide the authoritative, centralized, decision-making body demanded by businessmen on the cooperative committees. The *New York Times* described the formation of the WIB as "one of the most important steps in the effort to bring about the stabilization of all American markets. It will provide also a definite body with which producers of the many war-time commodities may treat, and put an end to whatever confusion may have existed because of the cumbersome size of the Council of National Defence."[88] McAdoo and Baruch knew better.

Throughout the spring and summer of 1917 the administration's business advisors had proven most sensitive to the great changes in traditional prerogatives demanded by industrial mobilization for war. They were by no means fully prescient in this endeavor, as Baruch's price-fixing proposals amply illustrate. Still, they recognized better than Baker and his generals the kinds of organizational changes required in the state bureaucracy, and they understood better than the Senate progressives that public and private institutions had to merge in the process of fighting a modern war. They searched for a coalition of men who shared their passion for a cooperative middle way between rigid federal control, on the one hand, and free-wheeling laissez-faire conduct on the other. Secretary Baker and Senator McKellar were symbolic of the men and values they had to overcome in forging the corporate war economy.[89]

For his part, President Wilson proved an ambiguous even enigmatic figure throughout these months. He was obviously reluctant to delegate authority to his business advisors, especially on pricing policy; determined to force Baker and Baruch to compromise; and anxious all the while to retain public confidence in his attitude toward major business interests. Yet at the same time he did cul-

---

[87]McAdoo to Wilson, July 30, 1917, *McAdoo Papers.*

[88]*New York Times*, July 29, 1917, p. 1.

[89]Herbert Hoover later noted: "These governmental activities were strange in American life and Congress was tardy, fearful and often inadequate in conferring the powers upon the President which were vital to enable the civilian agencies to contribute their part . . . ." Herbert Hoover, *The Ordeal of Woodrow Wilson* (New York: McGraw-Hill, 1958), p. 11.

tivate the advice of those business advisors whom he trusted, and he did leap to the defense of the cooperative system they were struggling to create, even to the point of clashing with the progressive wing of his party in Congress.

In some respects the president possessed greater power within his war administration at this point than he would have again until the end of the war. The permanent features of emergency administration had only begun to crystallize in these early months. Issues that would ultimately disappear into emergency boards for solution still found their way to the president's office. Problem-solving had not become fully formalized or institutionalized. The president possessed enormous personal influence in such policy areas as prices and purchasing for he had not yet delegated or centralized major authority for them. Time after time his advisors beseeched him to settle differences and allocate authority, and time after time he utilized his prerogative either to ignore or to heed such calls.

But the situation would not always be so malleable, or the president's impact so directly felt. The forms of administration would harden as the winter and spring wore on. And policies from prior decisions would take on a momentum of their own. Equally important, the politics of coalition warfare would prove a constant drain on the president's energies which when coupled with the sheer press of events at home ensured a gradual diminution of his personal role in industrial mobilization.

CHAPTER 5

THE WIB REAFFIRMED

In 1916 an organization like the War Industries Board might have at least encouraged Baruch and the institutional synthesizers in their work, but by the summer of 1917 it was a different story: a loosely structured advisory agency had absolutely no chance of disciplining an ongoing mobilization program. Though substantially more extensive than its predecessor agencies, and better designed to protect businessmen in government from public obloquy, the WIB was obviously ill-equipped to meet the goals which business advisors had set for the centralizing linchpin of America's economic mobilization.

The longer the administration postponed creation of a powerful coordinating organization the more difficult coordination and control became. An agency originating in the summer of 1917 confronted a far more bewildering organizational environment than one created in the early days of the war. Each succeeding administrative unit entered a thicker bureaucratic field. The impact of war generally facilitated organizational growth within the state and the economy, but with a paradoxical effect: it both extended the opportunity for central control and increased the strength of potential opposition.

While the board made piecemeal advances in specific policy areas in subsequent months, it was literally overwhelmed in its larger task of institutional coordination, and for a number of reasons. The causes of this failure derived partly from structural weaknesses in the board itself, and partly from the effective challenges of bureaucratic competitors in the state and in the economy. The uphill fight for concentrated, authoritative decision-making had not yet been won.

THE WIB DIVIDED: PURCHASES AND PRIORITIES

The War Industries Board, like the General Munitions Board it replaced, was a patchwork collection of semiautonomous functional fragments. Its business members, Brookings, Lovett, and Baruch, chased off after their own goals, just as the members of the Advisory Commission had done in the spring, and their individual accomplishments gave the board most of whatever strength it possessed. The entire membership did meet regularly to debate general policy (including the broad problems of civilian-military relations, price fixing, and Allied purchasing), but the board hardly existed as a collective entity. Moreover, it lacked the muscle to enforce its recommendations on either business groups or the military services. Personal animosities among the business advisors further weakened it. Baruch was still irritated by Scott's close relationship with Baker; he could never reconcile himself to the Clevelander's chairmanship. Lovett, on the other hand, never lost his wariness of the Wall Street speculator. He even refused to serve under Baruch on the Allied purchasing commission, and as a result, the commission hobbled along without a chairman. Baruch told Colonel House that "It hampers the work but it came to a question of either doing it in that way or losing the Judge's services."[1]

Frank Scott's health collapsed under the strain that fall and his loss severely injured the board. Although he did not resign offically until October 26, he was absent from Washington for most of September, and his departure deprived the board of its special relationship with the War Department. With his Cleveland friend gone, Baker had even less incentive to look to the WIB for assistance. Baruch and his allies might object to the close tie between Baker and Scott, but as long as the board remained subordinate to the Council of National Defense and under the thumb of the armed services, a man like Scott was very useful. The pay inspector of the navy regarded Scott's absence as "a real calamity," for Scott "clearly understood the extent of the law and the feelings of both services."[2] After Scott's departure, Lovett assumed the chairmanship on a tem-

[1] Edward M. House, diary (cited hereafter as *House Diary*), in Edward M. House Papers (cited hereafter as *House Papers*), Yale University, New Haven, Conn., September 23, 1917. Also see William G. McAdoo, *Crowded Years* (Boston: Houghton Mifflin, 1931), p. 401; and Joseph Tumulty to Wilson, September 17, 1917, Newton D. Baker Papers, Library of Congress, Washington, D.C. (hereafter cited as *Baker Papers*). The Allied purchasing commission set out its ground rules in August and began its negotiations with the Allies. *New York Times*, August 7 and 25, 1917; minutes of a meeting of the War Industries Board (hereafter cited as *WIB Minutes*), August 1, 10, and 29, 1917, Record Group 61, Records of the War Industries Board, Federal Records Center, Suitland, Md. (hereafter cited as *RG 61*), File 1–C1, boxes 72–74.

[2] Admiral Peoples to Scott, October 30, 1917, Frank A. Scott Papers, Princeton University, Princeton, N.J. Applauding Scott's appointment to the WIB two months before, William Hard of the *New Republic* wrote: "He has been a positively providential bridge between the civilian and the military ways of thinking." William Hard, "A Victory for Efficiency," *New Republic* 12 (August 11, 1917): 41. See the *New York Times*, October 27, 1917, p. 1, for Scott's formal resignation; and also Scott to Baker, October 25, 1917, Record Group 62, Records of the Council of National Defense, Federal Records Center, Suitland, Md. (cited hereafter as *RG 62*), File 2–A4, box 82. Scott had wanted to resign a month before, but Baker had persuaded him to stay on

porary basis in October, but he was distracted by his own priorities work and anxious to return to his railway.[3]

The civilian board members struggled on as best they could, but sporadic, individual triumphs could not produce a coherent mobilization program. The clearance committee, which originated in the GMB, tried to coordinate military purchasing through the WIB but never overcame interbureau competition and the board's own fragmented structure. It prepared a list of materials that were in short supply or subject to other difficulties and made committee "clearance" a condition for their purchase. The military bureaus were to refer their proposed contracts to the committee so that the GMB and WIB business experts could review them "with the object continually in mind of adjusting questions of delivery and distribution, and further preventing abnormal rises in prices due to competition between the Governmental agencies."[4] But the committee could compel neither military purchasers nor board members to follow this procedure. Baruch remained unenthusiastic about the committee because of its intimate association with the War Department, a tie encouraged by Chairman Chester Bolton, a reserve colonel and another Cleveland friend of Baker's. Some military purchasers would give no outside agency a veto over their ordering plans. The committee ultimately disappeared into the WIB's requirements division in the spring of 1918.[5]

Robert Brookings organized a number of commodity committees in his finished products division in the fall, with the assistance of Philadelphia banker Emmet Crawford.[6] By the end of November he had gained jurisdiction over

---

until the administration could find a replacement. Baker to Wilson, September 21, 1917, Woodrow Wilson Papers, Library of Congress, Washington, D.C. (cited hereafter as *Wilson Papers*).

[3] Joseph Tumulty to Daniel Willard, October 9, 1917, RG 62, File 1–A1, box 22. Lovett had been reluctant to come to Washington in July in the first place. He wanted the right to retire in a year if his railroad business made that necessary. Lovett to Baker, July 24 and 29, 1917, both in *Baker Papers.*

[4] "History of the Clearance Office of the War Industries Board," prepared by J. C. Musser, clearance secretary, requirements division, War Industries Board (n.d.), RG 61, File 21A–A2, box 61. The committee had representatives from the general staff, the navy department, the Allied purchasing commission (after August 1917), various army bureaus, and the General Munitions Board.

[5] *Ibid.* Bolton complained of noncooperation from the raw materials and supplies committees, in Bolton to WIB chairman, September 20, 1917, RG 61, File 21A–A2, box 61. Also see *WIB Minutes*, September 26, 1917. That a navy admiral (F. F. Fletcher) chaired the committee throughout its life suggests that it was probably more of a service agency than Baruch and his men would have liked. Bolton ultimately revealed his preferences by joining the ordnance department reserve.

[6] Crawford, a Princeton graduate and senior member in Crawford, Patton and Cannon of Philadelphia, volunteered to assist Arch Shaw's conservation program in April 1917, but found a post in Walter Gifford's office that spring instead, moving to Brookings's

Rosenwald's supplies committee and seven other product lines, including army vehicles, machine tools, locomotive cranes, and electrical equipment. Brookings and Crawford sought to coordinate demand and supply for these products by opening channels of communication to the military bureaus and promising reliable information on industrial capacity in return for forecasts of military requirements. Brookings advertised finished products as the best equipped organization to advise on orders, much as Baruch had done on behalf of the old cooperative committees. Brookings was hopeful the bureaus would regard finished products as a boon to their regular operations. But neither buyers nor sellers supported the division's requests. Private contractors and individual bureau chiefs dealt directly with one another, and competition among the service purchasers continued.[7] Crawford explained the unpopularity of Brookings's commodity chiefs this way:

> The reason, in my opinion, why men representing the trade are able to get as close, if not closer to the Departments than your various section heads, is due to the fact that the Departments themselves are naturally each one very anxious to make the best possible showing for his specific Department, and when a representative of any of the large . . . concerns go[es] to a Department he tries to give that Department the very best possible service and obtain for that Department, from his concern, the Department's requirements in the quickest and the best manner possible, irrespective of whether these requirements interfere with or hurt other Departments in any way. As against this your section heads occupy an entirely neutral ground. All their efforts are bent in aiding all of the Departments, insofar as they can to secure what all the Departments need in the way of equipment. They have no favorites to play and endeavor to ascertain the needs of all the Departments rather than advance the requirement of any specific one against the requirements of others. In this way, insofar as they are able, without having full cooperation from the Departments, they are acting as the coordinating agent of all the Departments' requirements.[8]

Crawford demanded more concentrated authority for his section heads. Following in the footsteps of Robert Downman and the cooperative committee

operation in the fall. He became one of George Peek's right-hand men when Peek took over the division in March 1918.

[7]Crawford to General William Black, chief of the engineer corps, October 16, 1917, RG 61, File 21A–A4, box 1211; Brookings to Major Seth Williams, November 22, 1917, RG 61, File 21A–A1, box 10 (contains a list of committees in finished products); "Memorandum of Sections under Commissioner of Finished Products. . . ," November 16, 1917, RG 61, File 21A–A1, box 10. Brookings lost the committee on supplies and its thirteen subcommittees to the quartermaster department in January 1918. See Crawford to Ralph B. Feagin, January 21, 1918, *ibid.*

[8]Crawford and Walter Robbins (in charge of electrical equipment) to Brookings, January 2 [1918], RG 62, File 2–A8, box 88.

chairmen, he argued that "either the men heading the various sections are honest and thoroughly capable of handling the work given them or else they should not be permitted to have charge of their section."[9] The section heads shared his frustration.[10]

Bernard Baruch also pushed his independent operations ahead in these months. He continued to lobby for a civilian-controlled, multipurpose purchasing agency. He also added several men to his personal staff, including Alexander Legge, an International Harvester executive who took over duties in Allied purchasing; J. Leonard Replogle, president of the Cambria Steel Company, who administered the rapidly growing steel section; and Pope Yeatman, a consulting engineer who moved into nonferrous metals. These men, and others who later joined them, helped propel Baruch to the center of the emergency bureaucracy and solidify his position there. Baruch worried that he would not obtain the WIB chairmanship, but Meyer and his friends were convinced that the extensive personal organization they all were creating assured his future in Washington.[11]

Baruch and his men intensified their crusade for stable, predictable relations among the raw materials industries, the military bureaus, and themselves, expending a large part of their time, as usual, trying to reform the War Department's purchasing habits. "For the purpose of facilitating the work of the Raw Materials Committee and in order that the Government requirements may not unnecessarily interfere with the industry of the country," Eugene Meyer, Jr., wrote Scott in a characteristic vein, ". . . it is necessary to provide for centralization of the raw material requirements of the Ordnance Department in the hands of one officer."[12] This kind of demand was coupled with a request for long-range forecasts: ". . . You should put me in possession of information regarding the probable amounts of materials you expect to need, as soon as you can and for as long a time ahead as it is possible . . . ," Meyer told one ordnance officer.[13] Baruch once again asked Scott to have the WIB coordinate the raw

[9]Crawford to Brookings, November 22, 1917, RG 61, File 21A–A1, box 2. Crawford was a staunch advocate of giving ultimate authority over all decisions affecting a commodity to the business supervisor in charge.

[10]See the demands of Brookings's supervisors for better cooperation from the services and the emergency fleet corporation, in Section Heads to Brookings, December 17, 1917, RG 61, File 21A–A1, box 10. "The use of the sections," they wrote, "is now largely called upon by the Government Departments only when said departments are in trouble. It is our desire to avoid trouble before it becomes an actual condition—which suggests this letter."

[11]Eugene Meyer, Jr., Memoir, Oral History Collection, Columbia University, New York.

[12]Eugene Meyer, Jr., to Frank Scott, August 3, 1917, RG 61, File 21A–A4, box 463.

[13]Eugene Meyer, Jr., to Major Douglas J. McKay, December 7, 1917, RG 61, File 21A–A4, box 785.

material demands of the various government boards. "I realize that this is attendant with some difficulties," he wrote, "but we should commence to acquaint these departments with the fact that they must look ahead and not come suddenly upon the War Industries Board for materials for immediate delivery. You will readily understand that sudden demands for large amounts of materials are attendant with serious dislocation to the industrial needs."[14]

A clash between the navy and Rosenwald's supplies committee in September 1917 illustrates the jealousies over military prerogatives which plagued board members. In the course of its regular work the supplies committee called a conference with the nation's bean growers and then asked the navy to forward its requirements so the committee could inform the assembled businessmen. The navy's paymaster general, Samuel McGowan, balked on two counts: first, the navy had not requested the supplies committee to act on this front; and second, the navy preferred to handle this commodity through the food administration.[15] The episode, rather petty in itself, raised the larger question of the WIB's jurisdiction vis-à-vis military supplies. Baruch had alluded to this question only a few days before. "After the formation of the War Industries Board," he had informed Scott, "I did not understand that to be the policy and I thought I heard you in a meeting of the various departments here so instruct or inform them."[16] Not so, responded McGowan. Congressional statutes, he said, clearly fixed responsibility for purchasing supplies in the military departments, and there it would remain. The WIB's functions were "wholly advisory and in no way administrative or supervisory."[17] "The War Industries Board can be of material assistance to the War and Navy Departments in making their purchases of war supplies," he wrote his chief, "but, as it appears that the impression has gained currency that individual committees of the Board are to act in an administrative and supervisory capacity, it is believed advisable that their attention be invited to the requirements of the statutes and that they be informed their functions must necessarily be advisory only."[18]

Daniels and his naval officers met with Scott and Rosenwald in late September to clarify their relationship. All parties agreed then that the WIB and its

---

[14] Baruch to Scott, August 6, 1917, RG 61, File 21A–A4, box 1210.

[15] McGowan to Secretary of the Navy, September 7, 1917, RG 61, File 21A–A3, box 35.

[16] Baruch's letter to Scott of August 30, 1917, is included in *ibid.*

[17] McGowan to Daniels, September 12, 1917, *ibid.*

[18] *Ibid.* Daniel Willard later recalled the dogmatism of Secretary Daniels on just this point. "I remember many conferences I had with Secretary Daniels. . . . His course was laid out by definite enactments and he had to follow them, and he could not shift his responsibility to me or to anybody else." U.S. Congress, *Hearings before the Commission Appointed under the Authority of Public Resolution No. 98* (cited hereafter as *War Policies Commission*), Res. 251, 71st Cong., 2nd sess., 1931, part 1, p. 178.

committees could recommend prices but could not make purchases. The navy promised that the board and Lovett's priority division could have jurisdiction over the precedence of navy orders,[19] but they forgot this promise in later weeks.

The WIB's generally subordinate position is clearly illustrated by the fact that it had no contact at all with some boards, not even in an informal or haphazard way. The lack of official liaison with the shipping board and the aircraft production board meant that even if the WIB were able to reach an agreement with the services on purchasing a product like copper, it still would have no idea how shipping and aircraft demands might affect that commodity. Inadequate information and circumscribed jurisdiction obviously undermined the clearance and priority committees—how could they properly decide precedence when they were uncertain as to the sources and timing of needs? The board's lawyers made a critical survey of the board's deficiencies in October and concluded on a pessimistic note. The WIB "was created (and its members know it) for the very purpose of wiping out for the time being artificial and largely historical distinctions between governmental departments. And yet it finds itself constantly hampered by new distinctions between departments. The result cannot fail to be depressing to the morale of the Board, especially to the morale of a Board composed mostly of business men, unused to public office and to its limitations."[20]

Judge Lovett encountered all these problems in his Washington work, and shared the board members' growing sense of futility. Lovett was a Texan, born in 1860, who entered the railroad business after obtaining his law degree. He made rapid headway, becoming general counsel for the Union Pacific and Southern Pacific in 1904, president of both lines in 1909, and then chairman of the executive committee of the Union Pacific System in 1913. He volunteered for the Red Cross when the United States entered the war, then joined the WIB in August 1917. An amendment to the Interstate Commerce Act, passed on August 10, 1917, authorized President Wilson to give priority to shipments vital to national defense, and Wilson chose Lovett to administer the act and ease the bottleneck in coal transport. Lovett immediately directed forty-six railroads to give bituminous coal shipments precedence over their other business.[21]

[19]"Jurisdiction of the War Industries Board. . .," September 28, 1917, RG 61, File 21A-A3, box 35.

[20]"Preliminary Memorandum . . . on Organization" (n.d.), RG 61, File 21A-A1, box 1. The lawyers recommended statutory power for WIB priorities, purchasing, and "somebody responsible under the President alone for the making of all large decisions and the formulation of all large policies."

[21]*New York Times*, May 21, July 29, August 21, 22, and 24, 1917; Wilson to Baker, August 17, 1917, *Baker Papers*; Wilson to Lovett, August 17, 1917, RG 61, File 21A-A4, box 1158. For the administrative details of the first order, see box 1158, *ibid.*

Lovett conceived his role as administrator of the Priority in Transportation Act as quite separate from his position as chief of priorities on the WIB. By January 1918, however, the former function had disappeared into the railroad administration. The WIB was then absorbing most of Lovett's energy as he struggled to overcome limited power, fragmented jurisdiction, and inadequate information. A priority committee had already been functioning when Lovett arrived in Washington, but his drive gave it a real forward thrust. He enlarged its administrative staff by luring a number of railroadmen to Washington, along with San Francisco businessman George Armsby, American Radiator executive Charles K. Foster and, most important of all, Houston lawyer Edwin B. Parker, who ultimately took over the program when Lovett quit Washington in March 1918.[22]

Lovett thoroughly reorganized the priorities administration in November on the basis of a survey undertaken by a Price-Waterhouse consultant. That reorganized structure remained the basic framework for priorities until the end of the war, and is worth outlining in some detail. To relieve the central administration of routine paper work, the consultant recommended formation of three principal subcommittees: a bureau of applications and issue; a bureau of investigation and research; and a bureau of contests, complaints and rehearings. The investigation bureau, organized along commodity lines, would undertake the vital task of scrutinizing manufacturers' claims for priority. The commodity investigators, to quote the Price-Waterhouse report, would be administered by "business men drawn from the respective Industries, who are thoroughly proficient in their respective lines and who also have a fairly wide acquaintance with the personnel of the Trade." To facilitate these investigations, a committee on trade conferences would supervise meetings with various industrial groups, "since it has already been found that the co-operation of the accredited representatives of the various Trades and Industries is desirable, if not essential, in order to deal intelligently with the broad and far-reaching questions which will require to be decided. . . ."[23]

[22] Lovett brought a young lawyer, Ralph B. Feagin, from the Houston firm of Baker, Botts, Parker and Garwood, to handle office routine at $200.00 a month. The Erie Railroad gave him their superintendent of transportation, who received $600.00 a month. Ralph B. Feagin to Congressional Directory Office and to Ruby Patton, October 5, 1917, and Lovett to Wilson, September 11, 1917, both in RG 61, File 21A–A4, box 1157. Also see the undated, unsigned memorandum on the history of the priorities committee in RG 61, File 7–B3, box 846.

[23] See the fairly extensive "Memorandum on Proposed Organization with Relative Exhibits and Appendix," November 8, 1917, RG 61, File 21A–A1, box 18. By this time Lovett had also received aid from the vice president, assistant controller, and chief statistician of the Union Pacific, and the Price-Waterhouse consultant remained with him throughout the fall. He then recruited the vice president of the Western Union Telegraph Company to head the bureau of application. See the undated, unsigned memorandum

Functional gains matched structural improvements when Lovett issued the first priority order, circular no. 1, on September 21, 1917. Henceforth, all steel orders would be divided into general classes, A, B, and C, in a descending scale of importance from 1 to 7, with work relating to class A contracts taking precedence over categories B and C. Class A comprised war work; class B was not essentially war work yet fell within the public interest; and class C was the catch-all category for which priority orders were barred. Government officials did not consider similar treatment for any other product at the time, so the steel action did not inaugurate a broad program of priority control. Nevertheless, circular no. 1 was a major precedent for federal intervention in the distribution process.[24]

Like Brookings and Baruch, then, Lovett took command of his area of interest and mounted an attack on disorder and competition. But also like them he never doubted that the handicaps and restraints would severely limit any gains he might make. Lack of legal authority inhibited the board in priorities as in purchases, and reinforced its dependency upon cooperation from business and military buyers and steel producers. Moreover, military bureaus retained the legal right to commandeer goods at will despite priority rulings, so they could always intervene if dissatisfied with the treatment accorded their orders. Edwin Parker lobbied strenuously to have all military orders routed through the priority division and to monopolize all commandeering authority for the board. He wrote this latter stipulation into priority circular no. 3, but the navy forced it out.[25] Parker and the WIB did not gain even the formal right to coordinate military commandeering orders until September 1918.

---

on the history of the priorities committee in RG 61, File 7-B3, box 846. Edwin Parker assumed the general task of recruitment for priorities and the nature of his appeal is admirably summed up in the following: "... You will ... readily realize the great importance of strong, active, experienced men, with executive ability, promptly organizing and directing this work along broad lines." Parker to A. H. Nairn, September 15, 1917, RG 61, File 21A-A1, box 17.

[24] Minutes of the Council of National Defense and joint meetings of the council and Advisory Commission (cited hereafter as *CND Minutes*), RG 62, File 2B-1, box 104, September 5, 1917; circular no. 1, "Directions as to Priority," September 21, 1917, RG 61, File 21A-A4, box 1157; *New York Times*, September 25, 1917, p. 1. On civilian-military relations, however, Lovett favored letting the services settle their own squabbles rather than injecting his priorities organization. This of course weakened its overall coordinating function. See Rear Admiral F. F. Fletcher and Colonel P. E. Pierce to Secretary of Navy and Secretary of War, November 24, 1917, Josephus Daniels Papers, Library of Congress, Washington, D.C. (cited hereafter as *Daniels Papers*), and "Statement of Judge R. S. Lovett," Bernard M. Baruch Papers, Princeton University, Princeton, N.J. (cited hereafter as *Baruch Papers*).

[25] Parker had written Admiral Fletcher: "There is obviously grave danger of delay if all applications by contractors and subcontractors are cleared through the various departments of the Government." But to no avail. Parker to Fletcher, January 23, 1918, RG

In the final analysis, buyers and sellers could use the division when it served their purposes, ignore it when it did not. Among federal agencies, the War Department submitted cases on occasion, but the navy and shipping board, among large buyers, paid no attention at all. Journalist George Soule offered an accurate judgment on its position at the end of October 1917:

It represents neither all the buying divisions nor all the sources of supply, but is a compromise between the two. It is supposed to coördinate the buying program of all departments, the Allies, and all the railroads and public necessities in private hands, to lay out on that basis policies of priority, to decide the conflicts passed up by the Clearance Committee, and to distribute to manufacturers classified priority certificates showing which orders are to be given precedence. . . . Here should be the nervous system to regulate our whole producing circulation. Perhaps the Priority Committee understands its vastly important and vastly perplexing function, but few others in Washington or elsewhere do understand it, and in consequence the Committee is not yet accomplishing a small fraction of what it should accomplish.[26]

THE PROBLEM OF PRICES

To break down institutional distinctions among government departments and between business and government, to reorder the bureaucratic structure of the state, and to alter the popular attitude toward competition and individualism proved as formidable in the area of prices as it did in purchases and priorities. That some of the chief skeptics of the WIB impulse were business interests themselves complicated matters further. Businessmen in government could be very explicit about their search for power to discipline the state on behalf of an integrated mobilization program. They could assert repeatedly that if only the government would centralize its decision-making, concentrate its power, and rationalize its structure, then friendly, continuous business-government relations were assured. But the assumption underlying this argument was that business interests could be depended upon to accede to government requests once the state finally put its house in order.

What if business leadership refused to cooperate? Businessmen in government were committed to the idea of proving what private corporate leadership could achieve in conjunction with a friendly, rationalized state. The cooperative committees of industry had been built on this principle. How then could they

_____

61, File 7-B3, box 846. Parker continued his campaign to centralize priority and commandeering decisions throughout the war, gaining more success after the WIB reorganization in March 1918.

[26] George Soule, "The War Industries Board," *New Republic* 12 (October 27, 1918): 356.

admit that industrial interests did not always accept WIB intervention willingly, at least not on the board's terms? Did this not raise serious doubts as to the viability of a mobilization program founded largely on the goodwill of American big business? Did it not justify outright government coercion? To admit that the WIB could not secure prompt agreement from business interests could only strengthen the very groups who threatened the system of institutional cooperation. Thus the business advisors were bound by an important ideological commitment, and its influence emerges most clearly in the debate over fixing prices on steel and copper in the summer and fall of 1917. In this instance businessmen in government protected hesitant business interests from groups within the state, the economy, and among the public who would willingly have abandoned a cooperative system for rigid, political control of spiraling prices.

Throughout the spring business advisors had waged an unsuccessful campaign for a concentrated, stable price policy. Their agitation had by no means ended with the WIB's formation. The board's mandate included the right to consider "price factors" but not to make policy or settle outstanding controversies. Thus, in a tone reminiscent of the special price committee of the previous May, the board informed the council only a week after its inauguration: "Business is suffering throughout the country today because of uncertainty as to Government policy with respect to prices and taxation. In this respect the business loss is serious, but even more serious is the bad effect on the spirit of manufacturers who would be willing, and glad, to work and make sacrifices for the benefit of the Government in its emergency if they felt sure of fair and equal treatment, based on a definite Government policy." With each military bureau and war board clinging to an independent policy "contractors supplying the various needs of the Government are not treated with equality and are not dealt with consistently on any established principle."[27]

WIB men grumbled about other things besides generally unsettled business conditions. The interrelationship of prices among private, governmental, and Allied buyers still required attention. The board was also anxious to disabuse military officials of the notion that their proper course lay in driving the best possible bargain, for from the board's point of view, seeking the lowest possible prices on military supplies merely forced up prices for the Allies and the public at large, and threatened to bring radical controls. It also discriminated against the manufacturers of government requirements and rewarded those who sold elsewhere.

The WIB wanted to make the price issue its own and so opposed giving jurisdiction to some other government agency, like the Federal Trade Commission, as some were suggesting. The FTC could contribute important data,

[27] "Memorandum on Proposed Powers of War Industries Board," August 9, 1917, enclosed in Baker to Wilson, August 9, 1917, *Baker Papers.*

perhaps, but "a knowledge of the cost of production, unaccompanied by the other facts which would be known to the War Industries Board, would not enable the Federal Trade Commission fairly to fix prices."[28] The general principles of price fixing also concerned the board. It specifically opposed the policy of pooling production and setting prices on the basis of cost, plus a percentage profit. This would mean a varying price scale, a complicated governmental administrative program, a large role for the agency that calculated costs (the FTC), and possibly less incentive for production. The board favored a flat price policy—the same price for every producer, with an excess profits tax skimming off the inordinate profits made by large, efficient firms. This approach required little administration, kept the federal government in the background, opened a wider avenue of negotiation between business and government, saved borderline producers, and generally served better to maintain the industrial status quo.

In its August brief, the board emphasized the need to coordinate pricing, purchasing, and priority decisions "so as to be able to assure manufacturers who accept the fixed reduced prices that their products are actually going to be used for the military and economic needs essential to the successful prosecution of the war."[29] Industrial equilibrium necessitated all segments of the mobilization program moving forward together. Only the board could serve this coordinating function; the sooner it had charge the better.

The practical suggestions which followed this lengthy brief on prices were remarkably mild. Recommendations for far-reaching federal controls and tough administrative practices were noticeably absent. The whole force of the board's recommendations moved in the opposite direction. The threat of drastic federal price control concerned the board most of all, and it reacted now, as before, to head off such action. The board, with the cooperation of other government departments, intended to "control prices generally by request, on patriotic grounds publicly endorsed by the President, that no one quote or pay prices in excess of those fixed by the Board." These prices could then be enforced "by the hint that those quoting higher prices in their private trade would have their capacity entirely used on Government orders so that their private customers would be obliged to look elsewhere." Such an approach required no change in the law. "Legislation may be desirable and even necessary later, but can best be suggested as the result of experience in the attempt above outlined."[30] Throughout the war the WIB men were well aware that only if certain kinds of preventative federal actions were taken in time could dangerous, radical experiments be

[28] *Ibid.* For an example of this anxiety over the FTC in the business press, see "The Matter of Prices," *Engineering and Mining Journal* 103 (June 30, 1917): 1166-67.
[29] "Memorandum on Proposed Powers of War Industries Board," August 9, 1917, enclosed in Baker to Wilson, August 9, 1917, *Baker Papers.*
[30] *Ibid.*

suppressed. Defensive tactics were central pillars of the WIB's offense during the war.

Since Secretary Baker sought to avoid large concentrations of emergency power and strict federal controls, he readily favored business proposals like the WIB's, especially when, as in this case, his own prerogatives were not so directly involved. He also shared the anxiety of WIB men that, unless some actions were taken, the voluntary, cooperative framework of business-government relations might collapse and make extensive federal intervention inevitable. Baker was optimistic about the WIB proposals and explained to Wilson that with presidential approval "they could . . . make rapid progress in settling some price controversies and give a sense of assurance to the business men with whom they have to deal on the subject."[31] Wilson remained unconvinced, reluctant to give up control and wary perhaps of appearing to yield to every business demand. He explained to Baker that while he valued the WIB's advice he could not give it "the power to determine prices."[32]

The price controversies which Baker mentioned included negotiations with the steel and copper industries that dragged on until late the next month.[33] Discussion had waxed and waned with the steel industry since late March, when Baruch visited the New York offices of Elbert H. Gary, chairman of the board of United States Steel, in search of an arrangement analogous to the agreement he had struck with the copper people. He was rebuffed, however, and relations between Gary and the administration's business advisors remained cool for many months. Several days after Baruch's mission, the industry did agree to supply structural steel to the military services below market prices, but did so reluctantly and only after it forced the issue right to the president. Gary's attitude angered Baruch; yet the lesson Baruch and the other business advisors derived from the episode was the absolute necessity of placing the whole price question firmly in their own hands and settling outstanding issues at once. This sentiment was evident in the report of the special price committee in May. Secretary Daniels and the steel industry had feuded over prices since before the war, and Baruch probably thought that Daniels's absence from direct negotiations might improve the atmosphere. Baruch and Scott also realized that the fear that private businessmen had of facing several different sources of government authority on price fixing also increased friction, an observation dramatically illustrated a week later when the industry and the shipping board clashed over steel plate prices. At this point the steelmakers proposed creation of a joint commission of army,

---

[31] Baker to Wilson, August 9, 1917, *Baker Papers.*

[32] Wilson to Baker, August 16, 1917, *ibid.*

[33] The following discussion of price negotiations with the steel industry is drawn largely from Robert D. Cuff and Melvin I. Urofsky, "The Steel Industry and Price-Fixing during World War I," *Business History Review* 44 (Autumn 1970): 291–306.

navy, and shipping board representatives, through which the American Iron and Steel Institute could negotiate prices. But the administration backed away from this proposal and decided instead to launch an FTC investigation. In the meantime it asked the industry to deliver the required amounts at prewar rates. Proper adjustments could be made later.

Wilson refused to act hastily over prices, but he could not still the press of events and the demands of war. Pressure for action built up within the war organization itself, as government purchasing bureaus found steel impossible to obtain. Mill owners eyed the market and contracts remained open. The public also grew restless as prices mounted through June and early July to their highest point since America entered the war. "Our opinion is that unless the question of price, and the necessary economic readjustment, can be settled without involving the military programme as seriously as at present," Baruch and Scott warned Baker, "we may well anticipate not only the gravest military results but also serious reaction of public and political opinion."[34] Baruch disliked the steel industry's uncooperative stance. He disliked even more the possibility that Congress would use the present impasse as an excuse to enact stringent controls. Steel had to bear a large share of the blame, but Scott and Baruch were convinced that governmental indecision had also contributed to hard feelings between the industry and government.

President Wilson was in a fighting mood by this time and, according to Daniels, informed Baker that if the steel producers refused to give "right" prices at their meeting on July 11, he would nationalize the mills and fix the rates himself.[35] He issued a public statement that day to strengthen the government's position and to quiet public and congressional criticism. Calling on American business to place patriotism above profits, he exclaimed that with men dying on the battlefields of Europe the least businessmen could do was yield up their money. He referred to the ancient concept of the "just price" but defined it in such a way as to reassure the country's producers that he was not about to undermine the profit motive.

By a just price I mean a price which will sustain the industries concerned in a high state of efficiency, provide a living for those who conduct them, enable them to pay good wages, and make possible the expansion of their enterprises which from time to time become necessary. . . . We could not wisely or reasonably do less than pay such prices. They are necessary for the maintenance and development of industry, and the maintenance and development of industry are necessary for the great task we have in hand.[36]

[34] Baruch and Scott to Baker, July 5, 1917, RG 61, File 21B–A3, box 166.

[35] E. David Cronon, ed., *The Cabinet Diaries of Josephus Daniels* (Lincoln: University of Nebraska Press, 1963), p. 174 (hereafter cited as *Daniels Diary*).

[36] *New York Times*, July 12, 1917, p. 1.

As part of the politics of his plea Wilson proclaimed that all prices quoted to the government had to extend to the public and the Allies as well. This idea had been abroad in Washington since the early spring, but this was the first time Wilson had publicly committed the administration to it.

Two aspects of this presidential address must be stressed. First, it was not a general attack on American business, for the president directed his harshest words at the primary producers, such as the steel and copper interests, who were identified in the public mind as the profiteers driving prices upward. Secondary manufacturers and leading business spokesmen greeted the appeal warmly.[37] *American Hatter* concluded that: "Some of the most forceful passages were unquestionably launched with particular interests in mind. . . ."[38] The second point to note is that the speech was more effective as an emotional catharsis for a current public crisis than as a substantial contribution to settling price policy. What was a "just price" after all? How were prices to be fixed? Who would administer them? With the market mechanism thus affected how would goods be distributed?[39] Wilson answered none of these questions, and government officials continued to predict disaster for the supply program; buyers, both public and private, pressed for action. The president had decided against any further move, however, until he received the results of his FTC investigation.

The parties to the steel conferences on July 11 and 12 decided to defer price fixing until the FTC inquiry was completed. To soothe the steelmakers in the meantime, government officials agreed that "the price, when fixed, would insure reasonable profits and be made with reference to the expanding needs of this vital and fundamental industry."[40] The administration and the industry

---

[37] See, for example, Charles-Piez (president, Link-Belt Company) to Wilson, July 13, 1917, RG 61, File 21B-A3, box 164; William H. Crosby (president, Crosby Company Sheet Metal Stamping) to Rosenwald, RG 61, File 21B-A3, box 166; John Fahey (U.S. Chamber of Commerce leader) to Wilson, July 16, 1917, *Wilson Papers*; A. C. Bedford (president, Standard Oil of New Jersey) to Wilson, July 17, 1917, *Wilson Papers*; statement of Waddill Catchings, U.S. Chamber of Commerce spokeman, in the *New York Times*, July 16, 1917, p. 3. *Iron Age*, the steel industry's trade journal, noted, "The Government is not alone in wanting regulation of steel prices. Many producers and buyers of steel have feared the consequences of the ungoverned upward movement of the past six months." See "Price Regulation at Hand," *Iron Age* 100 (July 19, 1917): 142. *Literary Digest* reported great enthusiasm throughout business groups generally; see *Literary Digest* 55 (July 28, 1917): 18. "The President's statement expresses the popular desire exactly," concluded the *Washington Post*, July 13, 1917.

[38] "President Wilson's Appeal to Business Men," *American Hatter* 47 (August 1917): 57.

[39] Waddill Catchings touched on these points in *New York Times*, July 16, 1917, p. 3, and in Catchings to Wilson, July 13, 1917, RG 62, File 2-A1, box 31. See also "The Controversy over Prices," *Engineering and Mining Journal* 104 (July 14, 1917): 100-101.

[40] This is taken from a statement put out by the War Department attached to minutes of a meeting of the General Munitions Board, July 12, 1917, in RG 62, File 5-B1, box 290;

were in the midst of hammering out a compromise on the one-price-for-all issue and still awaiting the FTC report when the WIB issued its August appeal for power in prices. Not until September 23 did a steel agreement finally emerge.

Business advisors might admit that steel and copper producers were dragging their heels, but they believed they understood the reasons for this far better than the administration's nonbusiness members. They could sympathize with producers who found themselves caught between rising public criticism on the one hand and a vacillating administration on the other. Baruch summed up this sentiment on August 6, 1917, at a conference on copper prices for the Allies: "Mr. Baruch," the minutes record, "brought out the fact that the copper people had been liberal and that the present situation was brought about through no fault of theirs but was due to the delay in decision of the Government as to the proper price that should be paid."[41] The cynic might argue that Baruch was merely showing a special warmness for the Guggenheims here, but even if this were true, it should not obscure the broader point involved. With copper, as with steel, the problem of identical prices for the Allies and the United States government formed a major barrier to amicable price fixing. At Baruch's suggestion, the board agreed to fix a temporary price a little lower than the copper interests wanted—22.5¢ instead of 25¢—and determine the final price when the FTC report arrived.[42] This permitted immediate purchases, pacified administration officials, and still left the way open for an upward revision whenever the regular price fixing agreement took place. On August 17, 1917, though, nine days after the board adopted this position, British and Canadian spokesmen asked Baruch to buy Allied copper "as an individual, independently of the Board,"[43] at the price the copper interests originally quoted. With so many buyers willing to pay almost any price for desperately needed materials, it was extremely difficult to hold the lid on prices.

In subsequent weeks the board, under Lovett's direction, scrutinized the FTC findings and decided that 22 cents was a proper price for all buyers. This did not sit at all well with the major producers, as they indicated on September 11. John Ryan of Anaconda, Baruch's major contact within the industry, argued that the small, high cost producers would never cooperate at that price. If the board had stuck to a 22 cent price, he said later, it would have had to find another group of producers to administer the agreement. The board and the

---

see also W.L.C., "The Readjustment of Steel Prices," *Iron Age* 100 (July 19, 1917): 168–70.

[41] *WIB Minutes*, August 6, 1917. Howard Coffin later testified that profiteering during the war was "largely the result of the Government's own uncertainty, vacillation, and lack of any intelligent prearrangement or plan in that direction." *War Policies Commission*, part 1, p. 302.

[42] *WIB Minutes*, August 8, 1917.

[43] *Ibid.*, August 17, 1917.

producers, however, agreed on a compromise price of 23.5 cents. A statement accompanying the formal agreement of September 21 claimed the government would take over the mills of any interests who failed to cooperate. But in light of Ryan's comments, this threat appears to have been aimed as much at the minor as at the major producers.[44]

Although there were conflicting reports as to how the industry greeted the final arrangement, no one could gainsay the fact that this agreement was a major advance toward a price fixing policy. "Those who have argued against Government prices, which they feared might be so low as to hinder production and disorganize the industry," commented the *New York Times,* "expressed the opinion tonight that the Government's copper price was an all-important step in the right direction, especially if it might be accepted as a forecast of action on other basic commodities."[45]

Interestingly enough, the copper agreement and the steel agreement two days later did not inaugurate a general price fixing program. The board received FTC information on various commodities and met with Wilson in November to discuss prices on lumber, lead, cement, zinc, tin, and supplementary steel items, but new agreements came only sporadically thereafter.[46] Special price arrangements between industry and the various emergency boards and the military bureaus continued, of course, but the WIB hesitated to recommend prices for the public and Allies as well. To some extent the board simply adhered to the recommendations against such moves that it received from the industries involved.[47] But the basic problem was the board's subordinate position and its lack of congressional or statutory authority over prices. This was one reason why the board had believed it so important to cast the steel and copper compromises in the form of voluntary agreements. Baruch recalled: "There was no doubt about [the legal authority of price fixing for] the Army and Navy, but there was

---

[44] *Ibid.,* September 5, 11, 12, and 21; Lovett to Wilson, September 19, 1917, *Wilson Papers;* *New York Times,* September 21 and 22, 1917, pp. 4 and 15, respectively. Lewis Kennedy Morse has much of the general detail in "The Price-Fixing of Copper," *Quarterly Journal of Economics* 23 (November 1918): 71-106.

[45] *New York Times,* September 21, 1917, p. 4.

[46] Wilson to Baruch, October 13, 1917, *Wilson Papers; WIB Minutes,* November 2, 7, 21, and 22, 1917.

[47] John Morron of Atlas Cement told Eugene Meyer, Jr., that his industry could not possibly supply private buyers at government prices (the president's July 11 statement notwithstanding). See Morron to Meyer, November 22, 1917, RG 61, File 21A-A4, box 312. Also see the discussion and announcement against lead price fixing, *WIB Minutes,* December 17, 1917. Baruch noted in his diary: "Board met to discuss advisability of fixing a maximum on Lead—decided not to. I think should have done so." Bernard M. Baruch, diary, in *Baruch Papers* (cited hereafter as *Baruch Diary*), December 17, 1917. See *WIB Minutes,* January 4, 1918, for the decision against fixing a maximum price on nickel.

some doubt about the Allies. But when you got to the point of fixing the price for the civilian population, we did not think we had anything in the law which would enable us to do that. In that situation, I think many times we perhaps paid a little bit more."[48] Ideological bias and practical necessity coincided in recommendations by business advisors on the price issue.

Baruch and the rest naturally shied away from arbitrary orders issued under legislative fiat, for that practice ran counter to the promise of harmonious business-government relations implicit in the corporate vision. Yet their own personal need for legal authority and administrative power remained. A real ambiguity pervaded the relationship between big business and central business administrators like Baruch, Lovett, and Brookings. Even while these men excused the intransigence of their colleagues in industry, they sought more power to save some of them from the folly of their own shortsightedness. The most effective way to protect corporate leadership in the long run, they reasoned, was to augment their own credibility with the private businessmen whose behavior threatened the broader goals they, the administrators, had entered government to realize. Better that those of them who were sympathetic to business interests firmly discipline the industrial economy than to permit one obdurate industry or firm to undermine the promise of business-government cooperation and thereby place them all at the mercy of hostile politicians.

But in the impasse over steel, for example, how could the WIB actually discipline an industry? It could threaten a takeover as a last resort, but what if its bluff were called? In reality, inadequate administrative resources compounded the legal flaw in the board's character. Daniel Willard referred to these problems in a letter he wrote to Wilson in December as the newly appointed WIB chairman. Lumber prices were a problem at the time, and without formal authority to limit prices for the public and Allies, Willard wondered what the board could do. In the case of copper and steel, Willard thought prices might possibly have been enforced by government seizure and operation of the mines and factories, but this tactic was out of the question in the sprawling lumber industry. To fix prices without even a hope of success would discredit all past agreements. "In short," Willard concluded on behalf of the WIB, "we think it wise to fix prices only in those cases where there is some means, direct or indirect, of compelling obedience."[49] War demands would ultimately make the board ignore its own advice, but in the meantime this lack of legal-administrative muscle acted

[48] U.S. Congress, Senate, Special Committee to Investigate the Munitions Industry, *Hearings, Munitions Industry*, 73rd–74th Cong., 1934–1937, part 22, pp. 6312–13 (hereafter cited as Nye Committee, *Hearings*).

[49] Willard to Wilson, December 7, 1917, *Wilson Papers*. See also *WIB Minutes*, December 6, 1917, and *CND Minutes*, December 7, 1917.

as a major constraint on its price fixing activities. The president fully concurred in the board's course of action.

BUSINESS PRESSURE FOR CHANGE

Within the business community itself, the United States Chamber of Commerce best expressed the sentiments then current among the administration's business advisors. The chamber was the most insistently vocal and well-informed business critic of the administration's mobilization program, and it played an important part as educator and advocate of advanced business opinion. In many instances it stated publicly what business advisors could only grouse about privately. The striking similarity between the WIB position and the chamber's policy statements was less a conspiracy between the two than an indication of how often the government's business experts merely expressed the conventional wisdom of enlightened business opinion.

The chamber had welcomed the creation of the WIB in July 1917. *Nation's Business* even claimed it as "one of the contributions of organized business to the nation."[50] Still, it was acutely aware of its deficiencies. It noted that the board did not actually procure supplies; that it confronted problems only after other departments revealed them; that it depended on others for information; that it lacked direct means of enforcement; and that it had to overcome insuperable problems in designing price and priority policies. The WIB would have to yield to a board with real power, "not power which comes from friendly cooperation—but the real power which compels action and can be judged by results."[51]

The chamber carried its message of centralization and control to business groups at the War Convention of American Business in September, and in a regular series of printed war bulletins.[52] As part of its program it recommended that price control legislation be administered by "*a small executive board appointed by the President.*" It also subscribed to the flat price policy and an

---

[50]*Nation's Business* 5 (August 1917): 8.

[51]The Chamber of Commerce statement on the WIB appeared in the *New York Times*, August 13, 1917, p. 6. The machine tool industry was also a persistent advocate of centralized mobilization. For a sample comment, see Fred H. Colvin, "Latest Advices from Our Washington Editor," *American Machinist* 47 (September 6, 1917): 436–37; and also "Wanted—a Master Hand," *ibid.* (September 20, 1917), pp. 518–19.

[52]The chamber convention of September 18, 19, 20, and 21, 1917, offered a dramatic demonstration of growing business pressure for concentrated authority in the Washington bureaucracy. *Nation's Business* 5 (October 1917) contains a comprehensive report, including reprints of the major addresses.

excess profits tax. The federal government ought not to delay matters, the chamber warned, for that could "create a situation which will lead state legislatures . . . to think it necessary to deal with prices, thus substituting a diversity of provisions in a subject so important as to demand the uniformity which federal legislation alone can give."[53]

The chamber stepped up the pressure in late October. It dispatched delegations to Washington and released a shower of memoranda on many government officials, including the president himself.[54] Unless the government exerted firm leadership, said a lengthy commentary which the chamber's directors prepared in mid-November, "serious dislocation is inevitable." The entire war organization required a complete overhaul. The crisis demanded an agency "designed to meet the emergency, to consider great problems as they arise with power to reach decisions, and to carry these decisions into effect." Without this kind of direction "democracy can not concentrate its scattered efforts or assemble its strength for war." Mobilization required a "Department of War Supplies" responsible for the government's entire purchasing program, with complete power to set prices, commandeer goods, and make deliveries.[55]

The protective theme associated earlier with Howard Coffin's preparedness campaign figured prominently in all of the chamber's statements. The federal government had both to win the war and "to maintain essential industrial life and to preserve so far as possible the normal industrial structure until the return of peace."[56]

The chamber had stood in advance of other business groups in its criticism of the existing war organization during the spring and summer of 1917, but it gained many adherents in the late fall and winter, as war needs increased and the prospects of a long war grew. Businessmen could no longer afford to regard the chamber's position papers as interesting but essentially theoretical statements.

[53] From "Referendum no. 22, On the Report of the Special Committee on Control of Prices during War," September 12, 1917, RG 61, File 21A-A4, box 1147.

[54] WIB Minutes, October 19, 1917; Daniels Diary, p. 230; Wilson to R. G. Rhett (chamber president), November 20, 1917, Wilson Papers. They visited Colonel House, too. House Diary, October 19, 1917.

[55] The Chamber of Commerce memorandum, "Government War Buying," is enclosed in R. G. Rhett to Wilson, November 15, 1917, Wilson Papers.

[56] Ibid. Daniel Willard had just become chairman of the WIB when the chamber brief and its sponsors were making the rounds in Washington that November, and he persuaded them to call off their proposed referendum and legislative campaign to give him a chance. They reluctantly agreed. Waddill Catchings (chairman of the chamber's war committee) to Willard, November 27, 1917, RG 61, File 21A-A3, box 44; Willard to Catchings, November 30, 1917, ibid.; Newton D. Baker to Willard, November 28, 1917, RG 61, File 21A-A3, box 35; WIB Minutes, November 30, 1917; Willard to Baker, December 7, 1917, Wilson Papers; Baker to Rhett, December 12, 1917, and R. G. Rhett to Wilson, December 14, 1917, both ibid.

Indeed, near panic swept American industry in the fall as rumors spread of an imminent program of restrictions on nonessential business. "Business men everywhere are wondering what is nonessential business," commented the chamber in one of its war bulletins. It resolutely opposed any nonessential-essential classification until "a general plan" was formulated and all industrial groups were consulted.[57]

The feeling that less essential industries would have to give way to war needs was not a new idea in November 1917. The Advisory Commission had forecast this possibility as early as March 1917, and Daniel Willard had told Walter Gifford in August that, "All activities which are in no sense related to the successful outcome of the war should be subordinated, if not wholly eliminated, during the continuance of the war."[58] With an eye on the European experience, Howard Coffin had addressed himself to just such a problem in his prewar campaign. If only the administration planned its course properly, he argued, no industry had to be sacrificed to the war effort, and needless to say, businessmen generally shared his conviction. Faced now with rumors of severe cutbacks, Coffin's feeling was that whatever happened, industry should not be made to suffer for the administration's shortsightedness.[59]

By November WIB executives wanted to scuttle the "business as usual" attitude once and for all, and begin a series of cutbacks in nonwar industry. This kind of sentiment motivated the board in late October to ask the producers of alloy steel to conserve their output for war industries only, and then to include on priority order no. 2 a list of nonessential industries which could not expect their usual access to rail transportation. The reaction showed how far the War Industries Board had strayed from general business opinion.

The automobile industry emitted a cry of outrage at these moves. The steel order came like a "flash from a clear sky,"[60] as a trade paper phrased it, and the priority circular which placed the industry in the same category as cosmetics and musical instruments only intensified the hostility. Trade journals trumpeted a

---

[57]United States Chamber of Commerce, "Non-Essential Business," War Bulletin no. 29, November 2, 1917, in the Edwin F. Gay Papers, Hoover Institute, Stanford University, Stanford, Cal.

[58]Willard to Gifford, August 21, 1917, RG 62, File 1–A1, box 22. See also *Daniels Diary*, p. 201; and *CND Minutes*, October 1, 1917.

[59]This sentiment comes through best in Coffin's comments in preliminary discussions about auto curtailment; see "Memorandum of Meeting in Mr. Baruch's Office," October 30, 1917, RG 61, File 21A–A1, box 2.

[60]"Washington Aims Destructive Blow at Dealer Industry," *Motor World* 53 (November 7, 1917): 5. Articles in *Iron Age* offer good descriptions of the order and its consequences; see "Eliminating the Unessentials," *Iron Age* 100 (November 8, 1917): 1130 (also pp. 1152–53 of this issue), and "Steel for the 'Unessentials'?" *Iron Age* 100 (November 29, 1917): 1304–5.

call to arms; auto men already in Washington rushed to the WIB's offices; and private delegations followed closely behind. The protest knocked the board completely off its feet. By November 24, Robert Lovett was contradicting himself publicly, and a week later the board hinted that the whole episode had been a terrible mistake. No alloy steel shortage existed after all.[61] There is no better example of the WIB's sorry state in the fall and winter of 1917, than the pounding it took on this issue. But the WIB itself was largely to blame, for its action had been precipitous, uncoordinated, issued with no prior consultation with the industry most heavily affected, and without any thought as to how the companies involved could shift to war work. The board seems to have been even naive enough to think it could work through the order without publicity. An entirely predictable complaint from one of the twenty-three steel companies involved blew the issue wide open.

As the board reeled from the first round in what became a long knock-down-drag-out fight with Detroit, it tried to reassure businessmen on the question of nonessential industry and regain its self-respect in the process. The board summoned George Peek to Washington to head a bureau of manufacturing resources that could advise on conversion problems and issue comforting statements that there were no "nonessential industries." Peek was an executive with Deere and Company, and an associational activist within the agricultural implements industry. He had worried privately for some time about the administration's haphazard industrial policies, and believed the time had come for more thoroughgoing cooperation between business and government. Once in Washington, Peek made the chamber of commerce his principal communication channel to industry, and enlisted Arch W. Shaw's Commercial Economy Board in his plans to have businessmen save themselves through streamlined operations.[62] Enthusiasm soon gave way to frustration, though, as Peek stumbled on the kinds of obstacles to coordination and control that had already confounded Brookings, Baruch, and the rest. He too became convinced that drastic innova-

---

[61] W.L.C., "Concentrating for Real War Work," *Iron Age* 100 (November 22, 1917): 1231-33; "Nothing Will Be Done To Upset the Motor Car Industry," *Automobile Trade Journal* 22 (December 1, 1917): 140; "Government Changes Attitude toward Car Industry," *Motor World* 53 (November 28, 1917): 39-40.

[62] Robert D. Cuff, "A 'Dollar-a-Year Man' in Government: George N. Peek and the War Industries Board," *Business History Review* 41 (Winter 1967): 404-20, especially pp. 405-11. For Peek's developing ties with the chamber and Shaw's board, see Peek to Waddill Catchings, December 31, 1917, and Shaw to Peek, December 17, 1917, both in George N. Peek Papers, Western Historical Manuscript Collection, University of Missouri Library, Columbia, Mo. (cited hereafter as *Peek Papers*). Peek's bureau of manufacturing resources and his ties with the chamber and Shaw received a good press through December, and helped momentarily to relieve business fears. See the *Washington Star*, December 19, 1917; *New York Women's Wear*, December 21, 1917; and other clippings in *Peek Papers*.

tions were required before government could offer American industry the scope for planning and protection it deserved.

THE WINTER CRISIS

"It seemed such a hopeless tangle," Baruch recalled of these winter months, "that men who were offered positions refused to take them and many of those who were connected with the civilian side of the war were leaving or expressed a desire to leave."[63] Baruch turned to his diary for solace; Lovett penned critical memoranda to Colonel House; and all the dollar-a-year men complained about the conduct of the War Department.[64] Never had the powerlessness of the WIB been so apparent. The entire war machine seemed to be grinding slowly to a halt. General Pershing forecast disaster for the spring offensive, given the present flow of supplies; the railroad snarl along the east coast brought federal control on December 26; training camp shortages had reached scandalous proportions; and on December 28, even the weather conspired against the administration, as the country suffered through its worst blizzard in forty-one years. When the sixty-fifth Congress reassembled on December 4, the critics launched an immediate inquest into the war program, an inquest that included five major investigations.

Though the situation that winter resembled the kind of convergence of forces that had produced the WIB in July 1917, the winter crisis was far more serious and complex. It also included a new factor—the widespread enthusiasm among business groups for centralized control of industrial mobilization. The war effort had penetrated the American economy far more deeply by this point. And because government intervention extended so much further in such areas as purchases, prices, and priorities, business interests were forced as never before to rethink and readjust their relationship to the state. In so doing they found it

---

[63]Nye Committee, *Hearings*, part 22, p. 6264. Homer L. Ferguson, president of the Newport News Shipbuilding and Drydock Company, turned down Daniels and Baker for the WIB chairmanship in early November. *Daniels Diary*, pp. 233, 236; Daniel R. Beaver, *Newton D. Baker and the American War Effort, 1917-1919* (Lincoln: University of Nebraska Press, 1966), pp. 76-77. And finally, see the pessimistic comments in Chandler P. Anderson's diary, Chandler P. Anderson Papers, Library of Congress, Washington, D.C. (cited hereafter as *Anderson Diary*), January 22, 24, and 25, 1918.

[64]"No one wants to give the power to one man," Baruch commented, "makes them less powerful and they think it makes him too powerful. Fiddle—Rome burns." *Baruch Diary*, November 26, 1917; and *ibid.*, November 27, December 7, 1917, and January 10, 1918. Lovett offered House a very pessimistic review of the WIB. Convinced the present system would ultimately break down, Lovett recommended a single munitions department in command of all purchasing, backed by strong legislation. Lovett to House, December 22, 1917, *House Papers*.

easy to subscribe to the long-standing recommendations of their colleagues in government. Extensive business support for a powerful, centralized mobilization agency was a development that significantly reinforced the protective thrust which had been part of the WIB's functions from its very inception.

In December and January, however, it seemed increasingly doubtful that the WIB would even last out the winter. Reverberations from the general failure in the war program deepened fissures in its rickety structure and undermined its disparate functions. Improvements in the military establishment also took their toll. For one thing, Secretary Baker proposed an agency to conduct weekly reviews of the war program composed of the Council of National Defense, the Secretary of the Treasury, and a number of civilian war administrators, including the WIB chairman. For another, he replaced his quartermaster and ordnance chiefs, created several new positions, established a war council, and pointed army supply in a more dynamic direction by ordering the redoubtable Peyton C. March to return from Europe as acting chief of staff.[65]

The army's successful reorganization demoralized and enraged WIB executives. "By the time you arrive here," Peek informed a friend about to come east in mid-January, "there may be no War Industries Board. . . ."[66] Brookings felt the effects of an energized War Department in his division of finished products when the quartermaster's department, under newly appointed George Goethals, engorged his cotton and leather committees. "The impression created by this casual move in disintegrating the War Industries Board organization has naturally caused a degree of uneasiness. . . ."[67] The clearance committee chastized the WIB executive for letting these commodity sections go to the army without a fight.[68] Howard Coffin informed a Senate committee that the army bureaus had ceased to consult the WIB altogether.[69] *Iron Age* predicted "the virtual abandon-

---

[65]*CND Minutes*, November 27, 1917; *New York Times*, November 28, 1917, p. 3, and January 26, 1918, p. 1; testimony of General Peyton V. March and General George Goethals before the U.S. Congress, Senate, Subcommittee of the Committee on Military Affairs, *Hearings, Reorganization of the Army*, 66th Cong., 2nd sess, 1919, part 1, pp. 79–81, 1026–28; Otto L. Nelson, Jr., *National Security and the General Staff* (Washington, D.C.: Infantry Journal Press, 1946), pp. 241–44; Erna Risch, *The Quartermaster Corps: Organization, Supply, and Services* (Washington, D.C.: Quartermaster Historian's Office, Office of the Quartermaster General, 1953), pp. 628–44; Beaver, *Newton D. Baker*, pp. 93–96; Paul A. C. Koistinen, "The 'Industrial-Military Complex' in Historical Perspective: World War I," *Business History Review* 41 (Winter 1967): 400–401.

[66]Peek to F. R. Todd, January 17, 1918, *Peek Papers*.

[67]Brookings to General Palmer E. Pierce, January 22, 1918, RG 61, File 21A–A1, box 28.

[68]Clearance Committee to WIB, February 7, 1918, RG 61, File 21A–A1, box 9.

[69]U.S. Congress, Senate, Committee on Military Affairs, *Hearings, Investigation of the War Department*, 65th Cong., 2nd sess., 1918 (cited hereafter as Chamberlain Committee *Hearings*), part 6, p. 2274.

ment of the War Industries Board."[70] The War Department's new look "has stripped the War Industries Board of its last reason to exist," wrote one of its columnists, "and an order abolishing it would surprise no experienced observer of Washington affairs."[71]

The chamber of commerce and WIB officials fought Baker's policies throughout January with the full support of leading trade papers. The *Engineering and Mining Journal* advocated "*a superior war council*"[72] to coordinate all requirements. *American Machinist* observed, "No business could survive such lack of coordination, and this is, or should be, the largest business enterprise in the world at the present time!"[73] The fuel administration's decision to shut down all industrial plants east of the Mississippi for nine consecutive Mondays beginning January 28 raised a storm of business protest that augmented the cries for centralized control. According to *Iron Age*, the fuel administrator's "extraordinary order" was "chiefly important as indicating the dangers to which the industries of the country are exposed under the present decentralized form of government by detached and irresponsible boards, commissions and 'administrations.' . . . The incident furnishes the strongest possible argument in favor of the creation of a supreme war council and the relegation to a director of munitions of all questions of importance to the manufacturers of the country."[74] Reform and reorganization within a single department could not meet business needs— something business advisors had been saying privately for some time. Thus *American Machinist* interpreted Baker's reorganization of the ordnance department as a step in the right direction, but "the sooner we secure complete centralized control, the sooner we can prepare for victory and peace."[75] Business sentiment was, of course, only part of a broad range of critical public opinion in December and January that demanded reform of the war administration. According to *Literary Digest*, editors "all over the country" demanded "the creation of a Department of Munitions, or a more thoroughgoing reorganization of the War Department, or the replacement of Secretary Baker by a man of more belligerent psychology."[76]

---

[70] "Future Government Buying of Steel," *Iron Age* 101 (January 31, 1918): 334.

[71] W.L.C., "More 'Advisory' Help in Buying for Army," *ibid.*, p. 339. The *New Republic*, one of the staunchest advocates of bureaucratic centralization, gave up on the WIB at this point; see "The Conduct of the War," *New Republic* 13 (December 8, 1917): 136–38. It wanted an "Organizer and Controller of American War Industry"; William Hard, "Retarding the Allies," *ibid.* (December 29, 1917), pp. 238–40.

[72] "Bill of Materials," *Engineering and Mining Journal* 104 (December 29, 1917): 238.

[73] "Go the Limit—NOW," *American Machinist* 48 (January 10, 1918): 78.

[74] "Dr. Garfield's Action as Viewed in Washington," *Iron Age* 101 (January 24, 1918): 249. Also see "Widespread Closing Down of Industry," *ibid.*

[75] "Go the Limit—NOW," p. 78.

[76] "The Call for a War-Lord," *Literary Digest* 56 (January 26, 1918): 10.

As pressure from editorial writers in the public and business press gathered force, WIB executives and chamber of commerce officials made a dramatic public appeal in mid-January on behalf of their goals before the Senate Military Affairs Committee. Even Baruch threw caution to the wind and publicly censured the administration's course, an action which suggests the enormity of discontent among WIB personnel. Willard, Baruch, Gifford, Coffin, and Waddill Catchings of the United States Chamber of Commerce all decried the absence of concentrated civilian power, central planning, and coordinated purchasing. Willard specifically criticized the competition for supplies, the lack of general overall view, and excess plant construction.[77] Walter Gifford warned that unless centralized authority was established, "we will wreck our industries."[78] Coffin repeated the thesis he had been developing since 1916: "The industrial prosperity of the Nation is a vital necessity for the consummation of [victory and peace]. We must not lose sight of our object in frantic and uncoordinated efforts on the part of every bureau and department of the Government to accomplish impossible programs."[79] With the administration's recent attempt at curtailment of the auto industry in mind, he added, "We must not rush blindly into the sacrifice of our commercial industries."[80] Catchings voiced the most direct plea for government intervention when he commented: "We are at sea without a chart. Our experience is no longer helpful. We have no longer the play of supply and demand to guide us. No man can foresee what conditions are going to exist in business in two or three months. He has no way of knowing. All of our experience is suddenly cast aside and we have been declaring for months that in this situation there is need for a definite, clear, positive program on the part of the Government. There must be some kind of leadership in this situation. We have a very great fear with regard to industry."[81]

Businessmen offered the same general remedy. Someone, somewhere had to have complete authority "so that we may have a 'Yes' and a 'No,' and a definite policy...."[82] Following the chamber line, Catchings mentioned a minister of munitions with cabinet rank who would rule over all military departments. "It seems to me that what is needed is some one who shall have power and responsibility for making decisions. The difficulty of getting decisions in Washington to-day is apparent to everyone. It is an extraordinarily difficult thing to have any matter definitely and positively decided."[83] Baruch also advocated "highly

---

[77]Chamberlain Committee, *Hearings*, part 3, p. 1823.

[78]*Ibid.*, p. 1863.

[79]*Ibid.*, part 6, p. 2289.

[80]*Ibid.*

[81]*Ibid.*, part 3, p. 1891.

[82]*Ibid.*, part 6, p. 2279.

[83]*Ibid.*, part 3, p. 1901.

centralized authority,"[84] and subscribed to the munitions ministry concept. Mobilization, commented Baruch, was "more than a military task; it it [sic] a huge industrial proposition that requires concentrated energy. One man, working at the head of the supply agencies, could do better than the agencies with lack of co-ordinated effort."[85]

There is no clearer public expression of discontent by businessmen in government than this testimony before the Senate Military Affairs Committee. The principles underlying the business dream of centralized control emerge with crystal clarity. Only through effective use of the state apparatus did business advisors believe they could achieve the institutional coordination required both to mobilize the economy for war and protect the long-run interests of the country's industrial structure. Though all business experts were united on this point, they did not all agree on the precise form a reorganization should take. Some differences emerge in the testimony of Daniel Willard that require attention.

Willard had accepted the WIB chairmanship in mid-November, but without enthusiasm.[86] He yielded to Baker's promises of military cooperation in subsequent weeks, but by early January had decided he could do more for the war effort at the Baltimore and Ohio than on the WIB. He had already decided to resign from the board when he testified on January 14, and his inclination now was to recommend creation of a post of supreme power along the lines of a munitions minister. The only reason he did not was a conversation he had had with President Wilson on the matter. "I would be willing to have a minister of munitions if I had a superman to put in the place," the president had told Willard, "but it requires a superman, and there is no superman."[87] Thus as Willard faced the committee he sought to balance presidential preferences with business needs.

When he had first arrived in Washington, Willard told the committee, he had felt the country should have a minister of munitions to rule over the industrial side of the war. He still believed in the necessity of a single, authoritative head,

---

[84]*Ibid.*, p. 1840.

[85]*New York Times*, January 15, 1918, p. 3.

[86]Secretary Baker had to argue long and hard to gain his acquiescence, for Willard was skeptical as to what the WIB could accomplish. Baruch was annoyed that no one had consulted him on the choice but believed Willard to be "a fine man generous and unselfish and it will be a pleasure to work with him." *Baruch Diary*, November 20, 1917; Baker to Wilson, November 17, 1917, and Wilson to Baker, November 19, 1917, both *Wilson Papers*; Willard to Baruch, December 23, 1918, Washington correspondence, *Baruch Papers*; Willard to Wilson, November 19, 1917, *Wilson Papers*; *New York Times*, November 20, 1917, p. 3.

[87]"Statement of Daniel Willard," *Baruch Papers*; *Baruch Diary*, December 22, 1917; *Daniels Diary*, p. 265; Willard to Grosvenor B. Clarkson, May 14, 1923, the Grosvenor B. Clarkson correspondence, *Wilson Papers*; Willard to Wilson, January 11, 1918, and

but now favored giving someone sufficient authority to coordinate the present organizational arrangements rather than going outside them altogether. Instead of transferring all purchasing power to this individual, as under the munitions minister scheme, Willard would give him jurisdiction only over those activities not covered adequately at present. "I would have a man at the head," said Willard, "and I would have the President authorized to give that man such authority at any time as the situation seemed to require so he could take over all or any part of it, but I do not think it would be wise for him to take over all of it."[88] Willard's position differed from that of the other business advisors in its moderate, temperate, and cautious tone, and the difference can be directly attributed to Willard's talk with Wilson.

Business advisors implied throughout their testimony that, whatever their effect, Baker's reforms in the War Department would not lessen the need for some form of overall direction. (Catchings characterized Baker's policies as "woefully chaotic.")[89] But Baker remained remarkably cool in the face of such criticism. He denied the inadequacy of the existing administration and argued that the WIB had the potential to accomplish the desired results. He even went so far as to suggest that the board be regarded as the functional equivalent of a munitions ministry. The president, "as the supreme executive and in control of the complete executive function, has directed that the subordinate executive agencies should pool their needs and accept the determination of the War Industries Board, and we do."[90] Baker was being either obdurate or obtuse, or perhaps both. Or else he was indicating the extent to which he was out of touch with the operations of his own department.

Unlike his business colleagues, Baker refused to consider discarding the WIB. "I think the difficulty with the War Industries Board has not been a lack of power, but has been a lack of facility to do all the things which it has been gradually and constantly preparing itself to do. To a certain extent, the War and Navy Departments have acted independently of the War Industries Board, but only in those fields of activity where the War Industries Board in the process of building its organization had not yet reached its ability to be of service."[91] This was a curious statement. On the one hand it largely qualified his idealistic portrait of military cooperation. On the other hand it blamed independent service action on the inadequacies of the WIB, while denying the legitimacy of business complaints about these inadequacies. Baker simply refused to admit

---

Wilson to Willard, January 17, 1918, both *Wilson Papers*; *War Policies Commission*, part 1, p. 170.

[88] Chamberlain Committee, *Hearings*, part 3, p. 1823.

[89] *New York Times*, January 17, 1918, p. 3.

[90] Chamberlain Committee, *Hearings*, part 5, p. 2106.

[91] *Ibid.*, pp. 2106-7.

that differences existed between him and the WIB businessmen. In a statement which completely disregarded business testimony, he claimed that WIB executives had given up on the idea of "a central purchasing agency." "I do not think there is a man in their midst now who would not regard that as a misfortune if it were done. I do not think there is one." And if there were, he continued, "then I respectfully dissent from every one.... I think that nothing would be more unfortunate than to start all over again with the building up of a central purchasing agency outside of the several using departments."[92] It should not be forgotten that the navy supported Baker's opposition to a central purchasing agency. When the committee asked Admiral McGowan for his comments on an agency superior to both services, he replied: "I hope that will be after I am dead."[93]

THE PRESIDENTIAL RESPONSE

How would President Wilson react to the forces that swirled about him in the winter crisis of 1917-1918? How could he silence his Republican and congressional critics, placate his business advisors, satisfy the military establishment, and all the while speed up the mobilization program? And what kind of changes could he realistically make without seeming at the same time to yield everything to his opponents? The fate of the WIB must be seen in the context of a presidential strategy designed to cope with the larger political crisis of these months. As it turned out, Wilson gave the board an ironic role to play in his subsequent tactics: having originally created it to protect his business advisors from public censure, he now chose to make it a buffer against business criticism and political pressure for administrative change. Wilson and Baker intensified their commitment to the board just as businessmen sought salvation elsewhere. The compromise embodied in the WIB of March 1918 did push the war organization in a direction favored by the administration's business advisors. But as we shall see, the reorganization could not transcend Wilson's fundamental commitment to organizational continuity in his mobilization program.

Stung by the attacks of his critics, the president bitterly denounced charges of organizational collapse in Washington and publicly opposed proposals for a war cabinet and munitions ministry. A drastic restructuring of the current adminis-

[92] *Ibid.*, p. 2107.

[93] U.S. Congress, House, Committee on Naval Affairs, *Hearings on Estimates Submitted by the Secretary of the Navy, 1918*, 65th Cong., 2nd sess., 1918, p. 317. "I could not possibly look on and see the Navy's supply system interfered with by elaboration, absorption, consolidation, or any other change whatever without making the most earnest effort to prevent it," McGowan told the committee. *Ibid.*, p. 316.

tration was out of the question, he averred. The resultant delays and loss of morale would far outstrip the advantages.[94] "Nobody who is not in direct contact with the problems of organization and cooperation as I am daily," the president wrote a chamber of commerce official, "can realize how imperfectly and crudely such propositions as are now being widely discussed for radical readjustments meet the difficulties and necessities of the case. The faith that some people put in machinery is child-like and touching, but machinery does not do the task; particularly is it impossible to do it if new and inexperienced elements are introduced."[95]

The entire debate left him in bad humor. He wrote Robert Brookings: "May I not say . . . how much I appreciate the course of action you have imposed upon yourself, of refraining from the almost universal habit of public discussion about things that must necessarily be handled by slow evolution?"[96] "The President has his blood up," exulted Josephus Daniels, "and in a veto message would say some things."[97]

In defusing the public furor Wilson shrewdly employed other strategies besides button-holing Senators and making public speeches. On February 1 the White House leaked hints of great administrative changes, and several days later Senator Overman introduced legislation designed to give the president a literal *carte blanche* in reordering his executive agencies. According to the *New York Times*, the far-reaching Overman bill "caused the most profound sensation of the entire legislative session, in which sensations have been frequent."[98] Cries of "dictatorship" from the proposal's critics would soon inflate the public's impression of the president's intentions, and thereby assist his strategy to contain pressure for a munitions ministry.

Presidential intentions aside, the crisis atmosphere of December and January provided just the kind of acute pressure for major administrative change that had eluded the business advisors for so long. Crisis alone could produce the organizational and ideological setting conducive to more extensive institutional manipulation. For a bureaucratic entrepreneur like Baruch, a serious administrative and political breakdown was an opportunity, not a disaster, and he made the most of it. It was at this point that Baruch attained his greatest personal influence in

[94] See Wilson to Senator George E. Chamberlain, January 11, 1918, *Wilson Papers*, for an exposition of Wilson's views.

[95] Wilson to John H. Fahey, January 26, 1918, *ibid.* Also see Wilson to Milton A. Romjue, January 26, 1918, *ibid.*

[96] Wilson to Brookings, February 18, 1918, *ibid.*

[97] *Daniels Diary*, p. 269.

[98] *New York Times*, February 7, 1918, p. 1; *Anderson Diary*, February 1, 1918; *New York Times*, February 2, 1918; "Defeat of War Cabinet Bill Predicted," *Iron Age* 101 (February 7, 1918): 423; James Miller Leake, "The Conflict Over Coördination," *American Political Science Review*, 12 (August 1918): 365–80; Beaver, *Newton D. Baker*, pp. 97–104.

presidential decision-making. The strains of war had finally turned policy sharply toward his version of institutional synthesis.

In a remarkable display of entrepreneurial talent, Baruch accelerated his quest for power and influence in the days following his testimony, and his negotiations with Secretary Baker at the end of January provided the most satisfying kind of personal victory. While publicly denying the need for change, Baker privately admitted the force of business criticism. Doubtless under a command from the White House, Baruch and Baker met and agreed that in the future the WIB should be "a legal, authoritative, responsible, centralized agency" with power "to commandeer plants, products, equipment, manufacturing facilities, mines and materials, and the additional power not now granted of distributing materials thus commandeered." Baker made a number of concessions, including an admission that the board was merely a debating society at the moment with power that was "consultative, and not final, except by consent." He also accepted a plan whereby all major purchasing programs would go to the WIB chairman for "his final allocation, distribution and judgment." At the same time he comforted himself with the contention that if "power were vested in the Chairman the agencies now established could continue to perform all of the work, except the final decisions which would then go to an individual." The chairman would neither administer specific contracts nor assume an actual purchasing function.[99] This Baker-Baruch document, which ultimately found its way into the president's final March announcement, enhanced the role of the WIB chairman, making him supreme within the WIB organization.

In coming to his final decision on administrative reorganization, the president also benefited from a resolution passed on to him from the Council of National Defense on February 21. This proposal recommended giving the WIB chairman full authority in matters of priority, conversion, conservation, allied purchasing, and advice on prices. (The Baker-Baruch agreement had urged formation of a committee on prices reporting directly to the president.) Wilson included these six functions in his final plan.[100]

By February, the president had to find a replacement for Daniel Willard, in addition to devising a political and administrative response to his critics. A

---

[99] Baker to Wilson, February 1, 1918, *Baker Papers*.

[100] *CND Minutes*, February 21, 1918. It is important to note that Secretary Baker himself carried this resolution to the president. Apparently he had accommodated himself to the WIB reorganization, though no doubt with some distaste. With his own department considerably strengthened, perhaps he no longer regarded an independent WIB as quite as much a threat. At a meeting with Daniels and Wilson at the White House on February 24, 1918, he assented to the president's redefinition of the board's functions and to his choice of Baruch as chairman. *Daniels Diary*, p. 283. In the postwar years Baker held to the idea that the military establishment had incorporated businessmen and business ideas for its own purposes, and had not simply leaned on outside agencies for direction. Thus the AC, CND, GMB, and WIB were part of the War Department,

number of candidates emerged, including Edward Stettinius, the recently appointed surveyor general of the War Department and former buyer for the J. P. Morgan Company; John D. Ryan of the Anaconda Copper Company; and Robert Woolley of the American Radiator Company, presently with the War Trade Board. Stettinius seems to have been the most serious contender in early February; Baker supported Ryan without great conviction; and William Redfield alone stood for Woolley. Ultimately, however, Stettinius's connection with the Morgans branded him as unsafe in the eyes of several Wilsonians, including Daniels, McAdoo, House, and Tumulty. Once again, Baruch emerged as the controversial frontrunner. Baker had never liked Baruch's style and wondered now about his executive, managerial ability; and others shared his concern, including Redfield, Houston, and Lane among the cabinet, and Lovett, Gifford, and USCC officials among businessmen. *Engineering and Mining Journal* touched upon their reservations: "If for the muddling of doctrinaires there be substituted a management of financiers and bankers, on the theory that they are the kind of businessmen who are needed, there will be no great step in advance. What we have on our hands is a great job of production, and what we need is a production management."[101]

Baruch was not without his supporters, however. McAdoo stressed Baruch's valuable war experience and his political loyalty, and he expressed the hope that Allied and domestic purchasing could be linked through Baruch's appointment. In any event he had a place for Baruch at the railroad administration if things did not work out. Both Daniels and Tumulty were also attracted to Baruch's demonstrable loyalty to the president and his administration.[102]

Baruch knew his appointment was in jeopardy, and he remained intensely anxious throughout February, optimistic and pessimistic in turn as he digested the latest Washington gossip. The president felt constrained from acting by the critical mood on Capitol Hill and the uncertain fate of his Overman bill. He did not want to risk another fight at the moment. He had already asked Judge Lovett to withhold his resignation "until we can relieve the hysteria which has taken hold for the time being of the United States Senate."[103]

---

according to Baker's perception. This reinforces the thought that once Baker believed he could no longer use the WIB as a stopgap, he was willing to see it move outside his jurisdiction. Baker to Thomas G. Frothingham, September 11, 1925, *Baker Papers.*

[101] "Turning Over a New Leaf," *Engineering and Mining Journal* 105 (February 16, 1918): 345; Baker to Wilson, January 24 and February 2, 1918, McAdoo to Wilson, January 27, 1918, Daniels to Wilson, January 26 and February 2, 1918, Wilson to Daniels, February 4, 1918, House to Wilson, February 6, 1918, Tumulty to Wilson, February 7, 1918, all in *Wilson Papers; Daniels Diary*, p. 271; *New York Times*, February 2, 1918, p. 1; Beaver, *Newton D. Baker*, pp. 104–7.

[102] See note 101 above.

[103] Wilson to Lovett, January 21, 1918, *Wilson Papers; Anderson Diary*, February 1, 7, and 8, 1918.

Despite his nervousness, Baruch never for a moment relented in his campaign for reorganization. He was committed to making the chairman the kingpin in the WIB and was now afraid that neither Baker nor the president really grasped what he had in mind. He wrote the Secretary of War only three days after their agreement: "I am wondering whether the letter was definite enough as to our thoughts that this agency should be an individual who decentralizes the execution of his authority. In the letter you speak of it as a body, which gives the impression that we thought it should be a board, whereas I understood we were both agreed it should be one man."[104] Baruch gained an interview with Wilson on February 7 to elaborate his views further. At this meeting he suggested that the president delineate the duties of the new WIB chairman in a public announcement. Baruch had never lost sight of his broad goal of achieving a stable environment for American industry, and he made his proposal in this context. A presidential statement would have "a very helpful effect, not alone from the military and naval but also from the industrial and financial standpoint." Baruch wanted the president to emphasize that wages, hours, and government orders would continue unchanged, "so there shall be as little dislocation and congestion as possible through competition for the same materials and facilities."[105] Baruch was satisfied by his meeting with the president, although he believed Stettinius would get the chairmanship. He told his Washington friends on February 8 that he wanted them with him if he did become chairman, but that he would join McAdoo at the railroad administration if he did not receive the nod.[106]

By the latter part of the month Baruch was much more optimistic about his appointment. Perhaps he had talked to Wilson himself, for by this time the president had reached his decision on the WIB's structure and its new chairman. He informed Baker and Daniels on February 24 that his choice was Baruch, and they dutifully approved the draft of his proposed public letter "as wise and applicable."[107] When McAdoo asked Wilson to send Baruch to either the war finance corporation or his railroad administration, Wilson vetoed his request arguing that, "He has trained now in the War Industries Board until he is thoroughly conversant with the activities of it from top to bottom, and as soon as I

---

[104] Baruch to Baker, February 4, 1918, *Wilson Papers.* Baker did not disagree. Baker to Baruch, February 5, 1918, selected correspondence, *Baruch Papers.*

[105] Baruch to Wilson, February 8, 1918, RG 61, File 21A–A1, box 2; *Anderson Diary*, February 6 and 7, 1918. Baruch also suggested that "even if all orders were not directed by this central agency, copies of all orders placed should be sent to him in order that someone would know, not alone what materials and facilities we had but to what extent they had been drawn upon by all consumers." Baruch to Wilson, February 8, 1918, RG 61, File 21A–A1, box 2.

[106] *Anderson Diary*, February 7 and 8, 1918.

[107] *Daniels Diary*, p. 283; *Anderson Diary*, February 21, 1918.

can do so without risking new issues on the Hill I am going to appoint him chairman of that board."[108] Baruch received his letter on March 4, 1918.

The president's public instructions clearly gave Bernard Baruch the last word in the WIB and elevated him to a place in the forefront of the Washington bureaucracy.[109] In this lies the chief innovative element of the president's response. Baruch would have "the ultimate decision of all questions, except the determination of prices . . . the other members acting in a cooperative and advisory capacity." No longer would the WIB be a debating society that relied on consensus for action. In place of an executive committee stood a single individual. As chairman, Baruch was to offer guidance whenever necessary, to settle conflicts between the departments on supply problems, to follow up contracts and deliveries, and to anticipate future military requirements. "In brief, he should act as the general eye of all supply departments in the field of industry." Wilson also directed the chairman to obtain advance information on military needs "in order that as definite an outlook and opportunity for planning as possible may be afforded the business men of the country."[110] The office of the chairman of the WIB now clearly provided possibilities for central coordination of supply activities.

Though the president's letter to Baruch was one of the most significant documents in the evolution of Wilsonian war government, it was not without its shortcomings. Indeed its impact, and that of the Overman act that followed in May, have been exaggerated by many commentators both then and since. Two points should be underlined to qualify the aura of optimism that enshrouds these two events in most accounts. First, the president's letter fell far short of creating the kind of centralization in Washington demanded by either the administration's critics or its business advisors; and the Overman act did not initiate any experiment in dictatorial control of industrial mobilization. The president specifically told Baruch to leave alone those areas which were running smoothly and to "interfere as little as possible with the present normal processes of purchase and delivery in the several Departments."[111] "The President's letter," commented William Hard of the *New Republic*, "seems to mark the end of any ambition that may ever have been cherished by the War Industries Board to become the United States government's Central Buyer."[112]

The second point to emphasize is that Baruch's position, no matter how elevated on paper, required operational definition. It was by no means clear in

[108] Wilson to McAdoo, February 26, 1918, *Wilson Papers*.

[109] Wilson heightened the effect of his decision by soliciting cooperation for Baruch and the WIB from every one of his top administrators. See Wilson to McAdoo *et al.*, undated, *ibid.*

[110] Wilson to Baruch, March 4, 1918, *ibid.*, attached to *WIB Minutes*, March 6, 1918.

[111] *Ibid.*

[112] William Hard, "Wilson Defines Baruch," *New Republic* 14 (March 23, 1918): 230.

March how the chairman of the WIB would be able to make his decisions felt on any of his constituencies—the military services, business groups, or his own organization. Furthermore, many of the difficulties which had hampered the board in the past were structural in nature and could hardly be dealt with through changes in a single office. Baruch would have to exercise his mandate, such as it was, within an organizational environment that remained largely unaffected by the president's letter, or by his use of the Overman act. Yet only changes in the entire organizational landscape of industrial mobilization could guarantee the concentration of power the president intended Baruch to have. What form these changes would take, or whether they would evolve at all, remained to be seen.

But more important than the organizational dimension of Baruch's mandate are the reasons why he received it in the first place. We must remember that Wilson promoted the WIB as a way to undermine the potential radical reordering of America's institutional system implicit in the idea of a munitions ministry. Wilson stood with Secretary Baker in his determination to maintain the traditional legal and functional roles of the military services in industrial mobilization for war. He was sensitive too to the popular political traditions that opposed concentration of all emergency power in a state agency dominated by businessmen. In one sense, the effect of the WIB of 1918 was partially to deflect the kind of organic ideal pursued by Baruch and the business advisors. As he awaited passage of the Overman bill, Wilson informed one correspondent: "I am afraid that great things will be expected of me by way of reorganization under the Overman Bill, because of the large amount of public attention it has attracted. My purposes under it are very modest, but I hope and believe that they will effect some very serviceable re-arrangements of authority."[113] Once the act passed Congress in May, Wilson separated the WIB from the CND and made it an executive agency reporting directly to him.[114] After elevating Baruch within the WIB organization, defining and enlarging the board's functions, and associating the agency closely with the presidential office, Wilson felt he had gone about as far as he could toward concentrated emergency authority without subverting his commitment to America's peacetime institutional structure. While he shared the cooperative impulse of his business advisors, Wilson proved less enthusiastic than they about a radical reordering of relationships between business and the state during wartime. Wilson may have realized that the gains which accrued to the government in any reorganization of the WIB did not accrue to government alone. Given the peculiar nature of the WIB, every triumph for the state signified a gain for business power.

[113] Wilson to Herbert Bayard Swope, May 1, 1918, *Wilson Papers.*

[114] In his comparative study of emergency governments Clinton Rossiter concludes that the president used the Overman act "as a sort of threat. . . . Actual resorts to it for authority were scarce." Clinton Rossiter, *Constitutional Dictatorship* (Princeton, N.J.: Princeton University Press, 1948), p. 249.

CHAPTER 6

THE STRUCTURAL REALITIES
OF INDUSTRIAL PLANNING

The War Industries Board of March 1918 was a constellation of diverse structures acting in a series of diverse processes, all of which evolved at different speeds over different routes. Purchasing controls, price administration, priority decisions, industrial-military cooperation, bureaucratic coordination and a number of other functions engaged all parts of the WIB, including the chairman's office, the price fixing committee and the priorities division. Every component of the WIB administrative system had a partially separate history, and the result was an extraordinarily multifaceted state agency.

Notwithstanding such diversity, however, the tension between traditional, peacetime impulses and the imperatives of a nation in modern war cut across all the WIB's structures and functions. There can be no doubt that the forces of rationalization, centralization, and bureaucratization inherent in capitalism and war accelerated rapidly in the crisis, and as we know, such long-range trends carried the future before them. At the same time, industrial mobilization embraced the past as well as the future, and traditions of another time also shaped America's response to war. Within this larger clash between traditional and modern trends there arose a number of questions which lay at the heart of the WIB experiment. Could a bundle of diverse structures and processes be integrated into a coherent, unified administrative system? Could that individual system then integrate the broader administrative-social setting in which it stood? And could the traditions derived from other times be reconciled with the innovations required of a corporate capitalist country at war?

Contrary to the general consensus in World War I historiography, the reorganized WIB of March 1918 did not achieve either internal or external integration. It did not entirely overcome the pull of traditional configurations. The images of a unified, highly integrated system of business-military-government relations which order the literature on mobilization are not sufficiently complex to capture the full historical significance of the WIB experiment.

148

The WIB and its administrative program were a bundle of paradoxes where decentralization vied with centralization, competition with combination, individualism with integration, freedom with coercion. A maturing capitalism and advancing technology had made the long-standing debate over these kinds of values particularly acute in the prewar years, and the business synthesizers who entered Washington after 1914 carried with them a significant amount of ideological baggage developed at that time. One of the many promises of upper class progressivism had been that American capitalism, if properly encouraged and administered, could bind together an individualistic past and a disciplined future. A corporate capitalism led by socially responsible men could resolve the tensions inherent in that clash between the democratic ideology of the nineteenth century and the hard realities of the twentieth. The war crisis altered the setting for the debate, but it only intensified the commitment of business ideologues to prove the virtues of corporate capitalism. As they struggled toward centralized decision-making and executive control, businessmen in government hoped to show that through voluntary effort and decentralized administration America could both mount a superior mobilization effort and avoid the hazards to private business enterprise they associated with a European-style state bureaucracy. With a properly rationalized state system directed by businessmen in government, America would be able to combine the traditional genius of individualism and free enterprise with the modern efficiency of administrative centralization and state regulation. This is the kind of idealized schema within which key business administrators lived their war experience and through which they interpreted it in the postwar years. It is a schema which severely distorts the structural realities that confronted them both before and after March 1918.

A discussion of the board's commodity sections provides an unusually fine opportunity to explore and illustrate these general themes of the WIB experience for several reasons. First, the evolution and operation of the commodity sections touch on the WIB's paradoxical nature by showing how modern bureaucratic trends existed side by side with the informal, highly personalized arrangements of a less bureaucratic age. Commodity section development also shows how specific political incidents influenced the nature and timing of broader, bureaucratic evolution. Second, this segment of the WIB's structure reveals the obstacles to industrial-military and business-government integration which the board encountered throughout its history. Third, the administrative actions of the commodity sections demonstrate that the WIB could not wholly fulfill the ideological promises proclaimed by businessmen in government. What in rhetoric was a unique blend of freedom and authority, decentralization and centralization, proved in practice to be an administrative system that rested upon a shifting coalition of private economic oligarchies. What in rhetoric became a decision to decentralize responsibility proved in practice to be a constant inability to centralize power. What in rhetoric became public control embraced a process whereby private interest groups enhanced their power through association with an emergency state agency.

EVOLUTION OF THE COMMODITY SECTIONS

All students of the WIB and industrial mobilization agree that the board's commodity sections were critical administrative units in the mobilization process. Sometimes referred to as the "backbone" of the board, they are generally regarded as the major operational arms of the chairman's office. Not infrequently the concept itself is attributed to Bernard Baruch as an example of the transformation he wrought in the WIB once he assumed command. Such an interpretation underestimates the element of continuity in the board's general development and both overestimates and misinterprets Baruch's role in the WIB's administrative program after March 1918.

As a legacy of the crisis over the cooperative committees of industry that occurred during the summer of 1917, the commodity sections should be regarded in part as the organizational process by which the administration sought to ward off the effects of section 3 of the food and fuel act. Passed on August 10, section 3 raised serious questions about the future of business-government relations under the committee system, and made business volunteers very uncertain as government lawyers discussed what could be done. Samuel M. Vauclain, senior vice president of the Baldwin Locomotive Works and chairman of the committee on navy and army artillery, lamented: "It would appear as though all those who are able to do things promptly and efficiently for the Government will be compelled to retire."[1] "I have been up against several tough propositions in my time," mused Vauclain, "but I do not want to get up against the penitentiary...."[2]

In an effort to ward off massive resignations, Secretary Baker asked the legal counsel of the Council of National Defense, the judge advocate general of the army, and the attorney general to prepare a resolution which would so clearly define the functions of the cooperative committees as to exempt them from prosecution under the present law. It was with knowledge that this was being done that government officials urged businessmen to stay on the job.[3]

---

[1] Vauclain to Boise Penrose, August 15, 1917, Record Group 62, Records of the Council of National Defense, Federal Records Center, Suitland, Md. (cited hereafter as RG 62), File 1–A1, box 14.

[2] Vauclain to Daniel Willard, August 15, 1917, RG 62, File 2–A4, box 82.

[3] Baker to Walter Gifford, August 20, 1917, and Gifford to Frank Scott, September 4, 1917, both *ibid.*; Baker to Vauclain, August 22, 1917, Record Group 61, Records of the War Industries Board, Federal Records Center, Suitland, Md. (cited hereafter as RG 61),

In the meantime, Frank Scott, as WIB chairman, put to the attorney general a series of questions the answers to which he hoped would clarify the status of advisors under section 3 once and for all. Attorney General Gregory's reply made it obvious, however, that he was very reluctant to give Scott the kind of blanket assurance he wanted. Taking each of the six questions in turn, Gregory made a number of pertinent observations, and from these it emerged that a committee member would comply with the law if he made a full disclosure of his interests whenever he recommended a contract. This was not only legal if such an interested person made a recommendation to the WIB or another similar council, but also if he made a recommendation directly to the contracting officer of the military department concerned. Had the attorney general let the matter rest here his opinion would likely have been interpreted as a green light for heavy committee traffic. However, in discussing the relation between the committeemen and a contracting officer, Gregory switched the light from green to amber. In view of "the narrow margin of difference" between "recommending" on the one hand, which was legal with a full disclosure, he added, and "*inducing, soliciting,* or *awarding*" on the other, which was not legal even with a disclosure, "it would be well as a practical matter for such persons to exercise great caution as to the kind of *recommendations* they shall make."[4]

The committeemen had won an uncertain victory. "After I got through reading his opinion," commented Thomas F. Manville, chairman of the committee on asbestos and roofing, "I don't know just where I am at." Manville was still not completely certain whether he ought to continue at his post. "Am I, as President of the H. W. Johns-Manville Company, who manufactures asbestos, magnesia and roofing, doing something I should not in serving on these committees?"[5] Eugene Meyer was also unhappy over the outcome, in part because he was not entirely certain that all members of the committee would be willing to disclose the extent of their interest in each case in which they acted. Furthermore he wondered whether corporation lawyers would feel their clients had sufficient guarantee of immunity under the act in event of possible legal suits. It was his own opinion that Gregory's statement "leaves the matter in a very unsatisfactory condition, so far as obtaining full benefit of the co-operative sub-committees. . . ."[6] The number of resignations proferred as a result of the

---

File 21A-A1, box 1; Wilson to Edgar Palmer, August 23, 1917, Woodrow Wilson Papers, Library of Congress, Washington, D.C. (cited hereafter as *Wilson Papers*).

[4] Gregory to Scott, August 29, 1917, *Wilson Papers*.

[5] Manville to Baruch, September 10, 1917, RG 61, File 21A-A1, box 5.

[6] Meyer to Baruch, September 4, 1917, RG 61, File 21A-A1, box 1. *Iron Age* noted that in the light of Gregory's answer the members of the steel committee would not act until they heard from their attorneys. "Status of Iron and Steel Advisers," *Iron Age* 100 (September 13, 1917): 631-32.

attorney general's reply bore out Meyer's concern. Edgar Palmer of the zinc committee, for example, informed the president that his battery of legal advisors felt the only practical course open to committee members like himself was to step down.[7]

The resolution passed by the CND on September 5 did little to resolve business fears. It merely stressed the difference between "inducing" or "soliciting," which were illegal, and "recommending," which was legal with a complete disclosure.[8] The council decided, however, to proceed on this basis, and warned the committee members to declare their interests. Meanwhile, resignations trickled in.[9]

Baruch refused to admit that section 3 demanded alteration in the committee system and actually fought the very developments that ultimately formalized business-government relations in the WIB's commodity sections. Aside from the personal slight involved, the attack on the cooperative committees threatened to undermine the functional base of his own power in Washington as head of an informal, voluntary business coalition in raw materials and metals. And it challenged the entire cooperative spirit on which it rested. Baruch had struggled valiantly to bind industry and the military services through his office, and just as he was beginning to lay a substantial groundwork, Congress decided to tear it up. His was a tenuous system, and anything that put big businessmen in bad humor threatened its destruction. Now the Senate was moving to reintroduce competitive business conduct just as business advisors were seeking to legitimize collusion. The government would get far lower prices by relying upon cooperative business volunteers, argued Baruch, "than by a process of bargaining by ourselves."[10]

Baruch charged that the main reason for the current imbroglio was the desire of various government purchasing bureaus to deal directly with individual firms instead of working through the WIB and subordinate agencies such as the

[7]Palmer to Wilson, September 20, 1917, *Wilson Papers*.

[8]Minutes of the Council of National Defense and joint meetings of the council and Advisory Commission (cited hereafter as *CND Minutes*), September 5, 1917, RG 62, File 2-B1, box 104.

[9]See the memo dated September 10, 1917, warning the committee members to declare their business interests, attached to a sample letter dated September 11, 1917, RG 61, File 21A-A1, box 1. For one example of such a declaration of interest, see the letters from members of the petroleum committee in RG 61, File 21A-A1, box 14. Pierre S. Du Pont was reluctant to let men from his company join the ordnance department as long as section 3 was on the books. See his testimony in U.S. Congress, Senate, Special Committee to Investigate the Munitions Industry, *Hearings, Munitions Industry*, 73rd-74th Cong., 1934-1937, part 15, pp. 3657-59. The brass committee resigned in a letter to Baruch on September 17, 1917, RG 61, File 21A-A1, box 1.

[10]Baruch to Dr. William H. Nichols (chairman of the committee on chemicals), November 26, 1917, RG 61, File 21A-A1, box 7.

raw materials committee. This practice of government agencies, more than anything else, opened businessmen to charges of conflict of interest. If the departments allowed his committees to communicate their advice and recommendations only through the WIB, Baruch could not see how they would in any way violate section 3. The problem lay with the military purchasing bureaus, not with his committees.[11]

This line of counterattack was very natural to Baruch, for it reflected his ongoing struggle with the competing military units. But his suggestion really offered no solution. Even businessmen to whom he outlined his plan of dealing solely through his office felt that the army and navy departments would adhere to their present course. Moreover, their own business was spread so far across the military establishment as to make it impossible to concentrate solely through Baruch's office. "In view of the demands made upon our company by the government for special materials," Thomas Manville wrote Baruch, " . . . the government officials insist upon dealing with us direct, [and] it would be most difficult to handle our transaction as you suggest."[12] Nor was there as yet any way to prevent defection from the business side. Section 3 was bound to take a heavy toll among committeemen, or at the very least prevent them from doing "justice" to their business interests.[13] Ambrose Monell told Baruch that since it was his "obvious duty" to represent his corporation, he would not blame people for being somewhat skeptical about his actions on the nickel committee—he was its sole member. He would have to resign.[14] Baruch personally refrained from accepting resignations as long as possible, but this delaying tactic was merely a preface to defeat. By November time had run out. On November 9, 1917, Walter Gifford, as director of the CND, specifically asked Baruch to disband his committees.[15]

[11]For various statements of this basic argument, see the following: Baruch to J. D. Laying (zinc committee), September 19, 1917, RG 61, File 21A-A1, box 30; Baruch to J. H. Markham, Jr. (petroleum committee), October 1, 1917, RG 61, File 21A-A1, box 14; Baruch to Ambrose Monell (nickel committee), October 11, 1917, RG 61, File 21A-A1, box 13; Baruch to Arthur V. Davis (aluminum committee), September 12, 1917, RG 61, File 21A-A1, box 20; Baruch to Thomas Manville (asbestos and roofing committee), September 14, 1917, RG 61, File 21A-A1, box 5; Leland Summers to W. D. Huntington (subcommittee on fertilizers), September 27, 1917, RG 61, File 21A-A1, box 8; and Alex Legge to Lewis W. Kingsley (subcommittee on mica), September 17, 1917, RG 61, File 21A-A1, box 13.

[12]Manville to Baruch, September 17, 1917, RG 61, File 21A-A1, box 5.

[13]To quote Lewis W. Kingsley (subcommittee on mica) to Baruch, September 12, 1917, RG 61, File 21A-A1, box 13.

[14]Monell to Baruch, September 12, 1917, *ibid.*

[15]Walter Gifford called for an end to the committees as early as October 6th, 1917, but he had to wait a few weeks before he had his way. Minutes of the Advisory Commission, RG 62, File 1B-1, box 25, October 6, 1917; *New York Times*, October 9, 1917, p. 1;

Given the public's suspicion of the cooperative committees, it became imperative to devise an alternate system that would permit businessmen easy access to the Washington bureaucracy, yet protect them from charges of graft and corruption. Business-government cooperation required a legitimizing tactic. Any subsequent forms would at least have to appear democratic and open, with private and public responsibilities clearly defined. The administration had to reassure the general public that their interest remained beyond the reach of selfish privateers, and after the section 3 episode it had to convince businessmen that it was "safe" to cooperate with government.

The administration turned directly to organized business for the solution. It praised business patriotism, but condemned the present committee system and inaugerated a campaign to have the business community organize itself into trade committees that could cooperate in a formal, regularized way with business advisors on the newly created WIB. These groups were ultimately called war service committees and later took up positions alongside the WIB's commodity sections. In effect, Washington returned to the scheme that Walter Gifford and the CND had recommended in April—open, formal, broad-based, and ostensibly democratic.

Gifford had already addressed the War Convention of American Business sponsored by the United States Chamber of Commerce in September 1917, with a broad appeal on behalf of the principles of associationalism. Let it be admitted that the cooperative committees did constitute a flawed system, argued Gifford, but it was a system that had developed only because American industry had not been sufficiently organized into trade associations to make any other approach feasible. The need for speed forced the government to pick committees without regard for representation. What industry had to do, therefore, was to form trade associations and so ensure equity to all producers. "We have never needed such organized industry as much as we need it now while we are engaged in this war," exclaimed Gifford, "and we never have needed it as much as we shall after the war is over, when we shall be in the midst of a world competition of unknown proportions." If associations built up a code of ethics and sharpened their sense of service, they could undermine popular schemes for socializing industry and prove that the antitrust laws were no longer necessary. "Business men undoubtedly know the mechanics and machinery of organization by which things may be accomplished, but have they yet proved their ability to be far-sighted and broadminded as to the relation of their individual business to the great economic and social scheme of modern society?"

Gifford also explicitly countered a suggestion that industry organize along regional lines, an idea that, as we shall see, the WIB eventually had to embrace.

Gifford to WIB, October 17, 1917, RG 62, File 2–A4, box 82; Robert S. Lovett to Gifford, October 31, 1917, *ibid.*; Gifford to Baruch, November 9, 1917, RG 61, File 21A–A1, box 1.

Each industry would best serve the government if it were organized on a nation-wide basis with complete representation of all members of the industry. Organization along state lines or by localities is admirable for chambers of commerce and local civic associations, but our industrial life is not so bounded. Industries are not largely affected by state lines. A national organization by industries is the form of organization that will best serve the government both in time of war and in time of peace.

"Business men must get away from provincialism," Gifford challenged his audience. They had a duty to support the spread of trade associations which, in turn, could elect executive committees to deal with government.[16]

In the fall of 1917 the government was so desperate for an organization representative of the nation's business groups that had a chamber of commerce not already existed the administration would have had to create one. Traditional democratic values had had a devastating impact on business-government ties, at least for the moment. In the meantime, the chamber's leadership could be counted upon to heed Gifford's plea, not only because patriotism demanded as much, but also because such cooperation might enhance its own organizational goals and prestige within the business community.

Founded in 1912, the chamber was the strongest and largest general business association to emerge from the organizational ferment of the progressive era, and its leaders had already tried to ingratiate themselves with the Wilson administration. John Fahey, a Boston businessman and one of the chamber's founders, corresponded frequently with the president, and Wilson's choice of the chamber's annual meeting in 1916 to outline a program for American business helped sustain fairly cordial relations.

It pleased the chamber very much to respond to Secretary Baker's request to assist the quartermaster's department in the early stages of mobilization, and it sponsored advisory business committees to assist the local purchasing agent at each of the army's quartermaster headquarters. The New York committee, for example, arranged financial loans to tide over the department until regular congressional appropriations came through.[17]

[16]Walter S. Gifford, "Organized Industry," address delivered before the War Convention of the Chamber of Commerce of the United States at Atlantic City, N.J., press release, October 14, 1917, RG 62, File 3–A5, box 171.

[17]Quartermaster General Henry G. Sharpe advised Baker to have the CND select these business advisors and Baker got in touch with the chamber of commerce. Sharpe to Baker, February 4, 1917, RG 62, File 2–A1, box 55; Baker to R. G. Rhett (chamber president), February 19, 1917, ibid.; CND Minutes, February 28, 1917; Elliot H. Goodwin (general secretary of the chamber) to Baker, March 1, 1917, RG 62, File 2–A1, box 31; New York Times, February 22, 28, and March 27, 1917, pp. 1, 11, and 1, respectively; "Work Done by Advisory Committees," RG 61, File 21A–A4, box 328; Henry G. Sharpe, The Quartermaster Corps, in the Year 1917 in the World War (New York: Century, 1921), pp. 135–36.

Throughout the spring and early summer the chamber hovered about the periphery of the national war organization, assisting in other small ways, proffering advice, and searching eagerly for a prestigious position beside the government. Walter Gifford proved more amenable to their ambition than most, always hopeful he could enlist them in his strategy of trade association development. A major step in a growing alliance between the chamber and Gifford's office came with the appointment of Waddill Catchings to Gifford's staff in June 1917. Catchings was formerly in the export department of the J. P. Morgan organization, and in 1917 was president of the Sloss-Sheffield Steel and Iron Works of Birmingham. He was a vigorous advocate of business service and responsibility, the central principles of an "enlightened" capitalism, and became a liaison between the national administration, the chamber of commerce, and the American business community for which the chamber believed itself the logical representative. Catchings remained with the council until November 1917, when the chamber's bitter criticism of the mobilization program forced his resignation.[18]

Not until the fall of 1917 did council policy fully coincide with the chamber's goals, but from then on their relationship proved very intimate indeed. According to the arrangements devised by Gifford and chamber officials, the chamber became responsible for organizing trade associations in American industry. It called general meetings, certified committees as truly representative, and even selected war service committees, the associations' executive bodies, when formation of a trade association proved impractical. The war service committees were to perform advisory, informational functions similar to those originally intended for the cooperative committees.[19]

American industry reacted favorably to Gifford's call on the whole, but several WIB members, including Baruch and Robert Lovett, remained skep-

[18]The chamber suggested that Catchings be appointed so he could inform their executive committee about the government's ongoing mobilization program. They in turn could offer authoritative information to the general business community. See "Minutes of Meeting between Committee Heads of the General Munitions Board and the Executive Committee of the Chamber of Commerce . . . June 13th," RG 62, File 5–C1, box 294; and "Information to Industries of the Country," attached; *CND Minutes*, June 8, 1917; Catchings to Gifford, August 9 and November 8, 1917, RG 62, File 2–A1, box 3. For Gifford-Catchings consultation on the chamber's war bulletins, see Catchings to Gifford, August 17 and September 6, 1917, RG 62, File 2–A1, box 31; and for an expression of Catchings's general ideology, see Waddill Catchings, *The Business Man's Responsibility in the Industrial Problems of the War* (New York, 1918).

[19]Chamber of Commerce of the United States, War Service Executive Committee, *War Service Committees, Plan of Organization, Their Scope and Duties*, RG 61, File 21A–A4, box 1573; Chamber of Commerce of the United States, *Sixth Annual Report* (Washington, D.C., 1917); Catchings to Gifford, September 22, 1917, RG 62, File 2–A1, box 31; War Service Committees (unsigned, February 1918), in RG 61, File 21A–A3, box 44.

tical.[20] Baruch had always favored a more informal, personal system, and Lovett had long suspected the motives and goals of trade associations in his private business career.[21] These differences came to a head when Gifford asked the CND and WIB to give the chamber's committees official recognition. This move would make one group solely responsible for all official dealings that a trade had in Washington and would generally tighten up administration all along the line. The chamber, of course, sided with Gifford. But Washington war agencies were reluctant to displace their own trade committees, and at Lovett's instigation the WIB refused as a matter of principle to offer certification.[22] Although in its later life the board often privately sanctioned specific war service committee agreements, it nevertheless intended to go on record against "any general license covering undefined and unforeseeable possibilities."[23] Commodity chiefs later appointed many war service committees, which the chamber promptly recognized, but WIB executives would not budge from their official position.

The WIB executive had been forced into this relationship with the chamber of commerce not through any real desire of its own, but out of the need for a legitimizing tactic to overcome public hostility to a covert, cooperative system of business-government relations. Public pressures had forced upon the administration the kind of bureaucratic, formalized procedures that Baruch for one had hoped to avoid. Neither Baruch nor Lovett intended to share power with the chamber of commerce, or to permit it to use them for any ulterior purposes. Insofar as Baruch had any use for the chamber, it was as a kind of organizational shell through which big business leaders could continue to communicate with their governmental colleagues. As Baruch well knew, actual control over the means of production still rested with private corporations, not with the chamber of commerce; and public sensitivity aside, it was with corporate leaders that Baruch had ultimately to negotiate. WIB officials intended the chamber to serve

[20]See examples of the positive response in C. A. Tupper, "The Spirit of Co-Operation," *Cement World* (September 1917), pp. 6–7; "Mobilizing American Industry," *Commercial America* 14 (October 1917): 11; and the certifications made by the chamber in RG 61, File 1–A2, box 33.

[21]"Statement of Judge R. S. Lovett," Bernard M. Baruch Papers, Princeton University, Princeton, N.J. (cited hereafter as *Baruch Papers*).

[22]Gifford to George Peek, January 9, 1918, RG 62, File 2–A4, box 83; Redfield to Gifford, February 8, 1918, Gifford to Hoover *et al.*, February 9, 1918, Hoover to Gifford, February 19, 1918, C. M. Woolley to Gifford, February 16, 1918, and Lovett to Gifford, February 12, 1918, all in RG 62, File 2–A1, box 32; Peek to Gifford, February 25, 1918, RG 62, File 2–A1, box 56.

[23]Lovett to Henry P. Fowler (secretary, war service executive committee), March 1, 1918, RG 61, File 21A–A3, box 44. Baruch continued this policy when he became chairman. Baruch to Harry A. Wheeler (president, United States Chamber of Commerce), October 29, 1918, RG 61, File 21A–A4, box 329.

primarily as a symbol of the change in business-government relations occasioned by passage of section 3. The chamber represented the private, business community with which the WIB as a public, official agency could legitimately arrange business affairs. The chamber, and not the board, had full responsibility for creating trade organizations and attesting to their representativeness. If they turned out to be exclusive clubs, responsibility lay with the chamber and not with the board. While war service committees might promote their trade, they could not be confused with official business advisors who operated on the other side of that imaginary line separating business and government, private and public institutions.[24]

The war service committees took up positions of even greater intimacy with the WIB than those recently vacated by the cooperative committees. They worked closely with the WIB's commodity chiefs, entering the administrative system in a way that involved a substantial transfer of public authority to them. The chamber provided a very porous buffer indeed between public officials and private business groups, and there was a partial continuation of the same kind of arrangements that many hoped section 3 would eliminate. While additional trade committees coalesced around the board in great numbers, and while the original cooperative committeemen were sometimes joined by fresh faces, the principle of informal, covert arrangements between business advisors within government with their colleagues in business was by no means at an end.

Even though letters of resignation were accepted from members of the old committees in the fall and winter of 1917, many of the committees themselves remained intact. Baruch asked several important industrial leaders to disband their groups, but he appealed to them to remain in Washington. He expressed his hope to John Morron, president of the Atlas-Portland Cement Company, that the former cement committee chairman would continue as the government's point of contact with the industry either by himself, or as part of another committee. Responding to this kind of appeal, the cement committee became the "Portland Cement Committee on Government Requirements" with essentially the same membership. The committee finally accepted the war service designation in June 1918, but strictly as a matter of form.[25] The WIB asked the

[24]Walter Gifford, whose convictions were more sincere than Baruch's in the matter, made the point this way: "We have talked to the business men. We have gotten them interested and enthusiastic over doing this on their own hook, and they are coming to us sitting on that side of the table representing the industry, we sitting on this side of the table representing the Government, and talking," U.S. Congress, Senate, Committee on Military Affairs, *Hearings, Investigation of the War Department*, 65th Cong., 2nd sess., 1918, part 3, p. 1872.

[25]Baruch to Morron, November 24, 1917, RG 61, File 21A–A1, box 7; M. A. Holman (secretary, cement committee) to Eugene Meyer, Jr., January 9, 1918, and Morron to Meyer, December 18, 1917, both in RG 61, File 21A–A4, box 312; M. A. Holman

petroleum committee to form a new committee and to "continue the same personnel as on the dissolved committee," adding any members it deemed advisable.[26] The members of the very influential chemical committee became the directors of the newly formed Chemical Alliance which continued the old committee's work under a different name, and, in theory at least, at arm's length from the government. The former subcommittee on fertilizers now became the committee on fertilizers of the Chemical Alliance, Inc.[27]

Although the original lead committee disbanded, explained the committee's final report, "it was nevertheless desired by Mr. Baruch, as represented by Mr. Eugene Meyer, Jr., . . . that some means should be arranged for supplying the direct pig lead requirements of the Government." The producers therefore appointed Irwin H. Cornell as their representative to allot government business. Cornell was vice president and sales manager of the St. Joseph Lead Company, and secretary of the cooperative committee in lead. "From time to time," as the same report explained further, "Mr. Clinton H. [Crane (president of the St. Joseph Lead Company and chairman of the cooperative committee)] called informal meetings of the producers for the purpose of discussing the work." Only in June 1918 did this committee formally become a war service committee affiliated with the chamber.[28] The lead producers, in other words, continued to

---

to Richard L. Humphrey, February 24, 1919, RG 61, File 21A–A4, box 316. Baruch also asked a member of the Prepared Roofing and Shingle Manufactures Association to remain behind after the committee on asbestos, magnesia, and roofing was disbanded. See Philip Allen (of the committee) to Baruch, October 17, 1917, RG 61, File 21A–A1, box 5.

[26] Unsigned letter to A. C. Bedford and members of the petroleum committee, December 4, 1917, RG 61, File 21A–A1, box 14. A notation on this copy reads: "This letter was originally drafted by Judge Parker and Mr. Beford; later corrected by Mr. Baruch and shown to Mr. Willard, who approved same."

[27] Leland Summers had urged Baruch in late October to act at once on the chemical front. Given section 3, the committee could no longer carry on as it once had, and because the council had spoken against forming new committees the industry was not yet fully organized. The industry designed the Chemical Alliance as a way out of the impasse. Summers to Baruch, October 23, 1917, and Baruch to Frank Scott, October 24, 1917, both in RG 61, File 1–A2, box 29; William H. Nichols (chairman, committee on chemicals) to Baruch, November 16, 1917, Baruch to Nichols, November 16, 1917, and Horace Bowker to Baruch, December 10, 1917, all in RG 61, File 21A–A1, box 8; Baruch to Nichols, November 26 and December 5, 1917, RG 61, File 21A–A1, box 7. The Chemical Alliance then became the war service committee for the chemical industry with the full approval of the chamber of commerce war service executive committee. See Summers to Catchings, January 21, 1918, and Catchings to Summers, January 25, 1918, both in RG 61, File 21A–A4, box 1573.

[28] "A Brief History of the War Service Committees of the United States Pig Lead Producers 1917–1918," a pamphlet in RG 61, File 21A–A4, box 786; Baruch to Crane, May 23, 1918, requesting the industry to form a WSC, RG 61, File 21A–A4, box 784.

conduct themselves after the passage of section 3 very much as they had before, and with the full encouragement of Meyer and Baruch. This was true for all the raw material industries.[29]

Secretary Baker came close to the truth of the matter when he explained to Quartermaster Sharpe that section 3 resulted in "rather a reorganization than a complete abandonment of the committee activities." And indeed Baker personally approved continuation of the old system. He urged Sharpe to reach a clear understanding with Rosenwald about the wool situation, for example, "so that the work will not be injuriously affected."[30] The wool committee did not quit Washington, and Sharpe assured Baker: "I do not think there will be any interruption in the proper handling of our wool supply."[31]

Senator McKellar (D., Tenn.), one of section 3's strongest supporters, was sufficiently disillusioned by the insubstantial impact of the Senate amendment as to introduce legislation in January to take mobilization out of the hands of dollar-a-year men altogether and to give it to fully compensated government employees. But he stood alone. The chamber of commerce and its war service committee system, allied with the image of disinterestedness cultivated by the civilian mobilizers themselves, proved adequate both to quiet public opposition and to maintain at the same time easy routes of access between the owners of the means of production and those government officials dependent upon them.[32] The exaggerated virtues of the war service committees—their openness, formality, and organizational coherence—marred a clear view of the more covert activities in which they engaged.

The events surrounding section 3 and the crisis in business-government relations it symbolized also forced changes on the public side of that elusive business-government divide. As the administration and WIB now encouraged business groups to organize themselves more effectively through the chamber of com-

---

[29] And it was true of committees dealing with segments of the Washington organization other than Baruch's raw materials committee. See H. L. Green (pressed steel committee) to Frank Scott, October 12, 1917, RG 61, File 21A-A4, box 1146; and Chester Bolton (captain, ordnance department) to Thomas Neal (concerning committee on paint and varnishes), October 15, 1917, RG 61, File 21A-A1, box 14.

[30] Baker to Sharpe, December 5, 1917, Newton D. Baker Papers, Library of Congress, Washington, D.C.

[31] Sharpe to Baker, December 20, 1917, *ibid.*

[32] Both Howard Coffin and Secretary Baker appealed personally to McKellar to withdraw his bill, and he complied with their wishes, being assured by Baker that established agencies like the War Department were taking over more and more of the work and voluntary committees were being steadily restricted to "an advisory function, with the final official acts performed by official persons." Baker to McKellar, and Coffin to McKellar, February 9, 1918, and McKellar to Baker, February 13, 1918, all in the Kenneth D. McKellar Papers, Memphis Public Library, Memphis, Tennessee. See also "The Washington Situation," *Motor World* 54 (January 9, 1918): 560.

merce, they by necessity had to formalize and augment their own internal organization. Political conditions led to a government demand that private business groups enhance their associational ties, which stimulated in turn the state's own bureaucratic growth. The WIB asked leading members of the old cooperative committees and the new war service committees to join the WIB organization and link their groups to the board's expanding, organizational network.

Consider the case of the lumber industry. In November the WIB executive told Baruch and Robert Downman that the lumber committee had fallen from favor,[33] and it recommended two complementary forms of action. The industry should establish a war service committee and Downman should leave his present post and join WIB officialdom. Some of Downman's constituency regarded the board's invitation as outright territorial invasion, which made Downman reluctant to take up his new assignment. But the WIB persisted and the lumber chieftain and his entourage entered the WIB's raw materials division, apparently ready to give exclusive attention to the government's interest.[34]

What the crisis over section 3 had done was to accelerate bureaucratic trends inherent in the mobilization process itself. It pushed forward the rationalization and functional specialization inherent in the WIB's organizational response to war. Matching the expert with his specialty within an emergency agency characterized every step in economic coordination from the Naval Consulting Board to the formation of the WIB. The commodity sections only formalized this approach within the WIB structure. It had already occurred to some degree within Rosenwald's supplies committee, Baruch's raw materials committee, and Brookings's finished products division. Each of these men brought commodity specialists into his organization. Brookings, for instance, chose businessmen to administer such commodities as army vehicles, machine tools, locomotive cranes, and automotive products.

Although a number of commodity units had emerged in the WIB's functional divisions by the fall and winter of 1917, the major step in their development occurred during the spring and summer of 1918. There are several reasons for their expansion at this time. For one thing differentiation and specialization was bound to increase as the board's jurisdiction and responsibilities expanded. The longer the board was in operation, the more finely drawn its organization

---

[33] In early October 1917, the army set out to purchase lumber through a group of mills outside the lumber committee's emergency bureaus. The WIB approved; Baruch objected. Downman appealed to the board for sole jurisdiction, and it was at this point that Lovett, the chairman, issued his policy statement against the cooperative committees. Minutes of a meeting of the War Industries Board (cited hereafter as *WIB Minutes*), in RG 61, File 1-C1, boxes 72-74, October 12 and November 1, 1917.

[34] *WIB Minutes*, November 1, 1917. Baruch promised Downman that he could "surround himself with men of his own choosing" if he came. Frank G. Wisner to E. A. Selfridge, November 3, 1917, RG 61, File 10A-A2, box 1031.

became. Moreover, since a greater number of commodities were affected by wartime demands at this point, more and more business groups were experiencing various kinds of economic disruption and beginning to see the advantages of cooperating with an agency that could help eliminate obstacles to their production plans. But it was the decision at this point to connect the commodity sections directly to the supply structure of the armed services that gave them much of their distinction, attraction, and impetus for development.

THE COMMODITY SECTIONS AND INDUSTRIAL-MILITARY RELATIONS

In his March letter, the president directed Baruch and the WIB "to anticipate the prospective needs of the several supply departments of the Government and their feasible adjustment to the industry of the country as far in advance as possible, in order that as definite an outlook and opportunity for planning as possible may be afforded the businessmen of the country."[35] This was an important response to the business search for economic stability, harkening back to Coffin's industrial preparedness campaign. Then it was only the hope of a few farsighted men; now it was settled government policy. WIB officials conferred with military officers in March and April in an effort to give the directive some meaning. On the basis of memoranda from both services and from various WIB officials, Edwin Parker of the board's priorities division drew up a plan for a requirements division and a series of commodity sections that served as the basic framework for the WIB's relationship with the services to the end of the war.[36]

Inability to predict future needs had long been a major stumbling block in economic mobilization and a special point of contention between civilian business advisors and military officials. Parker and the WIB executive hoped that this plan would settle the issue once and for all. It was decided that the military

[35] Wilson to Baruch, March 4, 1918, *Wilson Papers.*

[36] It is important to emphasize here that Parker's organizational design responded to and incorporated initiatives taken by the services. Admirals McGowan and Peoples submitted ideas for the navy, Stettinius for the army. McGowan and navy officials had introduced the commodity section concept as early as December. Both Stettinius and Peoples offered full sketches of a requirements division and Parker used the latter's draft as the basis for his memorandum. Baruch was noticeably absent from the mechanics of this construction process. See U.S. Congress, House, Committee on Naval Affairs, *Hearings on Estimates Submitted by the Secretary of the Navy, 1918,* 65th Cong., 2nd sess., 1918, pp. 315–22 and 327–30, for McGowan's ideas on purchasing in December 1917. Also see Alex Legge to McGowan, March 9, 1918, McGowan to Baruch, March 6, 1918, and Stettinius to Baruch, March 18, 1918, all in RG 61, File 21A–A1, box 1; *WIB Minutes,* March 19, 1918; Parker to Legge, March 30, 1918, Parker to Peoples, March 30, 1918, Parker to Peek, April 1, 1918, Parker to Thomas N. Perkins, March 30, 1918, Perkins to Parker, April 1, 1918, and Parker to James Inglis, April 2, 1918, all in RG 61, File 21A–A1, box 21.

services and the Allied purchasing commission should forward information on prospective needs to a requirements division which, after digesting the information, would be in a position to advise on shortages. The division was to be composed of Alexander Legge, chairman; James Inglis, executive secretary; Edwin Parker, from the priorities division; George Peek from finished products; Leonard Replogle from the steel division; Leland Summers from chemicals and explosives; Pope Yeatman from nonferrous metals; plus representatives of the Allied purchasing commission, the war and navy departments, the shipping board, the emergency fleet corporation and the railroad administration. The fuel and food administrations and the Red Cross could send representatives whenever their plans affected industry.[37]

The requirements division was a good idea, but it never quite met the expectations of its civilian sponsors. The very most WIB officials later claimed for it was its usefulness as a meeting place for various war administrators to discuss common problems. There was still no way to compel the armed services to submit information; as late as September 1918 Alexander Legge complained that the services still went about their business as if the WIB never existed. And in any case, the division was not an administrative unit. It exercised no control over those who actually arranged purchases, prices, and the steps which businessmen would take to overcome shortages. A forum where top level administrators could develop a community of interest and get a better idea of what they were all thinking was useful, no doubt, but in functional terms the division could not overcome its fragmented, decentralized organizational environment. The armistice precluded the hope that the division might ultimately become a formidable source of centralized control.[38]

Provisions for commodity administration were of far more immediate importance to the war effort. Military and WIB officials agreed that commodity sections should be established in the WIB for products where "there is an actual or threatened shortage, or the price and production of which should be controlled. . . ."[39] And WIB officials also conceived of them as working arms of the requirements division. The division would amass all the proper information from the services and other war agencies and then send along a prospective list of requirements to the proper commodity section, which could then determine how best to respond. This would give the chief and his business constituency

---

[37] "Organization and Functions of Requirements Division of War Industries Board," enclosed with Parker to Peek, April 1, 1918, RG 61, File 21A–A1, box 21.

[38] To quote George Peek: "Well, it did a great deal of good in the way of bringing people from the different departments together . . . , but so far as the actual detailed work is concerned, it was wholly unnecessary." "Statement of George N. Peek," *Baruch Papers*.

[39] From "Organization and Functions of Requirements Division of War Industries Board," enclosed with Parker to Peek, April 1, 1918, RG 61, File 21A–A1, box 21.

sufficient warning to develop a collective strategy. They could then consider the problems of increasing production through conversion, plant expansion, and so on. Hopefully the system would give businessmen that "opportunity for planning" which the president now wanted them to have.[40]

According to the final scheme (it was revised a number of times), each commodity section was to be composed of an administrative "chief" drawn from private industry and a representative of each of the military supply departments interested in the commodity at hand. The WIB had still not relinquished its hope of dominating the entire supply program, and Parker originally placed the civilian commodity chief in complete charge of the section, but the navy, as usual, had objected. Not only did Daniels insist that his men be regarded as full members with "an active voice in handling" section business, but to ensure further that the navy would be treated equitably, he and his men also insisted on the right of military representatives to appeal section decisions to their superiors in the service, although the final power of arbitration would rest in the hands of the WIB chairman.[41]

As drafted in April, the scheme did not define the rights of the section chiefs in the matter of prices. Various WIB personnel wanted final authority invested in its chiefs, but as could be expected, the services objected, and the issue remained a contentious point in subsequent months. The evidence suggests that the civilian chiefs were sometimes more tender to industry's interest than the services would have liked. The army members of some commodity sections felt particularly slighted, and complained well into the fall of 1918 that the commodity chiefs were moving ahead without proper consultation.[42] It stands to reason, of course, that a system involving so many competing jurisdictions and so many various officials could not be perfected overnight.

All the plans submitted in March for better integration of military and industrial operations recognized that the competitive conduct of the army bureaus would have to end. Admiral McGowan, for instance, a strong advocate of the commodity committee idea, noted that his particular proposal "contemplates centralizing the purchases of the Army";[43] and Edward Stettinius, who acted on the army's behalf in negotiations preceding the inauguration of the

[40]This of course was the perspective of the WIB group and not the military services, who had other motives for improving the supply system. Stettinius, for example, seized on the commodity section idea as a way to protect the army's own business advisors from public criticism. They would carry on their work for the army through the WIB. Diary of George Goethals, April 9 and 10, 1918, and May 6, 1918, in George Goethals Papers, Manuscript Division, Library of Congress, Washington, D.C. (hereafter cited as *Goethals Diary*).

[41]Daniels to Baruch, April 3, 1918, RG 61, File 21A–A1, box 21.

[42]Meeting of the Commodity Chiefs, September 16, 1918, RG 61, File 1–C2, box 80.

[43]"Memorandum," enclosed with McGowan to Baruch, March 6, 1918, RG 61, File 21A–A1, box 1.

scheme, observed in one brief: "In order that the foregoing plan might be carried out effectively, arrangements should be made by which the procurement activities of the War Department would be so centralized that competitive buying between the several supply bureaus of the War Department should be done away with."[44] What deserves emphasis here is the fact that a strong consensus had built up among important groups within the Washington bureaucracy for coordination of the Army supply system to parallel developments in the civilian economy. WIB officials participated in the process but by no means determined the outcome. Moreover, there was no intention on the part of either the army or navy to subordinate themselves to the WIB. The key was mutual cooperation and coordination, not WIB control.

The commodity section development can be regarded in some respects as a continuation of the army's response to new organizational requirements initiated in the winter of 1917. From this perspective, the WIB's commodity sections are less a victory for WIB mobilizers than one result of a successful fight waged by military institutions to maintain a wide area of discretion for themselves in the face of bureaucratic invasions by emergency agencies. This is especially the case when we remember that the army, under Baker, had forced the WIB and the government's civilian business advisors into a compromise over the broad control of the mobilization program. After all, while Wilson's March 4 letter made Baruch supreme within the WIB structure, it told him to leave alone the purchasing functions of the military departments. The board would assist the services in this task, but it would not supplant them. Even the trend toward coordination of the WIB and the services through the commodity sections led away from WIB supremacy to a WIB-military compromise based on mutual recognition of limitations as well as rights. The commodity sections reflect less the power of Baruch's position than the perilous organizational compromise on which it rested.

Faced with these stubborn facts, some WIB personnel moved to perfect the organizational compromise and make it operate as smoothly as possible. As chief of the finished products division, George Peek took the initiative for the WIB, and army Captain Hugh Johnson offered him sympathetic assistance from the military side. After meeting his army counterpart, Peek wrote a friend: "He was a lieutenant only a year ago; is a young man and one of the most forceful, active fellows I have met. Unless I am greatly mistaken in the man he will bring about vast improvements in the War Department."[45]

Peek was not wrong about Johnson's energy and enthusiasm. He shared many of the values of the civilian mobilizers and worked well with them as director of purchase and supplies and then as army representative on the WIB.

[44]"Memorandum," enclosed with Stettinius to Baruch, March 18, 1918, *ibid.*

[45]Peek to C. D. Velie, May 6, 1918, George N. Peek Papers, Western Historical Manuscript Collection, University of Missouri, Columbia, Mo. (cited hereafter as *Peek Papers*).

Deeply committed to the concepts of civilian-military coordination and centralization within the military supply system, he eagerly took up the challenge of McGowan and Stettinius and drove forward the movement for rationalization of the Washington supply structure. As determined to make his office the focal point of the army's supply organization as Baruch was to make the WIB predominate on the civilian side, Johnson was adamant that all requests from civilian mobilizers be directed through his office. He was as irritated when commodity chiefs went directly to his bureaus for information as WIB mobilizers were when military purchasing officials skirted the board and dealt directly with private manufacturers, and he expressed his objections about this several times. He complained too about insufficient contact between WIB men and his purchasing officers, and the tendency of commodity chiefs to present military representatives with faits accomplis. At the end of August he sent his friend Peek a cumulative list of grievances which was representative of the problems that beset the commodity organization. Thirteen army representatives had told Johnson that commodity chiefs had not consulted them; of the forty-eight sections formed to that point, seventeen had either held no meetings or at least had not notified army representatives about them; and most disturbing of all, Johnson found "a distinct and growing tendency of the Chairmen to control the situation as though all power were delegated to them rather than to the section."[46] Just two months before the armistice, in other words, the system was moving in quite the opposite direction from which its military participants had intended. The board and the services were far from successfully integrating their functional units.

To try to arrest this drift, Johnson sent out a circular on August 28 which must surely stand as the most succinct statement on behalf of military-industrial integration to emerge from the war. Johnson pursued a heady vision of organic unity in this document, a vision which coupled the WIB's "power to control resources" with the War Department's "power of purchase." In a typically didactic tone he urged the military representatives to consider themselves "as much a part of the [WIB] as the officers of the War Industries Board themselves. . . ." They had not merely to submit their needs to the WIB; they had to

---

[46] Johnson to Peek, August 16, 1918, attached to *WIB Minutes*, August 20, 1918. Also see Johnson to Baruch, May 16, 1918, RG 61, File 21A–A1, box 2, and P. E. Foerderer (executive secretary, requirements division) to Albert Brunker, May 27, 1918, RG 61, File 11A–B1, box 1147. Johnson emphasized more than once, moreover, that WIB officials were to have nothing to do with actually purchasing materials. See Meeting of the Commodity Chiefs, July 29, 1918, RG 61, File 1–C2, box 81; and *Goethals Diary*, June 14, 17, and 21, and July 30, 1918. One army representative in the automotive products section regarded the section as a "star chamber proceeding." Captain Belmont Corn to Chief, External Relations Branch of Office of Chief of Staff, September 20, 1918, RG 61, File 21A–A2, box 47.

participate actively in all its deliberations. "In a word, the delegation of power to sections of that board is not to their chairman but to the sections themselves."[47] The very need Johnson felt to issue this plea suggests the difficulty he had in persuading all army personnel to accept his plan for civilian-military cooperation through the WIB. He later recalled of the army bureaus: "They fought the exterior control of the War Industries Board at every step, even after we had contrived a plan of integration that put their men in control of practically every economic unit."[48]

George Peek echoed these pleas on the civilian side as the nationalizers and centralizers fought for systematization against independent-minded military bureaus and business interests. Peek asked his commodity chiefs to encourage each member of the sections to assume full responsibility for its activities.[49] But even within his own personal organization there were those who objected to the idea of equality within the commodity sections. His assistant Emmet Crawford, in fact, had absolutely opposed the integration of military officials and civilian mobilizers. He had written Alexander Legge in April 1918: "I desire to go on record again as saying that I believe the creation of commodity committees is fundamentally wrong, and that the section head should be made absolute chief of his department with the privilege of calling upon the Army and Navy representatives for aid."[50] Crawford could be expected to sympathize with those commodity chiefs who arrogated authority to themselves in subsequent months.

Tensions did ease, however. Johnson, Peek, and the other cooperators had considerable success. The commodity chiefs decided ultimately to have regular meetings in which all major transactions that had transpired during the previous week could be ratified. All coordinating members of the services were to be

[47]U.S. War Department, Purchase, Storage and Traffic Division, General Staff, Supply Bulletin no. 22, August 28, 1918. Found in RG 61, File 1–C2, box 81.

[48]Hugh S. Johnson, *The Blue Eagle from Egg to Earth* (Garden City, N.Y.: Doubleday, Doran, 1935), p. 92. Johnson forgot to mention in his memoirs that he too guarded against WIB control during the war.

[49]See, for example, Peek's sympathetic response to Johnson's August complaints in *WIB Minutes*, August 20, 1918; and Peek to J. W. Scott *et al.*, September 25, 1918, RG 61, File 21A–A2, box 86.

[50]Crawford to Legge, April 9, 1918, RG 61, File 21A–A1, box 9. Also see Crawford to Legge, March 14, 1918, *ibid.*, and Crawford to Peek, March 16, 1918, RG 61, File 21A–A4, box 1147. Crawford wanted the commodity chief and his section to purchase for all government departments. Crawford to Baruch, June 27, 1918, RG 61, File 21A–A1, box 28. Charles MacDowell told his men in the chemical division in April that if the WIB were to become more than an advisory board they would have to take full responsibility for the commodities they handled. The trend was toward constant aggression by the WIB's commodity chiefs to obtain complete control of the commodities in question. See "Chemical and Explosive By-Weekly Meeting–4/30/18," in RG 61, File 1–C2, box 76.

notified of meetings in writing.[51] Most section chiefs reconciled themselves to the need of taking the military officials into account, or at least working out mutually acceptable agreements with them, although they never gave up the hope for more power. "After surveying the Commodity Section members on their judgment of the War Department representatives and others," ran a summary of October 30, "the general feeling is that everything is satisfactory, save for the Emergency Fleet Representative in the Optical Glass section, and the Army man in the tobacco section."[52]

This uneasy détente between WIB businessmen and military representatives was part of the general readjustment of authority relationships that occurred in the war years, a readjustment that required some time to materialize despite the formal and immediate declarations of cooperation and good fellowship. One dimension of the clash between WIB businessmen and military representatives involved a challenge to a hierarchical system of authority. Authority within the military departments rested on rank; within the WIB on how you did your job. The traditional, peacetime distribution of authority in matters of military policy put the armed services in the top spot, for they had responsibility for drawing up war plans and overseeing the country's war-making capacities. Creation of emergency agencies such as the WIB challenged peacetime arrangements and authority relationships. Businessmen had the best working knowledge of the industrial side of the war, and as members of the emergency bureaucracy they wanted formal authority commensurate with their newfound responsibilities. When they did not receive it they carried on in a haphazard, illegal fashion as best they could, grasping all the time for more power and wider jurisdictions. This clash between specialized business knowledge and hierarchical military authority within the Washington bureaucracy was most bitter in the initial stages of mobilization, as businessmen, anxious for industry in an uncertain environment and with no understanding of military sensibilities, confronted career officers who by virtue of their social isolation were not wholly sympathetic to or at ease with businessmen, and yet were nevertheless in a position to accept or reject their advice. To reduce the military's area of discretion in such matters had been Baruch's goal from the very beginning. Relations became smoother as the army reorganized itself along commodity lines more congenial to communication with the WIB organization and as both military officers and business administrators became better acquainted with each other. Charles MacDowell, the WIB's chemicals division chief, believed that the situation also improved as more civilian businessmen entered the services. MacDowell had known the key people in the army's explosive and chemical program in private life, for instance. They were

[51] Meeting of the Commodity Chiefs, September 16, 1918, RG 61, File 1–C2, box 80.

[52] "Commodity Section Members Summary," October 30, 1918, RG 61, File 1–C2, box 86.

"good business men," he recalled, they "knew how to handle business." In the early days, in contrast, he had had to deal with "some of the old-line men."[53]

THE COMMODITY SECTIONS AND PERSONNEL RECRUITMENT

As mentioned earlier, the embryo of the commodity sections, albeit without their military component, existed within the raw materials committee, the old supplies committee, and in the finished products division. Some of the commodity groups, such as automotive products and lumber, sprang from the original cooperative committees; others originated after the system's demise (as was true with the optical glass and crane sections). But whatever their origin, all those sections contained within the three WIB units merged with the new commodity organization after March 1918 and provided some continuity to its evolution. Nine of the fourteen key personnel with the finished products commodity sections in November 1918 had been with the board since before January of that year. A rapid expansion in the chemical sections and personnel occurred during the spring and summer of 1918, but Leland Summers and Charles MacDowell provided links with earlier organizational efforts in that industry. Summers had been with Baruch from the beginning, and MacDowell had come in the winter of 1917. Although many of the sections in hides, leather and leather goods, and cotton goods sprang up in the WIB only after March 1918, they had actually existed as operating units in the quartermaster's department and were closely tied to Rosenwald's old supplies committee organization.

If the course by which the commodity sections found their berths in the WIB provided a great many variations, the manner in which they secured their navigators proved uniform indeed. In almost every case the fifty-seven sections were administered by men drawn from the industries involved. Trade associations and their war services committees provided a major source of personnel, and the board frequently asked United States Chamber of Commerce officials for advice. E. E. Parsonage, manager of the John Deere Wagon Company and chairman of the industry's wagon and vehicle committee, took charge of these products for the WIB. Alexander Brown, president of the Brown Hoisting Machinery Company of Cleveland and chairman of a war-inspired producers committee, administered the crane section. Murray Sargent, executive manager of the Hardware Manufacturers' Organization for War Service, became chief of the hardware and handtool section. John C. Schmidt, a member of the executive committee of the American Hardware Manufacturers' Association, became chief of the chain section; Charles F. C. Stout, president of the Morocco Manufac-

---

[53]"Statement of Charles H. MacDowell," *Baruch Papers.*

turers National Association, became director of the hide, leather and leather goods division. George Peek made it a regular practice to obtain a list of names from an industrial trade association from which he could select a chief, in consultation with leaders of the industry. Peek also solicited suggestions from chamber of commerce officials.

Nor did reliance on trade associations end with selection of section chiefs. The sections themselves turned to the associations to augment their administrative staffs. This factor of course strengthened ties between the sections and the war service committees. The board's silk section called on the secretary of the Silk Association of America to serve in a similar capacity for it. Walter Robbins of the electrical and power equipment section turned to the industry's war service committee in March 1918 when he needed additional help. Charles Hanch, who became chief of automotive products in June 1918, observed, "My position has been terribly strenuous since I have been here and I needed help very badly at times. However, between the assistance given by Al Reeves, George Graham and the staff of the Chamber [the National Automobile Chamber of Commerce] I have been able to get by."[54]

As a matter of official policy, the board did try to avoid taking trade association employees. That is, while the board would not deny a business-administrator his post because of a present affiliation with a trade association, it did try to bar permanent trade association employees. Charles Hanch ran afoul of this sentiment in the fall of 1918. Hanch wanted to add two men to his section and had in a mind a couple of chamber officials who had assisted him informally in the past. George Peek submitted their applications to Legge on Hanch's behalf. Legge and Baruch both made it clear, however, that they did not want to have the board take on this kind of person, even if he separated himself from the chamber and came in on a dollar-a-year basis. When Hanch objected, however, Baruch and Legge could do little, aside from making their personal opinions known. Ultimately they bowed to Hanch's wishes and he had his men.[55]

The basic problems in the recruitment of commodity chiefs can be clearly seen in negotiations that preceded the choice of men to head the rubber and silk sections.

Peek took the rubber situation in hand in May, and asked a number of business acquaintances for opinions about a man he had in mind for the job, Emmet A. Saunders of the Misawaka Woolen Manufacturing Company. Before

[54]Hanch to H. O. Smith, August 12, 1918, RG 61, File 21A–A2, box 47.

[55]Hanch to William M. Ritter (one of Peek's assistants), September 23, 1918, Peek to Legge, September 24, 1918, and Legge to Peek, September 26, 1918, all *ibid.* Hanch also appealed to John Dodge for administrative assistants. Hanch to Dodge, September 21, 1918, *ibid.*

he could progress very far in this case, however, the candidate objected to his prospective appointment and recommended instead Harvey Firestone, president of the Firestone Rubber and Tire Company. Firestone was obviously an imposing candidate and had the full support of his competitors within the industry. But while Firestone agreed that only someone familiar with the industry should be chosen, he himself would not accept. He did not want a position which would make him, "through modesty or over feeling of the nicities [sic] of the case" unable "to see that his Company has a fair chance in the business going on."[56]

Emmet Crawford suggested next that the WIB pick a commodity chief from a committee of four selected by the industry. Crawford hoped in this way to obtain some independence for the board, and at the same time reflect trade sentiment. Crawford also suggested that if this did not satisfy all interests Peek could assign a man of Firestone's stature as chief and then pacify any other segment of the trade by giving it a representative on Firestone's staff. Apparently the board sometimes found it necessary to enlarge its commodity section staff to win feuding factions to its side.[57]

After Firestone turned down the offer, a number of other candidates came into view. Peek's friend Saunders suggested Harry T. Dunn, president of the Fisk Rubber Company; Dunn himself mentioned the possibility of taking the former president of the Republic Rubber Company, presently retired. "I think it would be better, however," he cautioned, "to have some one more intimately familiar with the industry as it now stands in order to render the service you desire."[58]

Peek had been trying to find someone not directly connected with the industry, as his original choice of Saunders indicates. In taking this tack, however, Peek was conforming less with his own wishes than with those of Baruch, who after being embarrassed once by Congress over the conflict of interest problem did not want it to happen again. But to discover an outsider acceptable to an industry was a formidable task. Baruch had already asked a businessman not in the rubber business to take the post. Peek informed the candidate that it was "not desirable to have a man from the rubber industry administer this job for the reason that he would be put in an unfair position in the eyes of the public and subject to possible criticism from Congress."[59] The board did not object to such an appointment on the grounds that conflict of interest would in any way damage the administrator's performance. They never doubted that the best course, the most efficient course, was to have each trade administered by

---

[56]E. L. Crawford to Peek, June 20, 1918, Joseph D. Oliver to Peek, May 22, 1918, and Saunders to Crawford, June 6, 1918, all in RG 61, File 21A – A2, box 216.

[57]Crawford to Peek, June 20, 1918, *ibid.*

[58]Dunn to Crawford, June 27, 1918, and Saunders to Crawford, June 24, 1918, both *ibid.*

[59]Peek to Arthur C. Smith, July 19, 1918, *ibid.* Also see Peek to Edwin B. Parker, June 20, 1918, RG 61, File 21A–A2, box 215.

industry personnel. The point was to avoid unfavorable reactions from a public and Congress whose lack of sophistication in such matters would, as they saw it, only lead to unnecessary anxiety.

Baruch and Peek might agree on an outside choice, but the rubber industry was unimpressed. Both Firestone and Dunn had explicitly rejected the idea. Ultimately Peek asked the rubber war service committee to offer four names, as Crawford had suggested. They nominated H. S. Firestone, H. T. Dunn, F. A. Seiberling, president of Goodyear Tire & Rubber Company, and H. E. Sawyer, vice president of the United States Rubber Company. Peek talked the matter over with Firestone and Sawyer, and then asked Dunn to join the board. Dunn was duly appointed in August.[60] In this case, finding a commodity chief for rubber had consumed over two months of precious time, only to result finally in the WIB's acceptance of the industry's choice.

John Scott, who was director of the textile division under Peek, encountered some similar problems when he began thinking about an administrator for a proposed silk section. Added to the regular difficulties in this case was a division of opinion over Scott's desire for a specialist and the trade's insistence on a generalist. In June, Scott approached M. D. Migel, president of the Allied Silk Trading Corporation and treasurer of the American Silk Company, with a proposal to form a silk section, and Migel discussed the proposition with Charles Cheney, president of the Silk Association of America. Both men agreed to the wisdom of the move, "as questions are arising daily and should be settled by some authority familiar with the requirements of the industry."[61] The industry, in other words, favored the idea not because the mobilization program faced difficulties in its silk supply, but because the industry was encountering problems which it now found in its own interest to get some government agency to help it overcome. Cheney favored Scott's suggestion that Migel assume the task of organizing the section.[62]

While the industry proceeded to elaborate the details of the proposed section, Scott began his search for a suitable chief. After much thought he settled on a man for the job, only to hear that the Silk Association wanted to be consulted in the process. Happy with his prospective choice, Scott was reluctant now to open the question to the association and possibly have someone less qualified foisted upon him. But he could not deny the industry's request. The trade association would ultimately administer the silk program and its cooperation had to be assured. To extricate Scott from his dilemma, Peek recommended that the textile director try Crawford's tactic and have the Silk Association name

[60]M. L. Heminway to Peek, June 28, 1918, and Peek to John W. Scott, July 26, 1918, both in RG 61, File 21A–A2, box 216.

[61]Migel to Scott, June 19, 1918, and Migel to the WIB, June 10, 1918, both *ibid.*

[62]Migel to Scott, June 19, 1918, *ibid.*

three or four candidates. It did offer some choice, and also "put the request on a little different ground than as though we asked them to select a man for us."[63] Even small concessions became major victories for Peek.

While Scott and Peek tried to convince each other of their independence from the trade, support within the industry gathered for William Skinner, president of the Silk Association and scion of an old New England silk dynasty. Despite growing indications that Skinner was the trade's number one choice, Scott determined at least to put the name of his candidate before the industry. But to no avail.

Baruch observed the interminable discussions with growing concern, uncomfortable once again over the possible public criticism that could grow out of the appointment of an industry man. He repeated his warning against having a man like Skinner take charge of the silk section. "I advise you," he wrote Scott, "to surround yourself with as few men in the trade as possible."[64] But again it was only advice. Scott had to confront the power of the silk industry.

Scott tried to persuade the Silk Association from its course, but failed. True, Scott's man had superior technical training, but Skinner's silk firm was, as one correspondent put it, "one of the very oldest in the country."[65] He was president of the Silk Association, and his name in the trade was "something to conjure with."[66] No one else could possibly gain the same respect from the industry. Migel observed that as section chief Skinner "will have the unqualified sympathy and assistance of the entire silk industry."[67] In the end, Skinner became head of the silk section and the Silk Assosciation's secretary accompanied him into public life.[68]

There is no reason to suspect that the dynamics of choosing a commodity chief for other sections differed in essential respects from these two examples. In every case the WIB had to comply with the industry's desires, for without trade cooperation the section would be unable to function at all. Peek and Crawford might try to assert their authority by choosing from a select list of candidates, but the result—trade dominance—was the same. At all points the industry set the limits within which WIB officials could move. It is interesting to note, however, that Baruch for one did at least suggest that the board try to reduce the number of officials who supervised their own industries. It is easy to criticise him for not doing more to enforce this principle, but it is not clear what he could do. He was

---

[63] Peek to Scott, June 29, 1918, and Scott to Paul R. Hartman, June 25, 1918, both *ibid.*

[64] Baruch to Scott, June 29, 1918, *ibid.*

[65] Horace B. Cheney to Scott, July 8, 1918, *ibid.*

[66] Paul R. Hartman to Scott, June 24, 1918, *ibid.*

[67] Migel to Scott, August 1, 1918, *ibid.*

[68] Ramsay Peugnet (silk association secretary) to Scott, July 13, 1918, to Major Alfred Wendt, August 3, 1918, and to Scott, December 16, 1918, all *ibid.*

hardly in a position to dictate to anybody, including his fellow board members. His power extended only to the point where someone opposed it.

Baruch was neither fully informed of all activities in his less than coherent organization, nor able adequately to assess this information even when apprised. Technical skill was concentrated along the outer edges of the WIB, within the commodity sections. This had important consequences for the distribution of authority within the organization, for it meant that much of the daily decision-making affecting industry took place here through close consultation between industrial representatives and the various section heads. Decisions occurred, in other words, where the territory of the board and of industry overlapped, beyond the reach of central officials. Baruch and the men in the center were generalists, after all, and were at a severe disadvantage in arguing against commodity chiefs and their associates in private industry, who had a monopoly of current information. Indeed, the success of the whole enterprise from the point of view of Baruch and the central officials was due to the willingness of the commodity chiefs to place the needs of the whole war effort over the desires of a single industry. But if the commodity chief became a lobbyist for his industry (in conjunction with his former colleagues) there was little the board could do about it. Even the section chiefs depended upon industry for personnel, information, and administrative tools. It is true that the chairman's office held the greatest concentration of formal power in the WIB, but the board's extremities and ultimately industry itself held the far greater power of managerial capacity and technical expertise.

Both managerial and technical abilities were to be found among section personnel, but among the commodity chiefs themselves the managerial tone seems to have been predominant. Technical competence alone was not sufficient to win the commodity chief the confidence of his industry, as John Scott learned with regard to the silk industry. It had to be balanced with reputation, prestige, and acquaintance with the industry's leading figures. As politician and diplomat, the commodity chief supervised meetings, mediated between military officers and business representatives, won over friends for the board, and tried to pacify its enemies. The WIB needed the persuasive, likeable salesman who was sensitive to compromise, human feelings, and status; able to move through the delicate web of personalities and interest groups which linked business, government, and the military services. Walter Robbins, chief of manufactured electrical products, included among his qualifications for an assistant, "executive experience," "initiative," and "attractive presence."[69] Charles MacDowell of the chemical division searched in December 1917 for "a man with plenty of punch, of

[69]R. K. Sheppard to Walter Robbins, June 4, 1918, RG 61, File 21A–A1, box 10. Robbins had asked Sheppard, who was chairman of the electrical manufacturing industry's war service committee, to suggest some names. See Sheppard to Robbins, March 25, 1918, and Robbins to Sheppard, March 28, 1918, both *ibid.*

pleasing personality—and one who can work with others."[70] John Fahey recommended Everett Morss for the board's priorities committee less because he had a good grasp of the wire, cable, and electrical heating industry than because he had been active in civic associations such as the Boston Chamber of Commerce, and therefore had "rather a broad and liberal view of things," and because he had been "successful in handling men and getting on with them."[71] Morss ultimately became chief of the board's wire and cable section. Arch Shaw recommended Thomas E. Donnelly for the pulp and paper section because in addition to being head of the largest printing business in the country he was a "very keen student of business affairs. Able executive. Active in public work. Excellent in conducting conferences."[72] Of course, although a managerial tone prevailed among the commodity sections, its technocrats still believed themselves to be superior in specialized knowledge to the military officers with whom they dealt, and worthy of deference in matters affecting the industry they supervised.

Remarkably few formal attempts were made to deal with the conflict of interest problem. The general sentiment among businessmen held that it was really no problem at all, except for the need to appease public sentiment. The board passed a resolution in June requiring all its members to declare their interests,[73] but other than this rather perfunctory and generally meaningless step each man adapted to the situation as he saw fit. Whether a man formally resigned from his company or from his posts in various industry organizations was entirely up to him. George Peek was reluctant to drop his connections with his industry's trade group, and did so finally only because the trade association itself asked him to for purposes of internal reorganization.[74] Clearly, though, there was a trend toward more formal, regularized, and extensive procedures as the war progressed. A letter Charles K. Leith received from Alexander Legge when he joined the board's mica section in June could never have been written several months earlier. Legge informed him that "it is understood that you have professional and financial connections with certain mineral industries and that if at any time any of your recommendations should affect these industries and connections you will make them known to the Board at the time the recommendations are made."[75] It is not clear what Legge could or would say to Dunn and Skinner.

[70]MacDowell to Howard F. Chappell, December 20, 1917, *ibid.*

[71]John Fahey to Edwin Parker, October 9, 1917, RG 61, File 21A-A1, box 17.

[72]Shaw to Baruch, May 6, 1918, RG 61, File 21A-A1, box 19.

[73]Michael D. Reagan, "Serving Two Masters: Problems in the Employment of Dollar-a-Year and Without Compensation Personnel" (Ph.D. dissertation, Princeton University, 1959), p. 17.

[74]Peek to C. S. Brantingham, December 11, 1917, and Peek to G. A. Ranney, March 30, 1918, *Peek Papers.*

[75]Legge to Leith, June 5, 1918, RG 61, File 21A-A3, box 29.

Of course nobody investigated to ensure that Leith or others complied with this kind of directive. Walter Robbins of the electrical equipment section refused to pass on contracts that involved his own company,[76] and other men made their own kind of separate peace. The board also made gestures in the direction of refusing to take on men who remained on company payrolls, but there is no way to be sure that a man was not being compensated by his industry while in Washington, and every reason to suspect that most were. Toward the end of the war the board ultimately began to give its section staffs salaries of two to three thousand dollars a year when some personnel requested small salaries to help them with the extra living costs they encountered in Washington. But this occurred more at the assistant level than among the commodity chiefs themselves, where the dollar-a-year principle held sway. Baruch, of course, hoped every administrator could come to Washington on a dollar-a-year basis so he could trumpet the great patriotism of American businessmen.[77]

WIB members demonstrated a high tolerance for the fusion of private and public interests. Commodity chiefs might shed their formal memberships in specific trade groups, and they might avoid passing on decisions involving their own companies, but they could not ignore the needs of their industry. Indeed to protect and stabilize their industries was one of their central functions. In the course of their evolution, trade groups and commodity sections became interlocked. Regardless of how individual commodity sections specifically interacted with their industries, all of them shared a common dependence on their business clientele. Everett Morss, whom the board had in mind as chairman of the nonferrous tube section in April 1918, would not even consider the position unless he could be assured that he had the assistance of Henry Elton, vice president of the American Brass Company. When Elton became chairman of the brass manufac-

---

[76] Minutes of Clearance Committee Meeting, March 22, 1918, RG 61, File 1-C2, box 77.

[77] Charles K. Leith received a salary of $4,000 a year. The section chiefs in Stout's leather division received between $200 and $250 per month. See Martin to Alex Legge, July 23, 1918, and "Record of Outgoing Mail from April 1, 1918," Commissioner of Finished Products, both in RG 61, File 21A-A2, box 86. Charles Hanch of automotive products wrote Peek after a month in Washington: "I find that the cost of living in Washington is very much greater than the cost in South Bend and a salary allowance to partly cover the difference, would surely be very acceptable." Hanch to Peek, August 1, 1918, RG 61, File 21A-A2, box 47. Hanch was given $200 per month. See the addendum to Hanch to Peek, August 1, 1918, RG 61, File 21A-A2, box 47. Also see Charles Stout to Emmet Crawford, May 9, 1918, RG 61, File 21A-A2, box 96. In an effort to strengthen the WIB's dollar-a-year image Alex Legge asked Peek if he could not persuade Stout to have some of his men forgo their stipends from the quartermaster's department when they joined the board in May. "I understand that General Goethals has insisted upon a salary but we are not insistent on people accepting salaries in this organization. . . ." Legge to Peek, October 18, 1918, RG 61, File 21A-A2, box 47.

turers committee, Morss established a WIB section and cooperated with Elton's committee to the end of the war.[78] Henry Evans, president of a number of private insurance companies and chairman of the advisory commission to the fire prevention section, attended meetings of the fire prevention section and received reports on all section business. So powerful was Evans in the life of this section that its chief felt unable even to discuss the section's dissolution at the end of the war without his permission. "May I have the authority to take up with Mr. Peek and through him with Mr. Baruch the question of the immediate discontinuance of the work of this Section?"[79] This kind of question dramatically clarifies the power relationship between the commodity section and the industry it supervised. While not every commodity chief was a prisoner of his business constituency in quite this way, every one of them relied heavily upon powerful business groups in the course of their work. Administrative necessity alone encouraged commodity chiefs to hand over problems for solution to industry itself. Just as possession of specialized knowledge helped gain recognition for the WIB among traditional public organizations, so private industry's wealth of information gave it a large role in decision-making in the WIB. The WIB was a clearing house for the application of private knowledge for a combination of private and public purposes.

THE COMMODITY SECTIONS AND THE PROTECTION OF BUSINESS INTERESTS

When the chief of the fire prevention section asked the insurance executive for permission to disband his segment of the WIB, his chief goal was to avoid taking any step that would hurt the insurance interests. The implication of his question was that had the industry decided it was not a good idea to discuss the section's immediate dissolution, then the section chief would have put off the matter to another time. Some industry spokesmen were remarkably explicit about regarding a berth in the WIB's commodity organization as a protective device. To have a WIB man in Washington reduced the chances of arbitrary government actions and offered a pipeline to better sources of information. The industry would have a better opportunity to shape the directives that reached it. Joining the WIB coalition afforded an industry a good opportunity to develop a collective strategy. In the final analysis, it offered access to public sanctions and the tools of public planning which could be used for private purposes.

[78]"Report on Non-Ferrous Tube," Morss to Peek, May 27, 1918, RG 61, File 21A–A1, box 14; Minutes of a meeting with the brass and copper manufacturers, August 29, 1918, RG 61, File 21A–A4, box 258; Morss to Baruch, August 28, 1918, RG 61, File 21A–A4, box 258.

[79]W. H. Merrill to Henry Evans, November 11, 1918, RG 61, File 21A–A2, box 88.

Take the case of the locomotive crane section. By the summer of 1917 some men in the industry had become apprehensive lest the expanding war program play havoc with the industry's production (probably Allied) schedules. Alexander C. Brown of the Brown Hoisting Machinery Company of Cleveland spearheaded the drive for some kind of coherent approach to the situation. Brown was young (32 in 1917), well educated (Yale and the Case School of Applied Science), and was active in the Cleveland business community; he spent considerable time sounding out other members of the trade before taking his case to the WIB in October 1917. He then pointed out the dangers to both industry and government "if the problems were decided without a careful survey of the situation, or if they were left undecided."[80] His brief must have had effect for Robert Brookings soon asked him to join Brookings's "official family" in the finished products division.[81] In effect, Brown had invited himself to Washington, gaining a connection with a war board which he hoped would strengthen his private quest for order and stability in the crane industry. Whether the cause for instability was of prewar or immediate origins, the result was the same.

Brown organized his Washington office in early November, assuming he could get by with three or four days a week in Washington. But as the tempo of the war progressed and the industry became more harassed with growing demands, Brown had to find himself some assistants and devote himself to Washington work on a full time basis.[82]

Brown had come to Washington in October on behalf of the locomotive crane committee, and he relied upon it throughout his administration. He informed its chairman that "this Section was formed for the purpose of assisting the Government and the War Industries of the country to obtain their requirements in cranes and, at the same time, to accomplish the result without upsetting the crane industry to any greater extent than necessary."[83] Brown strove to strike a balance between government orders on the one hand and industrial capacity on the other, and he devoted himself to securing information on government requirements.

As of the end of November Brown's surveys showed that only twenty per cent of the industry's regular production was required to fill the government's anticipated needs.[84] It is true that these estimates were constantly revised upwards, but as of November the industry was obviously in no danger of being

[80] Brown to Peek, April 4, 1918, RG 61, File 21A-A1, box 9. Brown describes in this letter the origins of his Washington work.

[81] Brookings to Brown, November 9, 1917, ibid.

[82] Brown to Peek, April 4, 1918, ibid.

[83] Brown to Sheldon Cary, February 19, 1918, RG 61, File 21A-A3, box 19.

[84] Brown to Brookings, November 27, December 4, 11, and 28, 1917, RG 61, File 21A-A1, box 9.

overwhelmed, as far as Brown could see. Thus Brown and the crane industry had not come to Washington with proof that the industry required immediate coordination because of a threatened shortage. What Brown was concerned about, and what he had persuaded the WIB to become concerned about, was the possibility that a shortage might indeed occur at some future date and that some kind of investigation ought to be undertaken in anticipation of that possibility. Brown realized he had a far greater chance of getting the information he needed from the military services and the industry as a government official than as a private businessman. Private shipbuilders, for instance, would be reluctant to give out purchasing information to a supplier, just as other crane manufacturers might refuse to share selling information with their competitors. Brown's official position, however, gave him a certain leverage in the matter. He sent a letter to 130 shipbuilding companies and to 500 domestic crane producers to discover anticipated needs. He struggled, moreover, to obtain priority requests for the crane industry and to speed up delivery of the materials they required for production.[85] Brown had effectively employed the threat of a future crane shortage to win the ear of Washington officials in October, and he continued to follow this tactic in courting special favors for his industry with the military services: to persuade them to avoid regular competitive bidding, and to yield up classified information. According to the official statement creating the commodity organization, a shortage was supposed to be the *sine qua non* for creation of a commodity section. Faced with a shortage, so the argument ran, the government obviously had to relent on formalities and extend to an industry all the aid it possibly could. A shortage was the green light for assumption of extraordinary power by a commodity chief. While military purchasers were reluctant to forget competitive bidding and eager to search for low prices, Brown argued that such shortsighted actions only encouraged the very condition the WIB's crane section was trying to prevent. Military officials regarded Brown's claims with skepticism and given the kinds of estimates which Brown himself actually possessed, their skepticism was justified.[86] Brown believed he served the war effort best by vigorously representing the locomotive crane producers on whose behalf he had come to Washington in the first place.

The hide, leather, and leather goods division provides another good illustration of an industry's perception of the WIB as a protective haven. Originally, the old supplies committee had handled the leather interests, and the remnants of this committee had found a place in Brookings's finished products division after the breakup of the cooperative committees. During the War Department's winter reorganization, however, the supplies committee, including its hide and leather

---

[85] Brown to Brookings, January 26, February 16, and March 19, 1918, all *ibid.*

[86] For the debate between Brown and army buyers over shortages, see "Minutes of Meeting of Crane Section, June 21st, 1918," RG 61, File 1–C2, box 81.

component, moved into the quartermaster's department. The decision to do this was apparently based on the committee's reading of where power would rest in wartime Washington. In subsequent months the industry increased its representation and expanded its subcommittees. Charles F. Stout, president of a Philadelphia leather concern, and vice president of the Tanner's Council, took control of the department's hide and leather control board.[87] By the end of March Stout had become disillusioned with the War Department and recommended that the WIB create a branch for hide and leather control. The object of such an agency, he informed the board, would be "an intelligent and comprehensive regulation which will preserve the healthy status of the industry."[88] Stout now believed that his chief enemy was the military supply system itself. At the same time, the Tanner's Council pressed the board for "a plan to control prices under Governmental authority."[89] Responding to the industry's demand for greater coordination, the board sanctioned the transfer of the hide and leather units, an action regarded by the industry as "a step in the right direction."[90] "The Hide and Leather Control Board," commented a trade paper, "acting under the Quartermaster General's Department exclusively has not accomplished the objects desired."[91] What the trade paper referred to was the fact that the jurisdiction offered by one department had not been sufficiently wide to offer the industry the protective power it required. It needed a more general vantage point to coordinate all aspects of the trade. It had guessed incorrectly about the War Department, for after March 4 the future seemed to lie with the WIB.

The industry wanted access to greater power to protect itself, but it justified the move by the contribution that its own salvation would make to the war effort. "To my mind," wrote Stout to Edwin F. Gay of the United States Shipping Board, "it is vital that our economic interests be protected by governmental control of our hide and leather market."[92] Stout remained a staunch advocate of central coordination. "When all these departments can sit down as one Board around the same table," he observed, "they can work out their conclusions infinitely better than if there is any conflicting measure brought in by dividing the Board."[93] Originally Stout had been asked to Washington specifically to supervise leather and keep an eye on the shoe and harness business, but he had disagreed with this fragmented approach. He recalled, ". . . The way I saw

[87]*Shoe and Leather Reporter* 129 (March 7, 1918): 34.

[88]Stout to Peek, March 28, 1918, RG 61, File 1–A6, box 44.

[89]V. A. Wallin (president of the tanners' council) to Baruch, March 29, 1918, RG 61, File 21A–A4, box 706.

[90]"New Position for C. F. C. Stout," *Hide and Leather* 55 (March 30, 1918): 7.

[91]*Ibid.*

[92]Stout to Gay, April 12, 1918, RG 61, File 21A–A4, box 709.

[93]Stout to Legge and Peek, April 19, 1918, RG 61, File 21A–A1, box 11.

it, it was a great big proposition; that the whole tanning industry should be represented in the Government; that it was one of the most important of the industries. . . ."[94] It was this sentiment which ultimately propelled Stout to the WIB.

The creation of the fire protection section offers an extreme example of the use of the WIB organization for protective purposes. In this case WIB officials yielded to the importunings of an industry which did not legitimately belong to the commodity section organization in the first place. Private insurance interests initiated the scheme for this section in reaction to rumors of a federally-sponsored insurance program for plants engaged in war work. Henry Evans, president of a number of insurance companies and chairman of the insurance fire prevention committee of the chamber of commerce, and John R. Freeman, another insurance executive, visited Washington together to speak with treasury officials against such a government program of fire insurance. Evans also reminded Baruch, a personal friend, that the president's March letter was sufficiently broad to permit creation of a section in the WIB to deal with the whole question of fire hazards in plants engaged in war production. To do this would place this phase of the government's insurance program firmly in the hands of private interests. As a result of a meeting with a number of federal officials, insurance company executives drew up a plan which resulted in the WIB's fire protection section, administered by the insurance companies themselves. The section strove to reduce fire producing hazards and to recommend improvements which would reduce the number of claims made upon them. According to Evans, the insurance men were "merely good citizens having knowledge of a certain kind that we are putting at the disposal of the Government, and all idea of profit or loss to the insurance companies is put out of consideration."[95] Despite intraindustry squabbling and considerable tension over settling upon a suitable section chief, the insurance men were, as George Peek observed in April 1918, "very happy over the way the thing is lined up."[96] And with good reason. The willingness of Baruch, Peek, and other WIB officials to receive them into their public organization saved them from a serious federal intrusion into the insurance business.

The commodity sections were crucial segments of the WIB. They made recommendations on prices and priorities and had chief responsibility for administering central decisions on these issues when they touched their particular industries. Yet given the nature of their origins and the recruitment and ideology of their personnel, they could hardly be called efficient tools of centralized

[94] Minutes of a meeting with the Chestnut Extract Manufacturers, undated, RG 61, File 21A–A1, box 2.

[95] Evans offers the details in Evans to Colonel House, July 3, 1918, Edward M. House Papers, Yale University, New Haven, Conn.

[96] Peek to W. Butterworth, April 9, 1918, RG 61, File 21A–A1, box 11.

planning. Industry itself predominated in shaping these segments of the board's structure, and industry's needs largely determined the content of their actions. The section chiefs tried to develop some independence by playing military representatives and trade delegations off against each other, much as the board tried to do as a whole on another level. At the same time, it was difficult for a commodity chief to forget his allegiance to the trade when crucial conflicts arose with the military services.[97] The very logic of the commodity chief's position made him dependent upon and anxious about trade opinion. Certainly advice from Baruch or Peek or any other of the WIB's core executives meant far less to him than sentiment within the industry itself.

What the central WIB administration had done was simply to create a variation of an "imperial bureaucratic system," to borrow a phrase from Gordon Tullock.[98] In this kind of system the central authority does not so much try to enforce decisions as simply to appoint administrators of similar background whom it can trust, and then hope for the best. Such a system provides freedom from stultifying central directives, and a great opportunity for flexibility, but "it is not really an organizational system at all. It is a system for voluntary cooperation, but with little actual cooperation implied."[99] The system only works insofar as local administrators and the central administration share common values. In this case the basis of agreement throughout the entire WIB organization was the belief that industry deserved the very best protection and support the government could give it while it mobilized its resources for war.

RESOURCES AND CONVERSION: THE REGIONAL ORGANIZATION OF INDUSTRY

Throughout its career the WIB confronted values and organizational habits antithetical to its basic orientation. The passage of section 3 and Woodrow Wilson's aversion to a munitions ministry illustrate different aspects of this challenge as it existed in the political system; the method of army purchasing through the bureaus exemplifies its counterpart in the military system. Opposition was evident within the economy as well. The board subscribed to nationalizing, centralizing trends. It wanted businessmen to group themselves on a nationwide basis along commodity lines. Forming cartels throughout the entire industrial economy was the logical goal, a trend that would find its organizational reflection in

---

[97] See Alexander Brown's pleas to military buyers not to drive too hard a bargain with the crane manufacturers. Things had not gone well in the relations between the two sides, and Brown "said a question of considerable tact entered into the matter and that the problem of salesmanship could be emphasized more strongly than ever." Minutes of a meeting of the crane section, July 31, 1918, RG 61, File 1–C2, box 81.

[98] Gordon Tullock, *The Politics of Bureaucracy* (Washington, D.C.: Public Affairs Press, 1965), p. 170.

[99] *Ibid.*, p. 171.

a reordered military structure and the WIB's commodity sections. The oligopolistic and monopolistic parts of the economy provided the models for this development. But there were areas of economic life which still clung to a local or regional orientation, and they could not be ignored. Ultimately the board was forced to sanction an impulse within its commodity section structure which ran counter to its fundamental direction. The resources and conversion section established in the latter part of May 1918 symbolizes the persistence of an ideology of localism, decentralization, and regionalism that opposed the Washington centralizers during the mobilization.

The idea of economic decentralization and fragmentation attracted Josephus Daniels as a measure to counter the monopolizing of war supplies by a few giant firms, and his interest appears to have been the immediate stimulus for adding the resources and conversion section to the WIB. In a visit to Cleveland in April 1918, Daniels spoke with local businessman Charles A. Otis about a scheme to distribute war work to smaller manufacturers so as to help them through the war. This appealed to Daniels's feelings for the little man, and he asked Baruch to investigate the possibilities of the plan for the navy's purchasing organization. Baruch was not enthusiastic. "The great difficulty about the distribution of work among smaller manufacturers is the difficulty of getting the work done, and placing the responsibility for the work and delivery." He did point out, however, that the board had urged "a number of firms to consolidate" and distribute orders among themselves, but this, of course, was not exactly what Daniels had in mind.[100] In any case, Baruch acceded to Daniels's request. "Baruch has turned me loose to organize the country into districts as we have had under consideration so long," George Peek wrote a friend in early May.[101] And it was highly appropriate that Peek should be handed the assignment, for as Peek interpreted R and C, this would continue and expand the task which had brought him to Washington in the first place: heading off unwarranted plant expansion and saving nonessential industry from harm.

At the suggestion of Colonel Guy E. Tripp, former chairman of the Westinghouse Company and presently chief of the ordnance department's production division, the War Department had already decentralized some of its purchasing activities by locating ordnance headquarters in ten major industrial centers: Pittsburgh, Cleveland, Rochester, Boston, New Haven, Detroit, Chicago, New York and Philadelphia. As it turned out, the resources and conversion section complemented Tripp's scheme.[102]

[100]Baruch to Daniels, May 3, 1918, RG 61, File 21A-A4, box 727; Daniels to Baruch, April 27, 1918, *ibid.*

[101]Peek to L. B. Reed, May 11, 1918, *Peek Papers; WIB Minutes*, May 28, 1918.

[102]"Ten Munitions Districts Established," *American Machinist* 48 (March 28, 1918): 539–40; *New York Times*, March 4, 1918; James W. Fesler, "Areas for Industrial Mobilization, 1917–1938," *Public Administration Review* 1 (Winter 1941): 149–66.

To administer the regional organization program Peek called on Charles A. Otis of Cleveland, an interesting figure and typical of a significant type of business executive drawn to war work in Washington. Born into an old, established Cleveland family in 1868, Otis pursued the path of many an upper class youth through Andover and Yale and then to the traditional grand tour upon graduation. In the meantime, like the members of other "eastern establishments," he also had a fling in the West.[103] After traveling through Europe and being suitably impressed with the military prowess and general efficiency of the German state, he tried Columbia Law School for a year and then entered the steel brokerage business in Cleveland, where he took full advantage of the contacts his father had accumulated as president of the Otis Steel Company. When Otis Steel accompanied other small firms into the great maw of United States Steel in 1901, Otis followed his contacts to the world of finance. He bought a seat on the New York Stock Exchange and helped to found the Cleveland Stock Exchange, becoming closely associated with the J. P. Morgan Company in the process. Morgan sent many underwriting projects Otis's way; and Otis represented Morgan interests in various industrial reorganizations in Ohio. Active in the Cleveland business community, Otis became a newspaper owner, opponent of the reform mayor, Tom L. Johnson, and president of the Cleveland Chamber of Commerce in 1916 and 1917.[104]

Like members of urban elites elsewhere, Otis joined the preparedness movement and on April 4, 1917, accepted appointment to the mayor's advisory war board to plan Cleveland's war activities.[105] Meanwhile, he had already involved himself in a scheme to rationalize Allied war production in the Cleveland area. Responding to the increase in war orders after 1914 and their desire to avoid cross-hauling and unnecessary train shipments, Cleveland manufacturers divided northern Ohio into a number of districts and subregions to coordinate production for the whole area. Otis, who identified very strongly with this idea, wanted to extend the concept across the entire country. That spring and winter Otis accompanied other business-innovators to Washington to "sell" his particular proposal. As with the others, Otis sought out his own group of personal contacts. He talked with Cleveland friends like Benedict Crowell, then a major in the ordnance department, and business associates like Edward Stettinius of the War Department, whom Otis had known as a buyer at J. P. Morgan's. He also spoke with the WIB people, including Baruch, Legge, and Peek.[106]

[103] Edward G. White, *The Eastern Establishment and the Western Experience, the West of Frederic Remington, Theodore Roosevelt, and Owen Wister* (New Haven: Yale University Press, 1968).

[104] Charles Otis, *Here I Am: A Rambling Account of the Exciting Times of Yesteryear* (Cleveland, Ohio: Buehler Printcraft Corporation, 1951).

[105] William G. Rose, *Cleveland, the Making of a City* (Cleveland, Ohio: World Publishing Co., 1950), pp. 749, 761.

[106] Otis, *Here I Am*, pp. 122–23; "Statement of Chas. A. Otis," *Baruch Papers*.

In the meantime, the Cleveland manufacturers refined their collective strategy. They organized themselves into eight subregions with the eight regional chairmen forming the district's executive committee. The industries in each region divided along commodity lines, and the business leaders in charge constituted the executive committee for their region. The entire operation was sustained by voluntary contributions from the industries involved.[107]

Otis's own persistence, combined with some of the thinking and events already described, brought him to Washington in May as chief of resources and conversion. For administrative purposes, Otis and Peek divided the country into 19 (later 21) industrial regions, dividing the regions in turn along the lines of the Cleveland model. Consistent with emphasis on the scheme's local, decentralized nature, leading business associations in the major industrial center of each region provided the leadership, initiative, and staff, with the association's president serving as Otis's regional advisor. As it turned out, local chambers of commerce became most heavily involved, partly because both Otis and Peek were predisposed toward them, partly because they were the best organized national organization, and partly because the chamber's federated structure perfectly matched the regional vision. Peek had worked with the chamber before the war and then as the WIB's industrial representative. Otis had been both a local president and a national director. "The only real organization everywhere, or most everywhere," affirmed Otis, "is the chamber of commerce. That is usually the place where the business men of the community give themselves to community organization."[108] Some competition among business groups developed for predominance in the community,[109] but on the whole this segment of the plan seems to have gone fairly smoothly.

Otis directed his regional advisors to cooperate with the ordnance district officers and generally assist industries in conversion to war work. As in the case of other parts of the WIB structure, resources and conversion did not gain an altogether friendly welcome from military representatives. The local ordnance officer was naturally suspicious of the purposes of local business organizations and their cries for contracts, and reluctant to disturb established business ties. He did not want to distribute his business among several small concerns when he already had a large, reliable contractor in hand. Moreover, official regulations said only that he should "disseminate the manufacture of war material through as large a number of contractors as possible, if, and when, it can be done without any sacrifice of the prime consideration of production."[110]

---

[107]"The Cleveland War Industries Commission Plan," undated, RG 40, File 77452; also attached to Otis to George S. Oliver, June 3, 1918, RG 61, File 21A-A3, box 36.

[108]"Statement of Chas. A. Otis," *Baruch Papers*.

[109]Otis recalled that the Chicago Manufacturers Association resented the intrusion of Otis's organizational efforts; see *ibid.*

[110]Major Hayden Eames to Cincinnati District Ordnance Office, August 2, 1918, RG 61, File 21A-A3, box 36.

Peek and Hugh Johnson tried to ensure continued cooperation, and Tripp asked his men to place their orders with "small shops, who find their nonessential business drying up," and to "influence a beneficial distribution of subcontracts by Prime Contractors. . . . These small items are important," he stressed, "and though they will entail a large amount of detail work and perhaps in many cases more work then [sic] the actual dollars and cents involved appear to warrant, they may nevertheless prove to be important factors in preserving general industrial solvency."[111]

The keystone of Otis's administration both in recruiting regional advisors and in deciding which business concerns should be encouraged to undertake production of war goods was "personal relations."[112] For Otis, "personal acquaintanceship" was the secret to business success.[113] It was certainly true in his own case, of course. His whole career rested on strategic personal contacts. Hardly just a business technique, this was a way of life for Otis. Social success at parties and conventions or in the local chamber of commerce was more important to Otis than mastery of complex organizational or technical detail. Otis considered Herbert Hoover, for example, "the strict type of businessman, very nice but never particularly friendly."[114] Hoover did not know how to merchandize himself effectively. Otis sought men like himself to take charge of his various regions, men active in community affairs who were friendly and worked well with people. While Otis employed the rhetoric of bureaucratic organization, he thought in terms of a network of personalities bound together in good fellowship. In promoting his regional organization he emphasized the advantages of "personal contact and the personal knowledge of affairs" his men could offer.[115]

Otis was a natural enthusiast. Lured on by grand visions of national business organization, he called for an end to mutual antagonism among various business associations, and for friendly cooperation for the sake of the whole business community. He aimed for "the consolidation of every possible organization in every spot in America."[116] "It is plain that the whole story is to develop the business of this country as though it were one enormous concern with its various departments."[117] By his rhetoric America itself would be transformed into one vast chamber of commerce.

Consistent with this principle of business amalgamation, Otis pressured the WIB to let him coordinate his work with the chamber of commerce's war

[111] Brigadier General Guy E. Tripp, *Memorandum to Ordnance Chiefs*, September 13, 1918, *ibid.*

[112] "Statement of Chas. A. Otis," *Baruch Papers.*

[113] *Ibid.*

[114] Otis, *Here I Am*, p. 165.

[115] Otis to Colonel W. A. Starrett, September 27, 1918, RG 61, File 21A–A2, box 202.

[116] "Statement of Chas A. Otis," *Baruch Papers.*

[117] Address of Charles A. Otis, June 14, 1918, RG 61, File 21A–A2, box 202.

service organization. The scheme which he and Peek had outlined in May specifically stated that Otis's section should not interfere with these committees, but did suggest that it could "supplement the general plan of securing the cooperation of industry."[118] Otis wanted the chamber's WIB representative, Henry Manss, located in his office to obtain better coordination. "It is my opinion that everything done today to bring together various business organizations," Otis told Baruch, "will be to the quick development of efficiency in cooperation with the government agencies."[119] Otis argued that resources and conversion could inform the national trade associations with a more precise, local viewpoint. Baruch had no objections to this, and Otis and Manss, both old Yale grads, enjoyed each other's company in Washington until the armistice.

A protective theme ran through all Otis's passionate appeals for business unity. In the course of winning friends and influencing people, Otis promised all his audiences that "the policy of the departments of our government is to do everything that is possible to maintain the financial and industrial structure of our country...."[120] In practice, this protectionist theme was double-edged. On the one hand it implied that Otis and his men would encourage the military departments to make more effort to find qualified suppliers. Some regional advisors suggested, for example, that the ordnance department display their requirements at the district offices so as to educate local contractors to their needs.[121] At the same time, Otis tried very hard to prevent unwarranted plant expansion and to encourage conversion only in instances where it could be undertaken successfully. He wanted "to keep the poor fellow out and get the good ones in." He tried to discriminate between the new supplier who could produce, and the one who could only promise. "As I saw my position," he recalled, "it was to find out if that man, temperamentally, organizationally, and as to location, transportation, power, housing, and the rest of the things that go into the development of an industry, would ever be able, during a rational period that we were thinking the war might last, to get into business; and if he was not, not to give the poor devil encouragement and get him tangled up with something that he could not go through with. I thought my job just as important to the industry of the country to keep them in a sane condition of mind and not to undertake something that I could see could not be done as it was to get a concern into a job."[122]

[118] Peek to Otis, May 27, 1918, *ibid.*

[119] Otis to Baruch, September 6, 1918, *ibid.*; Otis to W. E. Guylee, August 23, 1918, RG 61, File 11A–A1, box 1145; Legge to Otis, September 7, 1918, RG 61, File 21A–A2; Legge to Baruch, September 7, 1918, RG 61, File 21A–A2, box 202; Otis to Edwin C. Gibbs, September 14, 1918, RG 61, File 21A–A4, box 1573.

[120] Address of Charles A. Otis, June 14, 1918, RG 61, File 21A–A2, box 202.

[121] See, for example, Bradford D. Pierce, Jr. [regional advisor, region no. 2 (Bridgeport, Conn.)], to Otis, August 22, 1918, *ibid.*

[122] "Statement of Chas. A. Otis," *Baruch Papers.*

Otis was involved in some nice calculations here. Most of his advice was obviously guesswork because he had no better access to military requirements than other WIB members. He relied essentially on what his regional advisors could tell him about the applicant who presented himself in his Washington office. The man's fate could turn on a word from Otis's contacts in specific districts, on the trust and faith he had in his regional advisors. The very personal, whimsical, and arbitrary nature of the arrangements was open to grave abuse. Prejudice could intervene anywhere along the communication network, and no controls existed to check it. It is not too much to suppose that the supplicant in Washington could be stigmatized by a negative voice from a competitor back home who wanted the market to himself, or from an oligopoly presently content with the distribution of market power. Whether Otis himself felt expansion was necessary or foolish depended solely on his personal estimation, based on a usually inadequate supply of information.

Ultimately, Otis's section rested on economic regionalism and metropolitanism. His organization reflected and stimulated a regional industrial self-consciousness which had already been aroused by the flood of Allied munitions orders after 1914. Like other sections of the WIB, resources and conversion incorporated and expanded ongoing experiments in industrial organization and control, Otis's own Cleveland experience being the chief model in this case. The impulse for community economic development, spearheaded by local business leaders, underlay the regional, localist orientation. In a manner reminiscent of battles for railroads in the mid-nineteenth century, regions and urban centers fought for their share of war contracts and turned the resources and conversion branch of the WIB into a series of regional lobbies. They gained a route of access by cooperation with Otis's office on the one hand and with district ordnance offices on the other.

The manufacturers of St. Paul, Minnesota, for example, decided in October 1917, "to pool their interests and attempt to secure Government contracts," and established "a Washington soliciting force" financed by the membership for this purpose. The chairman of the group joined Otis in July, using the same Washington office and staff. The old regional lobby was now magically transformed into the St. Paul War Industries Board and touted as "the balance wheel governing the machinery of wartime production" in the region (no. 16).[123] The Milwaukee County Council of Defense set up a department of manufacturers in June 1917 under the direction of August H. Vogel, an active member of the business community and president of the Pfister and Vogel Leather Company. The department endeavored to coordinate the city's war industries, to distribute any business overflow in the county, to maintain records of plant capacity, and

[123]"Report Covering the Activities of Region Sixteen, Resources and Conversion Section, War Industries Board," December 2, 1918, attached to D. R. Catton to Otis, December 4, 1918, RG 61, File 21A–A2, box 212.

to prevent labor unrest. To obtain maximum war business the department set up an industrial bureau in Washington, seeking advance notice of government requirements and every opportunity to direct contracts to Milwaukee industry. Otis called on Vogel to administer region number 17 centering on Milwaukee. Vogel resigned as chairman of the Milwaukee lobby to become a dollar-a-year man with the WIB organization, and the department of manufacturers selected a new chairman, but provided Vogel with his former secretary.[124] When Dallas businessman Louis Lipsitz received Otis's call in June 1918, he obtained the assistance of the Buy It Made in Texas Association, which loaned him its chief executive officer and office staff. This promotional outfit adopted a more suitable name for a quasi-official body and became the Associated Industries of Texas. It then formed a war industries department which later became the executive body of region number 18 in the resources and conversion network.[125]

Otis appears to have helped rationalize a chain of regional lobbies in resources and conversion, lobbies which of course provided a formidable obstacle to his idea of shaping America into a gigantic business federation. War encouraged the rhetoric of unity, uniformity, and giant organization, but it could not suddenly overcome the reality of regionalism, localism, and diversity. But Otis, who had once been part of an aggressive locally-orientated business group and now part of the core of Washington nationalizers, seemed to understand all this. He accepted regional, local aggressiveness as part of the business game. In fact, he rather enjoyed the challenge of confronting the claims of local chambers of commerce and regional representatives for a greater share of the wartime bonanza. He readily accepted the fact that each regional advisor was a boomer for his area. He admitted after the war that, "in nearly every instance, while the regional adviser [sic] was working for industry in his region, it was only natural and proper. He was trying to sell his region to me to sell to the Army."[126] Otis remained confident that he could charm his men out of unrealistic claims.

The economic impact of resources and conversion, or even the part it played in industrial mobilization, is difficult to measure. Some conversions were made under its auspices, and if the reports of the advisors themselves can be trusted, some small manufacturers did receive aid.[127] Yet in retrospect it seems clear that resources and conversion had little impact on the WIB's central operations and

[124] August H. Vogel to Otis, November 19, 1918, RG 61, File 21A–A2, box 213.

[125] "Report of Louis Lipsitz, Regional Advisor Resources and Conversion Section War Industries Board Region No. 18," December 6, 1918, *ibid.*

[126] "Statement of Chas. A. Otis," *Baruch Papers.*

[127] For a sample list, see "Partial List of Industrial Conversions Report No. 1," July 6, 1918, RG 61, File 21A–A4, box 727. The clay and pottery products industries, war casualties par excellence, greeted the formation of R and C enthusiastically. See Waldon Fawcett, "War-Time Help for the Clay Products Industry," *Brick and Clay Record* 52 (June 18, 1918): 1126–27; and "Industry Will Be Organized for War Production," *Pottery, Glass, and Brass Salesman* 17 (June 13, 1918): 20.

never became more than the sum of its parts. It never developed a high degree of central coordination and coherence. While it may have provided a useful protective function in sustaining small business through the latter part of the war, its contribution to significant industrial production is obscure. This rested in the hands of that big business elite originally represented on the cooperative committees of industry, which subsequently managed to maintain close cooperation with the WIB despite the passage of section 3 of the food and fuel act.

That an extensive regional program for industrial mobilization found its way into a segment of the WIB, which was based upon nationally organized commodity groups, exemplifies the ambiguities in the WIB's program. Since it was composed of a collection of semi-independent experiments in economic organization, the WIB's administrative system reflected a wide diversity of business schemes, from Baruch's elitist dream of centralized, civilian control to Otis's euphoric plans for local business prosperity. It also reflected a wide diversity of organizational styles, from the highly personal, informal approach of Baruch and Otis to the bureaucratic direction favored by Walter Gifford and demanded by the exigencies of politics and the imperatives of war.

The WIB never overcame its diversity to win centralized, autonomous power. Throughout its history it rested uneasily on a series of compromises between business and military, private and public groups. Nor was the measure of state power it did amass necessarily antithetical to the ambitions of those industries it was supposed to regulate. On the contrary, under the mounting strains of war various business spokesmen began to search for a coordinating public agency to provide them with the kind of administrative environment they required to design programs for industrial prosperity or industrial survival. Only a state agency possessed the public credibility necessary to permit the required merger of business and government and the inevitable confusion between private and public interest. Public spokesmen described at length the controls which protected the public from private business groups. In fact, these very groups partially defined the public interest through the WIB's commodity sections. The WIB's effectiveness as a public symbol helped protect private businessmen from traditional political pressures while the board's ineffectiveness as a bureaucratic power saved them from undue intrusion by the state.

CHAPTER 7

PRIORITIES ADMINISTRATION

According to the final report of the War Industries Board, "What came to be known as the priority system was destined to become the most characteristic feature of the whole scheme of wartime supervision over the industrial forces." Once established, priorities left no room for chance or favoritism. "The flow of materials had to be directed, to every extent possible, from one central authority whose eye was everywhere."[1] In later years, Bernard Baruch emphasized that priority administration lay at the heart of the WIB experience. On it "depended the allocation of men, money, materials and all other resources on the basis of their use toward the quickest winning of the war."[2] Priority offered power. "With priority control established, conservation programs could be enforced, rationing programs and curtailment could be made effective, necessary new undertakings could be materially encouraged; the regulations of the Board became enforceable, and that small minority, whose tendency to disobey rules which an overwhelming majority were ready to follow, could be brought into line without unreasonable delays."[3] Priority was, to quote Baruch, "the iron fist in the velvet glove."[4]

As with so many postwar effusions about the WIB's extraordinary achievements, rhetoric and reality diverged at crucial points; experience and dreams merged in the nostalgic afterglow. It is true that government intervention in

---

[1] Richard H. Hippelheuser, ed., *American Industry in the War: A Report of the War Industries Board, March 1921* (New York: Prentice-Hall, 1941), p. 47.

[2] Bernard M. Baruch, "Address on Economic Mobilization at Army War College, February 12, 1924," Bernard M. Baruch Papers, Princeton University, Princeton, N.J. (cited hereafter as *Baruch Papers*), Public Papers, Vol. 1.

[3] Hippelheuser, *American Industry in the War*, p. 47.

[4] Bernard M. Baruch, "Address on Economic Mobilization before Corps of Cadets, West Point, May 4, 1929," Public Papers of Bernard M. Baruch, Vol. 1, *Baruch Papers*.

production and distribution was one of the most serious departures from capital-istic orthodoxy brought about by the war emergency, and it is true, too, that priority was a significant function of the WIB organization. But nevertheless, the kind of received opinion quoted above does not fully capture all sides of the WIB's priorities program. In this area, as in so many others, campaigns for coherence and order achieved their greatest triumphs only after the sounds of the actual battles had faded away. What we must emphasize, therefore, are those aspects of the WIB experience which place the priorities administration in better historical perspective. What the WIB men lose in being denied a total victory, they gain from our fuller appreciation of the forces they struggled to overcome.

An analysis of priorities administration highlights several notable features of the WIB experiment. For one thing, the program's tentative, groping quality usefully qualifies the image of systematic integration which pervades final re-ports and traditional secondary descriptions. Similarly, the degree of continuous development and the obvious influence strategically placed businessmen and lawyers had on it helps further to qualify the popular impression that Bernard Baruch essentially designed the WIB program himself, and that his chairmanship fundamentally transformed the nature of America's economic mobilization. In-deed, the formation and administration of priority policy illustrates once again both the structural limits on the power of the WIB and its chairman, and the ambiguity of a public policy administered by private business groups.

A discussion of priorities administration is important, too, for what it re-veals about the broader goals of businessmen in government. The corporate vision of Baruch and the central administrators is evident, as is their commit-ment to a method of voluntary business-government cooperation which favored informal, friendly persuasion over public, arbitrary regulation. But equally evi-dent is the fact that the cooperative method did not prove effective in every case. Businessmen in government could not always convince industrial leaders that their own self-interest or the interest of the general mobilization program demanded attention to the WIB's definition of pressing war needs or cooperation in its projected response. And while in theory this kind of impasse should have signaled quick intervention by an iron fist, in fact, it summoned forth the muted sounds of the velvet glove.

The far-reaching implications of delegated presidential authority and the practical significance of decentralized administration are also evident in the evo-lution of priorities policy and need to be noted. Until he appointed Baruch to the WIB chairmanship and enlarged the tools of priority planning, President Wilson exercised a meaningful control over the whole process. But once he officially delegated his authority to Baruch and the WIB in March, he assumed an essentially passive role in this policy area, for he remained true to his habit of relying upon the judgment and actions of trusted lieutenants. Indeed Wilson's formalistic approach to administration reinforced the centrifugal force of events themselves, and our attention is directed to the daily negotiations at the periphery of war government where public plans and private interests most directly intersected.

PROBLEMS, METHODS, AIMS

Baruch and his colleagues on the WIB simply backed into priorities administration. The Advisory Commission offered general pronouncements about eliminating nonwar needs in the spring of 1917, the General Munitions Board established a primitive scheme of classification, and in the winter of 1917 WIB officials half hoped to inaugurate cutbacks in nonessential industries. But administrative confusion and general business resistance overwhelmed their vague sentiments about maximizing war production. Priority policies were slow in coming, and opportunistic and haphazard when they came. Once steel and copper prices were stabilized in September, some intervention into the distribution process was inevitable, and Lovett issued the first priority order "on steel" on September 25, 1917. He therewith laid out the administrative structure for priority functions, but only two other priority circulars followed in the next nine months.

The tentativeness of these early months reflects a number of general conditions about the WIB: its continuous struggle for survival in the fall and winter, its generally chaotic industrial policy, and its basic legal insecurity—a characteristic which acted like a creeping paralysis on Judge Lovett. Lovett was too acutely aware of the precarious nature of his decisions to embark on an aggressive campaign, and even while his WIB colleagues might not share his legal qualms, they too refused to proclaim plans they could not enforce. Three weeks before Lovett issued the steel circular, he advised the chairman of the WIB to discuss the legal problem with the secretary of war, the secretary of the navy and the Council of National Defense. "Of course there is no law compelling manufacturers and others to obey the circular;" he wrote, "therefore, you will observe that it takes the form merely of a *request*. I believe, however, the approval of the Secretary of War, the Secretary of the Navy and Council of National Defense will practically secure compliance with the same. I attach particular importance to the approval of the Secretary of War and Secretary of the Navy because of the powers they have under existing statutes to place orders for war material, etc., and compel preferential filling of the same."[5]

Concern for the legality, or illegality, of priority circulars was constant throughout the war. The WIB's legal section grew weary warning officials of the

---

[5] Lovett to Frank Scott, August 31, 1917, Record Group 61, Records of the War Industries Board, Federal Records Center, Suitland, Md. (cited hereafter as RG 61), File 1A-2, box 31.

dangers involved. "It would seem," concluded one memorandum, "that so intricate a system of priority, involving much inconvenience and financial sacrifice on the part of a large number of producers and manufacturers, could hardly be effectively administered without a firm legal basis."[6] In the opinion of the legal section, the priorities committee, as a subordinate body of the Council of National Defense, lacked this security. As Lovett recognized, the committee derived its authority solely from the approval given its requests by the secretaries of the army and the navy and the fleet corporation. The army, navy, and fleet corporation had statutory authority to place obligatory orders for the production of supplies, and by standing behind priority requests, they gave the priority committee the benefit of their power.[7]

In addition to the problem of enforcement, there was another weakness in the developing administration. Because a priority order from the priority committee was in fact only a request, compliance opened up the cooperative firm to charges of breach of contract from a third party. If a manufacturer displaced a private contract for a government order, he was liable for the loss sustained. The legal section recommended that the committee seek legislation so that it might issue compulsory orders. These would protect producers from liability or damages. As it stood, "The unwilling producer will receive a compulsory order and thus be protected from liability for damages. The willing producer remains exposed to loss."[8]

Thus when the priorities committee and the WIB sought greater power in this field they did so for two reasons. Without additional legislation, the committee doubted whether it could assure immunity from suits to persons who complied with its regulations. Second, the existing system was inadequate to control production and distribution across that wide range of essential commodities with

---

[6] "Memorandum for Consideration of Priority Committee," undated, RG 61, File 21A–A4, box 1163.

[7] In his article, "The War Industries Board, 1917–1918: A Study in Industrial Mobilization," *American Political Science Review* 34 (August 1940): 655–84, Randall B. Kester offers a very good, if brief, discussion of the WIB's legal status, and the statutes the board could draw upon.

[8] Legal Committee, "The Priority Problem and Its Solution," undated, RG 61, File 2D–A1, box 213. We can assume that under these circumstances some business firms would be reluctant to comply with priority requests. For example, Westinghouse Electric Company refused to observe a priority certificate until the customer being displaced agreed to the procedure. See *History* of the Priorities Committee of the War Industries Board, Vol. D, p. 471, RG 61, File 7 – B2, box 844. AT&T executives debated the same problem. "The question continually arising in our minds," commented a vice president, "is whether or not it would be proper for us to give people doing business for the Government preferential service." W. C. Kingsbury to Walter Gifford, December 17, 1917, Record Group 62, Records of the Council of National Defense, Federal Records Center, Suitland, Md. (cited hereafter as RG 62), File 2–A1, box 28.

which the committee gradually had to deal. Except for the limited class of goods covered by the food and fuel act, the committee had no direct means of control. As the legal section wrote in May 1918, "It has been necessary, therefore, to rely to a large extent upon the voluntary cooperation of manufacturers and other persons engaged in the industries concerned." Certainly the committee had indirect ways of enforcement, through presidential power over transportation, imports, exports, and fuel, and the administration's right to place compulsory orders. But in the opinion of the board's legal section such control often proved a clumsy and inadequate expedient: "It enables the President to exercise drastic control over certain industries but leaves him practically powerless with regard to other industries, control of which may be no less vital."[9] In one case, some lumber dealers were found using the names of government officials to secure priority certificates unfairly, but the judge advocate general, the Justice Department and the WIB's legal section all agreed that no law existed by which to prosecute such abuse.[10]

The struggle to establish an independent, powerful WIB during the fall and winter touched on priorities as well as purchasing and price fixing. The United States Chamber of Commerce directed special attention to this topic in its condemnation of the current organization in November 1917. It demanded vigorous control in all areas of mobilization to end confusion. "With the right to commandeer in the War and Navy Departments, the Shipping Board and the Food Administration; with no division of industries into essential and non-essential; with no program of supplying essential industries with labor and material, or of assisting non-essential business during the war . . . there is not an effective machinery for priority in production and distribution." The chamber was distressed at the scattered efforts of various government agencies. Under these conditions, the position of nonessential industries was especially precarious. "Undue hardship is inevitable unless comprehensive plans are promptly put into effect to determine non-essential business, and to bring about when advisable gradual contraction in the industries affected. Effort should be made to permit practical operation of these industries so that a nucleus may remain for development after the war, and in producing war essentials, the available facilities of non-essential industries should be used."[11]

[9] Legal Section to Judge Parker, May 18, 1918, RG 61, File 2D–A1, box 213. The board resolved in June "that everything possible must be done in order to protect manufacturers and others from liability of this kind." Minutes of a meeting of the War Industries Board (cited hereafter as *WIB Minutes*) in RG 61, File 1–C1, boxes 72–74, June 18, 1918.

[10] Legal Section to Mr. Powell, May 11, 1918, RG 61, File 2D–A1, box 209.

[11] R. G. Rhett to Wilson, November 15, 1917, Woodrow Wilson Papers, Library of Congress, Washington, D.C. (cited hereafter as *Wilson Papers*). For similar complaints and solutions, see A. N. Holcombe, "New Problems of Governmental Efficiency," *American*

The WIB worked toward these ends, but how could it convince the military services that centralization in a civilian agency was a worthwhile step? By the beginning of 1918, confusion in military procurement had become so acute that the services themselves consented to a verbal agreement permitting the priorities committee to adjust cases between the two departments. Officials in the military purchasing bureaus were first to try to resolve conflicts among themselves, and if this proved impossible, they were to allow the priorities committee to step in. Further appeal could then be made to the army and navy members of the WIB; if that failed, the priorities commissioner would make the final determination.[12]

The priorities committee wanted to go further than this and take initiative away from the military bureaus altogether. The committee argued that it alone could comprehend the total picture. Too often contractors worked on orders for a number of competing agencies without the full knowledge of even the departments involved. There was obviously "grave danger of delay" in such circumstances.[13] The priorities committee also sought full commandeering authority, a move which would naturally increase its power. The committee wrote this stipulation into priority circular no. 3 to be issued in January 1918, but the military balked, and the navy struck it out. Not until September 1918 did the WIB become officially responsible for coordinating all commandeering orders, although board officials arranged an informal agreement with the services in June.[14]

In March 1918, the president made the WIB responsible for "the determination, wherever necessary, of priorities of production and of delivery and of the proportions of any given article to be made immediately accessible to the several purchasing agencies when the supply of that article is insufficient, either temporarily or permanently."[15] The existing priorities organization would assist the WIB chairman in production priorities, while in priorities of delivery he would now have in addition to the existing organization the advice of the official

---

Economic Review 13 (March 1918): 271–80. Holcombe concluded that as of December 1917 "the Priority Committee of the War Industries Board is not much more than an adjunct to certain bureaus of the War Department."

[12] Admiral F. F. Fletcher, "Memorandum for the Secretary of the Navy," January 11, 1918, RG 61, File 21A–A4, box 1157. Also see General Palmer E. Pierce to Newton Baker, *ibid.*; and *WIB Minutes*, December 7, 1917.

[13] Edwin Parker to Fletcher, January 23, 1918, RG 61, File 7–B3, box 846; *WIB Minutes*, December 13, 1917.

[14] Edwin Parker to Fletcher, January 23, 1918, RG 61, File 7–B3, box 846; *WIB Minutes*, June 13 and 27, 1918; Baruch to Wilson, August 30, 1918 and Wilson to Baker *et al.*, September 3, 1918, both in RG 61, File 21–A3, box 4.

[15] Wilson to Baruch, March 4, 1918, *Wilson Papers.*

representatives of the food administration, the fuel administration, the railway administration, the shipping board and the war trade board. Army and navy representatives were subsequently added to this roster. The new priorities board was created on March 27. Edwin Parker was named chairman, and the other members were: Bernard M. Baruch, ex officio member; Brigadier General Palmer E. Pierce of the army; Rear Admiral F. F. Fletcher of the navy; Edward Chambers, director of traffic of the railroad administration; Charles R. Piez, vice president and general manager of the emergency fleet corporation, representing the United States Shipping Board as well; Clarence M. Woolley, representing the war trade board; P. B. Noyes, representing the fuel administration; C. W. Merrill, representing the food administration; and Alexander Legge, representing the Allied purchasing commission.[16]

That the priorities administration made real gains at this point there can be no doubt. It generated fifty-six circulars in the next six months, tightened restrictions on nonwar industries, tried to cut back unnecessary building construction, and developed a preference list, which in its final form covered seventy-three industries and seven thousand separate plants considered of exceptional importance to the war effort. On July 8, 1918, the board received 1,901 priority applications, the highest number in a single day, and on September 30, 1918, it issued the greatest number of certificates in a single day, 2,121.[17]

Despite this considerable achievement, the development of priorities administration was saddled with fundamental problems that no amount of improvised ingenuity could overcome, even after March 4, 1918. Aside from the legal burden already discussed, the WIB's priority policy suffered from inadequate control over transportation facilities. When President Wilson showed William McAdoo the draft of Baruch's March 4 mandate, McAdoo demanded that no one tamper with his authority as director of the railroad administration. He apparently interpreted Wilson's charge to the WIB to direct priority of deliveries as an encroachment on his prerogatives. Wilson suggested by his reply, however, that he was actually aiming less to end the independent jurisdiction of the railroad administration than to ensure coordination of exports and imports by setting up a liaison among the WIB, the shipping board and the war trade board. As long as Wilson's goal was simply to establish a committee "which will determine the question of priority of deliveries as between the various governmental depart-

---

[16] For the service appointments, see *WIB Minutes*, March 6, 1918. See also "Outline of Priorities Organization," March 13, 1918, RG 61, File 7–B3, box 846. Brigadier General Hugh Johnson later replaced Pierce as the army's representative; T. F. Whitmarsh later replaced C. W. Merrill as food administration representative; and Felix Frankfurter later came to the board to represent the War Labor Policies Board. See "Outline of Priorities Organization," *ibid.*

[17] Hippelheuser, *American Industry in the War*, pp. 54, 56–57, 58.

ments and agencies but will not determine priorities of transportation," McAdoo was satisfied.[18] Wilson may have had a more centralized and integrated plan in mind, but the fact of the matter is that power to determine priorities of transportation remained with the railroad administration and forced the WIB into a dependency relationship with this agency. The WIB could proclaim priority in delivery, and it could threaten to cut off transportation to plants that refused to accept priority certificates, but without cooperation from the railroad administration such decisions were mere abstractions. Insufficient numbers of rail cars or inadequate administration in its sister agency could render a large area of the WIB's priorities program hollow indeed. Discussing industrial control in the postwar years, Charles K. Foster, the vice chairman of the priorities committee, recalled that the board "had more trouble with the railroads than anything else—getting cars for coal and everything."[19] In October 1918, he observed: "The Priorities Committee was blamed, I think, for a good many things that it did not do, because everyone in the United States believed that we had entire charge of the transportation problem, which was the real problem at that time. But as a matter of fact, the Priorities Committee has never had anything to do with the handling of transportation."[20]

The second major handicap in priorities was also administrative in nature. To put it simply, the WIB proclaimed a program of restrictions beyond its organizational capacities to achieve. It could neither administer nor enforce the schemes envisaged by its leading spokesmen. By the summer of 1918 the priorities division faced a total breakdown as its staff grappled with the growing load of paperwork; in addition, various industries balked at the centralized control the board seemed to have in mind; and commodity chiefs continued their demand for the ultimate voice in all decisions affecting their particular commodities. In response to these administrative and political pressures, the board inaugurated a scheme of automatic priorities with circular no. 4 on July 1, 1918, and lost through administration what it had gained in policy.[21]

[18] McAdoo to Wilson, March 1, 1918, *Wilson Papers*; McAdoo to Wilson, February 27, 1918, William Gibbs McAdoo Papers, Library of Congress, Washington, D.C.; and Wilson to McAdoo, February 28, 1918, *Wilson Papers*.

[19] "Conference with Mr. Charles K. Foster, former Vice-Chairman, Priorities Committee, War Industries Board," undated, Record Group 179, Records of the War Production Board, War Resources Board Documents, National Archives, Washington, D.C.

[20] Charles K. Foster, "Priorities Regulations Are Now Being Modified," *Bulletin of the Merchants' Association* 7 (October 21, 1918): 1–3, enclosed as exhibit #16, in History of the Priorities Committee, RG 61, File 7–B1, box 843. Edwin Parker made the same point in Parker to Baruch, March 25, 1918, RG 61, File 12G–A1, box 1376.

[21] Charles Brantingham, spokesman for the National Implement and Vehicle Association, called for less centralized administration later in June. See Brantingham to George Peek and George Armsby, June 22, 1918, RG 61, File 21A–A4, box 1163. See the steel

All priority orders had been divided into five general classes: Class AA, Class A, Class B, Class C, and Class D, with subdivisions of the first three indicated by suffix numbers, as, for example, Classes AA - 1, AA - 2, etc. An order for steel, for example, which had a priority certificate of AA-1 classification attached gave its holder prior claim on a steel producer and a wide advantage over a competing manufacturer who could acquire for his order a certificate in only the Class B range. It was now decided that certain of the lower classes should gain priority ratings without application for a written priority certificate. Within the automatic classification it would be sufficient to attach an affidavit to the order setting forth the facts of the case and naming the war use for which the materials were needed. The automatic rating extended only to an A-4, leaving those above it under the exclusive jurisdiction of the priorities committee. In effect, priority circular no. 4 permitted a manufacturer to rate his own orders, just as the preference list provided a key against which industrial suppliers could rate the applications they received. No better example exists of the bureaucratic free enterprise that marked industrial mobilization under the WIB than this dimension of the priorities program. The drain on central control was also intensified by an exception made to the general rule of excluding ratings above A-4 from automatic priority. Orders for the War and Navy Departments and the emergency fleet corporation falling within Class A could be automatically rated A-5 by one of their officials and this would stand unless rerated by the express order of the priorities committee.[22]

In keeping with its diffuse administrative program, the board placed administrative responsibility for distribution for key commodities on the producers themselves either through a single company, as in the case of a monopoly market like aluminum (Aluminum Company of America) and nickel (International Nickel), or through a trade association, as in the case of farm implements and the steel industry. The farm implement committee of the National Implement and Vehicle Association scrutinized priority requests for farm implements from November 1917 forward. As the arrangements in this particular case became systematized, the Chicago-based farm implements committee analyzed priority applications before they arrived in Washington. The priorities committee made similar agreements with the American Railway Association's subcommittee on materials and supplies, and the pig tin and wire rope committees of the American Iron and Steel Institute. The distribution committee of the American Iron

industry's fight against a centralized licensing system in Melvin I. Urofsky, *Big Steel and the Wilson Administration* (Columbus: Ohio State University Press, 1969), pp. 187–90. Also see Foster, "Priorities Regulations Are Now Being Modified."

[22] Hippelheuser, *American Industry in the War*, pp. 53, 55; and C. J. Stark, *Priority in War Industry*, exhibit #20, in History of the Priorities Committee, RG 61, File 7–B1, box 843.

and Steel Institute cooperated closely with the WIB's steel administrator and priorities division in the distribution of iron and steel products. *Iron Age* commented in late July 1918: "The priority system, while there was a little danger at one time of its eventually breaking down of its own weight, should not be harshly criticized, for it was a necessary resort in the early stages of the war preparation. The wisdom was in providing for its gradual dismissal as the emergency passed and the steady grind was entered upon."[23]

Cooperation quieted the committee's fears about the weakness of its legal base and generally facilitated administration in every way. George Armsby who, in addition to working on the priorities committee, was also chief of the section on tin, wrote a senior executive of the American Sheet and Tin Plate Company:

How do you feel at this time regarding the advisability of working out a systematic plan to administer priority on tin plate? I know you rather opposed our doing so when the matter was up last Fall, but I am inclined to think that at this time we are in a position to aid the manufacturers of tin plate through priority, and assist in diverting the supply of tin plate to more essential uses. Before taking any steps in this matter, however, I would like to have the benefit of your views.[24]

It would have been an impossible situation if powerful industrial figures stood absolutely opposed to the committee's work. Regulations had to be planned in conference with them. When relations did work smoothly, Edwin Parker could write, as he did in the case of machine tools: "We are ... grateful to note that the manufacturers are appreciative of our efforts, and are realizing that instead of an impediment, the work of priorities will prove helpful to them."[25]

Administration by industrial trade groups encouraged a close relationship between the priorities committee and the WIB's section chiefs. It was only natural that the section chief should be consulted in any plans for curtailing or increasing an industry's production. He was the best source of information on the state of the industry, and more aware than the priorities board as to what the industry could or could not do. The large roles that some commodity chiefs

[23]"Steel Control by Producers," *Iron Age* 102 (July 18, 1918): 161. For a list of trade associations–priorities administrators, see History of the Priorities Committee from February 16, 1918, to March 15, 1918, Vol. L, RG 61, File 7–B1, box 843. For the specifics of the Implement and Vehicle Association plan see Edwin Parker to Charles Brantingham, October 11, 1918, George N. Peek Papers, Western Historical Manuscript Collection, University of Missouri, Columbia, Mo.

[24]George Armsby to J. I. Andrews, March 16, 1918, in History of the Priorities Committee from March 16, 1918, to April 10, 1918, Vol. C, RG 61, File 7–B1, box 842.

[25]Parker to Baruch, March 25, 1918, RG 61, File 12G–A1, box 1376. The industry was enthusiastic; see "How the Priority Board Works," *American Machinist* 48 (January 3, 1918): 7–8.

took in priorities administration tended to undermine the priorities committee's general scheme altogether. As brass section chief, for example, Everett Morss permitted no shipment of any materials on automatic ratings without his specific permission. "If this authority is reposed in all Commodity Sections," queried the priorities committee's secretary, "does it [not] now absolutely nullify automatic ratings and even tend to destroy the value of priority certificates?"[26] Not all commodity chiefs exercised Morrs's extensive control, but all of them played an important part and all sought to augment their administrative powers. The WIB's most centralizing function could not escape the decentralizing bias inherent in its own administrative structure.

Private industrial organization also entered into priorities administration through the board's commodity sections. Priority certificates administered by the section chief for the priorities committee were ultimately referred to a trade committee for practical administration. When the Aluminum Company of America applied to the priorities committee for its copper requirements, Everett Morss replied that the copper producers' committee would take care of its inquiry.[27] Pope Yeatman, chief of the nonferrous metal section, wrote to the general agent of the International Nickel Company: "Although in many cases priority certificates will be issued, I shall expect you to look after the distribution much more closely than we can, for the reason that, even with priority orders, some other companies may be in greater need of the nickel than those having priority orders . . . and this you are better informed of than we ourselves."[28] In other words, the section chief yielded to International Nickel the ultimate decision in the distribution of that commodity.

One of the most potentially explosive questions the WIB and priorities committee had to face was the problem of nonessential industry. By establishing priority and preference lists, the WIB declared in effect that some industries and purposes were less essential to the war program than others. The needs of these groups would have to give way to more important concerns. The board was well aware, of course, that to move recklessly in this direction entailed great economic and political risks. Any abrupt move to slash industries would endanger the entire spirit of patriotic cooperation upon which the WIB was so dependent. As a result, the administration and the WIB moved very cautiously: the board had constantly to reassure businessmen that it did not contemplate any drastic measures. In May 1918, it decided to enlist the services of the United States Chamber of Commerce to issue a bulletin explaining the board's policy in this area. Edwin Parker sent the chamber an authorized statement for general

[26] Maurice Hirsh to Edwin Parker, August 8, 1918, RG 61, File 21A–A4, box 258.

[27] Everett Morss to Aluminum Company of America, December 22, 1917, RG 61, File 21A–A4, box 165.

[28] Yeatman to William B. Lawson, August 5, 1918, RG 61, File 21A–A4, box 945.

circulation, inviting the chamber to make any supplementary statement if it wished. He wrote: "We do not wish to unnecessarily alarm industries or the public. Our policy is to disturb legitimate business as little as possible, but this note of warning in the form of a conservative statement is, we are convinced, due to the industries of the country."[29] War bulletin no. 35 explained the preference list system to businessmen, and urged nonwar industries, as the WIB preferred to call them, to plan their activities with curtailment in mind, and to convert their facilities, where possible, "for purposes entitled to preference treatment, thus reducing the damage to industry to a minimum, and at the same time relieve some of the war industries that are staggering under the abnormal burdens which they are carrying."[30]

A committee set up under presidential direction studied the whole question of nonessential industry in the spring, and reported in June 1918 that "no industry should be absolutely prohibited and destroyed."[31] As a result of this report an industrial adjustment committee of the priorities board came into being. It included Clarence M. Woolley, of the war trade board, as chairman; T. F. Whitmarsh of the food administration; Edward Chambers of the railroad administration; Edwin F. Gay of the shipping board; Felix Frankfurter of the war labor policies board; George O. May of the treasury; P. B. Noyes of the fuel administration; and Edwin B. Parker of the priorities division. According to the WIB's final report, this committee helped nonwar industries adapt to proposed curtailments.[32] As President Wilson told a worried Senator, "I can assure you that the various agencies of the Government have been going very slowly and cautiously." The action "of such agencies as the War Industries Board has been very conservative, I believe, and has been a constant subject of discussion amongst us, so that I think the best brains there are in the employment of the Government are being devoted to that subject, and the best consciences also."[33]

Pondering the conundrum of essential and nonessential industry in the summer of 1918, the *Pottery, Glass, and Brass Salesman* concluded that the only

[29]Parker to Elliot Goodwin (United States Chamber of Commerce secretary), May 16, 1918, in History of the Priorities Committee, Vol. E, RG 61, File 7–B2, box 844; see also the unsigned letter to Edwin Parker, April 30, 1918, RG 61, File 21A–A4, box 1157.

[30]Chamber of Commerce of the United States of America, "Priority Policies Affecting Industry," war bulletin no. 35, May 20, 1918, in History of the Priorities Committee, Vol. E, RG 61, File 7–B2, box 844.

[31]Hippelheuser, *American Industry in the War*, p. 59.

[32]*Ibid.*, pp. 59–60.

[33]Wilson to Senator Owen, July 23, 1918, *Wilson Papers*. According to Owen there was no such thing as a nonessential industry. "People labor to make the things they want, and the things that the people want are essential to their wants, and they have a right to gratify their desires and should not be denied because some official does not think they are essential." Owen to Wilson, September 9, 1918, *ibid.*

hope of a realistic solution lay in "close co-operation between Government officials cognizant of the country's needs and manufacturers sufficiently broad-minded to realize the importance of these needs when explained to them."[34] This, in essence, was what occurred under the priorities committee. The board gave trade representatives every opportunity to talk with the committee members and win a place for themselves on the preference list. By the end of July the priorities committee had received delegations from twenty-three industries. Included among them were representatives from the casket, corset, printers' rollers, household washing machine, and davenport bed industries. The committee was rapidly learning about the strategic importance of some of these industries.[35]

The priorities committee sought agreements with all these delegations on conservation, standardization, and curtailment policies. The general strategy was this: the priorities committee would grant a degree of preferential treatment in fuel supply or raw materials to an industry which pledged to pursue a conservation program. The ultimate goal was always to permit sufficient materials to members of an industry to keep the bulk of them alive through the war. Naturally, the committee and trade representatives disagreed on the amount of material this required, but everyone involved shared the assumption that enough should be available to permit successful adjustment to wartime conditions. In any case, the board would not act until the industry in question had been given a full hearing and every effort was made to meet its demands part way. The cement manufacturers, for example, received preferential treatment in fuel supplies by promising to curtail their production to a level sufficient to meet only direct and indirect war requirements and exceptionally important demands. The committee curtailed stove manufacturing for the last four calendar months of 1918 by 50 per cent of four-twelfths its 1917 production. It permitted the baby buggy industry to operate on 50 per cent of four-twelfths its 1917 production, and gave it Class C rating for enough metal to match stocks it had on hand, provided only discard steel was used. It afforded the gas appliance industry a certain amount of material in response to a pledge that the industry would cut at least 75 per cent of its sizes, models, and types. In many cases, standardization plans did not offer any problem in implementation, for many business leaders seized on the opportunity afforded by the war to rationalize the industry and end the confusion of a multitude of competing styles, sizes, and so on. "All this is in reality for the best interests of the trade," concluded one trade journal regarding a standardization proposal. "The number of shapes that have been

---

[34] "Essential and Non-Essential," *Pottery, Glass, and Brass Salesman* 18 (June 27, 1918): 20.

[35] For this list, see Edwin Parker to George Foster, July 22, 1918, in History of the Priorities Committee from June 18, 1918, to November 25, 1918, Vol. F, RG 61, File 7–B2, box 844.

produced and the number of decorations brought out and specially made and carried in open stock have been little short of reckless."[36]

The priorities committee intended to do what it could to help industry through the war. "It is a large part of our responsibility," said Rhodes Baker, who conducted a large number of the meetings with war service committees, "to see that the industry is not unduly disturbed and is not unduly starved, during the period. Just as much as it is part of our responsibility to see that materials are forthcoming for war purposes." But where to strike a balance? That was the problem. Baker explained further to the representatives of the wire fence industry that that industry could not be closed down entirely because the less self-contained manufacturers could not convert to another type of production. The strongly-placed firms could adapt and change, but the weaker ones would die under a rigid curtailment program.[37] Just as prices were fixed with an eye to saving as many high-cost producers as possible, so curtailment schedules were formed to underwrite less fortunately placed firms. The priorities committee would strike a bargain with the industry on the amount of material it required to keep most of its members in operation throughout the war.

THE CASE OF AUTOMOBILES

A case study of the interaction between WIB officials and the automobile industry will perhaps illustrate some of the salient aspects of the priorities function. Priorities, as we have stressed, could be employed for broadly protective purposes. But any plan to equalize burdens or to distribute scarce goods to hungry industries inevitably disturbed those private power centers destined to lose most in the WIB's overall scheme of industrial balance. To be wholly effective, then, even as a protective agency, the WIB had to subordinate aggressive challengers on behalf of its benign view of the entire industrial community. A small industry without strong organizational resources presented little problem; and success came easily over industries that had possessed little private market power in peacetime. The board could draw a fairly tight rope around it, given the proper kind of cooperation from an important supplier, such as the steel industry. But

---

[36] "A New Era in the Trade," *Pottery, Glass, and Brass Salesman* 18 (August 29, 1918): 21. Also see "Standardizing Production," *ibid.*, 18 (September 12, 1918): 20. For details of the various bargains cited, see Edwin Parker to Rhodes Baker and H. G. Phillipps, August 10, 1918, and Priorities Board to the Commodity Chiefs and Section Heads, September 24, 1918, both in History of the Priorities Committee from June 18, 1918, to November 25, 1918, Vol. F, RG 61, File 7–B2, box 844.

[37] "Meeting of the Steel Section of the War Industries Board with the Representatives of the Wire Fence Industry for the Purpose of Determining the Amount of Steel to be Allotted to the Industry," October 7, 1918, RG 61, File 18G–A1, box 2682.

what about an industry that as a private buyer wielded enormous power over a host of suppliers, and in wartime consumed an enormous amount of vital materials?

The auto industry presented just this kind of challenge. It drained off numerous supplies ranging from rubber through machine tools; it absorbed scores of skilled mechanics; and it produced in the car a symbol of peacetime leisure and luxury. Numerous munitions producers, secondary manufacturers, railroad officials, military and government personnel favored curtailment as the tempo of America's war involvement increased. As early as May 1917, locomotive producers complained about the industry's impact on the skilled labor market. Samuel Vauclain of the General Munitions Board's committee on locomotives charged: "We pay enormous wages for manufacturing things which the government and country needs in this war and permit the automobile people to pay large prices for labor and monopolize labor supply to build pleasure cars."[38]

In late October and early November 1917, rumors were rife throughout industry that Washington was about to embark upon a broad program of industrial cutbacks. The gloom deepened when Judge Lovett issued a priority order on October 27 that denied the use of open-top railroad cars for shipments of coal to eleven industries as of November 1, 1917. Detroit seemed to have special cause for alarm. Not only was it the only major industry among the eleven cited—the others included such commodities as candy, toys, and pottery—but it also learned simultaneously of a WIB order to have the steel industry divert all chrome steel from regular customers to war industry. When coupled with known hostility toward it among its competitors for skilled labor, the evidence suggested the beginning of a concerted campaign to end auto production.[39]

Those auto executives already in official positions, as well as those who happened to be in Washington on lobbying activities, reacted to the news very quickly and girded themselves for battle against the industry's enemies. A meeting which they had with WIB and military officials on October 30, however, made it clear that although government officials favored a plan for automobile cutbacks, they by no means possessed any clear strategy of implementation. Indeed, WIB officials seemed frankly embarrassed over the entire episode. Baruch and his associates, Replogle and Meyer, offered rationalizations for the steel order and received full support for their stand from the military officers present, but they argued without conviction. Howard Coffin, chairman of the Aircraft Production Board, took the initiative on the industry's behalf and overwhelmed government officials with his criticisms. He denounced the chrome order as an example of the shortsightedness in industrial mobilization which he

---

[38] "General Munitions Board, Meeting of the Committee on Locomotives," May 8, 1917, RG 61, File 1–C2, box 84.

[39] See pp. 133–34.

had personally fought against for the past two years. He lectured the board on the need to consult industry officials. How was the industry to convert to war production? How were dealerships to survive the war?

The WIB had no answers. Government officials asked Coffin to call a meeting with the manufacturers on November 2. The auto executive accepted the charge, but before leaving he gave a parting thrust:

Some of the first questions we will have to meet are unquestionably to be along the lines of the Government's accurate needs and we have got to show these men when they come here the debit and credit side of the ledger in pretty good shape. We have been trying to get the book-keeping of the War Department in shape for six months—in other words, the requirements of the Government and the capacities of the country in black and white, but our efforts have been to no avail. I should like to have the figures to show them. If they are to make this great sacrifice, there must be more than a statement along general lines. I wonder if the Priority Board knew the facts when they made this ruling. If they do, they are the first body in the City of Washington that I have found which does know it.[40]

Coffin and the representatives of the auto and accessories manufacturers concluded their subsequent meetings with a general statement that the industry was far too important to permit government interference without full consultation. To facilitate close business-government cooperation in the future, a committee was formed composed of Hugh Chalmers of the National Automobile Chamber of Commerce, A. W. Copland, representing the Motor and Accessories Association; and Ford executive John R. Lee, representing producers outside the NACC.[41]

Discontent in the auto industry was a major factor forcing the WIB to deal more systematically with the entire nonessential question in the fall and winter of 1917. It was at this time that the board summoned George Peek to Washington to head the newly-created bureau of manufacturing resources. Peek then began his abortive attempts to coordinate military requirements and private industrial capacity, hoping to attain systematic industrial conversion. In the meantime, he and other government spokesmen tried to scotch rumors of a vast curtailment program, rumors of the kind that had so disturbed the auto industry. Judge Lovett promised that he, personally, had had nothing in mind beyond the open-top order. "In other words," commented *Motor World* with some

[40]"Memorandum of Meeting in Mr. Baruch's Office, October 30, 1917," RG 61, File 21A–A1, box 2.

[41]See a report of the meeting in "Weekly Report of Automotive Products Section," H. L. Horning to Brookings, November 10, 1917, RG 61, File 21A–A2, box 46. For press reports, see "Automotive Industry Clippings," in RG 61, File 21A–A4, box 220.

relief, "there is no cloud hanging over the industry on the matter of railroad cars."[42] Both *Motor World* and the *Automobile Trade Journal* were extraordinarily pleased and in a self-congratulatory mood by the end of November. They were hopeful that in future the newly-formed auto committee could anticipate any misguided radical orders and solve any differences in the WIB's automotive products section.[43]

The WIB and the industry took the first step toward settled administrative procedures when they formalized their channel of communication through the automobile trade committee. As in the case of so many trade committees, however, the auto group was no more than a middleman between the board and powerful private producers. It could not actually commit the major manufacturers to a policy any more than it could guarantee the industry that the WIB would hold to its informal promises. It achieved little in subsequent weeks. Such a committee adhered so well to section 3 of the food bill, which passed Congress in August, that smooth administration became impossible. Productive relations required that the WIB treat not with messengers but with kings.

The WIB's own troubles in subsequent months weakened it to the point where it could not undertake an assault on Detroit, even while demands for steel accelerated. Only in March 1918 did the board feel sufficiently healthy to broach the subject once again. On the same day that Baruch became WIB chairman, some of the biggest names in the auto industry gathered in Washington for official talks. John Dodge of Dodge Brothers, John Willys of Willys-Overland, and W. C. Durant of General Motors finally made the trek to Washington. The meeting seemed to go well and concluded on a hopeful note. The manufacturers agreed to a 30 per cent reduction in passenger car production compared with their present plans for 1918, to begin July 1, 1918. They agreed further to consult the board before embarking upon future manufacturing plans for the 1918-1919 season. The industry's representatives had the agreement ratified at a NACC meeting in New York City three days later.[44]

There were a number of factors involved here which made the agreement less useful than it might appear. Howard Coffin himself had suggested in October that a reduction of production by 30 per cent was not out of the question. The natural decrease in raw materials since that time made the 30 per cent proposal

[42] "Government Changes Attitude toward Car Industry," *Motor World* 53 (November 28, 1917): 39.

[43] "The Week in Washington," *Motor World* 53 (December 5, 1917): 53-54; "No Restriction of Passenger Car Output by Government Probable," *Automobile Trade Journal* 22 (December 1, 1917): 125-26, and "The Automobile Field is Well Represented at Washington," *ibid.*, p. 126.

[44] "*Memoranda*," March 4, 1918, attached to George Peek to John Dodge *et al.*, RG 61, File 21A-A1, box 2; Peek to Palmer Pierce, March 8, 1918, *ibid.*; *New York Times*, March 8, 1918, p. 1.

far less impressive than it had been four months earlier. *Motor World* was candid enough to admit that such a reduction would have hardly any effect because nearly all major companies had already reduced their schedules. The industry seemed to believe that the 30 per cent reduction actually meant a guarantee of materials for 70 per cent regular output. They chose to interpret it as a stabilizing point for the entire industry. Daniel Willard cast further doubt on the significance of the informal agreement when he argued that according to his sources the proposed cut was based on a prospective output which contemplated a 30 per cent increase over 1917 so that real production would remain the same.[45]

As the full implications of the March agreement became evident, dissatisfaction among WIB men gave way to irritation and anger. Clearly the industry did not suffer for lack of steel. For one thing, it was rumored that Detroit had generally stocked up well in advance of threatened shortages. Willys-Overland had ten months' supply on hand, according to Washington gossip. This kind of action, however, could at least be attributed to business foresight, something which businessmen in government might even inwardly admire. But rumors that the industry had actually bought steel after the March agreement indicated complete disingenuousness on Detroit's part, and such suspicions seemed confirmed by its reluctance to submit production schedules. Relations between the board and Detroit deteriorated rapidly that spring.[46]

Such a state of mind insured an unhappy May meeting to discuss 1918-1919 production schedules. The crux of the matter was steel shortages. The board and Detroit divided over both causes and solutions. Auto spokesmen argued that inadequate transportation facilities were the central problem. The government, it claimed, could not actually ship the materials it already had on hand. So to cut back auto production under these circumstances indicated merely a failure to grapple with the larger and underlying flaw in the supply program. It was to make a scapegoat out of the innocent while letting the responsible parties go free. Industry spokesmen argued, moreover, that to make matters worse, government purchasers continued to stockpile materials with no hope of their actually being used; this further indicated a general failure of coordination in wartime Washington, a failure for which government agencies

[45] "No Startling Effect from Order to Curtail," *Motor World* 54 (March 13, 1918): 36, and "Fuel Agreement Big Benefit to Industry," *ibid.* p. 41; "Passenger Car Dealers Adding Truck and Tractors to Their Lines," *Automobile Trade Journal* 22 (April 1, 1918): 142-42A; and Minutes of the Council of National Defense and joint meetings of the council and Advisory Commission, April 1, 1918, RG 62, File 2-B1, box 104.

[46] For evidence of advanced steel buying, see "Meeting of the Distribution Committee of the American Iron and Steel Institute, May 17, 1918," attached to *WIB Minutes*, May 17, 1918. On July 2, 1918, Leonard Replogle, the board's steel administrator, stated that General Motors and Dodge were buying steel. *WIB Minutes*, July 2, 1918.

like the WIB were largely responsible. But even granting an actual steel shortage, the solution was not a passenger car cutback, it was enlarged steel capacity. "It takes little ability to get a crowd of men down and say, 'You must cease manufacturing automobiles,'" charged John Dodge, "but it takes a whole lot to speed up all the other industries." "If you will take the material that you actually need," he went on to say, "that you can use, not taking stuff and storing it up that wouldn't be shipped in five years—. . . and let us alone, we believe there will be plenty to keep us going." "I have been down here six months," added Hugh Chalmers of the NACC, "and I know that the Departments have orders, millions of dollars' worth of stuff, that can't possibly be shipped for two years. . . . The question for you and us to find out is whether the Government needs are immediate needs."

Leonard Replogle did not help the WIB case by agreeing with the auto men that indeed transportation and fuel shortages largely accounted for the present impasse in steel production. "In other words," observed John Dodge with growing impatience, "you mean to say that if the industry was supplied with transportation and fuel there would be more steel?" "Certainly," replied Replogle, "there would be enough. It would at least take care of a great portion of the commercial interests." This kind of admission came with embarrassing regularity in WIB negotiations and gave industry representatives all the ammunition they needed. The WIB was obviously aiming its wrath in the wrong direction. Build more coke ovens and blast furnaces, Dodge countered. "It appears to me that what you want is one big boss to get these departments together and shake them up and get results." This was hardly a tactful comment to make in the presence of Washington's newly emerging "industrial dictator."

The auto men were absolutely rigid and defiant. Even Baruch's personal charm could not overcome the impasse. In company with Legge, Parker, and the others, Baruch pleaded, cajoled, bluffed, and even hinted at a possible shutdown of the industry. "I know that if we've got to close the automobile industry," he said rather off-handedly at one juncture, "you will take your medicine." Government officials outlined international and national implications; relations with the Allies and with other war boards; the shipping situation; the railroad problems; and the state of the coal industry—all in an effort to educate these reluctant businessmen to the seriousness of the situation. "This is the problem as we see it," said Baruch, "you haven't seen it yet, but when you see the picture you may see it in a different slant; you might make a suggestion as to how we can turn it out." John Dort's observation was not encouraging. "I think it would be very much better to consider even dragging a bit on the Government program than to absolutely paralyze and destroy your own people here."

Seeing that the present state of mind made agreement impossible, Baruch asked the industry to appoint three men with whom the board could explain and discuss the situation in more detail. W. C. Durant agreed enthusiastically. He was very much interested in having an opportunity "to obtain the facts," doubting all the while, of course, that the WIB actually possessed any. Peek, Legge, Replogle, and Frayne met with Durant, Flanders, Willys, and Dort for further discussion. But this ploy did not work as Baruch had hoped. The subsequent meeting focused on transportation problems, not auto curtailment. The industry recommended expansion of truck production, which would have the practical effect of helping the industry maintain its production facilities and the patriotic effect of enlarging transportation capacity; WIB representatives pointed out that the industry could supply railroads with skilled mechanics and promised to serve as a liaison with the railroad administration toward that end. The admission at this meeting by both Edward Hurley of the United States Shipping Board and Edward Stettinius of the War Department that it was doubtful if auto curtailment would be wise given the state of the shipping industry, only strengthened Detroit's hand. The automobile executives left Washington with the understanding that their subcommittee would recommend a plan of action once they had received specific government requirements. It was a safe strategem, given the WIB's well-known difficulties in obtaining coherent information from the military services.[47]

Baruch and his men could only shake their heads in dismay. The industry had come to Washington ostensibly to reach an agreement about next year's production, but had gone away under no obligation whatsoever. Baruch commented pessimistically to the American Iron and Steel Institute a week or so later: "I am a little bit 'leary' of what has happened in the automobile trade. Those men came down here and made an agreement that they would not prepare for the next year's program until they had consulted with us. They just made us look foolish."[48]

WIB officials seemed of two minds in subsequent weeks. On the one hand, steel shortages and their personal anger moved them toward an arbitrary limitation of the fuel and steel supplies. Edwin Parker favored the "let's-get-tough" attitude, and at a meeting on June 18, advocated withdrawal of all preferences to the industry, save those given to manufacturers producing army trucks or otherwise engaged in legitimate war work.[49] But evidently Baruch preferred to wait and see what the industry might offer on its own accord. In the meantime,

[47] "Meeting of the War Industries Board with Representatives of the Automobile Industry for the Determination of What Action Is To Be Taken with Regard to Steel Situation, Insofar as That Industry Is Concerned," May 7, 1918, attached to *WIB Minutes*, May 7, 1918; Memorandum to Baruch, May 7, 1918, attached to *WIB Minutes*, July 9, 1918; Peek to Baruch, May 8, 1918, attached to *WIB Minutes*, May 8, 1918; *WIB Minutes*, May 7, 8, and 9, 1918.

[48] "Meeting of the Distribution Committee of the American Iron and Steel Institute, May 17, 1918," attached to *WIB Minutes*, May 17, 1918.

[49] *WIB Minutes*, June 18, 1918.

the *Automobile Trade Journal* made a realistic prediction of what the future would bring in automobile curtailment. "The probable outcome, it is believed, is that the industry will not be arbitrarily limited, but that it will be naturally limited by its inability to get all the material that it would like. . . . What curtailment there will be will not be by legislative restrictions, probably, but by inability to get raw material."[50]

On July 10, Charles Hanch, chief of the WIB's automotive products section, traveled to Detroit to sound out the manufacturers. Hanch, who had been connected with the financial end of the industry as treasurer of Studebaker Company of South Bend, Indiana, had come to Washington that month to succeed Harry L. Horning as chief of the WIB's auto section. He had not figured prominently in negotiations, though, because of his position on the periphery of both Detroit and the WIB. Like any commodity chief caught in a crossfire between his industry and the government, Hanch was in an unhappy, ambiguous position. Moreover, in this particular case, Hanch lacked a private source of personal power since he was not a major executive in peacetime. He had far less leverage to use than would have been the case had he been a well-known member of the industry. As an interpreter between public and private power, Hanch intended to tell the manufacturers "what the industry ought to do and what it will probably have to do in order to get in good with the public."[51] But he could be little more than a messenger boy, and his entrance at this stage is indicative of the deterioration rather than solidification of relations between the WIB and Detroit.

Hanch made his report to the board on July 16, and the news was not good. First, the board learned that the former automobile committee had now been dissolved because its members refused to "accept any responsibility for anything that would put their fellow members out of business."[52] Direct communications between manufacturers and the WIB had come to an end. A new committee of the NACC was now in charge, and Hugh Chalmers was its chief spokesman. He and other NACC officials accompanied Hanch to the July 16 WIB meeting. Unfortunately, as Hugh Chalmers pointed out, he was not authorized to commit the auto manufacturers to anything. Chalmers held that there was a very specific cause for the manufacturers' withdrawal at this point in the negotiations. According to him, the manufacturers had understood that the agreement to cut back by 30 per cent included a WIB guarantee for materials necessary in 70 per cent production so they could liquidate their inventories. Chalmers admitted

---

[50]"The Threatened Production Curtailment," *Automobile Trade Journal* 22 (June 1, 1918): 130.

[51]Hanch to Hugh Chalmers, July 3, 1918, RG 61, File 21A–A2, box 47.

[52]From the minutes of the meeting between Chalmers, Hanch and WIB officials on July 16, 1918, attached to *WIB Minutes*, July 16, 1918.

that the WIB had signed no binding agreement to this effect, but he claimed Replogle and Peek had promised as much in an informal way. Then the WIB had turned around and tightened up its distribution of steel through its steel division and the American Iron and Steel Institute. Chalmers insisted upon gaining time for the industry to liquidate its stocks and balance out its inventory. He dogmatically opposed any move to curtail production or to take labor away from Detroit until the industry had accomplished this task. "I think, in all fairness, that the automobile companies should be given some time to liquidate these inventories which was promised to be done. I think these inventories in dollars and cents should be submitted to Mr. Hanch as your chief and that recommendations from him ought to be made to your steel section and other sections as to what these companies can get with reference to these materials."

When Parker had informed an automobile president of the way in which manufacturers were presently accumulating materials, the manufacturer had said, "Of course we have; we would be damn fools if we hadn't." Chalmers could not wholly deny such a charge, although he claimed only a minority were guilty. Exasperation among the WIB men, particularly Edwin Parker, showed itself clearly at this meeting. As priorities commissioner, Parker was most directly affected by the issue. He was personally very angry and ready at least to threaten bold steps. The board, Parker announced after a short break in the discussion, had decided that it would assist the industry in liquidating its stock provided that "no one manufacturer shall produce any passenger automobiles exceeding 25% of what he produced in the corresponding period of 1917."

It was the strongest proposal the WIB had made to date and brought an angry response from Chalmers. "That is the beginning of the end," he exclaimed. "You may not pay any attention to what I say, but this is the most serious mistake you have made down here. . . . It is absolutely confiscation of the industry." Chalmers forecast nationwide unrest and bankruptcy for the state of Michigan. Automobiles would disappear; labor would flee Detroit; dealers would all go under. Chalmers was both indignant and defiant. The manufacturers would simply not agree to any such order, he told the board. "I am telling you this, and I think it is my business to tell you because we are not going to sit here and bow our heads. We are the third largest industry in this country, and with all the men we employ and all the obligations we have to our parts people, all the money we owe our banks, we can not surrender to this."

In fact, the WIB was not after surrender. It sought a bargain. It had offered the industry a deal whereby it would assist Detroit to get raw materials to clear out stocks if the industry would reduce its production to the specified amounts. Chalmers had balked. To try and strengthen its case, the board hoped to convince Chalmer that, given the steel shortage and WIB control, the industry could not possibly obtain required materials to close out stocks without WIB assistance. Chalmers, however, remained unpersuaded, unconvinced both about the shortage and about the control that the board exercised over the steel industry. Before Parker had gotten into his proposal, Chalmers had observed: "Well, I am inclined to think . . . several steel manufacturers are prone to look out for their old customers whose financial responsibility is beyond question and whose business will continue after this war is over." This was all too true, unfortunately, as the WIB was well aware, but nothing could be done. At the same time, too, growing steel shortages gave Chalmers an opening to argue that the WIB, despite its promise of assistance, could not in fact guarantee the industry any steel, so why should it agree to join the bargain? The manufacturers would rather take their chances on getting steel in the future than enter into such an unfavorable bargain. "The thing might break in some way; production might increase and the steel be available." "But you can't get the steel," Baruch argued, "we can't give it to you. If you would like for us to say, 'We don't want any restrictions; we will do the best we can,' we can say that, but you won't get your steel; that is all. If you simply want to go along on a hand to mouth policy, very well. We have shut down on the steel. You won't get any more one way than the other." This kind of comment no doubt relieved Chalmers considerably, for it implied that Baruch had no intention of issuing restrictions until he had gained an agreement with the industry. Moreover, as discussion proceeded Parker modified his initial proposal. He suggested that beginning July 1, no manufacturer could produce more than 25 per cent of 1917 in the coming year. This was 25 per cent of production not for the corresponding period of 1917, but for the entire period of 1917. He further offered the industry the right to take the 25 per cent in two or three months. Chalmers seemed intrigued by the idea but then raised further objections. If a man had materials on hand for 50 per cent of 1917 production, it would take him two years to clear up stocks at this 25 per cent a year restriction. This would discriminate against those who had had the foresight to stockpile. To Parker, however, foresight was simply a euphemism for hoarding and ought not to be given any kind of approval. He suggested the likelihood of government seizure of excess stocks coupled with a pooling plan to aid manufacturers to reach the 25 per cent level. Chalmers remained adamant to the end. "We are willing to take our chances. Get your 100% war program. We will take our chances of the situation in steel breaking. You are going to force a situation of starved industries in this country; you are accumulating a lot of war materials that cannot be shipped and when that is shown and the industries are killed you will find yourselves in a storm of criticism."

One would have thought that after these charges and counter-charges the parties would have broken off negotiations altogether and the WIB would have proceeded arbitrarily to curtail auto production. Instead, Hugh Johnson suggested that Chalmers find out exactly what the automobile industry required to clean out its stocks, and Chalmers hinted that he might be able to talk about 30 to 40 per cent restricted business, the original figure incorporated in the informal understanding of March. The meeting ended on a conciliatory note. Baruch, bluffing to the end, promised that the board would not discriminate against the industry despite its refusal to enter an agreement.[53]

The auto producers were in no hurry to send in their reports on the materials they needed to convert their inventories into stock, and a thoroughly frustrated Judge Parker submitted a resolution to the WIB on August 6, 1918, prohibiting all steel to the industry until they submitted the information, "that this Board may intelligently deal with the industry as a whole."[54]

Initiative remained with the industry, however, and at a meeting in Detroit on August 6, the NACC reached an agreement to make a voluntary reduction of 50 per cent of 1916 or 1917 production.[55] On August 8 Chalmers returned to Washington with the news. Chalmers was in a much better mood by now and intended to enlist the board's sympathy for the industry's latest move. "Perhaps you feel that they have been dilly-dallying along with this, but you must bear in mind, with an industry as large as this, with different elements composing its membership, it is pretty hard to harmonize these elements into an effective agreement. We have done that in this." Chalmers coupled his soft tone with an emphasis on the industry's willingness to take all the war work it could get. But it required retention of its labor force until those orders came in. To disperse labor from Detroit now would only endanger munitions production in automobile plants in the long run, and anything more than a 50 per cent reduction in automobile manufacturing would make retention of labor and facilities impossible.

Baruch and the board reciprocated Chalmers's conciliatory approach. "I want to say on behalf of myself and the Board that we are going to meet you in this is [sic] a fair spirit. Any feeling that anyone has had in the past has gone. . . . Acting for the Government, we have no feelings, and when we come quietly down to cases, we know that the automobile industry will do its share."[56]

That same day, August 8, the WIB issued a public warning to the auto industry that seemed to belie the good spirits evident in the board's private discussions with Chalmers. It called the offer of 50 per cent curtailment a "step in the right direction" but warned that the industry could not expect future

---

[53] *Ibid.*; and *WIB Minutes*, July 16, 1918.

[54] *WIB Minutes*, August 6, 1918. In the meantime market forces brought passenger car production to a low ebb and dealers were moving into trucks and farm implements. See "Your Major Business," *Motor World* 56 (August 14, 1918): 28.

[55] *WIB Minutes*, August 8, 1918.

[56] "Meeting with representatives of the National Automobile Chamber of Commerce," August 8, 1918, attached to *ibid.*

supplies of steel or rubber and other raw materials. Its best interests demanded conversion to 100 per cent war work not later than January 1, 1919, "for in no other way can you be sure of the continuance of your industry and the preservation of your organization." The board was evidently still angered at the industry's refusal to submit production schedules or to cooperate more quickly, and it stated that, "no material will be furnished to any passenger automobile manufacturer until it has filed with this Board a sworn statement embodying the information requested on July 16, coupled with an agreement to furnish this Board with such additional information from time to time as it may require."[57]

It was a tough, forceful statement with an unyielding tone out of character with the discussions that preceded its release. Several motivations were at work on the board at this point. Most important, the board could cover up its weaknesses and gain credibility with the public by taking a strong rhetorical stand. Such a statement secured the impression that the WIB had the automobile situation firmly in hand. The board also hoped that this kind of statement would impress Detroit with the seriousness of the situation and force them to at least go along with the 50 per cent agreement. Hopefully its belligerent tone would have a healthy shock value. Hugh Chalmers had apparently agreed to the statement for this latter reason, but with the understanding that he would deliver the message to industry privately. He now felt double-crossed and especially upset because the statement gave a false impression to the public that the industry was going out of business by January 1; ". . . but you and I both know," he wrote Hanch, "that that was not the intention, but it was the intention to give the manufacturers warning to take on war work."[58] The WIB had never presented Chalmers with a demand for 100 per cent curtailment in their private negotiations; Chalmers knew it, the board knew it, the public did not.

Once again the WIB received greater opposition to an impulsive press release than it had bargained for: this time from the dealership sector of the auto industry. From the outset, spokesmen for the automobile dealers had reacted hysterically over potential cutbacks, an indication of their distance from the ultimate sources of information and power in Detroit and Washington. *Motor World*, the dealers' journal, made the most extreme defense of the status quo for auto production. That every American should have the right to own a car seemed to be the essence of the journal's critique. Those who pointed out that European countries had curtailed production did not faze this journal's editors. Only the upper classes owned cars in Europe, so that indeed the automobile

---

[57]WIB to National Automobile Chamber of Commerce, August 8, 1918, attached to *WIB Minutes*, August 13, 1918. See also "What Happened in Washington about Shutting off the Industry," *Motor World* 56 (August 14, 1918): 42–43.

[58]Chalmers to Hanch, August 12, 1918, RG 61, File 21A–A2, box 47.

ought to be condemned there as a class phenomenon. But in America, everyone had a car and thus auto production was in fact a force for the democratic way of life. "America has made the motor car for the masses rather than for the classes. The American car is an uplifter of masses which is unique to our industry. . . ."[59]

Motor World, though dogmatic, was not naive. It coupled ideological rationalizations with warnings to its constituency to organize and take its case to Washington and to the American people.[60] The National Automobile Dealers' Association was formed that fall and embarked upon a campaign for voluntary conservation to show that cutbacks were unnecessary. F. W. A. Vesper, a St. Louis Buick distributor and head of the St. Louis Automobile Association, spearheaded the drive. The association allied itself with the United States Chamber of Commerce and received the support of Waddill Catchings and the chamber's war service committee organization. Typically, too, Vesper encouraged a liaison with Arch Shaw's conservation division. They inaugurated gasless Sundays and a scheme of closing service stations on specified evenings to show that the automobile industry had the national interest at heart. Like all such attempts at voluntary regulation through the conservation division, however, enforcement depended upon the ability of the trade associations to enforce informal agreements.[61]

The NADA no doubt helped create a favorable image for the auto industry, but its major service to Detroit came in response to the WIB's August prediction of 100 per cent curtailment by January 1, 1919. The association roused its members to an all-out lobbying effort, winning an audience with the board on August 16. *Motor World*, now in tune with the motives of the WIB, urged its readers to remain calm, for "when all the facts are considered, the situation is not so definite as one might believe."[62] As Vesper and the dealers soon discovered, the WIB statement was indeed more rhetoric than reality. Ironically, Baruch's play for public pressure on Detroit was partially responsible for mobilizing thousands of dealers firmly against the WIB.

Several points emerged from the August meeting between the board and thirty-five auto dealers. First, WIB officials were definitely not intent upon a

---

[59]"Is This Industry Non-Essential?" *Motor World* 53 (November 7, 1917): 10, and "Convince Washington or Be a Non-Essential," *ibid.*, pp. 36–37.

[60]See *Motor World* 53 (November 21, 1917): 11, 12, 28, 41.

[61]F. W. A. Vesper to Catchings, January 22, 1918 and other evidence of the association's conservation efforts in RG 61, File 21A–A4, box 219. Also see *Motor World* 56 (July 10, 1918): 6–7, 42, 47, (July 17, 1918), pp. 14–16, (July 24, 1918), pp. 8–9, 44, and (August 7, 1918), pp. 10–11, 37.

[62]"What Happened in Washington about Shutting off the Industry," *Motor World* 56 (August 14, 1918): 42.

100 per cent curtailment. No order had actually gone out to that effect, Baruch assured the dealers. The statement expressed a belief, not a policy. Second, in the future the board would not act without the industry's consent. The dealers derived great relief from Alexander Legge's observation: "The regulation has got to originate by the men in the business that know how and where and when it can be regulated. I don't think we can do that here, but we can start to help you do it. In all these industries the real practical solution has not been worked out by the War Industries Board, or any genius in Washington: it has been worked out by the industries themselves. People who know the business can always come to the front if there is anything to be done."

Vesper was out front to speak for the industry. He and his men wanted only enough production to "get by" and regarded 75 per cent curtailment as a workable figure. The WIB executives were sympathetic to this level but refrained from explicit promises until the manufacturers submitted all their figures. It was a gain of 25 per cent over the manufacturers' pledge of some weeks before. The board quite wisely placed upon the manufacturers the onus for its present inability to give a firm promise on a 75 per cent figure, as well as for the general bad feelings between government and the industry.[63]

The association representatives parted from the conference amicably, grateful to learn that they might expect to receive 25 per cent production, and that the WIB harbored no grievance against them. A correspondent for *Motor World* believed that through their cooperative spirit the dealers "gave the motor car industry the standing of legitimacy it has sought. . . ."[64] For its part, the WIB had made a distinct gain during this conference. Not only had it been able to play off segments of the industry against each other, but it had managed to ally itself with the dealers against the manufacturers and isolate the latter as the obstructive force.

By August 21, only GM and Dodge had failed to submit their anticipated production schedules,[65] but they must have submitted them soon thereafter, for the board and the industry finally agreed to settle the issue before the end of the month. The board, the NACC, and the NADA agreed to restrict passenger car production during the last six months of 1918 to 25 per cent of the number of cars produced during 1917. The priorities division promised preference to all manufacturers who pledged to abide by the agreement. Manufacturers were to

[63] "Meeting of the War Industries Board with Representatives of the Automobile Dealers of the United States for Consultation as to What Steps Might Be Taken to Preserve Their Organization in View of the Curtailment of the Manufacture of Automobiles," August 16, 1918, in RG 61, File 21A–A4, box 220.

[64] Ray W. Sherman, "Probability Is Dealers Will Get 25% of Cars," *Motor World* 56 (August 21, 1918):7.

[65] Jensen to George Peek, August 21, 1918, RG 61, File 21A–A2, box 47.

promise to conserve and economize on steel in every way possible; submit reports under oath on request; and release any excess stocks which the board could then reroute and redirect.[66]

The WIB had to threaten, plead, and suffer through various retreats and humiliations before it managed to get a curtailment agreement down on paper. And yet the compromise could provide no excuse for WIB exultation. It had taken far too long to accomplish. If the WIB's prognostications about steel shortages in past months were in any way accurate, it meant that this long drawn-out episode must have damaged the overall war program. Moreover, one cannot help but surmise that, as the *Trade Journal* predicted in the fall of 1917, auto curtailment depended as much upon the natural disappearance of raw materials as upon WIB regulations.[67] Some plants were already cut back to 25 per cent of 1917 production. In mid-August, for example, *Motor World* reported that the Ford Motor Company and Dodge Brothers were largely devoted to war work.[68] It is impossible to tell accurately to what extent WIB pressure actually affected the conversion process. We have every reason to believe that the industry moved in its own time, according to its own purposes and calculations of market conditions. And as it turned out, the armistice arrived before the industry actually produced its total allotment.[69]

Admittedly, a single case does not provide an adequate basis for generalizing about the WIB's priorities administration. It does, however, throw a sharp light on certain aspects of the program, and it does reflect upon the broader dimension of business-government relations under the WIB. Business administrators clearly favored persuasion to arbitrary regulation in their relationship with the auto industry. They did so for at least two reasons. On the one hand, they had little alternative. Administrative obstacles and organizational deficiencies weakened their threats and reduced their alternatives. Hugh Chalmers touched on this theme when he shoved aside Baruch's vow to cut off Detroit's steel supplies. Both Chalmers and Baruch knew that the WIB's total panoply of controls lacked

---

[66]"Restrict Passenger Car Manufacture 50 Per Cent for Remainder of Year," *Motor World* 56 (August 28, 1918): 5-6.

[67]John B. Rae comes to this conclusion in *The American Automobile: A Brief History* (Chicago: University of Chicago Press, 1965), p. 71.

[68]*Motor World* 56 (August 14, 1918): 41. Nevins and Hill note that war projects completely engaged Ford's production lines by this time. Allan Nevins and Frank Ernest Hill, *Ford: Expansion and Challenge, 1915-1933* (New York: Scribner's, 1957), p. 77.

[69]According to the automotive products section, the industry had a production allotment of 295,468 cars for the last six months of 1918. 186,178 cars were produced July through September, leaving 109,290 cars for the last quarter. See "Final Report, Automotive Products Section, WIB," undated, RG 61, File 1-D1, box 89. Also see War Industries Board, Division of Planning and Statistics, Preliminary Report on the Automobile Industry, no. 3, RG 61, File 21A-A2, box 46.

the necessary integration to assure the operation of any of its major parts. Could Baruch count on cooperation from the railroad administration to deny shipment? Could he depend upon the steel industry to deny supplies? Could he and the WIB realistically withstand the political consequences of abrupt curtailment? In practice, priorities was a series of question marks.

Baruch's actual conduct in the automobile case, on the other hand, raises yet a further question: would he have recommended arbitrary curtailment even if he had been able to make the policy stick? The evidence adduced here suggests not. Baruch and his colleagues were committed to proving that business-government cooperation could sustain a mobilization program once the state concentrated its authority and defined its policies. On one level, Baruch could argue that the debate over auto curtailment only illustrated that the state had not fulfilled its share of the bargain: it had failed to centralize all strands of the mobilization process. Yet on another level, is it not the case that this same debate showed that the WIB's commitment to proving that informal, friendly persuasion far surpassed legislative or arbitrary regulation as the optimum relationship between business and the state actually restrained its search for administrative alternatives?

In the postwar years, central business administrators could not admit either to themselves or to the public at large the extent to which the promise of voluntary business-government cooperation was not always fulfilled, or the extent to which that failure hindered the general mobilization program. As a consequence, they promoted an image of systematic integration and dictatorial power which both understated the degree of failure in their program and denied even in theory the possibility of effective business opposition.

CHAPTER 8

THE PRICE FIXING PROCESS

Price fixing and priorities both portray in microcosm several characteristics of the War Industries Board experience which deserve closer scrutiny. Attention to their evolution makes clear that although Baruch's elevation to the WIB chairmanship guaranteed the reduction of presidential intervention in administrative detail, it by no means produced an integrated system of industrial mobilization. A single individual could not even coordinate the WIB organization, let alone the total bureaucratic structure of wartime Washington. Insufficient legal authority encouraged a wide range of bargaining between the board and its business constituencies, and the concentration of expertise in the commodity sections, the lack of administrative resources, and an ideology that favored control through cooperation resulted in price and priorities programs that were less than coherent or fully centralized.

The price fixing process also illuminates the protective thrust of industrial policy under the WIB. Its evolution shows how business advisors sought government power, first, to strengthen industry through the adoption of concepts and values associated with modern corporate capitalism, and second, to maintain the country's industrial structure in anticipation of postwar trade battles. The price fixing committee, established in March 1918, also exemplifies the board's efforts to stabilize the economy in order to head off the kind of social unrest that could ultimately lead to a demand for harsh government regulations. And finally, the evolution and administration of price fixing once again demonstrates the tremendous difficulties confronting businessmen in the center of wartime Washington as they urged their colleagues in industry to accept specific WIB schemes for industrial salvation.

The search for a stable, centralized federal price policy had been central to business demands for a rationalized mobilization process. Price negotiations with steel and copper had dragged on intermittently in an uncertain, chilly atmosphere throughout the fall of 1917, and WIB men consistently prodded the administration to settle all issues associated with the price question, anxious all the while to ensure that this power did not fall into the wrong hands, and eager to place it securely in a strong, coordinating agency. Neither the WIB of July 1917 nor the reorganized board of March 1918 satisfied business advisors on this score. Internal organizational problems, military independence, and inadequate legal foundations marred both agencies. President Wilson had refused to lodge price fixing within the WIB in August, and he had not changed his mind by March. He asked the WIB to advise government purchasing bureaus on prices, but he set up a separate committee for this task. It was to be composed of the WIB chairman, the members of the board concerned with raw materials and manufactured products, the board's labor member, the Federal Trade Commission chairman, the Tariff Commission chairman, and the fuel administrator. Furthermore, the president's letter to Baruch and the passage of the Overman act in May by no means remedied the legal weakness of the board or its new committee. The act permitted the president to delegate executive powers to administrative agencies. But while everyone knew that the powers of the commander-in-chief were formidable, not everyone agreed on what in practice they legally covered. The need for specific congressional price fixing legislation remained.[1]

Wilson had a number of reasons for not lodging price fixing authority directly in the WIB. The debate over the munitions ministry had already revealed his aversion to concentrating responsibility for all industrial policy within a single emergency agency, and perhaps he believed that a degree of administrative fragmentation could counter the growth of overweening business power. He had good political reasons, moreover, to appease the antimonopoly sentiment so popular in the southern and western parts of the nation. He was sensitive, too, to the possible conflict-of-interest charge if price fixing were lodged directly in an agency so associated in the public mind with dollar-a-year men.

The very fact that prices touched the general public so directly made a price fixing committee especially vulnerable, and its integrity had to be protected at all costs. The press release accompanying the committee's formation in March underlined its "quasi-judicial" nature. The administration aimed to concoct the image of a sanctified committee devoted to the public interest. The committee,

---

[1] Wilson to Newton Baker, August 16, 1917, Newton D. Baker Papers, Library of Congress, Washington, D.C.; and Wilson to Baruch, March 4, 1918, Woodrow Wilson Papers, Library of Congress, Washington, D.C. (cited hereafter as *Wilson Papers*). A number of efforts were made in subsequent months to enlarge the committee's legal authority. See, for example, Edwin Parker to Robert Bulkley, March 18, 1918, Record Group 61, Records of the War Industries Board, Federal Records Center, Suitland, Md. (cited hereafter as RG 61), File 21A–A4, box 1147. Baruch's legal advisor, Albert Ritchie, questioned the legal scope of the president's power in Ritchie to Baruch, July 8, 1918, RG 61, File 1–A5, box 41.

ran the public announcement, was composed "of men separated so completely from industrial interests that their motives and actions in the determination of prices can be subject to no suspicion of mercenary interest."[2] Bernard Baruch underscored the public relations tone of the PFC in a typically self-congratulatory talk at the War College in 1925.

The make-up of the price-fixing committee was thoroughly satisfactory. You cannot go around and take this man or that man because in dealing with these problems there is a question of what the civilians are going to think about it and the civilian people who stay at home are much more important than we generally give them credit for, because they write to the soldiers in the field and tell them how everything is going in the home country.[3]

By the time the PFC came into public view it had gained representatives of both services, and the former governor of Virginia was added in July. Secretary Daniels insisted on giving the navy a voice in any recommendations, and Governor Stuart was placed on the committee in reaction to agricultural criticism of industrial prices. The other members of the committee included Dr. Harry A. Garfield of the fuel administration; Frank W. Taussig, chairman of the Tariff Commission and a well-known Harvard economist; Hugh Frayne, the WIB labor representative; and William J. Harris of the Federal Trade Commission. Baruch was an ex-officio member.[4]

The appointment of Robert Brookings to the chairmanship of the PFC was most appropriate, for he possessed several characteristics which made him an ideal candidate to preside over a price fixing "court". With several million dollars

[2] Press release, March 19, 1918, RG 61, File 21A–A1, box 15; *New York Times*, March 20, 1918, p. 8. See the same emphasis on the committee's "quasi-judicial" nature in Bernard Baruch, "The War Industries Board," a lecture before the Army War College, December 2, 1925, doc. no. 2 in *Course at the War College*, p. 5.

[3] Bernard Baruch, Lecture on Economic Mobilization at Army War College, January 15, 1925, Bernard M. Baruch Papers, Princeton University, Princeton, N.J. (cited hereafter as *Baruch Papers*), Public Papers.

[4] Daniels to Wilson, March 11, 1918, Josephus Daniels Papers, Library of Congress, Washington, D.C. (cited hereafter as *Daniels Papers*); Wilson to Daniels, March 12, 1918, *Wilson Papers*; E. David Cronon, ed., *The Cabinet Diaries of Josephus Daniels* (Lincoln: University of Nebraska Press, 1963), p. 289; Wilson to Baruch, March 12, 1918, and Baruch to Wilson, March 13, 1918, both in *Wilson Papers*. Baruch said Edward Hurley of the shipping board wanted that agency represented as well, but Wilson disagreed. "If we are to have a representative there of the farmers, why not representatives of many other classes of producers, and if the Shipping Board is to be represented, why not all the other purchasing agencies of the Government? I think we ought to go very slowly in this matter." But he did yield on an agricultural representative. Wilson to Baruch, July 1, 1918, and Baruch to Wilson, June 27, 1918, both in *ibid.*

in hand, Brookings had retired from business in 1895 at the age of 45. He had then devoted himself to public service, giving special attention to the expansion of Washington University, and as a member of the National Civic Federation in the prewar years he had long espoused the ideology of social cooperation and enlightened capitalism. Brookings had long been divorced from active business, then, long associated with public service, and fully cognizant of the need for business-government cooperation. His white beard and his patriarchal bearing even gave him the appearance of an understanding but impartial judge.[5]

A not unimportant sidelight to Brookings's appointment is the fact that Baruch wanted to eject him from the central WIB organization as soon as he took up his chairmanship, and make Peek head of finished products. Baruch and his close colleagues had a low regard for Brookings, considering him not much more than a fussy, "ladylike old bachelor"[6] who talked far too much to get things done efficiently. Personal friction between Brookings and Baruch underlined the separation between the PFC and the WIB. More than once Brookings vigorously explained to visiting businessmen that he, and not Baruch, had the final word in all matters of prices. "You are only one of the Price Fixing Committee," he admonished Baruch at one heated meeting, "and you have no more authority than any other member of the Committee, and you ought to attend the meetings of the Committee. . . ."[7]

The question of authority was of special concern to Brookings in March. In accepting the committee chairmanship, he wrote Wilson: "I am of the opinion, Mr. President, that this price-fixing problem without additional legislation is likely to become more and more involved. However, I am willing to assume to the best of my ability any responsibility when sustained by your authority."[8] To give his activities more force in subsequent months, Brookings had Wilson publicly proclaim a number of major price agreements, but the legal implication of this method remained unclear and unsettled. The uncertainty and restraint characteristic of WIB action on prices in the fall and winter of 1917–1918 never wholly disappeared after March 1918.

Whether or not the WIB should actively seek to remedy its legal deficiencies remained a moot point. Lovett, Brookings, and Parker supported the idea as it

[5] Hermann Hagedorn, *Brookings: A Biography* (New York: Macmillan, 1937); James Weinstein, *The Corporate Ideal in the Liberal State* (Boston: Beacon, 1968), chapter 8.

[6] Chandler P. Anderson, diary, January 22, 1918, in Chandler P. Anderson Papers, Library of Congress, Washington, D.C.. See also *ibid.*, March 6 and 15, 1918; Brookings to Wilson, March 11, 1918, *Wilson Papers.*

[7] Meeting of the Price Fixing Committee with the Representatives of the Cotton Fabrics Industry to Fix a Price on Their Product, July 1, 1918, RG 61, File 4–B1, boxes 529–31, Vol. 5.

[8] Brookings to Wilson, March 11, 1918, *Wilson Papers.*

arose, but Baruch's legal advisor, Albert Ritchie, remained opposed. Ritchie always granted the usefulness of further legislation but objected to a WIB-led campaign. He argued his case most explicitly with regard to priorities legislation, but the same arguments pertained to prices. The difficulty the WIB faced in priorities was one of providing protection for private producers who displaced their regular contracts with military orders, for under existing law such producers had no protection against liability from those displaced. The need for a legal remedy was obvious, but Ritchie refused to budge. He argued that the board had already been ordering priorities on nongovernment contracts (and fixing prices also) without its legal power being questioned, so why anticipate any challenge in the future? He dismissed out of hand the speculation that board members faced personal liability for exceeding their authority. But the central point, and the one which Ritchie always came back to in his brief against a legislative campaign, was that to advocate such legislation would reveal all too clearly just how much the board's work had actually been illegal, and then compound this trouble further by risking a legislative defeat. Ritchie asked Baruch: ". . . Is it wise to apply for legislation which must apparently concede the Board's lack of authority to do what it has been doing, and which may open up the question whether Congress will grant such power?"[9] Ritchie thought not, and apparently convinced Baruch. The WIB chairman had at this time lined up Congressman W. A. Ayres of Kansas to introduce a bill of sweeping power in priorities and prices, originally drafted by Lovett and fully supported by Parker and Brookings.[10] But it never emerged into public view. The debate about whether or not to introduce strong supplemental legislation waxed and waned to the war's end without resolution. Parker remained enthusiastic, Ritchie counseled caution, and Baruch, the speculator, was content to take his chances.

For his part, Robert Brookings ultimately made a virtue out of weakness, a consistent tactic of all WIB administrators. He informed visiting delegations many times that he would much rather rely upon close association with the president of the United States for power than upon any congressional statute. And it is true, of course, that presidential announcements strengthened the hands of producers who agreed with the PFC and augmented the social pressure which could be brought upon sellers to enforce compliance.[11]

[9] Ritchie to Baruch, August 19, 1918, RG 61, File 1–A5, box 41.

[10] See the bill attached to Brookings to Baruch, August 9, 1918, RG 61, File 1–A5, box 40. Also see the related correspondence: Parker to Brookings, March 11, 1918, Ayres to Brookings, August 3, 1918, Brookings to Ayres, August 9, 1918, Brookings to Baruch, August 9, 1918, and Ritchie to Baruch, August 14, 1918, all *ibid.*

[11] Meeting of the Price Fixing Committee with the Representatives of the Cotton Fabrics Industry to Fix a Price on Their Product, July 1, 1918, RG 61, File 4–B1, boxes 529–31, Vol. 5. One contemporary analyst argued that the success of wartime price fixing rested more on social values than economic factors; see Benjamin M. Anderson,

The board's price fixing committee was assigned four major duties in March. It was to advise on prices for "basic materials," to act as a coordinating body for price policies, to scrutinize specific military contracts upon request, and to fix prices on commandeered goods.[12] Brookings hoped the committee could expand beyond these functions to become the linchpin of all Washington price administration.[13] Herbert Hoover had certainly regarded formation of the PFC in this light and told Baruch of his wish "to have this power consolidated in one place, as the whole economic fabric must hold together."[14] Baruch shared Hoover's sentiments, but felt that the president's charge would not permit the PFC to take up food prices as Hoover hoped.[15] Clearly the price fixing committee could not become the kind of coordinating body business advisors wanted. Indeed it was soon obvious that the committee would not even be able to fulfill adequately the functions assigned to it, for like the WIB proper it fell among competing jurisdictions and partook of the compromise between military and civilian institutions that had emerged from the WIB reorganization of March 1918.

Since the administration's general approach to prices had evolved in a halting, haphazard fashion, much to the chagrin of its business advisors, the PFC possessed no comprehensive scheme of either principles or administration by which to plot its course. As with all WIB functions, price fixing was an evolutionary process based less on an initial guiding conception than on political conditions, bureaucratic infighting, and force of circumstance. Whether or not formal prerogatives expanded or contracted defied prediction. One price fixer put it this way: ". . . Government price-fixing during the war was not uniform in its objects, and was little guided by principles or deliberate policies. In the main it was opportunist, feeling its way from case to case."[16] Brookings explained to the copper producers in May 1918: ". . . We have [n't] a cut and dried principle or theory upon which we act, but we simply get together, advise together and discuss the problem as it is today without any particular regard to what we did six months ago." Whether a base price was to be raised or dropped did not depend on any objective neutral body of price fixing rules. A base price was, as

Jr., "Value and Price Theory in Relation to Price-Fixing and War Finance," *American Economic Review* 8 (March 1918): 239–56.

[12] Minutes of a meeting of the War Industries Board, March 14, 1918, in RG 61, File 1-C1, boxes 72–74 (cited hereafter as *WIB Minutes*).

[13] Brookings to Wilson, May 2, 1918, *Wilson Papers.*

[14] Hoover to Baruch, April 4, 1918, RG 61, File 21A-A1, box 1.

[15] Baruch to Hoover, April 5, 1918, *ibid.*

[16] Frank W. Taussig, "Price-Fixing as Seen by a Price-Fixer," *Quarterly Journal of Economics* 33 (February 1919): 238. Harold J. Tobin and Percy W. Bidwell make the same point in *Mobilizing Civilian America* (New York: Council on Foreign Relations, 1940), p. 169.

Brookings explained, "a price, after hearing all the evidence and getting all the information we can, which we think is fair and seems to you to be fair. . . ."[17] In other words, a base price for any commodity was whatever the committee and the industry could agree upon. Brookings believed that most businessmen would seek the highest price they thought they could get away with, so as a matter of course he always aimed to knock off a few points and yet come close enough to make some kind of agreement possible.

The image of the PFC as a judicial court is misleading.[18] A number of tactical considerations affected the committee's decision-making. Lewis Haney, an FTC economist during the war, summarized this point in the following manner.

Sometimes a particular government department, such as the Navy, was immediately interested in securing a lower price, and then the tendency was for the Price-Fixing Committee to drive a sharper bargain. If there was considerable public interest in the price, the article concerned being of wide, general use, the same tendency existed. If the quantity involved was small, no great part of the total output being concerned, it was easy to reach an agreement, and in such cases concessions were sometimes made to the government, while in others, possibly the government did not make so careful an investigation or attempt to ascertain accurately the lowest possible price.[19]

Since it was involved in a bargaining situation, the committee also had to take into account the odds of winning in any one instance. Daniel Willard had had this factor on his mind in December when he told President Wilson that the board would avoid trying to fix prices on widely scattered industries.[20] The strength of the industrial trade group, the practicality of gaining consent, and the possibility of gaining cooperation from another arm of the Washington bureaucracy were all factors that entered PFC calculations.[21]

The PFC turned to the WIB's commodity sections and various trade groups to administer its price agreements. The commodity chiefs were especially active in the price fixing process, despite the apparent concentration of this activity in

[17] Meeting of the Price Fixing Committee with the Representatives of the Copper Industry to Determine what Action Is To Be Taken in Regard to the Price of Copper, May 22, 1918, RG 61, File 4–B1, boxes 529–31, Vol. 4.

[18] Brookings used the metaphor of a court in Brookings to Wilson, October 4, 1918, *Wilson Papers.*

[19] Lewis H. Haney, "Price-Fixing in the United States during the War, III," *Political Science Quarterly* 34 (September 1919): 447.

[20] Willard to Wilson, December 7, 1917, *Wilson Papers.*

[21] Lewis H. Haney offers the best analysis of these and other variables in WIB price administration in his three articles for the *Political Science Quarterly* 34 (March, June, September, 1919): 104–26, 262–89, 434–53.

the PFC. Specific military items were always open to negotiation, of course, and the commodity chiefs were intimately involved at this level. In some cases a commodity chief might make a recommendation after his own investigation; sometimes the central committee delegated the task of gaining an agreement to him.

As might be expected, the commodity chiefs pressured for the right to take care of all price fixing activities that concerned the products under their charge.[22] The members of the PFC were generalists, after all, more interested in broad principles than specific, detailed analysis. As an extension of this line of argument some trade groups questioned the committee's ability to fix specific prices altogether. The *Engineering and Mining Journal* never relented in its opposition to price fixing throughout the war.[23] *Engineering and Cement World* observed sardonically: "One might create a committee of bishops to pass upon certain industrial problems and it could be well said that the highest type of men were represented on the committee."[24] All industries, no matter how much they agreed with central guidelines, naturally preferred to work out the details among themselves in cooperation with the WIB specialist.

The kind of arrangements devised by the WIB's hide and leather division to police price agreements on hides and skins is indicative of commodity section-industry cooperation in price administration. The division divided the country into ten districts and selected the leading hide dealer in each district to organize the trade, relying ultimately on the power of a private group to oversee this particular semipublic agreement. Such a system had severe limitations; Charles Stout, the divisional chief, estimated that 25 per cent of the operators ignored the WIB ruling as of the summer of 1918, and predicted that unless the WIB gained some form of sanction and punishment the entire system would go down in defeat.[25]

With its own program in mind, the *Shoe and Leather Reporter* commented upon the inevitable dilution of administrative regulations as they passed through the WIB emergency organization. "From President Wilson down commands have

---

[22] The military bureaus fought off WIB pressure in this area, and resolutions appeared periodically to the effect that the board's commodity sections could not actually fix prices on government purchases. See "Be It Resolved...," June 25, 1918, RG 61, File 1-A5, box 41; "Office Memorandum no. 4," RG 61, File 21A-A4, box 1147; Minutes of Commodity Section Meeting, July 18, 1918, RG 61, File 21A-A4, box 1147. This latter meeting modified the rule to the point that WIB sections could fix prices as long as the military bureaus involved were adequately represented at price discussions.

[23] For sample editorials, see "Tampering with the Machinery," *Engineering and Mining Journal* 104 (August 4, 1917): 225-26, and "Fixing the Price for Platinum," 105 (May 25, 1918): 976-77.

[24] "The Raw Materials Committee," *Engineering and Cement World* 12 (May 1, 1918): 6.

[25] Charles Stout to Albert Ritchie, October 25, 1918, RG 61, File 2D-A1, box 207.

been softened into recommendations and suggestions." But as a booster for price regulation, it added defiantly: "But there are claws under the velvet paw and it will be dangerous for members of our trade if they mistake courtesy for weakness."[26] Bernard Baruch indicated his awareness of the significance of decentralized administration within the WIB when he remarked after the war: ". . . Fixing the price was not such an important item in itself. The administration of the article whose price was fixed was the important thing." He firmly believed that "the section chief was the man who made the price that was fixed."[27]

Brookings brought all his considerable loquacious powers to bear on visiting businessmen. Exuding a warm confidence and paternalistic tone, he conducted negotiations with drama and zest, thoroughly enjoying the chance to lecture his captive audience on the principles of sound business enterprise. Brookings was so well known for his preaching to trade delegations as to move the *Paper Trade Journal* to comment: "Mr. Brookings calls the men of the industry into conference to get their advice and when they arrive they get little or no chance to give their advice, the time being taken up listening to Mr. Brookings's theories on the subject."[28] At every turn the WIB urged trade groups to see that their own best interests lay in business-government cooperation and in the adoption of sophisticated business conduct. Brookings was passionately committed to the idea of economic stabilization through price control. No trade delegation escaped his exhortations on this score. "We meet together as one organization, one group, one industry," Brookings told the cotton manufacturers. "The Government becomes your partner in trying to do something that you couldn't do alone very well, in assisting you to stabilize the market."[29] Brookings naturally had to stress this theme most strenuously with industries like cotton that remained skeptical, reluctant, and hostile. Only through an agreement, he assured the cotton representatives, could they gain stable, continuous prices. "Everything will be kept sound and kept safe; I don't say running along on 'ragged edge'; that isn't conserving the industry. I mean keeping it in good healthy condition. It is

[26] "Relations between the Government and Our Industry," *Shoe and Leather Reporter* 131 (August 22, 1918): 20–21.

[27] Baruch to Grosvenor Clarkson, January 12, 1921, general correspondence, *Baruch Papers.* This comment is particularly appropriate regarding the role which the section chiefs took in building up a differentiated price structure from the basic raw material price negotiated through the central committee. As an example of this process in the leather industry, see Charles Stout to A. J. Sweet, June 20, 1918, RG 61, File 21A–A4, box 1150.

[28] *Paper Trade Journal* 68 (July 25, 1918): 9.

[29] Meeting of the Price Fixing Committee of the War Industries Board with Special Committee Representing the Cotton Fabrics Industry To Consider the Advisability of Fixing a Price on Cotton Fabrics, May 29, 1918, RG 61, File 4–B1, boxes 529–31, Vol. 4.

the best thing for the Nation at large, if all industries were gradually brought into line, and I think they will. . . ."[30] Brookings sought to "keep values down to some sort of reasonable basis, not to grind the last drop of blood out of an industry, but to keep things down to a normal basis." The object of the PFC, he believed, was "to stabilize industry and to keep sufficiently near the earth so that when the war is over things will be able to take their normal course again."[31]

If Brookings had not had a talent for lecturing he would have had to develop it, for he was so largely dependent upon persuasion for results. As could be expected, his greatest successes came with businessmen experienced in oligopoly or monopoly. Fixing prices on aluminum transpired especially well, as the following brief dialogue between the president of the Aluminum Company of America and Brookings shows.

Davis: How long do you want to make that for—three months or six months?
Brookings: What would you like?[32]

Brookings wrote Wilson after the aluminum agreement of May 1918: "The production of aluminum is practically a monopoly in the hands of one very large and very strong corporation, whose attitude, however, toward the Government has been patriotic and liberal to a degree."[33] Davis requested an advance in August but acquiesced immediately when Brookings advised against it. Brookings congratulated Davis on his "fine, broad spirit."[34] Elbert Gary of United States Steel also shared Brookings's commitment to long-range stability and his aversion to competitive activity and short-run profits. The early hostility between the Wilson administration and the steel industry gave way to an aura of good fellowship and camaraderie under Brookings's price fixing committee. Both men shared the same regard for the long-range implications of their war work and fought off challenges to their price structure from both small independent producers and government buyers.[35]

[30] *Ibid.*

[31] Meeting of the Price Fixing Committee of the War Industries Board Held Wednesday, August 7th, *ibid.*, Vol. 7.

[32] Meeting of the Price Fixing Committee To Fix the Price on Aluminum for the Next Four [*sic*] Beginning June 1st, May 9, 1918, *ibid.*, Vol. 3.

[33] Brookings to Wilson, May 27, 1918, *Wilson Papers.*

[34] Meeting of the Price Fixing Committee of the War Industries Board with a Representative of the Aluminum Industry for the Purpose of Fixing the Price of Aluminum, August 20, 1918, RG 61, File 4-B1, boxes 529-31, Vol. 7.

[35] Robert D. Cuff and Melvin I. Urofsky, "The Steel Industry and Price-Fixing during World War I," *Business History Review* 44 (Autumn 1970): 291-306.

Pressure against price fixing from small producers was a common problem, as was the general hostility from intensely competitive industries. "If some of your competitors whom we haven't met are not disposed to do the right thing and the fair thing by you," Brookings told the cotton manufacturers, "why, we want to be kept in touch with that because we must protect you, those of you who we know want to do the right thing."[36] Part of a letter which Brookings wrote to Wilson in regard to the cotton industry is worth quoting on this theme.

Owing to the very large number of mills in the country and the great variety of good [sic] produced, this has been the most difficult price fixing problem we have been called upon to solve. Without going into details, it has been practically impossible for us to use the indirect pressure which we could bring to bear on such industries as steel and copper, so that we have had to resort to the slow process of reason. . . .[37]

Brookings was, of course, in no position to impose any arbitrary settlement no matter how strongly he felt about any matter. All he could do was to urge trade leaders to organize the industry more effectively, form a small negotiating group, and try to come to some agreement with him on a sensible schedule of prices.[38]

As they remembered or testified about their war experience, all business administrators distinguished between enlightened and unenlightened industrialists, and naturally underscored the predominance of the former in the WIB enterprise. By that time, in the postwar years, the dollar-a-year men possessed a vested interest in asserting that businessmen who sought stability and valued cooperative arrangements were the rule, and backward-looking, individualistic, uncooperative men proved the exception. To say otherwise would have been to cast doubt not only on business patriotism, but on the efficiency of the WIB organization as well. Such testimony overlooked the bitter conflicts among business groups and the board during the war. Still, there was much truth in the kind of distinction WIB administrators made among businessmen. The army representative on the PFC commented to his colleagues on the kind of businessmen he had seen before the committee.

It is interesting to note the attitude of men in some of these conferences. The conservative business man, who has been in the market for years and years and

---

[36] Meeting of the Price Fixing Committee of the War Industries Board with Representatives of the Cotton Fabrics Industry, September 6, 1918, RG 61, File 4-B1, boxes 529-31, Vol. 8.

[37] Brookings to Wilson, July 3, 1918, RG 61, File 21A-A4, box 1148.

[38] Louis Galambos traces these developments for the cotton industry in *Competition and Cooperation: The Emergence of a National Trade Association* (Baltimore, Md.: Johns Hopkins Press, 1966), pp. 65-66.

years—he argues for the stable price constantly, and they dominate in all meetings by the way; but the young, energetic hustler, who is willing to take chances, starts off in the meeting with the market price as a basis, and he argues that right out to the finish. Sometimes he doesn't give up until the decision is rendered, but he is willing to take his chances in a speculative market. There are very few of them, I may say.[39]

Brookings spoke to this same point at a meeting of the PFC.

There are some men who feel they can make an additional amount of profit in a few months and salt it away. They are willing to do that because then they know they have that much, but I don't think any large corporations that expect to live for years likes that kind of a market. All of their supplies go up and their basis of values go up. It is an unhealthy condition. When the war ends they will have to face a difficult problem.[40]

The hustlers and the new market entries had good economic reasons to avoid stabilization at moderate prices. The older and larger firms could more easily recognize the value of cooperating with the committee as a way to maintain the status quo and retain their market power. Stabilization favored those who were dominant before prices were fixed. One zinc ore producer summed up sentiment on behalf of the price fixing enthusiasts this way: "It has a wonderful effect of stabilizing and that is the end we seek; it has a wonderful effect, and we sure appreciate the Government's action."[41] Brookings and the PFC had been instrumental in this case in bringing the producers and smelters together into an informal price agreement, and the producers were particularly happy about the results. This was the kind of arrangement that Brookings had in mind when he told one trade delegation: "We get behind you and enable you to do some things for which you would be criticized if you didn't have our assistance."[42]

In the postwar years Baruch, Brookings, and other WIB men put great emphasis upon business patriotism as a central force in their wartime success, but we should not let this obscure the extent to which hard power was in fact

[39] Special Meeting of Representatives of Army, Navy, and Shipping Board with Representatives of the Lumber Dealers To Fix Prices for Handling Lumber for Government, May 10, 1918, RG 61, File 21A–A1, box 12.

[40] Meeting of the Price Fixing Committee of the War Industries Board, March 26, 1918, "Concerning Cotton Goods," RG 61, File 4–B1, boxes 529–31, Vol. 1.

[41] Meeting of the Price Fixing Committee with the Producers of Zinc Ore and Plate and Sheet Zinc to Determine the Advisability of Revising the Prices on Plate and Sheet Zinc, May 17, 1918, *ibid.*, Vol. 4.

[42] A Meeting of the Price Fixing Committee of the War Industries Board with Representatives of the Cotton Fabrics Industry for the Purpose of Fixing a Maximum Price on Cotton Fabrics, June 8, 1918, *ibid.*, Vol. 4.

operative in WIB regulatory activities, even though it was the power of private rather than public administration. The private economic governments that cooperated with the WIB through its price fixing committee and other functional units exercised supervisory functions on the board's behalf. Without its own independent source of legal, bureaucratic authority, the PFC and the entire WIB organization relied upon traditional authority in American industry: on great corporations and powerfully organized trade associations, many of which came to life under the stimulus of war. The more highly organized an industry, the easier the process of regulation in any field. Brookings was most explicit about negotiating with such private power centers. "Now I think that is really up to you leaders," he informed one delegation, "the bigger men in the business. . . ."[43] It was up to them to administer agreements and bring the rest of the trade into line.

The PFC minutes underscore the delicate nature of the committee's relationship with private economic groups. Because of the absence of precise rules, procedures, and so on, there was a great deal of vagueness and wide room for misunderstanding. The PFC certainly helped to formalize and institutionalize procedures by setting out precedents for price fixing operations. But its activities were nevertheless marked by the kind of informality characteristic of the WIB's earlier ventures into the field. Given the general instability of the entire process, good feelings and hostilities could and did alternate with great rapidity. The entire situation was so thoroughly unpredictable that new issues could arise at any moment to endanger a promising entente between an industry and the committee. In groping toward a modus vivendi, or testing the nature of an evolving relationship, Brookings and the industrial representatives deported themselves much as diplomats facing a perpetually explosive issue. Both sides were well aware of the danger involved in any explosion. While anxious to settle the problem to their own advantage, they still hoped to avoid an all-out war. A single, unpleasant bargaining incident could undermine many days of tangled negotiations. Conversely, tempers would subside and good feelings resume after the proper exchange of formalized compliments.

Toward the end of the war the WIB and its price fixing committee were attracted to a problem far more complicated than fixing prices on industrial raw materials and military purchases. Brookings, Baruch, and the men in the board's administrative center were concerned ultimately to stabilize the country's entire industrial structure, and this ambitious aim brought them face to face with the whole complex issue of social order and the cost of living question. Such concern was far beyond any function specifically assigned the board, yet the inter-

[43] Meeting of the Price Fixing Committee with the Representatives of the Cotton Fabrics Industry To Fix a Price on Their Product, July 1, 1918, *ibid.*, Vol. 5.

connection between social order and a stable industrial price policy necessitated some kind of action.

Robert Brookings had long advocated close cooperation between business, labor and the federal government on behalf of social peace and a stable expanding economy, and rising wartime prices and unsettled social conditions only emphasized the utility of a cooperative effort for industrial stabilization.[44] In April 1918, he wrote Wilson that "The prices of cotton, wool and leather products largely involve the cost of living, and necessarily in turn involve the great problem of labor wage. The labor wage and cost of living are inseparable. It is probably our most important economic problem. I understand that Great Britain has so stabilized the cost of living," he continued, ". . . as to establish a more or less basic relation between the cost of living and the scale of wages, in preparation for the inevitable competition between nations after the war. It is perfectly evident that unless we make some effort in this direction we will soon find our values (including wages) established on a basis that will practically destroy the great advantage which our raw materials and merchant marine should give us in competing for the world's trade after the war."[45] Brookings believed there was no "greater stimulus to strikes for advanced wages than the constantly advancing price of shoes and clothing,"[46] so that without effective stabilization violence across the labor front was inevitable. Brookings was the most advanced social thinker on the WIB, and he was willing to go much further than his colleagues in the direction of government controls to achieve an integrated, stable industrial policy embracing both labor and business.

Brookings's interest in negotiating prices in the leather, cotton, and woolen industries stemmed largely from his interest in the cost of living problem. He advocated government sponsorship of a number of mass-produced, standardized lines of goods designated "Liberty" items designed especially for "the working people."[47] President Wilson wondered whether large firms would not monopolize production under Brookings's scheme, and whether the plan would not produce a formidable inspection system, but he did not discourage Brookings's speculation.[48]

By late summer the WIB was formally on record as favoring a price fixing program in consumer goods.[49] It set up a committee to discuss the cost of living issue, and Baruch personally spoke with Felix Frankfurter of the war labor

[44] For an analysis of this ideology, see Weinstein, *Corporate Ideal*, chap. 1.

[45] Brookings to Wilson, April 20, 1918, *Wilson Papers*.

[46] Brookings to Wilson, May 2, 1918, *ibid.*

[47] *Ibid.*

[48] Wilson to Brookings, May 3, 1918, *Wilson Papers*.

[49] *WIB Minutes*, August 1, 6, 13, 1918.

policies board, who had already urged action upon the WIB and food administration.[50] Fears grew up within the WIB inner group that, in the words of George Peek, "unless the business men of the country awaken to the situation and take some constructive steps to meet the new conditions, . . . they are going to force upon themselves Government control of every line of business dealing in the essentials of life."[51] Personally Peek seemed more haunted by the specter of growing radicalism and state control than most of his colleagues on the board. He also lacked Brookings's more humanitarian motives. The inability of the population to buy the necessities of life could have only one result, according to Peek, the hard-nosed realist: "It would mean a riot from within our own country. It would mean an intolerable situation which would force not only State ownership but Government ownership or control of practically all the basic industries of the country—and that is no theory."[52]

A general stabilization program would have been only a leap in the dark at this point, so the board decided first to test the possibility on a small scale by setting prices on shoes. The industry had already agreed to rationalize and standardize its product lines through the board's conservation division, and on August 7 the priorities division issued a circular requiring each boot and shoe manufacturer to practice mutually agreeable economies for a place on the preference list. The industry was enthusiastic about the scheme, particularly since it could draw up its own kinds of regulations.[53] Arch Shaw explained the method of conservation regulation this way:

The function of the Commercial Economy Board [the name of Shaw's committee before March 1918] was to conserve our resources and our facilities. No board and no individual was qualified to perform that function in all the diverse industries and trades of the United States. So the Commerical Economy Board simply called in these various industries and told them the Government's needs

---

[50] Herbert B. Swope to Baruch, undated, and Swope to John W. Scott (director, textile and rubber division), October 17, 1918, both in RG 61, File 21A–A4, box 1147; Baruch to Swope, October 16, 1918, and Swope to Peek, October 30, 1918, both in RG 61, File 1–A4, box 37; and Felix Frankfurter to Swope, September 19, 1918, RG 61, File 21A–A3, box 34.

[51] Peek to Judge Nathaniel French, August 21, 1918, George N. Peek Papers, Western Historical Manuscript Collection, University of Missouri, Columbia, Mo.

[52] Meeting of the Hide, Leather & Leather Goods Section of the War Industries Board with Representatives of the Shoe Industry for the Purpose of Discussing a Proposed "Liberty Shoe," August 19, 1918, RG 61, File 21A–A2, box 100.

[53] Richard H. Hippelheuser, ed., *American Industry in the War, A Report of the War Industries Board, March 1921* (New York: Prentice-Hall, 1941), p. 269; "Reformation of Trade Practices" and "Priority for Essential Industries," *Shoe and Leather Reporter* 131 (July 18, 1918): 20–21; and "Relations between the Government and Our Industry," *ibid.*, 131 (August 22, 1918): 20–21.

and enlisted them as Government officials so far as their industries were concerned.[54]

The *Shoe and Leather Reporter* noted apropos this point that: "It has frequently happened that severe restrictions which met with vigorous opposition at the outset were later found to have been conceived in wisdom . . . ."[55] The industry realized that conservation was far less threatening than helpful. Hopefully through these measures the industry could make sufficient cutbacks to prove that radical controls were unnecessary. The conservation division was motivated to help industry avoid tough, politically imposed restrictions by helping industry to help itself. The industry was satisfied under these conditions that "the administration of hide, leather and shoe affairs in Washington is conducted in a spirit of equity."[56]

From August onward, editorials in the trade journal took a sharp turn to the right. In a series of vitriolic explosions, the journal charged the WIB with political grandstanding and making a scapegoat of the shoe industry. "Despite the fact that many industrial leaders are members of the War Industries Board political fallacy frequently overcomes business sense."[57] The occasion for this bitterness was the board's decision to have the industry actually curtail production of many of its lines and concentrate instead on a standardized, low-cost product. The industry now confronted the challenge of government intervention, fixed low prices, and close supervision of the production process.

Fortunately for the trade, division among WIB officials themselves offered considerable room to maneuver. Apparently Brookings was the only WIB spokesman absolutely committed to a government-licensed, wholly standardized, Liberty Shoe, and significantly enough he was largely excluded from the subsequent negotiations. Baruch favored the idea of a low-cost working class shoe but was open to a number of low-cost lines, opposed to direct government supervision, and willing to leave to industry all decisions on styles and prices, although he did favor stamping on the retail prices. Buyers would then have a clear guideline of suggested prices, and sellers would have to explain to the consumer why they had strayed over any stamped price. This strategy put the retailer under real social pressure and eliminated any need for a large state inspectorate—something that had bothered President Wilson with Brookings's plans. But Baruch remained flexible throughout all discussions, trying to find a way be-

[54] "Statement of A. W. Shaw," *Baruch Papers.*

[55] "Relations between the Government and Our Industry," *Shoe and Leather Reporter* 131 (August 22, 1918): 20–21.

[56] *Ibid.*

[57] "The Conservation of Industries," *Shoe and Leather Reporter* 131 (September 12, 1918): 20.

tween the Brookings ideal, on the one hand, and the laissez faire dogmas of a large number of reluctant manufacturers, on the other.

George Peek shared Baruch's aversion to Brookings's suggestion, but he differed over the point at which they ought to set the price. Baruch favored letting the retailer put on the final public price; Peek thought it better to stamp on the cost for the public to see. As a manufacturer, Peek relished the idea of giving the producer the option of putting the price on his own goods to ensure against being used by greedy middlemen or retailers. Charles Stout, the industry's Washington representative in the WIB, seemed to act as a mediator among all parties. He shared the WIB's feeling that the industry should cooperate in helping to keep the cost of living down, but he was equally desirous that industry be afforded the greatest freedom to make up its own plans. After a long struggle, the board ultimately adopted his moderate scheme of standardized lines with price floors and ceilings for each category.[58]

The bitter conflict between the WIB and the shoe industry offers a classic example of the battle constantly waged in wartime Washington between the broad-gauged, system-conscious WIB executives and the more narrowly-based, interest-conscious spokesmen from the industrial community. Baruch and Peek shared the industry's aversion to government control, but they were sufficiently attuned to a hostile public opinion and to the obvious need to coordinate all segments of society on behalf of social peace and the war effort to see that the industry would at the very minimum have to meet them in some half-way house of cooperative regulation.

George Peek was most vocal in his opposition to the competitive ideal harbored by the manufacturers. The following dialogue between Peek and J. F. McElwain, a major shoe manufacturer, provides a useful example of Peek's position:

Mr. Peek: Let me ask you, all these conditions which you outline are the result of a highly competitive situation which has been going on for many, many years, are they not?

Mr. McElwain: Yes.

Mr. Peek: If you gentlemen were the board of directors of the industry instead of representing your separate companies you wouldn't run your business that way, would you?

Mr. McElwain: No.

Mr. Peek: If there was one company, if you gentlemen were running one company and had an absolute monopoly, you would not do what you are doing now?

[58]These policy positions are derived from Meeting of the Hide, Leather & Leather Goods Section of the War Industries Board with Representatives of the Shoe Industry for the

Mr. McElwain: That is correct.

Mr. Peek: Now, I contend that the law of supply and demand and competitive conditions must be suspended and that we must issue a rain check on this competitive situation and cash it in after the war, and in the meantime run the industry as you would run one company if you were the directors of that one industry instead of representing the separate companies. Now, I don't know how to make it any clearer than that.[59]

Baruch and Peek pleaded, argued, and even threatened presidential intervention if the manufacturers stood against the cooperative effort. The manufacturers had to forget profits, to forget even the hope of getting everyone through the war intact. They had to think of the future, of their role in postwar industrial competition. Baruch brought a number of these themes together in one of his more expansive presentations:

I am really only putting my ideas of what I think ought to be done for your benefit, and my only idea is that we should speedily work this problem out for the benefit of the country at large. I don't want you to accept this as Baruch's or the War Industries' or the United States Government's, but it is the shoe industry and ourselves together, and I am looking ahead, perhaps I may flatter myself that I am looking a little bit further, because I have got to in the interest of the industry. The War Industries Board is not for the purpose of only helping the war program but to also help for the purpose of protecting so far as it is possible and compatible, protecting the various industries so that they will be in a position after the war to speedily adjust themselves. If we can get into a position where we can skeletonize and preserve an industry so that after the war we will be able to go along through regular lines of business that is just what we are after. It seems rather funny for a man knowing nothing about this business to tell you what you ought to do. I am only giving the line along which I would like to have you go. Perhaps I am entirely too radical in this, but I believe we are going to get further with the public and get a bit further with the large masses and I believe we will greatly help the war program if you will stabilize the price of shoes and standardize the styles.[60]

Meetings continued through September. Business protests mounted as WIB pressure increased. The *Shoe and Leather Reporter* complained of the board's

---

Purpose of Discussing a Proposed "Liberty Shoe," August 19, 1918, and WIB Meeting with Shoe Manufacturers, August 20, 1918, both in RG 61, File 21A–A2, box 100.

[59] Meeting of the Hide, Leather & Leather Goods Section of the War Industries Board with Representatives of the Shoe Industry for the Purpose of Discussing a Proposed "Liberty Shoe," August 19, 1918, *ibid.*

[60] *Ibid.*

"socialistic suggestions,"[61] and its "shifting policies and impossible demands."[62] The WIB, the paper charged at one point, "is exceeding its powers and establishing a system of paternalism which threatens our constitutional government."[63] These attacks outraged Baruch, and rightly so, for they grossly misrepresented his motives and his style.[64] Such accusations did, however, have the positive effect of reinforcing his power image with the public and other business groups.

The upshot of it all was, as might be expected, a compromise. The industry avoided the Liberty Shoe, government inspection, and even stamped wholesale and retail prices, but it did agree to certain kinds of price constraints and to a reduction of styles. The plan as it ultimately passed through negotiations decreed that all shoes were to be reduced to four classes—A, B, C, D—each with a varying price range—$9.00 to $12.00, $6.00 to $8.95, $3.00 to $5.95, and below $3.00 respectively. Each shoe was to be stamped with a number and the purchaser would discover the price range from a key provided by the retailer. The whole plan was to go into effect in the spring of 1919.[65]

The WIB had successfully forced the shoe industry to go further toward conservation and price stabilization than it would have had it been left alone to its own devices. Its spokesmen had fought the board's proposals every step of the way, while seizing on those options that permitted it the greatest freedom to design palatable regulations. It was particularly annoyed by the way in which the WIB had placed it under the glare of publicity and had it labeled an opponent of the public interest. The episode raised public expectations to a level that was simply not justified by the nature of the ultimate arrangements. This, of course, was one of the board's favorite tactics, to direct public opinion to an industry and force it to go to greater lengths to appease those expectations. The trade journal observed that the final plan "fell far short of the desire of Bernard M. Baruch and the radical members of the War Industries Board. They are mild and tame compared with the original plans, but enough remained to form the basis of sensational reports which have been furnished to the daily papers telling how the

[61] "The New Shoe Conservation Agreement," *Shoe and Leather Reporter* 131 (September 19, 1918): 20.

[62] "What Is the Matter with the War Industries Board?" *Shoe and Leather Reporter* 132 (October 3, 1918): 23.

[63] *Ibid.*

[64] Baruch drafted a stinging rebuke to the *Shoe and Leather Reporter* but did not send it. See the draft of Baruch to Editor, *Shoe and Leather Reporter*, October 18, 1918, RG 61, File 21A–A3, box 20.

[65] For a full chronology of the negotiations between the board and the industry, see George R. Wheeler, assistant chief of the boot and shoe section, to H. P. Ingels, December 7, 1918, RG 61, File 21A–A2, box 104.

Board has whipped the shoe manufacturers into line. . . ."[66] The *Dry Goods Reporter* also recognized how modest the final plan was compared to the original Liberty Shoe concept and the reports that circulated in the press. "The regulation of shoe prices," it concluded, ". . . is not going to hurt anybody materially because the restrictions thus far are not very drastic."[67] Actual implementation would not begin for almost a full year and the enforcement of the agreement rested upon only voluntary pledges from the manufacturers involved.

It was highly unlikely that the agreement would have uniform success given the number of groups involved, the geographic area covered, and the insubstantial quality of its administration. The entire program rested ultimately on whatever social pressure the WIB could whip up among the public at large, allied with a cooperative spirit among some members of the industry, which in this case was minimal indeed. Baruch admitted that "The matter of the final price to the consumer will have to be left more or less to the retailer. The success of this is going to depend upon the shoe people. . . ."[68] He hoped that they could see that it was to their own interest as an industry and in the interest of the industrial community as a whole to support the compromise.

The armistice precluded testing the WIB's new program, and it was a test the WIB was fortunate to have avoided, because it is highly probable that the whole system would have broken down in the end. The WIB avoided a failure which would have pointed up not only the limits of its powers but also the extent to which its regulations were in fact designed to meet the need for control without affecting a dramatic shift in the distribution of power.

The experiment in the shoe industry was the WIB's only systematic venture into the cost of living issue. Some discussion of standardizing and fixing prices on "workingmen's garments"[69] occurred in the summer and fall of 1918 but nothing developed before the end of the war. Yet the shoe experiment was a significant step. It illuminates the ideology of the WIB mobilizers, the deficiencies in their administrative organization, and the kind of opposition their plans encountered. The WIB men feared social unrest, and desired to protect and stabi-

[66]"Politics and the War Industries Board," *Shoe and Leather Reporter* 132 (October 10, 1918): 20. See also "The New Government Shoe Regulations," *ibid.*, pp. 21–22, for the same point.

[67]"The Regulation of Retail Prices," *Dry Goods Reporter* 47 (October 19, 1918): 7.

[68]Draft of a letter, Baruch to Peek, September 19, 1918, RG 61, File 21A–A3, box 21. Brookings adhered to his original concept and recommended the liberty shoe once again at the end of October; see Brookings to Baruch, October 21, 1918, RG 61, File 21A–A3, box 20.

[69]John Scott to R. S. Ely (executive secretary, war service committee of the garment industry), September 9, 1918, RG 61, File 4–B1, box 528. Scott suggested a "liberty" overalls in this letter to Ely.

lize American business through a system of institutional coordination. Some among them were eager to seek legislative authority in support of their long-range goals, but Baruch disagreed. Unwilling to open up any aspect of his administration to congressional probing, he preferred to gamble with his talent for bargaining and the good sense of his colleagues in private industry—the essence of the cooperative, middle way. The result was an unstable, tenuous, haphazard price fixing program that stumbled over both bureaucratic fragmentation and business suspicion.

Not all business groups agreed with Baruch's version of their best interest. Elbert Gary of U.S. Steel had hesitated many months before he accepted a compromise with the WIB in September 1917, and many weeks passed after that before the steel industry and price fixing committee routinized their relationship. The cotton industry took even longer to adjust to government price fixing, despite all the ideological fervor of Robert Brookings. The shoe manufacturers proved more difficult still. Indeed, the debate over shoe prices provides good evidence to support the older, progressive interpretation of conflict between business and government in the process of public regulation. The political economy of war never closed all the gaps in its drive for integration. In the last analysis, the WIB's price fixing program and its grander vision of institutional integration could not overcome the deficiencies in its own organization or the resistance it encountered in both the state and the economy. The WIB embodied an impulse for order far beyond its capacities to achieve.

CHAPTER 9

THE WIB DISSOLVES

Despite the extension of its commodity sections and its enlarged programs of priority and price control, the WIB never achieved the internal consistency and external dominance required to fulfill the Hamiltonian dreams of its early sponsors, even after March 1918. Baruch did not even try to enforce his formal authority throughout the board. Had he done so he would have risked the mass exodus of strong-minded business experts, and the destruction of his hopes for voluntary business administration. The board's emergency nature made it virtually impossible to routinize and integrate procedures. And since none of his administrators considered the agency a full time career he could hardly employ the sanctions available to executives in regular bureaucratic organizations.

As for its external search for stability and predictability, after March 1918 the WIB had to satisfy itself with compromise, not dominance; with power that was shared, and not absolute. In the case of the military services, the board shared power largely out of necessity. Baruch simply failed to displace the military bureaus from their regular purchasing functions. In the case of major business interests, the board shared power not only out of necessity, although that was an ever present reality, but also out of choice. The board's imperative need for private administrative resources was reinforced by its hostility toward outright state control and its enthusiasm for the public image of voluntary business-government cooperation for war. Negotiations over auto conversion and shoe price fixing make clear the board's reluctance to take arbitrary steps against an industry even in the face of serious provocation.

What would have happened had the war continued beyond November 11 is impossible to say. But there is some reason to believe that in the face of intensified social and economic crisis the WIB and its administrative program would have ultimately cracked apart. The conduct of Baruch and the board just before and just after the armistice offers good evidence for this thesis. Why, for example, did Baruch and the WIB fail to intervene forcefully during this period to coordinate and control the transition to peace? Why did they fail to integrate military and industrial policies of demobilization? Why did they fail to contain the competitive pressures then breaking out within the economy? The answers to these questions provide yet another perspective on the WIB's weaknesses as an organization, the precarious nature of its relationship with external groups, and finally, and most important, the highly political character of its leaders' long-range goals.

THE ABSENCE OF POSTWAR PLANNING

Few voices had been raised on behalf of postwar planning within the Washington bureaucracy during the war. Grosvenor Clarkson was anxious to regain some prestige as director of the languishing Council of National Defense and put the council forward as a locus for postwar planning activity. He set up a small staff under the direction of Harvard finance expert, Professor O. M. W. Sprague, dispatched a variety of memoranda to government officials in the summer of 1918, and gained support from a number of export associations.[1] Felix Frankfurter pressed for studies on demobilization and reconstruction and ultimately had his War Labor Policies Board initiate some investigations.[2] Walter Gifford and Department of Commerce representatives set out as early as June to estimate the effects of the war on American industry.[3] And the WIB's Arch Shaw, pursuing a long-standing interest in European economic developments, analyzed the economics of postwar adjustment.[4] But these were piecemeal actions and a

[1] Grosvenor B. Clarkson, "A memorandum on the past and future functions of the Council of National Defense," March 22, 1918, in the Newton D. Baker Papers, Library of Congress, Washington, D.C. (cited hereafter as *Baker Papers*); Wilson to Clarkson, March 26, 1918, and Baker to Clarkson, April 17, 1918, both *ibid.* See also Grosvenor B. Clarkson, "Plan for the Peace-Time Organization of the United States Council of National Defence," May 9, 1918, *ibid.*; Clarkson to Baruch, July 17, 1918, Record Group 62, Records of the Council of National Defense, Federal Records Center, Suitland, Md. (cited hereafter as RG 62), File 2–A5, box 83; Clarkson to Baker, November 4, 1918, *Baker Papers*; Stanley J. Quinn (American Manufacturers Export Association) to Clarkson, August 30, 1918, RG 62, File 2–A1, box 58; Clarkson to Gifford, May 23, 1918, RG 62, File 2–A1, box 49; and Clarkson to Baruch, July 17, 1918, RG 62, File 2–A5, box 83.

[2] See [Walton Hamilton] to Frankfurter, October 21, 1918, and Frankfurter to William B. Wilson, October 22, 1918, both in Record Group 1, Records of the War Labor Policies Board, National Archives, Washington, D.C., box 30.

[3] Minutes of the Council of National Defense and joint meetings of the council and Advisory Commission (cited hereafter as *CND Minutes*), June 24, 1918, RG 62, File 2–B1, box 104.

[4] For some of the material that Shaw forwarded to his colleagues in the WIB, see Record Group 61, Records of the War Industries Board, Federal Records Center, Suitland, Md. (cited hereafter as RG 61), File 1–A5, box 41.

striking contrast to the experience in European countries. Both France and Germany had established commissions to study postwar problems as early as 1916, and England set up a Ministry of Reconstruction in 1917.[5] In the light of these events, American planning enthusiasts could rightly charge the administration with "an unnecessarily timid attitude."[6] A correspondent for *Hardware Age* observed "both in the Cabinet and out of it, a general impatience toward suggestions that there is a need of preparedness for peace."[7] In sum, the United States government made no more preparations to leave the war than it had to enter it.

President Wilson was well aware of both reconstruction planning in Europe and the pressures for it within his own administration. In June he acceded to the CND's request to coordinate independent reconstruction studies and to collect all recommendations.[8] But as he told Colonel House in August, he did not envision the council becoming a committee on reconstruction.[9] He also opposed a measure introduced in the Senate by Senator John W. Weeks (R., Mass.) on September 27 which called for a congressionally appointed joint committee on reconstruction to be composed of six senators and six representatives. Senator Lee S. Overman (D., Tenn.) countered this threat to presidential prerogatives with a proposal for an executive-appointed committee, but even in this instance Wilson appealed to Overman to restrict the charge of any commission to reasonable limits, to "merely make a premininary [*sic*] survey."[10] Wilson had expressed his skepticism about the grandiose nature of some European inquiries on other occasions, and he simply reaffirmed his doubts to Overman.[11] He apparently believed that unless an investigation were narrowly defined and confined specifically to war-related problems it would inevitably design a program for fundamental and permanent changes in the structure and function of peacetime government, much of which would only play into the hands of conservative critics.

[5] William H. Moore, *Dissolution of the War Industries Board and Release of Its Industry Controls, 1918* (no. 56 in Historical Studies Series, U.S. Department of Labor, Bureau of Labor Statistics, December 1942), p. 8, in Record Group 179, Records of the War Production Board, National Archives, Washington, D.C., File 002.

[6] "Preliminary to Reconstruction," *New Republic* 16 (October 12, 1918): 304–5, a clipping in RG 61, File 1–A5, box 41.

[7] W. L. Crounse, "Washington News," *Hardware Age* 102 (October 24, 1918): 61.

[8] Moore, *Dissolution of the War Industries Board*, p. 10.

[9] Diary of Edward M. House, August 17, 1918, Edward M. House Papers, Yale University, New Haven, Conn.

[10] Wilson to Lee S. Overman, October 5, 1918, Woodrow Wilson Papers, Library of Congress, Washington, D.C. (cited hereafter as *Wilson Papers*); Charles G. Washburn, *The Life of John W. Weeks* (Boston: Houghton Mifflin, 1928), pp. 213–16; "Preliminary to Reconstruction," pp. 304–5.

[11] Wilson to Edward A. Filene, September 7, 1918, *Wilson Papers*.

A cautious approach toward emergency government had been evident in Wilson's thinking from the outset, and despite all the innovations and unprecedented changes induced by the war he never relinquished his commitment to regular forms of federal administration, firmly embedded in legal authority. Wilson intended to restrict emergency agencies to the war period itself, though he might exempt some of their functions from a general proscription. Wilson was not inflexible on the subject of continuing some wartime regulations or agreements. He was forthright, however, in his opposition to new departures in emergency government during the postarmistice period. He wrote Anna Howard Shaw of the CND's Women's Committee on November 18 with regard to reconstruction planning:

I doubt if I shall appoint a new and separate Reconstruction Commission. I have been trying to get the reconstruction work in hand through existing instrumentalities, altered in their direction and changed a bit in their organization, because I feel that it would take longer to start a new commission than would be wise.[12]

Those functions of war agencies like the WIB which might prove beneficial in the postwar period Wilson wanted transferred to regular departments.

While Wilson's predisposition against new experiments in emergency government was evident before mid-November 1918, it was confirmed by the results of the mid-term elections. In spite of—indeed, many argued, because of—a public presidential appeal for a Democratic Congress in late October, the elections produced Republican majorities in both houses. The defeat held grave implications for Wilson's leadership in foreign policy, of course, but it also raised questions about the fate of administration initiatives in domestic policy as well. Moreover, pressure mounted in both parties for retrenchment and economy, which placed further limits on executive action on the home front.[13]

These general political factors as well as the president's own predisposition naturally set significant constraints on Baruch's actions throughout the late fall. Sensitivity to presidential preferences had been a chief source of Baruch's wartime success. Yet these general circumstances, important though they are, do not entirely explain the behavior of the WIB chairman in the armistice period.

BUSINESS PRESSURES AND WIB RESPONSE

Throughout the war, organized business had never hesitated to call upon the state for aid when it was in its interest to do so. Business groups had stood in the vanguard of public demand for a munitions ministry in the winter crisis of

[12]Quoted in Moore, *Dissolution of the War Industries Board*, p. 11.
[13]*Ibid.*

1917-1918, for example, and they had campaigned for a rationalized state system thereafter. Faced now with the prospect of postwar chaos, the chamber of commerce once again designated itself as industry's spokesman, and propelled by widespread business apprehension, set about to secure federal intervention for postwar planning. American businessmen had concerned themselves about the peace long before they entered the war, of course, and the tempo of speculation increased tremendously as the conflict moved into the fall of 1918. The *Brick and Clay Record* expressed a typical plea that summer when it asked its readers to "resolve that the coming of peace will not find us unprepared for the battle of hustling for business after the war."[14] "Our country at the moment," wrote Emmet Crawford on November 4, "may be likened to the passengers on the Pennsylvania train that has passed through Newark on its way to New York. They have not arrived at New York, but they are all standing up."[15]

As with so many groups, the chamber rested its hopes on a reconstruction commission. According to the chamber, this body would represent "the social, agricultural, commercial and labor interests of the nation"[16] to "forestall the formulation of a number of separate and conflicting class programs."[17] Such was the distillation of cooperative sentiments encouraged by the war. Guided by a consensus approach to the country's major economic blocs, the chamber sought to head off the social tensions which would not only make planning more difficult, but would also endanger the system itself. In pursuit of its reconstruction strategy, the chamber decided in October to call a meeting of all the war service committees for early December and immediately ran into opposition from WIB officials who were concerned lest business attention be diverted from war production. But the chamber persisted. "You and I know," chamber president Harry Wheeler wrote Baruch, "unless we wish to delude ourselves, that business men have been thinking seriously of the readjustment period for many months," and "some sections of American business may get some very wrong ideas if left without guidance."[18] One of the major questions of the armistice

[14] "Now is the Time to Prepare for the After-War Period," *Brick and Clay Record* 53 (August 27, 1918): 365. For similar comments, see "Business after the War" and "War Board May Control Trade," *Dry Goods Reporter* 47 (September 14, 1918): 7, and 47 (November 2, 1918): 5; "If Peace Came—" *Iron Age* 102 (October 31, 1918): 978–79; "Will Machine Shops Decentralize after the War?" *American Machinist* 49(October 31, 1918): 822; and "In Time of War Prepare for Peace," *American Industries* 19 (November 1918): 7.

[15] Emmet L. Crawford to George Peek, November 4, 1918, RG 61, File 21A–A2, box 87.

[16] Harry A. Wheeler (president of the chamber of commerce) to Wilson, October 3, 1918, *Wilson Papers*.

[17] Edward A. Filene (chamber of commerce director) to Wilson, September 4, 1918, *ibid.*

[18] Wheeler to Baruch, October 28, 1918, RG 61, File 21A–A4, box 328. Also see Minutes of a Meeting of the Requirements Division, October 26, 1918, RG 61, File 11A–B1, box 1148 (hereafter cited as *Requirements Division Minutes*).

period is why Baruch persistently refused to have the WIB undertake the degree of state intervention demanded by the chamber of commerce.

The WIB could hardly remain aloof from mounting fears over postwar conditions, and reconstruction inevitably became a chief topic of conversation in the board's offices, especially among the section chiefs. A wide variety of proposals designed to help industry filtered in to Baruch from this source. Most popular among them were plans for overseas trade expansion, revision of the antitrust laws, allocation of raw materials during the transitional phase, maintenance of conservation and standardization programs, a controlled process of contract cancellations and military demobilization, and the pragmatic use of federal controls.[19] In the first few days of November, none of the WIB men seemed to doubt the utility and feasibility of federal intervention during the demobilization period: only the timing and the issues remained in question. Commodity chiefs generally felt that since the WIB had helped ease industry into the war it now had the responsibility to supervise the reverse process. Albert Ritchie reflected the general consensus in a memorandum which he submitted to Baruch on November 6. Since many of the same powers that the WIB had employed during the war would be required during the peacetime adjustment, the board's organization was "the logical one to undertake this work, under an appropriate new name," Ritchie commented. The remnants of the other emergency boards could then be merged with it. Unlike some of his colleagues, however, the lawyer added a note of caution which forecast the future far more accurately than his initial observations. Stay away from a substantial regulatory program, Ritchie warned. "At best we can now only surmise what conditions

---

[19]Some commodity section heads had agreed in August 1918 that they should prepare industry "for greater export business when the War is over." See the Memorandum Minutes of Commodity Section Heads of Finished Products Division held August 7, 1918, RG 61, File 1 - C2, box 83. This sentiment intensified as the end of the war approached. On this point, see "Report of Hardware and Hand Tool Section," November 4, 1918, RG 61, File 21A - A2, box 91; C. F. C. Stout (director, hide, leather and leather goods division) to Baruch, November 8, 1918, RG 61, File 21A–A2, box 103; W. B. Eisendrath (chief, upper & harness leather section) to Stout, November 9, 1918, RG 61, File 21A - A2, box 106; Bi-Weekly Meeting of Chemical Division, November 5 and 12, 1918, RG 61, File 1 - C2, box 76; E. L. Crawford to Baruch, November 9, 1918, RG 61, File 21A–A2, box 87.

Demand for a continuation of conservation and standardization programs was by all odds the most universally recommended proposal throughout November. For example, see "Report of Hardware and Hand Tool Section," November 4, 1918, RG 61, File 21A–A2, box 91; "Hardware and Hand Tool Section Meetings," November 7 and 14, 1918, RG 61, File 1–C2, box 83; Charles A. Rogers (chief, harness, saddlery and other leather equipment) to C. F. C. Stout, November 6, 1918, RG 61, File 21A–A2, box 96; W. B. Eisendrath to C. F. C. Stout, November 9, 1918, RG 61, File 21A–A2, box 106; George R. Wheeler (assistant chief, boot and shoe section) to C. F. C. Stout, November 12, 1918, File 21A–A2, box 96; Thomas E. Donnelly (director, pulp and paper division) to Baruch, November 7, 1918, RG 61, File 21A–A2, box 197.

will be. Industry may be prepared to handle it better than we think." And even more to the point, industry "generally is going to be very much less willing to submit" to government rulings "than was the case in war times."[20]

We have no comments from Baruch at this point, but his subsequent actions suggest that while he wanted to keep his options open, he nevertheless inclined in Ritchie's direction as much as a week before the actual armistice. He could not relay this stand to his section chiefs, or to American industry in general, especially in light of the panic which seized businessmen during the false armistice of November 7. On November 8, he announced that government contracts must continue, a policy to which Secretary Baker subscribed that same day; that the WIB would continue to allocate raw materials to prevent market demoralization; and that the board would exercise all its functions until a peace treaty was signed. He could say no less. Still even on this occasion he promised simultaneously that restrictions and curtailments would be gradually lifted "so as to allow as promptly as possible free flow of all supplies into peace channels."[21] And it was this part of the statement with which he chose to align himself in subsequent weeks.

The armistice on November 11 made the board's policy of pacifying industry's emotions all the more imperative. On the twelfth the *New York Times* reported that WIB officials foresaw "no serious industrial disturbance with the Government's grip on all industries and materials held tight." "The Board," the *Times* observed, "retains its authority until peace is formally proclaimed."[22]

Business pressure for central direction was most intense in the few days before and after the eleventh. Harry Wheeler had summed up business fears in a long letter to Wilson and Baruch on the ninth. He wrote of widespread anxiety that the government would cancel all outstanding contracts and immediately lift all controls so as to flood postwar markets and send prices tumbling downward. Some clearance committee was necessary to oversee the demobilization process, Wheeler advised.[23] Baruch assured the president that he had already suggested a common adjustment policy for all government agencies and that the WIB would clear contracts and allocate raw materials.[24] Such a reply, however, was a play for the president's confidence, not an accurate reflection of WIB achievements or capabilities.

Public pronouncements and private thinking diverged in early and mid-November. The administration and WIB leadership showed a real reluctance to yield to demands for intensified state intervention, a principle implicit in their

[20] Ritchie to Baruch, November 6, 1918, RG 61, File 1-A5, box 42.

[21] Press release, November 8, 1918, RG 61, File 1-A5, box 41; *New York Times*, November 9, 1918, p. 8.

[22] *New York Times*, November 12, 1918, p. 20.

[23] Wheeler to Wilson, November 9, 1918, *Wilson Papers*.

[24] Baruch to Wilson, November 11, 1918, *ibid.*

earlier aversion to postwar planning. The administration possessed no settled reconstruction program on November 11 and it refused to design one thereafter. WIB officials were at least prepared to discuss the future with CND representatives in Washington on armistice day, but on Baker's advice Wilson asked Baruch to leave off any such theorizing.[25]

Baruch was probably not unhappy at this turn of events, for sometime between the sixth of November, when he received Ritchie's memorandum, and a few days after the armistice, he decided he would leave Washington as soon as discretion allowed. A host of factors led him to this decision. Foremost among them was his estimation of what the board could undertake in the changed context of postwar America. Clearly, it could no longer rely upon the cooperative impulse of wartime to underwrite its regulatory activity. Baruch knew far better than the general public how tenuous many of his agreements were and that any attempt to duplicate them in peacetime would mean certain defeat. Baruch no doubt shared the feeling of division chiefs Shaw and Stout, who argued that the board would either have to create a full-fledged state bureaucracy and secure congressional statutes to enforce its program effectively in the future or would have to forget them altogether.[26] This was a crucial consideration. The absence of statutory authority had dogged the WIB throughout its history even though Baruch seemed personally to enjoy operating in the atmosphere of illegality it produced. So the inevitable question arose once again. Should the WIB lobby for enabling legislation with the president and Congress? The answer was no on at least two grounds. Neither Wilson nor Congress would be receptive. But not even a sympathetic Wilson and congenial Congress would have eliminated all doubts. Baruch probably shared the concern of some of his colleagues that with the peace an agency like the WIB might very easily fall prey to politicians or unsympathetic government officials. The very flexibility which an informal emergency agency like the WIB offered business interests as a protective device during the crisis was one of its great appeals to business synthesizers. To transform it into the strong arm of a regulatory state beyond the reach of voluntary business personnel was in some ways the very antithesis of the WIB experience.

Nor could Baruch fail to consider how his own reputation would fare if he prolonged the board's life. As he pointed out to steel representatives on the thirteenth, congressional investigations were a certainty now and the kinds of extralegal activity characteristic of the war years were simply out of the question.[27] Cries for retrenchment and Republican victories in the congressional

[25] Baker to Wilson, November 9, 1918, *ibid.*; "Meeting with the Representatives of the State Councils of Defense," November 11, 1918, RG 61, File 1–C2, box 85.

[26] *Requirements Division Minutes*, November 11, 1918, RG 61, File 21A–A1, box 21.

[27] "Special Meeting with Committee Representing the American Iron and Steel Institute with Members of the War Industries Board for the Purpose of Discussing Means for

elections that month suggested both the futility of making plans and the likelihood of intense criticism of those who did.[28] And then there was the hope that Wilson would take him to Versailles. "You must be on the Peace Commission," Ritchie told Baruch on November 15. "You are not only needed there because of your knowledge of conditions here, but this would be a wonderful way to end, and end now, while the going is at its very best, & when the work is really over, your work here."[29]

Baruch early recognized his limited future in postwar Washington, but he never relinquished his goal of protecting the country's industrial structure, and throughout November and December he did everything within his limited power to secure economic stability and prosperity. He encouraged the Department of Commerce to adopt several of the board's wartime functions, including its standardization and conservation programs. He consistently urged the War Department to coordinate contract cancellations with the Labor Department and with the WIB's commodity sections. He hoped private industrial leaders and the war service committees would continue to allocate materials and fix prices; and he had Wilson ask the military services to retain all excess stocks until the market could safely absorb them. He continued, too, to hope that business groups would keep consumer costs down lest the cost of living question force Congress to enact stringent controls.[30]

A number of other factors ensured that Baruch would make only a gradual retreat. For one thing, he worried about the board's image. He had to save face

---

Stabilizing the Industry during the Transition Period Following the Signing of the Armistice," November 13, 1918, a copy in Bernard M. Baruch Papers, Princeton University, Princeton, N.J. (cited hereafter as *Baruch Papers*).

[28] *Ibid.*

[29] Ritchie to Baruch, November 15, 1918, *Baruch Papers*, General Correspondence.

[30] On the transfer of conservation, standardization, and statistical projects to the Department of Commerce, see Redfield to Wilson, November 15, 1918, Wilson to Baruch, November 16, 1918, Baruch to Wilson, November 18, 1918, Wilson to Baruch, November 18, 1918, Wilson to Redfield, November 26, 1918, and Baruch to Wilson, November 27, 1918, all in the *Wilson Papers*; Baruch to Redfield, November 16, 1918, and related correspondence in Record Group 40, General Records of the Department of Commerce, National Archives, Washington, D.C., File 67009/72 and File 78253; *New York Times*, November 15, 1918, p. 1; William C. Redfield, *With Congress and Cabinet* (New York: Doubleday, Page, 1924), pp. 216–19; and Robert F. Himmelberg, "Business, Antitrust Policy, and the Industrial Board of the Department of Commerce, 1919," *Business History Review* 42 (Spring 1968): 4–5. President Wilson was fully in accord with these functional transfers.

On the formalities of army–WIB cooperation in contract cancellations, see Minutes of a Meeting of the War Industries Board, RG 61, File 1 – C1, boxes 72–74 (cited hereafter as *WIB Minutes*), November 19, 1918; "Memorandum," November 21, 1918, RG 61, File 21A–A3, box 3; George W. Goethals, Supply Circular no. 112, "Instructions to Supply Bureaus of the Army on Reduction and Cancellation of Contracts," November 9, 1918, RG 61, File 11A–A1, box 1144; "Memorandum for

with both his business clientele and with the general public. He had made moral commitments to American industry, offering them assistance in return for patriotic cooperation in the war, and now business groups were coming to claim their debts. Baruch could not openly admit he had nothing much to offer. He could only assure business that the WIB stood firm and that it was doing everything necessary to calm the troubled waters. He probably felt that if he asserted his optimism frequently enough, some business fears would indeed melt away. He also had to consider his commitments to the American public. He had boasted of the WIB's successes in lowering prices and modifying the cost of living, and to have values now suddenly shoot out of sight would raise some questions about the process by which they were fixed in the first place. Moreover, he had touted the WIB as the linchpin of economic mobilization, and to openly admit now that it could play no such role after November 11, despite the unchanged nature of its formal position, cast some doubt on its capacities and performance in the previous months.[31] Baruch still wanted—even required—the benefits of intraindustry cooperation and military-industrial-civilian coordination, but his board could no longer attempt its former legitimizing and coordinating functions. He continued to encourage private and semipublic strategems for stability and prosperity, but he was determined to withdraw the WIB from active service. He believed that the kind of state intervention generated by the war crisis was no longer likely or possibly even desirable during the peace.

While in the spring and summer of 1917 Baruch had prodded business interests to come into price and purchasing agreements with the state, in November 1918 he tried to convince many of the same interests that in the changed political circumstances of a nonwar period they could no longer expect state support. Where once Baruch had persistently sought responsibility in Washington he now as persistently sought to escape it.

At the heart of Baruch's postwar strategy for economic stability and prosperity at home lay the idea of a concerted drive for trade expansion abroad.

---

the Chief of Staff," November [?], 1918, Record Group 165, Records of the War College Division of the General Staff, National Archives, Washington, D.C., box 202, doc. no. 7564–22.

Wilson agreed with Baruch's suggestion to have the military departments keep their excess stocks off the market; see Baruch to Wilson, November 15, 1918, and Wilson to Baker et al., November 18, 1918, in Wilson Papers. For an example of Baruch's efforts with industrial leaders, see Baruch to Clinton H. Crane, November 21, 1918, RG 61, File 21A–A4, box 784.

[31] These comments are based in part on the report of a conversation between Baruch and a group of leading shoe manufacturers. One of them believed that "Mr. Baruch himself seems to be fishing around for something that would let him out with the public. He came out to the public saying that shoes would be reduced. . . . Now he is afraid that if restrictions are removed that the price will go right up in the air." "Meeting of the Hide & Leather Goods Section of the War Industries Board with Representatives of the

Business groups could obtain their basic goal of ordered prosperity without state regulation by enlarging their export trade. Baruch was a true Wilsonian in this respect. He shared the Wilsonian vision that linked business expansionism, the national interest, and the spread of liberal, capitalist values. Wilson had set the stage for this aspect of postwar policy as early as 1916. In the course of allying himself at that time with business proposals for trade expansion he had observed:

Somebody must keep the great stable foundations of the life of nations untouched and undisturbed. Somebody must keep the great economic processes of the world of business alive. Somebody must see to it that we stand ready to repair the enormous damage and the incalculable losses which will ensue from this war.[32]

Baruch took up this challenge in November 1918, both because he deeply believed in the assumptions on which it rested and because it served his immediate self-interest as chairman of a weakened war agency.

Baruch wove many of these themes together in his discussions with steel industry representatives on November 13. There is no better example of Baruch's determination to refuse responsibilities he could not successfully discharge, and of his belief that vigorous business expansion might obviate the need for politically dangerous state controls. Gary and the steel industry came to Washington to urge an activist role on the WIB. According to Gary, the Board should coordinate all contract cancellations, both for the Allied and United States governments, maintain all price agreements, encourage a large program of government buying, and generally do everything necessary to ensure an orderly transition to a peacetime economy. A hands-off policy, warned the steel spokesman, could only result in a great market demoralization. The conferees spent a great deal of time on the price question. Gary specifically requested the WIB to continue to back maximum prices so as not to give buyers the impression that they could expect an immediate drop, and thus tempt them to hold off purchases.

Baruch had reservations about every one of these requests. The industry's fears were partially unfounded, he asserted, and their remedies were impractical and undesirable. At the center of his optimism for steel specifically and business generally lay the conviction that "someone will have to supply an enormous amount of material particularly the steel, [sic] to every country in the world.

Shoe Manufacturers and Allied Industry for the Purpose of Considering the Removal of Restrictions and Regulations," November 14, 1918, RG 61, File 21A–A2, box 100.

[32] Quoted in N. Gordon Levin, Jr., *Woodrow Wilson and World Politics, America's Response to War and Revolution* (New York: Oxford University Press, 1969), p. 21. Levin expands upon this interpretation of Wilsonian ideology in chap. 1.

There is really one country today that is able to supply those and that is the United States." Business self-interest, service to humanity, and the national interest all led in the direction of trade expansion, he avowed. American business could serve its own cause in postwar America by reconstructing Europe. It could relieve suffering and gain prosperity at the same time. It could advance America's national interest and head off the revolutionary spirit already sweeping that continent. Baruch offered the steel industry a place in an international political economy in which America would have hegemony by virtue of her great wealth and healthy industrial plant. "We have our Army which we have got to supply; we have the great civilian population which are now engaged in revolution. It seems that the civilization and Government are rocked to the very bottom. Secondary to the establishment of food is the establishment of materials. . . . Unless they get the materials to get them work, they will have idle hands and idle minds and you know what the result of that is." Several corollary thoughts followed. To facilitate export, the industry should investigate "the possibility of arranging a combination" under the Webb bill. Above all it should lower prices to make itself competitive. Wartime price agreements, in other words, were positively detrimental at this point if they supported schedules that cut industry off from the very means to bring prosperity at home and peace abroad. "Would it be the wise thing to say reduce prices now to some point or would it be better for us to try to hold the situation and wait until those foreign orders come in, whether by reduction of price that would attract the orders here or some other country. That is the problem you have got to face." On the other hand, a precipitous decline in prices could be equally dangerous. And if that really seemed imminent, as the industry believed, well then, of course, "we may have to determine some minimum price legislation somewhat along the lines, we might say, of the Gary dinners under Government supervision. . . ."[33]

Baruch's emphasis upon low prices and expansive foreign trade was rooted in his analysis of the American political and social scene. On the one hand there were the inevitable excess supplies that would come with contract cancellations. On the other hand, there was a possibility that without prosperity social unrest could bring radical legislative measures. Baruch's own assessment had convinced him that the WIB could do little. "Don't forget, gentlemen," he warned, "we have all got politics in front of us." The opportunity for extralegal deals was now sharply reduced and, in addition, Congress would not underwrite the measures that industry had demanded and received during the war. "You say the President ought to do that, he ought to do this. It is a question of how far the President can go when we are out of the war and how far the country will back

---

[33] "Special Meeting with Committee Representing the American Iron and Steel Institute with Members of the War Industries Board for the Purpose of Discussing Means for Stabilizing the Industry during the Transition Period Following the Signing of the Armistice," November 13, 1918, a copy in *Baruch Papers*.

him up in conditions of peace and holding what the people think are false prices."[34]

Gary would not or could not lift his vision above specifics, and Baruch could do nothing else in the circumstances except issue a bland statement at the conclusion of the meeting which combined Gary's wishes for WIB controls and Baruch's conviction that business demand was sure to increase in the immediate weeks.

At this point (November 13) many commodity chiefs shared steel's desire for continued supervision and expected to have a major part in guiding their industry into a peacetime economy. They maintained this conception far longer than Baruch, largely because they were closer to the trades and partial to the cooperative agreements they had devised under the WIB's protective wing. Moreover, their daily work with industry had involved personal promises and strong moral commitments which they could not now suddenly dismiss. The commodity chiefs had good reason to worry about industries they would soon reenter; Baruch, on the other hand, would escape to Paris. Some tension developed between the center and periphery of the board over lifting restrictions. The *Dry Goods Reporter* observed "that while the big 'dollar-a-year' men are anxious to go home, those occupying positions of less importance in the same bodies express a very strong realization of the need for the continuance of such boards and administrations."[35] *Iron Age* noted that major officials definitely wanted to drop price fixing, but "some of the section chiefs have different ideas."[36]

Still it would be wrong to exaggerate either the division between the section chiefs and top WIB men, or the unanimity among the section chiefs themselves. By no means were all commodity chiefs willing to remain in Washington. According to one, ". . . There appears to be a lassitude, that in effect, means no one wants the responsibility of the clean-up. It is a question of getting out from under and going home."[37] The chief of the electrodes and abrasive section commented: "I feel very strongly and I think a number of other Section Heads feel the same way about it that I do, that none of us should be expected to volunteer our services during the readjustment time. All of the members of your staff have made tremendous sacrifices to serve the War Industries Board . . . and it would be rather unfair to expect them to still further neglect their private business. . . ."[38] Commodity chiefs also differed among themselves as to exactly

[34]*Ibid.*

[35] "For and Against Quick Action," *Dry Goods Reporter* 47 (November 23, 1918): 7.

[36]O.F.S., "Ending Government Regulations of Steel," *Iron Age* 102 (December 5, 1918): 1394.

[37]E. E. Parsonage to C. S. Brantingham, November 16, 1918, RG 61, File 21A–A4, box 1163.

[38]H. C. DuBois to Charles MacDowell, November 11, 1918, RG 61, File 21A–A2, box 59.

when and on what issues they favored a continuation of WIB controls. The WIB was a pluralistic, even chaotic organization, so it was difficult to obtain any overall consensus on an issue as controversial as reconstruction policy. Each man looked to the best interests of his particular industry. Only central officials like Ritchie, Baruch, and Peek worried about the board's general reputation. Baruch had asked all division heads to poll their sections on reconstruction in early November, and the replies of the chemical division are typical of the wide variety of responses he received. The paint section chief recommended that "return to normal conditions can be brought about more quickly by removal of restrictions than by their continued imposition." The abrasive section demanded that "all supervision" cease. The creosote section agreed. On the other hand, an overproduction of sulphuric acids made the acids and heavy chemicals section reluctant to end controls, and the sulphur and pyrites sections shared its concern. The tanning materials and natural dyes section hoped for a release on castor oil and waxes but requested restriction on the importation and allocation of tanning materials, fixed maximum prices on domestic tanning extracts, and a new allocation policy for harder fats.[39] We should not forget the effect of this variegated opinion in persuading Baruch and the board's inner group that regulated demobilization through the WIB, at least, was simply out of the question.

As early as the 10th, Baruch had indicated that how long a man remained in Washington was, in the words of George Peek, "largely a question for each man to determine for himself." "When [a Commodity Chief] has done everything possible and discharged his obiligation not only to the Government but to his industries which he has tied up then he may consider his task completed."[40] This kind of comment set the stage for an anarchic dissolution. Central controls simply faded away and prime responsibility fell to the section chiefs. Peek informed his section heads on the 12th that government purchasing agencies would listen to WIB recommendations on requirements and cancellations, and he strengthened his promise with a lengthy circular on November 22. A circular of November 15 gave full responsibility to the commodity chiefs for all permit systems and conservation programs and asked them to serve as spokesmen for their industries in all dealings with government departments. Peek and the board's central officials encouraged their men to do all within their power to aid

---

[39] Charles MacDowell to Baruch, November 14, 1918, *ibid.*, contains a digest of these opinions.

[40] *Requirements Division Minutes*, November 11, 1918, RG 61, File 21A–A1, box 21. The director of the WIB's building materials division told his group: "Mr. Baruch has stated that each section was a law practically unto itself. It [*sic*] work ceased when in its judgement it had ceased." "Meeting of the Building Materials Section," November 19, 1918, RG 61, File 1–C2, box 75.

industry. But they made it clear at the same time that the board could only act in an advisory capacity.[41]

The near panic among business groups in the days before and after the armistice began to lift after the middle of the month, and this development assisted the WIB in its course. By the sixteenth George Peek was personally convinced that much of the dismay over contract cancellation was "fear of what may happen and what has happened, and little has been done to disturb [sic] the country."[42] Secretary Baker commented on the twenty-fifth:

The business situation in the United States is giving me less concern than it did immediately after the armistice was signed. At the first blush there was much apprehension lest the sudden cession of war orders and the rapid demobilization of war industry as well as of military men would create a depression and labor disturbances. The indications now seem on every hand to be of very great readiness on the part of business to readapt itself to the changed conditions, and if I am at all a good judge, we are going to find business men everywhere launching out along old lines or new ones with little loss of time.[43]

Everyone granted that a gigantic building boom was in the offing and those industries that expected to participate were especially cheerful. The *American Paint and Oil Dealer* exclaimed, "There is scant doubt that the final cessation of fighting will bring building activities, the like of which has not before been seen in the United States."[44] The clothing industry anticipated release of pent-up consumer demands. In the opinion of *The American Hatter*, "Nothing but prosperity can await this nation in the years to come."[45] The National Association of Manufacturers' "Committee on Readjustment after the War" concluded that "the factories and stores of the United States are at present almost depleted of their usual stock and that our country is on the threshold of a most unprecedented business expansion owing to this domestic condition."[46]

[41] George N. Peek, "Reduced Requirements," memorandum to all section heads, November 12, 1918, RG 61, File 21A–A3, box 3; George N. Peek to all section heads of War Industries Board, November 15, 1918, *ibid.*; George N. Peek, "To All Divisional and Section Heads of the War Industries Board," November 22, 1918, RG 61, File 1–A5, box 41.

[42] *Requirements Division Minutes*, November 16, 1918, RG 61, File 21A–A1, box 21.

[43] Baker to Edward R. Stettinius, November 25, 1918, *Baker Papers.*

[44] *American Paint and Oil Dealer* 11 (November 1918): 15.

[45] "Peace on Earth!" *American Hatter* 49 (November 1918): 43. Also see "Now What?" *Brick and Clay Record* 53 (November 19, 1918): 868–71; "The War is Over–Now What?" *Dry Goods Reporter* 47 (November 16, 1918): 7; "Peace and its Possibilities," *Hardware Age 102* (November 21, 1918): 70–71.

[46] Quoted in *American Industries* 19 (January 1919): 7.

WIB leadership was more attuned to the subtleties, complications, and flaws in this glowing portrait, but determined nevertheless to release restrictions as soon as possible; and the section chiefs seemed increasingly to agree with this course. All of them could use the prognostications of an anticipated business boom as justification for their actions. The board placed the onus squarely upon industry to explain why restrictions and regulations should not be lifted. On November 22, 1918, the board officially requested the section chiefs to arrange consultation with all industries under their supervision and to discuss the withdrawal of all restrictions and the future of conservation programs. Once more the chiefs were to emphasize the advisory nature of WIB activity. They were to inform industry that all price agreements would expire as they came up; and that all priority rulings had ended except on contracts placed directly by the shipping board, navy, railroad administration, and telephone and telegraph companies. The board operated on the assumption that unless they heard to the contrary they would release industry from restriction. In any case, all agreements would have to terminate automatically by January 1, 1919.[47] When a colleague asked George Peek whether the WIB should be represented at the chamber of commerce's convention in December, Peek replied that some general statement might be necessary "because everyone is wondering what we are going to have to do with reconstruction and, as a matter of fact, we are going to have nothing."[48] Peek wrote a friend on the eighteenth of November, "We have about come to the conclusion that we will bring industries in and confer with them on the matter so as to have their concurrence in our action, but really we have in mind that there is nothing for us to do but to release all the restrictions we have imposed upon industries."[49]

As these sentiments crystallized into settled policy, WIB officials adamantly opposed business pressure to continue regulations beyond January 1 or to take on new responsibilities. Common sense and diplomatic niceties prevented the blunt expression of this course to business groups, but the strategy was fully revealed in private meetings, private correspondence, and above all in WIB inaction. Industries, of course, had been given some room to maneuver within the WIB's general guidelines. They had until January 1 to take advantage of any WIB

[47]George N. Peek, "To All Divisional and Section Heads of the War Industries Board," November 22, 1918; *Requirements Division Minutes*, November 22, 1918, RG 61, File 1–C2, box 86; George N. Peek, "Suggested Telegram to All Divisional and Section Heads of the War Industries Board," November 22, 1918, George N. Peek Papers, Western Historical Manuscript Collection, University of Missouri, Columbia, Mo. (cited hereafter as *Peek Papers*).

[48]"Meeting of Division Heads," November 23, 1918, RG 61, File 1–C2, box 81.

[49]Peek to Frank Silloway, November 18, 1918, *Peek Papers*. Judge Parker was reported as saying that day that "industries should be given as free rein as they want." George K. Burgess to Redfield, November 19, 1918, RG 40, File 67009/72.

agreements, and the section chiefs intended to do everything they could to help them along. One chief explained to his trade that "this Section stands ready to continue the present relations and to do all within its power to assist the industry in getting back to normal status."[50] Keeping industries informed of government policy and urging the purchasing departments to design their cutbacks to dovetail with industrial requirements were two common functions.[51] Some would have done more: they would have retained price fixing agreements beyond January 1, they would have extended pooling operations, and they would have lobbied for liberal contract readjustments. But all such moves would have entangled the board in postwar controversy and extended its capabilities beyond the breaking point. As a result, Baruch formally tried to bar the sections from sanctioning pooling plans or price fixing agreements without explicit approval from the central office. "Mr. Baruch is being urged to take on all kinds of new responsibilities for the War Industries Board," Peek observed on November 21, "but up to this time we have quite successfully escaped them."[52]

Of the new responsibilities to come before the board in November, none was more popular among business groups than a WIB-led campaign to amend the Sherman antitrust law. There was strong support for this goal within the board itself, and commodity chiefs recommended action throughout November. Baruch, however, wisely rejected all such overtures, for the same kinds of reasons which had led him to favor a speedy exit from the Washington stage: the WIB's vulnerability in a changed political and social climate; the possibility of congressional challenge to the board's entire operations; and a desire to avoid tarnishing his reputation.[53]

The WIB men also refrained from making a public issue of troop demobilization. This policy was of more immediate importance to the reconstruction period, and more within the WIB's legitimate concerns. On November 6, George Peek suggested that the board consider demobilization plans "in order that men

[50]"Minutes of the Meeting of the American Extract Manufacturers in Conjunction with the Tanning Material and Natural Dye Section of the War Industries Board," November 21, 1918, RG 61, File 1-C1, box 86. Also see "Meeting of the Woolen Division of the War Industries Board with the Representatives of the Wool Stock Graders Association and the National Association of Waste Dealers to Discuss the Condition of Their Industries," December 2, 1918, RG 61, File 1-C2, box 87.

[51]For examples of these activities, see E. E. Parsonage to C. S. Brantingham, November 16, 1918, RG 61, File 21A-A4, box 1163; Walter Robbins to Edwin B. Parker, November 20, 1918, RG 61, File 21A-A3, box 16; Charles C. Hanch to Rhodes S. Baker, November 20, 1918, RG 61, File 21A-A4, box 221; Alex C. Brown to The Brown Hoisting Machinery Company, November 22, 1918, RG 61, File 21A-A3, box 13.

[52]Peek to Frank Silloway, November 21, 1918, *Peek Papers*.

[53]Robert F. Himmelberg traces these developments in "The War Industries Board and the Antitrust Question in November 1918," *Journal of American History* 52 (June 1965): 59-74.

may be sent back to the particular lines of industry most needed."[54] He wanted to synchronize the human and material factors of production for an orderly and predictable business expansion. He recommended release of a hundred thousand highly skilled workers at once, along with farmers, executives, small business owners and all professional people. Peek would have then combed the army camps for workers in the food, fuel, mining, railroad, and ship building industries, using a furlough system to place only as many as the market could bear. Cooperation between the local draft boards and the U.S. Employment Service could organize the process to prevent a "mad scramble for overpaid jobs."[55] Peek enlisted the support of Baruch and Hugh Frayne, the WIB's labor representative, for this scheme, but General March of the army would not involve his service in such a discriminatory program. Baker promised War Department cooperation where possible, but as with so many such promises, this one was honored only in the breach. "I asked Mr. Baruch if this meant that we could make such requests as we pleased," observed Peek, "and that they would consider them and probably do nothing with them, and he said that would probably be the result."[56] Baruch and Peek might have been tempted at this point to generate support among business groups to try and bring the army to heel. But if this thought occurred to them, they gave it short shrift and yielded to the military's decision to demobilize en masse. At the war's end, the military services exercised prerogatives in demobilization of manpower and contract cancellation in a way that suggests that the onslaught against them by emergency boards such as the WIB was not as successful as we have been led to believe.

The WIB's central controls disappeared soon after November 11. The priorities division voted unanimously on November 19 to lift all restrictions,[57] and that same day Baruch and Wilson decided no price agreements could extend beyond their current termination dates. This latter step was something of a compromise between those who recommended immediate withdrawal and those who wanted the option to continue such agreements indefinitely. Brookings approved this compromise strategy when Baruch passed the word along to him.[58] Josephus Daniels noted in his diary that at a meeting of top-level policy

[54] Peek to Baruch, November 6, 1918, *Peek Papers.*

[55] Peek to Baruch, November 18, 1918, RG 61, File 21A–A3, box 14.

[56] Geroge N. Peek, "Memorandum on Demobilization," November 20, 1918, *ibid.* Also see Edward M. Coffman, *The Hilt of the Sword: The Career of Peyton C. March* (Madison: University of Wisconsin Press, 1966), pp. 152–156.

[57] History of Priorities from June 18, 1918, to November 25, 1918, Vol. F, RG 61, File 7–B2, box 844. As in all WIB divisions, disagreements preceded such actions; on November 15, the committee secretary specifically recommended against cancelling outstanding priority regulations en masse. Secretary, Priorities Committee to Priorities Commissioner, November 15, 1918, RG 61, File 21A–A4, box 1163.

[58] Brookings had been under pressure from the hides and leather division to lift price restrictions immediately, but he favored letting all price agreements run their course

makers on November 19, Baruch and McAdoo had said that "reconstruction would take care of itself."[59]

On November 27, Baruch officially informed Wilson that the WIB's life was really over and asked him to set the terminal date at January 1, 1919. Baruch's key argument in this letter was simply that future WIB programs were now impractical. The board would fail, and this failure would bring the entire government into disrespect. "The American people would resent, I believe," he wrote, "the continuance of apparent war powers; and further continuance of the War Industries Board, shorn as it is of its powers, would create a lack of respect for the government which sought to maintain unenforcible regulations. Therefore, I think the sooner it closes up its work and leaves, the better it will be for all concerned."[60]

Baruch attended an important meeting of war administrators three days later and further elaborated his position. Secretary Baker and the CND evidently decided on their own initiative to formulate recommendations on reconstruction, and they invited a number of advisors, including Baruch, to their meeting on the thirtieth. The group concluded that "in general the problem of reconstruction was rather one of removing restrictions imposed during the progress of the war than of formulating any new policy, it being the thought of all present that American industry and commerce would reassert itself and undertake peace time occupations as soon as the raw material and labor of the country were

---

and would not act unless specifically asked to do so by Baruch. Baruch declined, preferring to let the section heads and their industries work it out among themselves on the assumption that no agreements would continue beyond established expiry dates save under extraordinary conditions. As the days passed, the WIB refused to recognize any exceptions. The steel industry pressed for an extension of their agreement in December, for example, but Brookings refused. "Recommendations to the Price Fixing Committee Made by the Hide, Leather & Leather Goods Division of the War Industries Board on November 13th, 1918," G. C. Howe (chief, hide and skin section) to Baruch, November 18, 1918, and C. F. C. Stout to Brookings, November 20, 1918, all in RG 61, File 21A–A4, box 706; Brookings to Baruch, November 14, 1918, and Stout to Baruch, November 19, 1918, both in RG 61, File 21–A4, box 704; Baruch to Brookings, November 16, 1918, RG 61, File 4 – B1, box 528; Stout to Brookings, November 21, 1918, RG 61, File 21A – A4, box 1150; *WIB Minutes*, November 21, 1918; Brookings to Wilson, November 22, 1918, RG 61, File 21B–A3, box 163; Wilson to Brookings, November 26, 1918, *Wilson Papers*; Brookings to W. B. Colver, November 27, 1918, RG 61, File 21A–A4, box 1147; Brookings to Baruch, November 29, 1918, RG 61, File 21A–A3, box 34. On the steel episode, see Melvin I. Urofsky, *Big Steel and the Wilson Administration* (Columbus: Ohio State University Press, 1969), pp. 306 – 7 and O. F. S., "Refusal to Consider Prices Emphasized," and "War Board Did Not Consider Steel Prices," *Iron Age* 102 (December 19, 1918): 1513–14, 1512–13.

[59] E. David Cronon, ed., *The Cabinet Diaries of Josephus Daniels* (Lincoln: University of Nebraska Press, 1963), p. 350.

[60] Baruch to Wilson, November 27, 1918, *Wilson Papers*.

available for such resumption."[61] As council chairman, Baker drew up the official statement, but Baruch penned some emendations to the first draft. Baker and Baruch varied in their emphasis on the role of the state during the immediate postwar period. Baker believed it should now withdraw to its proper narrow and inactive position; Baruch sought to enlist its support in some areas, even while anxious to reduce its overall wartime role. His was a middle position between the laissez-faire orientation of Baker and the interventionist orientation of some of his business clientele. What was required, according to Baruch, were policies to develop domestic sources of raw materials, to increase industrial production generally, and to ensure America "an equal opportunity to enjoy the world's trade. . . ."[62]

Baruch's request of the twenty-seventh and the council meeting three days later dovetailed nicely with the president's own strategy for reconstruction. He had already informed the U.S. Chamber of Commerce that he had no message for their Atlantic City meeting;[63] he agreed to Baruch's proposal to end the WIB;[64] and his address to Congress on December 2, two days before he sailed for Europe, fully reflected the spirit of the council's summation.[65] Indeed, Wilson leaned more toward Baker than Baruch in this speech. The American "readjustment" would be far less serious than in European countries, he told Congress, and thus required very little in the way of state intervention. The American people did not like "to be coached and led." Now that the war was over Wilson was convinced the public would refuse to conform to regulations "and go their own way." He pointed to events of the past few weeks to buttress his case, arguing that the process of lifting restrictions "promises to outrun any inquiry that may be instituted and any aid that may be offered. It will not be easy to direct it any better than it will direct itself."[66] The president offered not even a hint of state aid or direction in the coming months. As the *New Republic* noted, "Those who hoped that the President's address would promise vigorous leadership for the period of reconstruction must now be thoroughly disillusioned."[67]

In tone and substance the president's address was thoroughly reminiscent of the New Freedom rhetoric of the 1912 campaign. As an actual description of the role of the state in the nation's economy in December 1918, however, it was very misleading. The railroads, the shipping industry, the merchant marine, and

[61] *CND Minutes*, November 29, 1918.

[62] See Baruch's suggestions in Baruch to Baker, November 30, 1918, and the final draft, Baker to Wilson, November 30, 1918, both in *Baker Papers*.

[63] Wilson to Harry A. Wheeler, November 26, 1918, *Wilson Papers*.

[64] Wilson to Baruch, November 30, 1918, *Wilson Papers*.

[65] Wilson to Baker, December 2, 1918, *Baker Papers*.

[66] *New York Times*, December 3, 1918, p. 1.

[67] *New Republic* 17 (December 7, 1918): 146.

the coal industry all continued under state regulation, and a guaranteed price for the 1919 wheat crop remained in effect. Moreover, as the WIB's experience in November makes clear, some business interests wanted very much to be coached and led. Indeed in the spring of 1919 the Department of Commerce would launch an abortive program of price agreements under an Industrial Board in response to just such business pressure.[68] Still, the president's sentiments were unmistakable.

Members of the WIB tried in various ways to mitigate the transition from war to peace, but the broad guidelines had been set. Moreover, the strain on the WIB lessened as business demands for federal direction decreased in the later part of November. By early December the chamber of commerce's "Reconstruction Congress" could agree that all regulations should be immediately revoked and all war restrictions removed "as speedily as practicable."[69] According to Robert Brookings this kind of resolution confirmed Baruch's "good judgement" in "letting the industries take care of themselves."[70]

Individual WIB members lingered on in the capital in December for various reasons—to lobby on behalf of special interests, to write up final reports, to transfer WIB functions to regular government departments,[71] or to ensure the passage of legislation that would legalize all informal government contracts in order to assure producers and manufacturers of legal protection—but most commodity sections had simply disintegrated by January 1, 1919. Baruch designated Albert Ritchie the board's liquidating officer before he set sail for the peace conference on December 31, and Ritchie devoted much of the next three months to tidying up administrative details, arranging for the transfer of WIB records to the Council of National Defense and lobbying for the legalization of

---

[68] For the Industrial Board experiment, see Robert F. Himmelberg, "Business, Antitrust Policy, and the Industrial Board of the Department of Commerce, 1919," *Business History Review* 42 (Spring 1968): 1–23; and E. Jay Howenstine, Jr., "The Industrial Board, Precursor of the N.R.A.: The Price–Reduction Movement after World War I," *Journal of Political Economy*, 51 (June 1943): 235–50.

[69] The Chamber of Commerce of the United States, "A Digest of the Reconstruction Congress of American Industries, Atlantic City, December 3rd, 4th, 5th and 6th, 1918," RG 61, File 21A–A4, box 328.

[70] Brookings to Baruch, December 11, 1918, *Baruch Papers*. To one lumber buyer who requested a continuation of government prices Baruch wrote: "Neither do I see what reason we can have for regulating the price of lumber, as the war has practically terminated." Baruch to George H. Hodges, December 2, 1918, RG 61, File 21A–A4, box 838.

[71] The Department of Interior, for example, would take over functions relating to the WIB's work in minerals under a new minerals act designed by Leland Summers, Charles MacDowell (chemical division), and other WIB men. See C. K. Leith (mica section) to Charles MacDowell, November 16, 1918, RG 61, File 1–C2, box 85, and correspondence relating to the origins of the mineral bill in RG 61, File 1–A5, box 40.

informal contracts.[72] Businessmen no longer scurried along the government corridors as they had done just weeks before. The emergency organization which Baruch, Lovett, Brookings, and the others had erected during 1917-1918 was now gone, along with the emotional élan that had bound its personnel together.

The WIB's rapid demise grew out of a complex interplay of factors, but surely among the most significant were the broadly political calculations of its chairman. For one thing, Baruch realized that during the months of mobilization the myth-making process of wartime propaganda had transformed him and his colleagues into symbols of the very corporate structure they aimed to strengthen and protect, and he realized further how important it was to guard their collective image during the armistice period and after. He could not afford to take any steps which might undermine the positive image of public control which he and the board had fashioned so well. Throughout the war Baruch consistently sidestepped political campaigns which might have either revealed the weakness of the WIB as a regulatory body or associated it too closely with special interests in the mind of either the president or the public. And he remained true to this policy during demobilization.

It is true that in part Baruch simply shared the conventional wisdom of the Wilsonians and responded to the president's desire to transfer continuing functions to the regular departments rather than extend emergency government. When Wilson accepted Baruch's resignation on November 30 he wrote:

> As I have told you orally, I think that just the right course is being followed in handing over to the proper permanent Departments those activities of the Board with which the Government ought not permanently to dispense.[73]

If Baruch had other convictions, he kept them well hidden during the armistice period. He had always preferred intervention behind the scenes to public crusades. But during the transition period even his room for private maneuvering suddenly narrowed, for with the billows of patriotic rhetoric clearing away, a curious public could now see more clearly the kind of covert activity at which he had been so adept in the past. He felt that Congress and the public would no longer tolerate the inroads which he and other mobilizers had made in tradi-

---

[72] George Peek assisted Ritchie in lobbying on behalf of the legislation on informal contracts, and their exertions from December 1918 to February 1919 can be traced from the documents in RG 61, File 1-A5, box 40. See also Peek to L. B. Reed, January 13, 1919, and to Samuel P. Bush, January 24, 1919, both in the *Peek Papers*; and Chandler P. Anderson, diary, in Chandler P. Anderson Papers, Library of Congress, Washington, D. C., December 13, 1918. Ritchie remained with WIB duties until April 1919. The bill to validate informal contracts passed on March 2, 1919, and was known as the Dent Act.

[73] Wilson to Baruch, November 30, 1918, *Wilson Papers*.

tional institutional relationships under the press of wartime crisis. Thus rather than expose publicly the extent to which some business groups had indeed found their uses for the state, Baruch disbanded his agency as fast as discretion would allow and quit Washington for the glories of Versailles.

One of the central goals of the business synthesizers throughout the war, after all, had been to prove what private corporate leadership could do in conjunction with a friendly state. What European countries might achieve through extensive state controls, so the argument ran, America would surpass by a process of private-public cooperation administered by businessmen in government. To suggest that a state-based officialdom may have proved important to the outcome would have raised some question about the viability and legitimacy of private corporate leadership in the postwar world. In the early weeks after the armistice, Baruch and some of the WIB men wondered whether businessmen could really afford to sanction an enlargement of the state in peacetime when they would no longer be in government to supervise the expansion. To retain something like a WIB in peacetime might lead to politically imposed controls rather than to the kinds of bargained compromises permitted under friendly business-government cooperation. The total absence of state administration could harm a corporate economy in peacetime, but a powerful public bureaucracy dominated by politicians would be a far greater menace.

But ideological and political considerations were not the only factors that restrained Baruch from an activist role after November 11. There was an organizational dimension as well. Far better than the planning enthusiasts Baruch knew the limits of his emergency administration. He had never secured firm central control of the WIB system, and the early rush to demobilize had weakened his position further. Much of his direction had rested upon interest group consensus and social pressure, and both weakened substantially during the armistice period. Businessmen reassessed their needs; and the pull of patriotic cooperation, such as it was, largely disappeared. Since Baruch was unwilling to sanction a thorough-going state expansion and rationalized public control, he had little alternative but to scuttle his agency before it fell on its own.

The WIB had never evolved to the point where it could consistently and reliably overcome the groups that might in future oppose its coordinating functions. In November, for example, the military services refused to yield ground on their traditional prerogatives over military decision-making, even when their decisions seriously impinged on the industrial economy, as in the case of troop demobilization. Within the economy itself an incredible number of forces precluded coherent, continuous coordination—the most important of which was simply the vast spectrum of opinion then extant on the future and nature of economic controls. Not all business groups shared Elbert Gary's enthusiasm for continued price controls, as the December meeting of the U.S. Chamber of Commerce indicates. Baruch refused to encourage the kind of state control required to still the competitive forces then breaking out within the economy and society. President Wilson strongly concurred in this course.

Finally, Baruch realized better than many businessmen that the opportunity for major institutional coordination depended upon the existence of continuing crisis. Only a national emergency could sustain the momentum and mask the inadequacies of a mobilization program so fundamentally dependent upon voluntary administration and the private cooperation of corporate interest groups. Now that the war had ended, the excuse for institutional synthesis had disappeared.

Abandoning the WIB was one of the most significant decisions Baruch ever made as chairman. In this way he not only preserved the reputation of himself and the board, a fact to which American historiography bears eloquent testimony, but of far greater consequence, his act of apparent self-denial also strengthened public reverence for America's industrial system and for the place of private corporate leadership within it. In this development lies one of the most important historical consequences of the entire WIB experience.

CHAPTER 10

CONCLUSION

BUSINESSMEN IN THE WIB:
SYMBOL AND CEREMONY IN STATE ADMINISTRATION

The WIB men of World War I directed one of the most ambitious attempts at institutional coordination in American history. Sophisticated in their ideology and skilled in their managerial ability, they set out to mobilize the country's economic resources for war and to protect its industrial economy for peace. They achieved a great deal in the short time available to them and built up a fund of experience and knowledge for the crisis managers of the future. In the end, however, the institutional realities of Progressive America overcame the rhetoric of integration and synthesis. The imperatives of modern war forced significant shifts in traditional institutional patterns, but the WIB men were unable to assert complete control over this process.

Commentators have not fully appreciated, however, the gap between the rhetoric and reality of the WIB experiment. Some have interpreted the WIB under Baruch's direction as an exercise in dictatorial state control; others have made it an example of the success of voluntary cooperation in overcoming a national crisis; and still others have found in the board the paradox of an agency exemplifying aspects of both dictatorship and cooperation. The enthusiastic, even congratulatory, tone of so much of the contemporary literature on industrial mobilization helps to account for the persistence of these images in the literature of the interwar years, and in some current textbook accounts. What this points to in the final analysis, however, is how successful the WIB was in maintaining the symbol and myth of an integrated system which in reality lay beyond its grasp.

Every administrative system is charged with symbolic qualities that arise out of the struggle to reduce the tension between the myths of its existence and the reality of its operation. Each organization resorts to symbols and ceremony to reconcile its actual conduct with its ideals, or the ideals imputed to it.[1] This principle, operative at all times, is accentuated during periods of national crisis, when the self-conscious manipulation of images and values becomes part of a struggle for national survival. Because wartime conduct is so antithetical to democratic values, the generation of symbols and rituals is especially significant to a democracy at war.

To gain legitimacy in the eyes of the American public the WIB had to prove that it could harness the nation's economic units to a mobilization program designed to serve the national interest. There were major obstacles to convincing the public it was successful in this, including the nature of its personnel and the principles of its administration: after all, it drew its staff and administrative resources largely from the very economic groups it promised to regulate; and it encouraged organizational trends that were antithetical to long standing popular suspicions toward concentrations of private political and economic power. As with most regulatory activity, the WIB's relationships with its business clientele in practice assumed the nature of a gaming process marked by loose, informal understandings, *ad hoc* arrangements, calculated risks of infringement, and pervasive bargaining.[2] Yet while these and other breaches of orthodoxy occurred, the board had to assure the public that the national interest received adequate protection and that in the last analysis economic interest groups yielded to the public need.

Under these circumstances it was not easy for the administrators to admit either at the time or later that they really required more power to deal with business groups. At its simplest level, such an admission would have contradicted the official doctrine of the board and such business associations as the chamber of commerce. According to this canon, American business was playing an outstanding wartime role, making sacrifices at every turn, subordinating self-interest to national interest, and generally giving itself entirely to the cause. WIB administrators wanted to promote this image, so that industry would emerge from the conflict in public favor. Noncooperation, speculation, and reckless business behavior bothered them not just as wartime administrators trying to get a job done, but as business leaders anxious to prove that industry deserved the public's respect and trust. They felt responsible for proving that American business did indeed harbor the spirit of service and community conscience its publicists had so often claimed for it. They also wanted to prove that industry could achieve a degree of mobilization through voluntary cooperation which wartime critics argued could come only through extensive government take-overs. They set out

---

[1]This concept is derived from Murray Edelman, *The Symbolic Uses of Politics* (Urbana: University of Illinois Press, 1964), especially chaps. 2 and 3, and Thurman Arnold, *The Folklore of Capitalism* (New Haven: Yale University Press, 1962).

[2]Edelman, *Symbolic Uses of Politics*, pp. 44–51.

to show that with proper treatment by Washington agencies, American business could plan for a nation at war without disturbing in any fundamental way the basic structure of the corporate capitalist state.

To posit an outpouring of goodwill from American industry may have been useful for propaganda purposes, but how could one rationalize the obvious reluctance of many business groups to accept WIB policy without extended negotiations and hard bargaining? If businessmen were so patriotic why could the board not secure lower prices? If cooperation was the spirit of the day why did the board introduce vague threats of government takeovers in discussions with the steel and copper industries in September 1917?[3] An obvious answer to such questions, and a popular one among all business administrators, was simply to distinguish between enlightened and unenlightened industrialists, and under-score the predominance of the former in the board's work. Those who sought stability and valued scientific management and the cooperative spirit proved the rule, while backward looking, individualistic, noncooperative groups proved the exception. Only a few short-sighted men required threats. When the Nye Com-mittee asked Baruch if industrialists cooperated fully in price fixing, Baruch replied: "The largest proportion of the manufacturers did come along, just like the largest proportion of labor. There are always some chislers. . . ."[4]

But although Baruch distinguished between the cooperative majority and the few "chislers," he also explained that the WIB could not have existed on the cooperative spirit alone. "You have got to have the power undoubtedly," he told the Senators. "You cannot leave any of these things to men's emotions or wishes at the time."[5] When questioned sharply about the first formal copper agreement of September 1917, Baruch exclaimed, "Do not for a moment let me be put in the position of defending their patriotism, and all that kind of thing, because I realize that we had to use a club."[6] Although in this case Baruch felt

---

[3] Baruch confronted these kinds of questions before the Graham and Nye committee hear-ings and the War Policies Commission.

[4] U.S. Congress, Senate, Special Committee to Investigate the Munitions Industry, *Hearings, Munitions Industry*, 73rd–74th Cong., 1934–1937 (cited hereafter as Nye Committee, *Hearings*), part 22, p. 6272. Baruch praised the whole-hearted cooperation of American business "that alone made my work possible" before the War Policies Commission in 1930. See U.S. Congress, *Hearings before the Commission Appointed under the Author-ity of Public Resolution no. 98*, Res. 251, 71st Cong., 2nd sess., 1931 (cited hereafter as *War Policies Commission*), part 3, p. 815.

[5] Nye Committee, *Hearings*, part 22, p. 6273. Likewise, in his testimony before the War Policies Commission, Baruch emphasized that he had had to struggle hard over many price agreements. In this latter argument he reduced considerably his claim of the number of those who had joined the ranks of the willing. "Agreement there was in the sense of acceptance of a Federal price determination by a few leaders in each industry." *War Policies Commission*, part 3, p. 816.

[6] Nye Committee, *Hearings*, part 22, pp. 6299–6300.

obliged to disassociate himself from a business group coming under attack by the Senate committee, this was not the "real" interpretation of industrial mobilization he wanted to leave with his audience. The lesson he wanted inquisitive legislators to draw was how well business and government worked together without coercion or federally imposed controls. No administrator-businessman wanted to admit that he had had less than the full cooperation of American industry, although he might be willing to mention some exceptions. Baruch was forced to admit the most exceptions because he was the one most often asked in postwar years to explain the discord evident in the WIB minutes. Simultaneously with admitting conflict, however, Baruch asserted an impressive power for the board, so that he could argue that the public interest was always saved in the crunch—that noncooperators ultimately had to yield.[7]

Businessmen in the WIB sometimes tried in practice to exercise powers that they claimed both then and later they did not need. During the war, their wish to believe in business patriotism, as symbolized in the public image of the WIB, restrained their search for a firmer institutional basis of industrial mobilization. Devoted to the premise that businessmen did not require coercion, they compromised with industry when they might have fought. Yet, since coercion could not be completely avoided, all that really happened was that coercion occurred under private rather than public supervision. It was sporadic, haphazard, and largely uncontrolled. After the war, the desire of these administrator-businessmen to believe that a cooperative consensus was sufficient for industrial mobilization caused them to deemphasize the fact that only their extensive compromises with powerful groups had permitted resolution of the actual and potential business-government conflicts that marked their administrative program.

The WIB men were, in fact, unable to co-opt all groups into their emerging war system. Although opposition within the economy proved most difficult to rationalize from an ideological and political point of view, opposition from other institutions was no less damaging to systematic control. The military services also upset WIB plans for organizational coherence and control. Businessmen in government had searched for ways to displace traditional military prerogatives from the very first meetings of the Advisory Commission, but as in the case of leading economic institutions, the board had to settle for compromise and shared power. The army and navy worked their way into the WIB's administrative system in such a way as to make the WIB as dependent upon military cooperation as it was on business good will. The WIB straddled public and private institutions, and its power varied with the degree of harmony it established among them.

In the late thirties, as the United States geared up for the catastrophe of World War II, some members of the Roosevelt administration "wondered how

[7] *War Policies Commission*, part 3, pp. 814–17.

far the President would go or permit others to go in abdicating in favor of big business, as Wilson did at the time of the First World War."[8] Harold Ickes, Robert Jackson, and other liberal New Dealers had every reason to worry about the dollar-a-year men of World War II, but their anxiety made them unfairly hostile to the memory of Woodrow Wilson. There is not sufficient evidence in this study to generalize with confidence about Wilson's overall role in mobilizing America for war. But we have shown that he did not simply abdicate to big business in the evolution of the WIB. His caution in delegating authority, especially over prices, his reluctance to yield to business demands for a munitions ministry, and his refusal to undermine the traditional role of military institutions, suggest that 'abdication' is too easy an answer to explain what New Dealers quite accurately discerned as the extraordinary wartime inroads that business groups made into the state. It is more realistic to look for an explanation in the nature of the political economy and of the state itself. Wilson, after all, possessed only a small and inexperienced peacetime bureaucracy with which to mobilize the country's major economic institutions. Moreover, he shared a variety of Progressive thought that was deeply suspicious of the statist element in national planning. While Wilson might go so far as to advise and coordinate private economic decision-making, he had no wish to supplant it. So, given a commitment to the basic structure and prerogatives of corporate capitalism and an aversion to the growth of an extensive and powerful state bureaucracy, even when faced with the institutional requirements of modern war, it was largely inevitable that mobilization went forward by means of a voluntary expert staff and the private administration of public policy.

Bernard Baruch was the perfect choice as institutional middleman. Baruch, the self-made millionaire who had beaten the money moguls at their own game, brought the traditional habits and values of individualism to an emerging bureaucratic system. Economic planning is a bureaucratic phenomenon founded on values of predictability, teamwork, and prescribed functions. In the WIB, Baruch was associated with an historic trend he really did not understand and would have fought against if he had. Baruch and those Wilsonians he spoke for favored voluntary cooperation over political coercion, and informal agreements among like-minded men over formal, bureaucratic order. Baruch was able to retain for mobilization the image of old-fashioned freedom and independence. He seemed able to reconcile American individualism and scientific control. One might think that, given these circumstances, Baruch was actually an anomaly in a process whose force and direction would ultimately leave him behind. This in fact might have been the case had America suffered through the same prolonged crisis that affected European nations, and had Wilsonian liberalism succumbed to a strong

[8] Harold L. Ickes, *The Secret Diaries of Harold Ickes* (New York: Simon and Schuster, 1954), 2: 716.

challenge from a radical left or an alienated right.[9] Victory for a socialist or fascist impulse would have brought the kind of political controls that were repugnant to the men who led the WIB and its sister agencies. But this is only speculation. As America's war government evolved in the short time between April 1917 and November 1918, Baruch's style, personality, and values matched perfectly the informal, fragmented system of American industrial mobilization.

As one of the organizational pioneers of American preparedness, Baruch showed an early awareness of the institutional requirements of mobilization for modern war. But he possessed no clearer conception of the detailed complexities of the process than many other individuals who were drawn into public life in 1915 and 1916. Baruch was not a technician of institutional synthesis. He was one of its statesmen. He gravitated to the center of power as a politician, not as a technocrat. Howard Coffin and Frank Scott knew far more about munitions production and military requirements; and Walter Gifford had more appreciation for the virtues of a sound organization chart. But Baruch outdid them all in cultivating strategically placed individuals in business and politics. Moreover, unlike some businessmen in government, Baruch gave himself over completely to public life. He had come to Washington early and he intended to stay a long time. He would still be there after others like Frank Scott, Daniel Willard, and Robert Lovett returned to business, weary of the bureaucratic battles of wartime Washington. Baruch had committed his time and his money to wartime success. As others fell by the wayside, Baruch persisted in his drive for power. He was everywhere with his briefs for concentrated authority. A sweeping usurpation of traditional prerogatives and responsibilities was out of the question in the early stages of the war, but Baruch's chances improved as the crisis deepened, and his mandate finally came in March 1918.

Thurman Arnold once observed that "the roles of the actor on the stage and the technician who directs the play are entirely different. Ability in one of these lines has little relation to ability in the other. The creed of any institution is public presentation of a drama in which the institution is the hero. The play is spoiled unless the machinery behind the scenes is carefully concealed."[10] While the technicians in Baruch's informal group of Washington friends helped catapult him to the forefront of economic mobilization, and while the technocrats in the WIB's functional units moved the organization ahead, Baruch took up a position on the center stage of industrial mobilization which with remarkable tenacity he has retained to this very day. That both contemporaries and subsequent interpreters have been so attracted to him as WIB chairman is a tribute to the skill of his performance. Baruch and the WIB have since come to represent the greatest

[9] Arno J. Mayer explores this dynamic in the European context in *Wilson vs. Lenin: Political Origins of the New Diplomacy 1917-1918* (Cleveland and New York: Meridian, 1964).

[10] Arnold, *Folklore of Capitalism*, p. 357.

concentration of delegated authority in American history, while at the time, Baruch and his men floundered in an organizational maze over which they never had sufficient control. Baruch has since taken on the aura of economic dictator,[11] although at the time, economic interest groups and the military service bureaus reached into the WIB organization to shape specific programs, oftentimes against his will. The symbol of Bernard Baruch, the WIB's high priest of ceremony, has given an image of unity and form to what in retrospect was an extraordinarily chaotic, disjointed process. But more importantly, it is through the symbol of Bernard Baruch that the vision of a stable, cooperative system of industrial mobilization finally found the kind of fulfillment denied it during World War I.

THE WIB AND BUSINESS-GOVERNMENT RELATIONS DURING WORLD WAR I

Recent research offers several competing approaches to the study of the political economy of the Progressive era, and each one of them is also useful in understanding business-government relations in the war period. Interest groups crisscrossed the business community in a manner described by Robert Wiebe in *Businessmen and Reform.* The pull of region, for instance, is exemplified very well by the resources and conversion section of the WIB's commodity organization. Likewise, a corporate ideology characterized key WIB administrators, as James Weinstein indicates in *The Corporate Ideal and the Liberal State.* The antidemocratic tendency of business-sponsored administrative reform, which Samuel Hays documents for the Progressive years, also finds many parallels during the war, and is certainly true in the case of the WIB. And finally, some American industries called for state intervention to obtain the rationalization

[11]For references to Baruch as an industrial or economic dictator in college textbooks, see Oscar T. Barck, Jr., and Nelson M. Blake, *Since 1900: A History of the United States in Our Times* (New York: Macmillan, 1965), pp. 226–27; Arthur S. Link, *American Epoch* (New York: Knopf, 1963), p. 203; Richard Hofstadter, William Miller, and Daniel Aaron, *The United States: The History of a Republic* (Englewood Cliffs, N.J.: Prentice-Hall, 1967), p. 677; and Forrest McDonald, *The Torch Is Passed: The United States in the 20th Century* (Reading, Mass.: Addison-Wesley, 1968), p. 163. For similar, if more ambiguous, comments in specialized accounts, see Grosvenor B. Clarkson, *Industrial America in the World War: The Strategy behind the Line, 1917-1918* (Boston: Houghton Mifflin, 1923), chap. 5; Benedict Crowell and Robert F. Wilson, *The Giant Hand: Our Mobilization and Control of Industry and National Resources, 1917-1918,* Vol. 1 of *How America Went to War* (New Haven: Yale University Press, 1921), pp. 7–8; Pendleton Herring, *The Impact of War: Our American Democracy under Arms* (New York: Farrar & Rinehart, 1941), p. 175; Edward M. Coffman, *The War To End All Wars: The American Military Experience in World War I* (New York: Oxford University Press, 1968), pp. 163–66.

and stability they could not guarantee on their own, a theme which Gabriel Kolko develops for the Progressive era as a whole.

Interest group politics, corporate ideology, and the structural imperatives of the economy and the state are among the major processes that defined business-government relations both before and during World War I. No single one of them can be disregarded for a comprehensive account of the problem for the war years. They operated side by side throughout the conflict, and their interaction provides one of the central determinants of the WIB's evolution and operation.

While it is clear that all these characterizations are useful to an account of business-government relations in the WIB, it would be highly unsatisfactory to let the matter rest there. It is necessary to say a word about their relative value as approaches to the problem, and to point out the danger of relying upon any single one of them for a comprehensive account. Any history of business-government relations for the war period, for instance, that was written exclusively within a framework of interest-group politics would underestimate the process which gave some elite corporations comparatively greater influence over the formulation of public policy. The WIB experience demonstrates the significance of interest group pressures on state policy. In fact, because the war so accelerated the growth of business organizations, state agencies like the WIB had to take them into account as never before. In terms of comparative influence, however, there is no doubt about the crucial significance of giant corporations. Negotiations between the WIB and the corset manufacturers' association were of almost no consequence to the mobilization program compared to the outcome of discussions with big steel over prices, or with General Motors over automobile curtailments. The exigencies of war favored industrial consolidation and placed a premium upon the managerial and productive capacities of major American corporations. Even when the WIB struck up a continuing relationship with a business association such as the United States Chamber of Commerce, it did so largely to satisfy public demand for regularized, democratic procedures while maintaining easy access to big business interests.

Corporate ideology as a general approach to business-government relations under the WIB reveals many more limitations than interest group politics. Carriers of corporate ideology did stand at the center of the WIB's administrative complex, and they showed a proper appreciation of the interdependent nature of modern society and the need for cooperative values to make it function. But the command posts of the WIB were staffed by a special group of men. They were business politicians rather than economic entrepreneurs; and they should not be confused with the actual owners and managers of giant enterprise. Indeed, it was their very separation from centers of private economic power that made men like Brookings and Baruch so attractive to the Wilson administration.

A thoroughgoing pragmatism far more than ideological commitment to the ideal of business-government cooperation characterized private business leaders who negotiated with the WIB in Washington. Judge Gary, for instance, hesitated over price agreements in the spring and summer of 1917 lest they reduce his prerogatives and profits, but in December 1918 he was first in line for an agreement with the state as a way to guarantee price stability and profits during an anticipated market decline. The cooperative ideal did become systematized into ideology during the Progressive period, and the impact of war refined it further, but it would be misleading to call it a guiding force of big business action. Moreover, given the trend toward institutional coordination generated by the war itself, there was every reason to expect cooperation among institutional blocs such as business and government irrespective of the ideological predilections of those caught up in the process.

Although pressure group politics and corporate thinking affected the evolution of business-government relations under the WIB, the structural dimensions of the economy and the state proved a more important influence than either. The structure of an industry largely determined the nature of its interest group representation, just as it set real limits on the practicality of realizing corporate ideals. The state bureaucracy itself partially reflected characteristics of the country's underlying economic structure. The search for coordination and control through the WIB, for instance, stemmed in part from American industry's need for a stable administrative environment conducive to private corporate planning; and reorganization of the army's purchasing system was undertaken to match a national economy organized along commodity lines. We must be careful, however, not to make the state bureaucracy simply a dependent variable of the country's economic structure, for that would overlook the significant ways in which the state itself influenced its relationship with specific business groups. For instance, bureaucratic disorganization and inadequate administration were contributing factors to business-government tension in the early months. When state bureaus fought among themselves over jurisdiction and policy, business firms suffered the consequences. And further, the relationships between industry and government improved as the state rationalized its administrative procedures and substituted business volunteers for its regular civilian and military personnel. However, conflict between state advisors and private businessmen did not entirely disappear. While they all agreed they should do everything possible to protect America's industrial structure, they argued over the best means of doing this. Values and structure interacted at this point. Men who considered the needs of the whole system, as members of an agency of coordination, clashed with private managers whose interest-conscious views were appropriate to those in command of particular parts of the national economy.

In a situation tending by its very nature toward centralization and integration, the trends toward the growth of economic interest groups, giant corporations, corporate ideology, and intimate alliances between businessmen and the state all received widespread encouragement. The rhetoric of war itself reflected this organizational impulse as "cooperation" and "consolidation" replaced "individualism" and "competition" as rhetorical ideals. There is as yet no definitive study of the trade association movement, for instance, but what evidence is presently available points to a tremendous increase as a result of the war.[12] The policies of emergency agencies like the WIB both necessitated and legitimized associational activities. More significantly, the large industrial firms that stood at the heart of mobilization discovered new support and a wide area of freedom for cooperation with state bureaus. The *Wall Street Journal* noted in 1917 that the frequently slandered "trusts," although "technically extinct," were enjoying the liberties of the "old Days."[13] "Washington dispatches in these days," exclaimed the *Engineering and Mining Journal*, "often cause us to rub our eyes in amazement and wonder whether we are living in the same country that we lived in a few years ago."[14]

It is possible to recognize the important acceleration of centralizing, consolidating, integrating trends, however, without ignoring or underestimating the

[12] For comments on this point in secondary sources, see Joseph H. Foth, *Trade Associations, Their Service to Industry* (New York: Ronald Press, 1930), pp. 21-22, 32-35, 229; and Thomas C. Cochran, *The American Business System: A Historical Perspective 1900-1955* (New York: Harper & Bros., 1962), pp. 61-62. Robert F. Himmelberg argues that the rate of trade association formation was more rapid between 1915 and 1920 than in either the preceding or succeeding five-year periods. See n. 5 in Robert F. Himmelberg, "The War Industries Board and the Antitrust Question in November 1918," *Journal of American History* 53 (June 1965): 59-74. The House committee investigating expenditures in the ordnance department in the immediate postwar period concluded that "under the fostering hand of the Government . . . trusts and combinations sprung up like weeds, until, at the end of the war, there was hardly an industry or business interest that was not thoroughly and completely organized; competition was at an end." U.S. Congress, House, Select Committee on Expenditures in the War Department, *Report no. 1400*, 66th Cong., 3rd sess., 1921, p. 83. Studies of trade associations in three industries assess the war's positive impact: R. C. Fraunberger, "Lumber Trade Associations, Their Economic and Social Significance" (Master's Thesis, Temple University, 1951), pp. 15-16; Harry J. Brown, "The National Association of Wool Manufacturers, 1864-1897" (Ph.D. dissertation, Cornell University, 1949), pp. 454-57; Louis Galambos, *Competition and Cooperation: The Emergence of a National Trade Association* (Baltimore, Md.: Johns Hopkins Press, 1966), pp. 67, 292.

[13] "War Has Given Trusts a New Freedom," *Wall Street Journal*, September 28, 1917, p. 1.

[14] "Respecting Combinations," *Engineering and Mining Journal* 104 (July 7, 1917): 32. While agencies like the WIB provided an institutional environment favorable to corporate consolidation, rising prices and increased production provided the necessary economic incentives. Ralph L. Nelson estimates that in 1917 the number of firms disappearing by merger reached a level not exceeded since 1905, and that the period 1915-1920 is one of the two greatest periods of merger activity between 1895 and 1920. Ralph L. Nelson, *Merger Movements in American Industry, 1895-1956* (Princeton, N.J.: Princeton University Press, 1959), p. 35.

strength of those forces within the state, the economy, and society which opposed them. The evidence adduced in this study should caution us against a premature declaration of their defeat. In large part, the problem is simply one of balance and perspective. In the long run the future lay with the trends associated with modern war, but the specific nature of business-government relations during World War I cannot be understood without recognizing the impact of traditions from an earlier era.

The degree of close, continuing integration implied by phrases like the "New Nationalism," "political capitalism," or "corporate liberalism" varied in practice during the war according to the segments of the economy and state involved and the issues on which they joined. The better organized an industry in peacetime, the smoother the adjustment was likely to be in war, although clashes over particular policy decisions could quickly cancel structural advantages. Much depended on the kinds of issues involved. It is fairly easy, for example, to compose a glowing portrait of business-government cooperation based on the interaction of business interests and the WIB's conservation division. Throughout its work, the division relied exclusively upon voluntary adoption of conservation programs designed by industries themselves. Such reforms could hardly become an occasion for conflict between businessmen and the state, because they were obviously aimed at helping industry through the war and strengthening its competitive position for peace. Moreover, they raised no vital questions of authority. Prices and priorities, on the other hand, involved substantive questions of power and control and in these issue areas relations could be ambiguous, tense, and sometimes bitter. In most cases the agreements which ultimately followed the threats and counterthreats of negotiation were remarkably mild. But even so, the outcome was not determined by the prewar structure of business thought and business-government relations alone. The process of role definition between businessmen and the state evolved partly out of the war crisis itself.

What the WIB experience suggests, in conclusion, is that the phrase "business-government relations" embraces a whole series of processes which are shaped at any one time by a complex interplay of fluctuating variables. The processes themselves may display contradictory tendencies and differential rates of growth; and important new factors can enter the general flow of change at any point. A large constellation of business groups compose the business community, for example, and distinctions can be drawn between small and large corporations, public ideologues and private managers, specific trade organizations and general business associations, and so on. The character of business-government relations varies directly with the kinds of groups that intersect with the state. Similarly, the government's constituent parts must be taken into account—the Congress, the executive, the courts, the military services, the administrative agencies, and so forth—for the nature of business-government relations reflects the structure of the state as well as the structure of business enterprise. It is only by making explicit the structures and processes which compose a concept as vague as business-government relations that we can understand what it signifies at any one stage of its historical development. Obviously, the permutations and combinations which are possible in this kind of conceptualization could, if taken to the extreme, confuse more than they clarify. But despite this admitted danger, only a model of greater complexity than those discussed here can order the evidence of business-government relations under the WIB.

BIBLIOGRAPHY

BOOKS AND DISSERTATIONS

Arnold, Thurman. *The Folklore of Capitalism.* New Haven: Yale University Press, 1962.
Ayres, Leonard P. *The War with Germany: A Statistical Summary.* Washington, D.C.: U.S. Government Printing Office, 1919.
Baker, Charles W. *Government Control and Operation of Industry in Great Britain and the United States during the World War.* New York: Oxford University Press, 1921.
Baker, Liva. *Felix Frankfurter.* New York: Coward-McCann, 1969.
Baker, Ray Stannard. *Woodrow Wilson: Life and Letters.* 8 vols. Garden City, N.Y.: Doubleday, Page, 1927; and Doubleday, Doran, 1927–1939.
——, and Dodd, William E., eds. *The Public Papers of Woodrow Wilson.* 6 vols. New York: Harper & Bros., 1925–1927.
Barck, Oscar T., Jr., and Blake, Nelson M. *Since 1900: A History of the United States in Our Times.* New York: Macmillan, 1965.
Baritz, Loren. *The Servants of Power: A History of the Use of Social Science in American Industry.* Middletown, Conn.: Wesleyan University Press, 1960.
Baruch, Bernard M. *Baruch: My Own Story.* New York: Henry Holt, 1957.
——. *Baruch: The Public Years.* New York: Holt, Rinehart and Winston, 1960.
Bates, J. Leonard. *The Origins of Teapot Dome: Progressives, Parties and Petroleum, 1909–1921.* Urbana: University of Illinois Press, 1963.
Beaver, Daniel R. *Newton D. Baker and the American War Effort, 1917–1919.* Lincoln: University of Nebraska Press, 1966.
Billington, Monroe L. *Thomas P. Gore, the Blind Senator from Oklahoma.* Lawrence: University of Kansas Press, 1967.
Blum, John M. *Joe Tumulty and the Wilson Era.* Boston: Houghton, Mifflin, 1951.
——. *Woodrow Wilson and the Politics of Morality.* Boston: Little, Brown, 1956.
Boulding, Kenneth E. *The Organizational Revolution: A Study in the Ethics of Economic Organization.* Chicago: Quadrangle, 1968.
Bourne, Randolph. *Untimely Papers,* ed. James Oppenheim. New York: B. W. Huebsch, 1919.
Bradley, Joseph F. *The Role of Trade Associations and Professional Business Societies in America.* University Park, Pa.: Pennsylvania State University Press, 1965.
Bragdon, Henry W. *Woodrow Wilson: The Academic Years.* Cambridge, Mass.: Harvard University Press, 1967.

Breen, William J. "The Council of National Defense: 1916–1921." Ph.D. dissertation, Duke University, 1968.

Brooks, Edward H. "The National Defense Policy of the Wilson Administration, 1913–1917." Ph.D. dissertation, Stanford University, 1950.

Brookings, Robert S. *Economic Democracy.* New York: Macmillan, 1929.

Brown, Harry J. "The National Association of Wool Manufacturers, 1864–1897." Ph.D. dissertation, Cornell University, 1949.

Bullard, Robert L. *Personalities and Reminiscences of the War.* Garden City, N.Y.: Doubleday, Page, 1925.

Calvert, Monte A. *The Mechanical Engineer in America, 1830–1910: Professional Cultures in Conflict.* Baltimore, Md.: Johns Hopkins Press, 1967.

Catchings, Waddill. *The Business Man's Responsibility in the Industrial Problems of the War.* New York: 1918.

Chamber of Commerce of the United States of America. *Annual Report.* Fifth Annual Meeting, Board of Directors. Washington, D.C., 1917.

_____. *Speeches on Anti-trust Legislation Delivered at Second Annual Meeting.* Washington, D.C., 1914.

_____. *War Convention of the National Association of Commercial Organization Secretaries.* Chicago, 1918.

_____. War Service Executive Committee. *War Service Committees. List of Committees.* Washington, D.C., 1918.

_____. *War Service Committees. Organization, Their Scope and Duties.* Washington, D.C., 1918.

_____. *War Service Committees. War Service Committees of the Nation's Industries as an Aid to the War Program.* Washington, D.C., 1918.

Chambers, Frank P. *The War Behind the War, 1914–1918: A History of the Political and Civilian Fronts.* New York: Harcourt, Brace, 1939.

Chandler, Alfred D., Jr., and Salsbury, Stephen. *Pierre S. Du Pont and the Making of the Modern Corporation.* New York: Harper & Row, 1971.

Clark, J. Maurice; Hamilton, Walton H.; and Moulton, Harold G., eds. *Readings in the Economics of War.* Chicago: University of Chicago Press, 1918.

Clark, John M. *The Costs of the World War to the American People.* New Haven: Yale University Press, 1931.

Clarkson, Grosvenor B. *Industrial America in the World War: The Strategy behind the Line, 1917–1918.* Boston: Houghton Mifflin, 1923.

Cochran, Thomas C. *The American Business System: A Historical Perspective, 1900–1955.* New York: Harper & Row, 1962.

Coffman, Edward M. *The Hilt of the Sword: The Career of Peyton C. March.* Madison: University of Wisconsin Press, 1966.

_____. *The War To End All Wars: The American Military Experience in World War I.* New York: Oxford University Press, 1968.

Coit, Margaret L. *Mr. Baruch.* Boston: Houghton Mifflin, 1957.

Collins, Francis A. *The Fighting Engineers: The Minute Men of Our Industrial Army.* New York: Century, 1918.

Copeland, Melvin T. *And Mark an Era: The Story of the Harvard Business School.* Boston: Little, Brown, 1958.

Cramer, C. H. *Newton D. Baker: A Biography.* Cleveland: World Publishing Co., 1961.

Creel, George. *How We Advertised America.* New York: Harper & Bros., 1920.

Crissey, Forrest. *Alexander Legge, 1866–1933.* Chicago: Alexander Legge Memorial Committee, 1936.

Cronon, E. David, ed. *The Cabinet Diaries of Josephus Daniels, 1913-1921*. Lincoln: University of Nebraska Press, 1963.

Crowder, Enoch H. *The Spirit of Selective Service*. New York: Century, 1920.

Crowell, Benedict, and Wilson, Robert F. *How America Went to War*. 6 vols. New Haven: Yale University Press, 1921.

Crowell, J. Franklin. *Government War Contracts*. New York: Oxford University Press, 1920.

Crozier, Michael. *The Bureaucratic Phenomenon*. Chicago: University of Chicago Press, 1964.

Crozier, William. *Ordnance and the World War*. New York: Scribner's, 1920.

Cummins, Cedric C. *Indiana Public Opinion and the World War 1914-1917*. Indianapolis: Indiana Historical Bureau, 1945.

Daniels, Josephus. *The Wilson Era: Years of Peace, 1910-1917*. Chapel Hill: University of North Carolina Press, 1944.

——. *The Wilson Era: Years of War and After, 1917-1923*. Chapel Hill: University of North Carolina Press, 1946.

De Weerd, Harvey A. *President Wilson Fights His War*. New York: Macmillan, 1968.

Diamond, William. *The Economic Thought of Woodrow Wilson*. Baltimore, Md.: Johns Hopkins Press, 1943.

Dodd, William E. *Woodrow Wilson and His Work*. Garden City, N.Y.: Doubleday, Page, 1920.

Downs, Anthony. *Inside Bureaucracy*. Boston: Little, Brown, 1967.

Eckstein, Harry, and Apter, David E., eds. *Comparative Politics: A Reader*. New York: Free Press, 1965.

Eddy, Arthur J. *The New Competition*. Chicago: McGlurg, 1913.

Edelman, Murray. *The Symbolic Uses of Politics*. Urbana: University of Illinois Press, 1964.

Eisenhower, Dwight D. *At Ease: Stories I Tell to Friends*. Garden City, N.Y.: Doubleday, 1967.

Fainsod, Merle, and Gordon, Lincoln. *Government and the American Economy*. New York: Norton, 1941.

Field, Carter. *Bernard Baruch, Park Bench Statesmen*. New York: McGraw-Hill, 1944.

Fite, Gilbert C. *George N. Peek and the Fight for Farm Parity*. Norman: University of Oklahoma Press, 1954.

Fitzpatrick, F. Stuart. *A Study of Business Men's Associations*. Olean, N.Y.: Olean Times Publishing Company, 1925.

Foth, Joseph H. *Trade Associations: Their Service to Industry*. New York: Ronald Press, 1930.

Fraunberger, R. C. "Lumber Trade Associations: Their Economic and Social Significance." Master's thesis, Temple University, 1951.

Fredericks, Pierce G. *The Great Adventure: America in the First World War*. New York: Dutton, 1960.

Freidel, Frank. *Franklin D. Roosevelt: The Apprenticeship*. Boston: Little, Brown, 1952.

Frothingham, Thomas G. *The American Reinforcement in the World War*. New York: Doubleday, Page, 1927.

Galambos, Louis. *Competition and Cooperation: The Emergence of a National Trade Association*. Baltimore, Md.: Johns Hopkins Press, 1966.

Ganoe, William A. *The History of the United States Army*. New York: Appleton-Century, 1942.

Gilbert, Clinton W. *The Mirrors of Washington*. New York: Putnam's, 1921.

Godfrey, Hollis. *Dave Morrell's Battery*. Boston: Little, Brown, 1912.

——. *For the Norton Name*. Boston: Little, Brown, 1909.

_____. *Jack Collerton's Engine*. Boston: Little, Brown, 1910.
_____. *The Man Who Ended War*. Boston: Little, Brown, 1908.
Gompers, Samuel. *Seventy Years of Life and Labor: An Autobiography*. 2 vols. New York: E. P. Dutton, 1925.
Gray, Howard C. *War Time Control of Industry: The Experience of England*. New York: Macmillan, 1918.
Greene, Francis V. *Our First Year in the Great War*. New York: Putnam's, 1918.
Haber, Samuel. *Efficiency and Uplift: Scientific Management in the Progressive Era 1890-1920*. Chicago: University of Chicago Press, 1964.
Hagedorn, Hermann. *Leonard Wood*. 2 vols. New York: Harper & Bros., 1931.
_____. *Brookings: A Biography*. New York: Macmillan, 1937.
Hammond, John Hays. *The Autobiography of John Hays Hammond*. 2 vols. New York: Farrar & Rinehart, 1935.
Hammond, Paul Y. *Organizing for Defense: The American Military Establishment in the Twentieth Century*. Princeton, N.J.: Princeton University Press, 1961.
Hardy, Charles O. *Wartime Control of Prices*. Washington, D.C.: The Brookings Institution, 1940.
Haynes, William. *Chemical Pioneers: The Founders of the American Chemical Industry*. New York: Van Nostrand, 1939.
Hays, Samuel P. *Conservation and the Gospel of Efficiency: The Progressive Conservation Movement 1890-1920*. Cambridge, Mass.: Harvard University Press, 1959.
Heaton, Herbert. *A Scholar in Action: Edwin F. Gay*. Cambridge, Mass.: Harvard University Press, 1952.
Herman, Sondra R. *Eleven against War: Studies in American International Thought, 1898-1921*. Stanford, Calif.: Hoover Institution Press, 1969.
Herring, Pendleton. *The Impact of War: Our American Democracy under Arms*. New York: Farrar & Rinehart, 1941.
Himmelberg, Robert F. "Relaxation of the Federal Anti-Trust Policies as a Goal of the Business Community during the period 1918-1933." Ph.D. dissertation, Pennsylvania State University, 1963.
Hippelheuser, Richard H., ed. *American Industry in the War: A Report of the War Industries Board, March 1921*. New York: Prentice-Hall, 1941.
Hofstadter, Richard. *The Age of Reform: From Bryan to F.D.R.* New York: Knopf, 1955.
Hofstadter, Richard; Miller, William; and Aaron, Daniel. *The United States: The History of a Republic*. Englewood Cliffs, N.J.: Prentice-Hall, 1967.
Holley, I. B., Jr., *Ideas and Weapons: Exploitation of the Aerial Weapon by the United States during World War I: A Study in the Relationship of Technological Advance, Military Doctrine, and the Development of Weapons*. New Haven: Yale University Press, 1953.
Holmes, William F. *The White Chief: James Kimble Vardaman*. Baton Rouge: Louisiana State University Press, 1970.
Hoover, Herbert. *The Memoirs of Herbert Hoover: Years of Adventure, 1874-1920*. New York: Macmillan, 1951.
_____. *The Ordeal of Woodrow Wilson*. New York: McGraw-Hill, 1958.
Houston, David F. *Eight Years with Wilson's Cabinet, 1913 to 1920*. 2 vols. Garden City, N.Y.: Doubleday, Page, 1926.
"How Business Men Stand on National Defense," n.p., n.d. Pamphlet in the library of the Chamber of Commerce of the United States of America, Washington, D.C.
Hoyt, Edwin P., Jr. *The Guggenheims and the American Dream*. New York: Funk & Wagnalls, 1967.

Hungerford, Edward. *Daniel Willard Rides the Line: The Story of the Great Railroad Man.* New York: Putnam's, 1938.

Huntington, Samuel P. *The Soldier and the State: The Theory and Politics of Civil-Military Relations.* Cambridge, Mass.: Harvard University Press, 1957.

Hurley, Edward N. *The Bridge To France.* Philadelphia: J. B. Lippincott, 1927.

Ickes, Harold L. *The Secret Diaries of Harold Ickes.* New York: Simon & Schuster, 1954.

Jenkins, Innis L. "Josephus Daniels and the Navy Department, 1913-1916: A Study in Military Administration." Ph.D. dissertation, University of Maryland, 1960.

Jensen, Gordon M. "The National Civic Federation: American Business in an Age of Social Change and Social Reform, 1900-1910." Ph.D. dissertation, Princeton University, 1956.

Johnson, Hugh S. *The Blue Eagle from Egg to Earth.* Garden City, N.Y.: Doubleday, Doran, 1935.

Josephson, Matthew. *Edison.* New York: McGraw-Hill, 1959.

Kahn, E. J., Jr. *The World of Swope.* New York: Simon & Schuster, 1965.

Kerr, K. Austin. *American Railroad Politics 1914-1920: Rates, Wages, and Efficiency.* Pittsburgh: University of Pittsburgh Press, 1968.

Knoeppel, Charles Edward. *Industrial Preparedness.* New York: The Engineering Magazine Company, 1916.

Kolko, Gabriel. *The Triumph of Conservatism: A Reinterpretation of American History, 1900-1916.* New York: Free Press, 1963.

――――. *Railroads and Regulation, 1877-1916.* Princeton, N.J.: Princeton University Press, 1965.

Kreidberg, Marvin A., and Henry, Merton G. *History of the Military Mobilization in the United States Army, 1775-1945.* Washington, D.C.: Department of the Army, 1955.

Lane, Anne W., and Wall, Louise Herrick, eds. *The Letters of Franklin K. Lane, Personal and Political.* Boston: Houghton Mifflin, 1922.

Lansing, Robert. *War Memoirs of Robert Lansing.* Indianapolis, Ind.: Bobbs-Merrill, 1935.

Lasch, Christopher. *The New Radicalism in America, 1889-1963: The Intellectual as a Social Type.* New York: Knopf, 1965.

Layton, Edwin T. "The American Engineering Profession and the Idea of Social Responsibility." Ph.D. dissertation, University of California, Los Angeles, 1956.

Leland, Waldo G., and Mereness, Newton D. *Introduction to the American Official Sources for the Economic and Social History of the World War.* New Haven, Conn.: Yale University Press, 1926.

Levin, N. Gordon, Jr. *Woodrow Wilson and World Politics: America's Response to War and Revolution.* New York: Oxford University Press, 1968.

Link, Arthur S. *Wilson: Campaigns for Progressivism and Peace 1916-1917.* Princeton, N.J.: Princeton University Press, 1965.

――――. *Wilson: Confusions and Crises, 1915-1916.* Princeton, N.J.: Princeton University Press, 1964.

――――. *Wilson: The New Freedom.* Princeton, N.J.: Princeton University Press, 1956.

――――. *Wilson: The Struggle for Neutrality, 1914-1915.* Princeton, N.J.: Princeton University Press, 1960.

――――. *Woodrow Wilson and the Progressive Era, 1910-1917.* New York: Harper & Bros., 1963.

――――, and Catton, William B. *American Epoch: A History of the United States since the 1890's.* New York: Knopf, 1963.

Litman, Simon. *Prices and Price Control in Great Britain and the United States during the World War.* New York: Oxford University Press, 1920.

Livermore, Seward W. *Politics Is Adjourned: Woodrow Wilson and the War Congress, 1916-1918.* Middletown, Conn.: Wesleyan University Press, 1966.

Lockmiller, David A. *Enoch H. Crowder: Soldier, Lawyer and Statesman.* Columbia: University of Missouri Press, 1955.

Lowi, Theodore J. *The End of Liberalism: Ideology, Policy, and the Crisis of Public Authority.* New York: Norton, 1969.

March, Peyton C. *The Nation at War.* Garden City, N.Y.: Doubleday, Doran, 1932.

Marcosson, Isaac F. *Leonard Wood, Prophet of Preparedness.* New York: John Lane, 1917.

Martin, Franklin H. *The Joy of Living: An Autobiography.* 2 vols. Garden City, N.Y.: Doubleday, Doran, 1933.

Mayer, Arno J. *Wilson vs. Lenin: Political Origins of the New Diplomacy 1917-1918.* Cleveland and New York: Meridian, 1964.

McAdoo, William G. *Crowded Years: The Reminiscences of William Gibbs McAdoo.* Boston: Houghton Mifflin, 1931.

McConnell, Grant. *Private Power and American Democracy.* New York: Knopf, 1966.

McDonald, Forrest. *The Torch Is Passed: The United States in the 20th Century.* Reading, Mass.: Addison-Wesley, 1968.

Mê Hsin Chiang. "The United States War Industries Board, 1917-1918." Master's thesis, Stanford University, 1937.

Merton, Robert K., *et al.,* eds. *Reader in Bureaucracy.* Glencoe, Ill.: Free Press, 1952.

Meyer, Eugene, Jr. *War Profiteering: Some Practical Aspects of its Control.* Washington, D.C.: 1917.

Millis, Walter. *Arms and Men: A Study of American Military History.* New York: Mentor, 1956.

Mock, James R., and Larson, Cedric. *Words That Won the War: The Story of the Committee on Public Information 1917-1919.* Princeton, N.J.: Princeton University Press, 1939.

Morrison, Joseph L. *Josephus Daniels, the Small-d Democrat.* Chapel Hill: University of North Carolina Press, 1966.

National Association of Manufacturers. *Governmental War Agencies Affecting Business.* N.p., 1918.

Nelson, Otto L., Jr. *National Security and the General Staff.* Washington, D.C.: Infantry Journal Press, 1946.

Nelson, Ralph L. *Merger Movements in American Industry, 1895-1956.* Princeton, N.J.: Princeton University Press, 1959.

Nevins, Allan, and Hill, Frank Ernest. *Ford: Expansion and Challenge, 1915-1933.* New York: Scribner's, 1957.

O'Connor, Harvey. *The Guggenheims: The Making of an American Dynasty.* New York: Covici Friede, 1937.

Otis, Charles. *Here I Am: A Rambling Account of the Exciting Times of Yesteryear.* Cleveland, Ohio: Buehler Printcraft Corporation, 1951.

Palmer, Frederick. *Newton D. Baker.* 2 vols. New York: Dodd, Mead, 1931.

Parrini, Carl P. *Heir to Empire: United States Economic Diplomacy, 1916-1923.* Pittsburgh: University of Pittsburgh Press, 1969.

Paxson, Frederick L. *American Democracy and the World War.* 3 vols. Boston and Berkeley: Houghton, Mifflin and the University of California Press, 1936-1948.

Payne, John W., Jr. "David F. Houston: A Biography." Ph.D. dissertation, University of Texas, 1953.

Peoples, John M. "The Genesis of the War Industries Board." Ph.D. dissertation, University of California, 1942.

Perry, Ralph B. *The Plattsburg Movement: A Chapter of America's Participation in the World War.* New York: Dutton, 1921.

Pigou, Arthur C. *The Political Economy of War*. New York: Macmillan, 1941.

Porter, John. *The Vertical Mosaic: An Analysis of Social Class and Power in Canada*. Toronto: University of Toronto Press, 1965.

Pound, Arthur, and Moore, Samuel Taylor, eds. *They Told Barron: Conversations and Revelations of an American Pepys in Wall Street*. New York: Harper & Bros., 1930.

Powell, E. Alexander. *The Army behind the Army*. New York: Scribner's, 1919.

Presthus, Robert. *The Organizational Society: An Analysis and a Theory*. New York: Vintage, 1962.

Rae, John B. *The American Automobile: A Brief History*. Chicago: University of Chicago Press, 1965.

Ratner, Sidney. *American Taxation: Its History as a Social Force in Democracy*. New York: Norton, 1942.

Reagan, Michael D. "Serving Two Masters: Problems in the Employment of Dollar-a-Year and Without Compensation Personnel." Ph.D. dissertation, Princeton University, 1959.

Redfield, William C. *With Congress and Cabinet*. New York: Doubleday, Page, 1924.

Riggs, Fred W. *The Ecology of Public Administration*. Issued under the auspices of the Indian Institute of Public Administration, New Delhi. London: Asia Publishing House, 1961.

Risch, Erna. *The Quartermaster Corps: Organization, Supply, and Services*. Washington, D.C.: Quartermaster Historian's Office, Office of the Quartermaster General, 1953.

——. *Quartermaster Support of the Army: A History of the Corps, 1775-1939*. Washington, D.C.: Government Printing Office, 1962.

Rollins, Alfred B., Jr. *Roosevelt and Howe*. New York: Knopf, 1962.

Rose, William G. *Cleveland, the Making of a City*. Cleveland, Ohio: World Publishing Co., 1950.

Rossiter, Clinton. *Constitutional Dictatorship*. Princeton, N.J.: Princeton University Press, 1948.

Schuyler, Hamilton. *The Roeblings: A Century of Engineers, Bridge-builders and Industrialists*. Princeton, N.J.: Princeton University Press, 1931.

Scott, Hugh L. *Some Memories of a Soldier*. New York: Century, 1928.

Scott, Lloyd N. *Naval Consulting Board of the United States*. Washington, D.C.: Government Printing Office, 1920.

Selznick, Philip. *TVA and the Grass Roots: A Study in the Sociology of Formal Organization*. New York: Harper & Row, 1966.

Sharpe, Henry G. *The Quartermaster Corps, in the Year 1917 in the World War*. New York: Century, 1921.

Shaw, Arch W. *An Approach to Business Problems*. Cambridge, Mass.: Harvard University Press, 1926.

——. *Some Problems in Market Distribution*. Cambridge, Mass.: Harvard University Press, 1915.

Short, Lloyd M. *The Development of National Administrative Organization in the United States*. Baltimore, Md.: Johns Hopkins Press, 1923.

Simon, Herbert A. *Administrative Behavior*. New York: Macmillan, 1963.

Simon, Herbert A.; Smithburg, Donald W.; and Thompson, Victor A. *Public Administration*. New York: Knopf, 1961.

Slosson, Preston W. *The Great Crusade and After 1914-1928*. New York: Macmillan, 1930.

Speier, Hans. *Social Order and the Risks of War*. Cambridge, Mass.: M.I.T. Press, 1964.

Sprout, Harold, and Sprout, Margaret. *The Rise of American Naval Power 1776-1918*. Princeton, N.J.: Princeton University Press, 1946.

Staley, Eugene. *Raw Materials in Peace and War*. New York: Council on Foreign Relations, 1937.

Steigerwalt, Albert K. *The National Association of Manufacturers, 1895-1914: A Study on Business Leadership.* Ann Arbor: University of Michigan Press, 1964.

Stein, Herbert. *Government Price Policy in the United States during the World War.* Williamstown, Mass.: Williams College, 1939.

Sullivan, Mark. *Our Times: The United States 1900-1925.* 6 vols. New York: Scribner's, 1926-1935.

Tarbell, Ida M. *The Life of Elbert H. Gary: The Story of Steel.* New York: Appleton, 1925.

————. *Owen D. Young: A New Type of Industrial Leader.* New York: Macmillan, 1932.

Thompson, Victor. *The Regulatory Process in OPA Rationing.* New York: Columbia University Press, 1950.

————. *Modern Organization.* New York: Knopf, 1961.

Thorelli, Hans B. *The Federal Antitrust Policy: Organization of an American Tradition.* Baltimore, Md.: Johns Hopkins Press, 1955.

Tindall, George Brown. *The Emergence of the New South, 1913-1945.* Baton Rouge: Louisiana State University Press, 1967.

Tobin, Harold J., and Bidwell, Percy W. *Mobilizing Civilian America.* New York: Council on Foreign Relations, 1940.

Trombley, Kenneth E. *The Life and Times of a Happy Liberal: A Biography of Morris Llewellyn Cooke.* New York: Harper and Brothers, 1954.

Tullock, Gordon. *The Politics of Bureaucracy.* Washington, D.C.: Public Affairs Press, 1965.

Tumulty, Joseph P. *Woodrow Wilson as I Know Him.* Garden City, N.Y.: Doubleday, Page, 1921.

Urofsky, Melvin I. *Big Steel and the Wilson Administration.* Columbus: Ohio State University Press, 1969.

Vauclain, Samuel M., with May, Earl Chapin. *Steaming Up! The Autobiography of Samuel M. Vauclain.* New York: Brewer & Warren, 1930.

Wagoner, Harless D. *The U.S. Machine Tool Industry from 1900 to 1950.* Cambridge, Mass.: M.I.T. Press, 1968.

Waldman, Seymour. *Death and Profits: A Study of the War Policies Commission.* New York: Brewer, Warren & Putnam, 1932.

Waldo, Dwight. *The Administrative State: A Study of the Political Theory of American Public Administration.* New York: Ronald Press, 1948.

Washburn, Charles C. *The Life of John W. Weeks.* Boston: Houghton Mifflin, 1928.

Wehle, Louis B. *Hidden Threads of History: Wilson through Roosevelt.* New York: Macmillan, 1953.

Weinstein, James. *The Corporate Ideal in the Liberal State.* Boston: Beacon, 1968.

White, Edward G. *The Eastern Establishment and the Western Experience: The West of Frederic Remington, Theodore Roosevelt, and Owen Wister.* New Haven: Yale University Press, 1968.

Wiebe, Robert H. *Businessmen and Reform: A Study of the Progressive Movement.* Cambridge, Mass.: Harvard University Press, 1962.

————. *The Search for Order, 1877-1920.* New York: Hill and Wang, 1967.

Williams, William Appleman. *The Contours of American History.* Chicago: Quadrangle, 1966.

Willoughby, William F. *Government Organization in War Time and After.* New York: Appleton, 1919.

Wiltz, John E. *In Search of Peace: The Senate Munitions Inquiry, 1934-1936.* Baton Rouge: Louisiana State University Press, 1963.

Wright, Helen. *Explorer of the Universe: A Biography of George Ellery Hale.* New York: Dutton, 1966.

SIGNED ARTICLES AND LECTURES

Addicks, L. "Presidential Address," *Metallurgical and Chemical Engineering* 14 (May 1, 1916): 475-76.

Anderson, Benjamin M., Jr. "Value and Price Theory in Relation to Price-Fixing and War Finance," *American Economic Review* 8 (March 1918): 239-56.

Ayres, Leonard P. "Statistics in War." Lecture delivered at the Army Industrial College, Washington, D.C., May 2, 1929, *Army Industrial College (1928-1929)*, pp. 326-42.

Baekeland, L. H. "The Naval Consulting Board of the United States," *Metallurgical and Chemical Engineering* 13 (December 15, 1915): 943-46.

Baruch, Bernard M. "The Control of Our Economic and Industrial Resources and Activities in War." Lecture delivered at the Army War College, Washington, D.C., December 13, 1927, *Course at the War College*, Vol. 5 (1927-1928), doc. no. 5.

_____. "Economic Mobilization of the United States." Lecture delivered at the Army War College, Washington, D.C., March 6, 1930, *Course at the War College*, Vol. 4 (1929-1930), doc. no. 17.

_____. "Economic Planning and Government Control," *Memorial Addresses Delivered at the Brookings Institution, May 19, 1933*, pp. 11-18. Washington, D.C.: Brookings Institution, 1933.

_____. "The Economics of Modern War." Address before the Convention of Reserve Officers Association, Indianapolis, April 22, 1929. *Bernard M. Baruch Papers* (Princeton University), *Public Papers*, Vol. 1 (1919-1930).

_____. "Industrial Preparedness." Lecture delivered at the Army War College, Washington, D.C., December 14, 1926, *Course at the War College*, Vol. 5 (1926-1927), doc. no. 6.

_____. "Industrial Support of War." Lecture delivered at the Army War College, Washington, D.C., November 16, 1931, *Course at the War College*, Vol. 4 (1931-1932), doc. no. 16.

_____. "Industry in War." Lecture delivered at the Army War College, Washington, D.C., October 31, 1933, *Course at the War College*, Vol. 4 (1933), doc. no. 7.

_____. "The War Industries Board." Lecture delivered at the Army War College, Washington, D.C., December 2, 1925, *Course at the War College*, Vol. 5 (1926-1927), doc. no. 2.

Beaver, Daniel R. "Newton D. Baker and the Genesis of the War Industries Board, 1917-1918," *Journal of American History* 52 (June 1965): 43-58.

Berglund, Abraham. "Price Fixing in the Iron and Steel Industry," *Quarterly Journal of Economics* 32 (August 1918): 597-620.

Brookings, Robert S. "Industrial Defense." Address at the graduation exercises of the Army Industrial College, Washington, D.C., March 25th, 1924. Reprinted in *Economic Democracy*, pp. 127-56. New York: Macmillan, 1929.

C., W. L. "Concentrating for Real War Work," *Iron Age* 100 (November 22, 1917): 1231-33.

_____. "Government Control of Iron and Steel," *Iron Age* 100 (August 16, 1917): 378.

_____. "Investigation of Cost of Steel Manufacture," *Iron Age* 99 (June 28, 1917): 1560-61.

_____. "More 'Advisory' Help in Buying for Army," *Iron Age* 101 (January 31, 1918): 338-39.

_____. "The Readjustment of Steel Prices," *Iron Age* 100 (July 19, 1917): 168-70.

_____. "Varying Prices for Steel Are Favored," *Iron Age* 100 (September 13, 1917): 604-5.

Chandler, Alfred D., Jr. "The Beginnings of 'Big Business' in American Industry," *Business History Review* 33 (Spring 1959): 1-31.

Chandler, Alfred D., Jr., and Galambos, Louis. "The Development of Large-Scale Economic Organizations in Modern America," *Journal of Economic History* 30 (March 1970): 201-17.

Clarke, E. A. S. "Steel in War." Lecture delivered at the Army War College, Washington, D.C., May 7, 1926, *Course at the War College*, Vol. 5 (1925-1926), doc. no. 16.

Coffin, Howard E. "The Automobile Engineer and Preparedness," *S.A.E. Bulletin* 10 (July 1916): 461-74.

_____. "The Council of National Defense." Lecture delivered at the Army Industrial College, Washington, D.C., September 14, 1932, *Army Industrial College* 9 (1931-1933): 12-23.

_____. "Teaching the Manufacturer of United States Munitions," *American Machinist* 45 (October 12, 1916): 617.

Coffman, Edward M. "The Battle against Red Tape: Business Methods of the War Department General Staff 1917-1918," *Military Affairs* 26 (Spring 1962): 1-10.

Colvin, Fred H. "Latest Advices [*sic*] from Our Washington Editor," *American Machinist* 47 (September 6, 1917): 436-37.

Constantine, Earl. "Organization and Leadership in Business," *American Industries* 18 (May 1918): 18-19.

Crounse, W. L. "Washington News," *Hardware Age* 102 (October 24, 1918): 61.

Crowell, Benedict. "Procurement in War." Lecture delivered at the Army War College, Washington, D.C., December 10, 1926, *Course at the War College*, Vol. 5 (1926-1927), doc. no. 4.

_____. "Organization and Functions of the Industries Board." Lecture delivered at the Army Industrial College, Washington, D.C., January 14, 1925, *Army Industrial College* 1 (February 1924-June 1925), 101-4.

Cuff, Robert D. "Bernard Baruch: Symbol and Myth in Industrial Mobilization," *Business History Review* 43 (Summer 1969): 115-33.

_____. "A 'Dollar-a-Year Man' in Government: George N. Peek and the War Industries Board," *Business History Review* 41 (Winter 1967): 404-20.

_____. "The Dollar-a-Year Men of the Great War," *Princeton University Library Chronicle* 30 (Autumn 1968): 10-24.

_____. "Newton D. Baker, Frank A. Scott, and 'The American Reinforcement in the World War'," *Military Affairs* 34 (February 1970): 11-13.

_____. "Organizing for War: Canada and the United States During World War I," in Canadian Historical Association, *Historical Papers, 1969*.

_____. "Woodrow Wilson and Business-Government Relations during World War I," *Review of Politics* 31 (July 1969): 385-407.

_____, and Urofsky, Melvin I. "The Steel Industry and Price-Fixing during World War I," *Business History Review* 44 (Autumn 1970): 291-306.

_____. "Business, the State, and World War I: The American Experience," in J. L. Granatstein and R. D. Cuff, eds., *War and Society in North America*, pp. 1-19. Toronto: Thomas Nelson, 1971.

_____. "The Cooperative Impulse and War: The Origins of the Council of National Defense and Advisory Commission," in Jerry Israel, ed., *Building the Organizational Society*. New York: Free Press, 1972.

Davies, Joseph E. "Price Control," *The Annals* 74 (November 1917): 288-93.

Davis, Allen F. "Welfare, Reform and World War I," *American Quarterly* 14 (Fall 1967): 516-33.

DeNovo, John A. "The Movement for an Aggressive American Oil Policy Abroad, 1918-1920," *American Historical Review* 61 (July 1956): 854-76.

Eckstein, Harry. "Group Theory and the Comparative Study of Pressure Groups" in Harry Eckstein and David E. Apter, eds., *Comparative Politics: A Reader*, pp. 389-97. New York: Free Press, 1965.

_____. "The Determinants of Pressure Group Politics" in Harry Eckstein and David E. Apter, eds., *Comparative Politics: A Reader*, pp. 408-21. New York: Free Press, 1965.

Etherington, Leonard. "Shoe Business Permanently Strengthened by War's Restrictions," *Printer's Ink* 105 (November 28, 1917): 134, 136-38, 141.

Evans, J. Wainright. "Business Charts Its Course," *Nation's Business* 5 (October 1917): 9.

Fawcett, Walton. "Some of the Clay Products Industry's 'War Profits,' " *Brick and Clay Record* 53 (December 31, 1919): 1132-34.

_____. "War-Time Help for the Clay Products Industry," *Brick and Clay Record* 52 (June 18, 1918): 1126-27.

Fesler, James W. "Areas for Industrial Mobilization, 1917-1938," *Public Administration Review* 1 (Winter 1941): 149-66.

Fish, Frederick P. "Adequate Definition of Terms Absolutely Necessary," in Chamber of Commerce of the United States of America, *Speeches on Antitrust Legislation Delivered at Second Annual Meeting* (Washington, 1914), pp. 35-55.

Foster, Charles K. "Priorities Regulations Are Now Being Modified," *Bulletin of the Merchants Association* 7 (October 21, 1918): 1-3.

Gifford, Walter S. "The Communication Industry of the United States." Lecture delivered at the Army Industrial College, Washington, D.C., December 10, 1936, *Army Industrial College* 13 (1936-1937): 279-89.

_____. "Realizing Industrial Preparedness: An Inventory of Our Resources," *Scientific American* 114 (June 3, 1916): 598-99.

Glad, Paul W. "Progressives and the Business Culture of the 1920's," *Journal of American History* 53 (June 1966): 75-89.

Godfrey, Hollis. "Application of Engineering Methods to the Problems of the Executive, Director and Trustee," in American Society of Mechanical Engineers, *Transactions* 37 (1915): 633-51.

Hall, Henry N. "Edison on Science Applied to Warfare," *New York World*, May 30, 1915, p. 1E.

Haney, Lewis H. "Price-Fixing in the United States during the War," *Political Science Quarterly* 34 (March, June, September 1919): 104-26, 262-89, 434-53.

Hard, William. "America Prepares," *New Republic* 10 (March 31, 1917): 253-55.

_____. "Retarding the Allies," *New Republic* 13 (December 29, 1917): 238-40.

_____. "A Victory for Efficiency," *New Republic* 12 (August 11, 1917): 40-42.

_____. "Wilson Defines Baruch," *New Republic* 14 (March 23, 1918): 229-32.

Hardy, Charles O. "Adjustments and Maladjustments in the United States after the First World War," *American Economic Review* 32 (March 1942): 24-30.

Hays, Samuel P. "Politics of Reform in Municipal Government in the Progressive Era," *Pacific Northwest Quarterly* 55 (October 1964): 157-69.

_____. "The Social Analysis of American Political History, 1880-1920," *Political Science Quarterly*, 80 (September 1965): 373-94.

Himmelberg, Robert F. "Business, Antitrust Policy, and the Industrial Board of the Department of Commerce, 1919," *Business History Review* 42 (Spring 1968): 1-23.

_____. "The War Industries Board and the Antitrust Question in November 1918," *Journal of American History* 52 (June 1965): 59-74.

Holcombe, A. N. "New Problems of Governmental Efficiency," *American Economic Review* 13 (March 1918): 271-80.

Howenstine, E. Jay, Jr. "The Industrial Board, Precursor of the N.R.A.: The Price-Reduction Movement after World War I," *Journal of Political Economy* 51 (June 1943): 235-50.

Howland, Ellis L. "When Business and the Government Get Together," *American Industries* 18 (October 1917): 15-16.

Hughes, Thomas Parke. "Early Government Research and Development: The Naval Consulting Board during World War I." Paper delivered at the annual meeting of the Organization of American Historians, Dallas, Texas, April 18, 1968.

Hurley, Edward N. "Co-operation and Efficiency in Developing our Foreign Trade," American Iron and Steel Institute, *Yearbook, 1916* (New York, 1916), pp. 177-96.

Kerr, Austin K. "Decision for Federal Control: Wilson, McAdoo, and the Railroads, 1917," *Journal of American History* 54 (December 1967): 550-60.

Kester, Randall B. "The War Industries Board, 1917-1918: A Study in Industrial Mobilization," *American Political Science Review* 34 (August 1940): 655-84.

Kevles, Daniel J. "George Ellery Hale, the First World War, and the Advancement of Science in America," *Isis* 59 (Winter 1968): 427-37.

Koistinen, Paul A. C. "The 'Industrial-Military Complex' in Historical Perspective: The Interwar Years," *Journal of American History* 56 (March 1970): 819-39.

_____. "The 'Industrial-Military Complex' in Historical Perspective: World War I," *Business History Review* 41 (Winter 1967): 378-403.

Leake, James Miller. "The Conflict Over Coördination," *American Political Science Review* 12 (August 1918): 365-80.

Leuchtenburg, William E. "The New Deal and the Analogue of War," in John Braeman, Robert H. Bremner, and Everett Walters, eds., *Change and Continuity in Twentieth-Century America*, pp. 81-143. New York: Harper & Row, 1966.

Lidbury, F. Austin. "The American Electrochemical Society in Its External Relations," *Metallurgical and Chemical Engineering* 13 (May 1915): 277-79.

Marshall, Edward. "Edison's Plan for Preparedness," *New York Times Magazine*, May 30, 1915, pp. 6-7.

May, Ernest R. "The Development of Political-Military Consultation in the United States," *Political Science Quarterly* 70 (June 1955): 161-80.

Miller, Spencer. "Organizing for Industrial Preparedness," in American Society of Mechanical Engineers, *Transactions* 36 (1916): 47-54.

Mitchell, Wesley C. "Prices and Reconstruction," *American Economic Review, Supplement* 10 (March 1920): 129-56.

Morrow, James B. "This Breakfast Made History," *Nation's Business* 5 (May 1917): 28-30.

Morse, Lewis Kennedy. "The Price-Fixing of Copper," *Quarterly Journal of Economics* 23 (November 1918): 71-106.

Nash, Gerald D. "Experiments in Industrial Mobilization: WIB and NRA," *Mid-America* 45 (July 1963): 157-74.

Odell, "Notes from Washington," *American Lumberman* 2193 (May 26, 1917): 42.

Paxson, Frederick L. "The American War Government, 1917-1918," *American Historical Review* 26 (October 1920): 54-76.

Peek, George N. "The Development of the Organization of the War Industries Board." Lecture delivered at the Army Industrial College, Washington, D.C., November 7, 1934, *Army Industrial College* 2 (1933-1935): 73-81.

Perry, Barton. "A Plattsburg of the Sea," *The Outlook* 113 (May 10, 1916): 51.

Pope, George. "The Outlook for Manufacturers," *American Industries* 16 (February 1916): 20-22.

Roberts, Merrill J. "The Motor Transportation Revolution," *Business History Review* 30 (March 1956): 57-95.

Robins, Thomas. "America's Industrial Organization for National Defense," *Scientific American* 115 (July 8, 1916): 40, 48-49.

S., O. F. "Evading Government Regulations of Steel," *Iron Age* 102 (December 5, 1918): 1394.

————. "Refusal to Consider Prices Emphasized," *Iron Age* 102 (December 19, 1918): 1513-14.

————. "War Board Did not Consider Steel Prices," *Iron Age* 102 (December 19, 1918): 1512-13.

Scheiber, Harry N. "World War I as Entrepreneurial Opportunity: Willard Straight and the American International Corporation," *Political Science Quarterly* 84 (September 1969): 486-511.

Schelling, Warner R. "Civil-Naval Policies in World War I," *World Politics* 7 (July 1955): 572-91.

Scott, Frank A. Lectures, bound in the Scott Papers, Princeton University: "Address by Colonel Frank A. Scott, O.R.C., before the Army Industrial College," February 1, 1926; "Address to the Graduating Class of the Army Industrial College," June 22, 1936; "Artillery Procurement in 1917," December 10, 1925; "The Development of the General Munitions Board," April 30, 1925; "How the United States Should Plan for Industrial Mobilization," lecture delivered at the Army War College, December 16, 1927; "Improvisation as a Resource in Modern War," April 9, 1926; "Industrial Mobilization," March 19, 1927; "Industrial Mobilization for a Great War," October 29, 1926; "Industrial Mobilization for a Great War," lecture delivered at the Army War College, December 16, 1926; "Informal Address," October 13, 1932; "Organization of the War Industries Board," January 15, 1925.

Sharfman, I. L. "The Trade Association Movement," *American Economic Review* 16 (March 1926): 203-18.

Sherman, Ray W. "Probability Is Dealers Will Get 25% of Cars," *Motor World* 56 (August 21, 1918): 5-8.

Soule, George. "The War Industries Board," *New Republic* 12 (October 27, 1917): 354-56.

Summers, Leland L. "Some Experience while a Member of the War Industries Board." Lecture delivered at the Army Industrial College, Washington, D.C., May 27, 1926, *Army Industrial College* 2 (September 1925-June 1926): 385-91.

Swisher, Carl B. "The Control of War Preparations in the United States," *American Political Science Review* 34 (December 1940): 1085-1103.

Syrett, Harold C. "The Business Press and American Neutrality, 1914-1917," *Mississippi Valley Historical Review* 32 (September 1945): 215-30.

Taussig, Frank W. "Price-Fixing as Seen by a Price-Fixer," *Quarterly Journal of Economics* 33 (February 1919): 205-41.

Thompson, George V. "Intercompany Technical Standardization in the Early American Automobile Industry," *Journal of Economic History* 14 (Winter 1954): 1-20.

Thompson, James D., and McEwen, William J. "Organizational Goals and Environment: Goal Setting as an Interaction Process," *American Sociological Review* 23 (February 1958): 23-31.

Tupper, C. A. "The Spirit of Co-operation," *Cement World*, September 1917, pp. 6-7.

Urofsky, Melvin I. "Josephus Daniels and the Armor Trust," *North Carolina Historical Review* 45 (July 1968): 237-63.

————. "Wilson, Brandeis and the Trust Issue, 1912-1914," *Mid-America* 49 (January 1967): 3-28.

Vauclain, Samuel M. "Some Phases of Industrial Mobilization." Lecture delivered at the Army Industrial College, Washington, D.C., December 11, 1925, *Army Industrial College* 2 (September 1925-June 1926): 116-29.

Wiebe, Robert H. "Business Disunity and the Progressive Movement, 1901–1914," *Mississippi Valley Historical Review* 44 (March 1958): 664–85.

———. "The House of Morgan and the Executive, 1905–1913," *American Historical Review* 65 (October 1959): 49–60.

Wildman, Edwin. "Howard Coffin and the Air War in the Air," *Forum* 59 (March 1918): 260.

Willard, Daniel. "The Advisory Commission and the Council of National Defense during the World War." Lecture delivered at the Army Industrial College, Washington, D.C., May 14, 1937, *Army Industrial College* 13 (1936–1937): 972–79.

UNSIGNED ARTICLES

"After We Have Won the War," *American Silk Journal* 28 (May 1918): 45–46.

"Agreed Prices on Semi-finished Lines," *Iron Age* 100 (October 18, 1918): 944–45.

"The American Zinc Institute," *Engineering and Mining Journal* 106 (July 13, 1918): 81.

"Antagonisms Lost in the War Crisis," *Iron Age* 99 (February 22, 1917): 489.

"Antagonisms Lost in the War Crisis," *Hardware Age* 99 (March 1, 1917): 87.

"Anti-Trust Suits to Be Pressed," *Iron Age* 100 (October 11, 1917): 890.

"The Automobile Field is Well Represented at Washington," *Automobile Trade Journal* 22 (December 1, 1917): 126.

"Better Made Goods One Result of the War," *The Pottery, Glass, and Brass Salesman* 17 (May 23, 1918): 20.

"Bill of Materials," *Engineering and Mining Journal* 104 (December 29, 1917): 1138.

"Business after the War," *Dry Goods Reporter* 47 (September 14, 1918): 7.

"The Business Lessons of the War," *Printers' Ink* 105 (November 14, 1918): 144.

"Business Men for Preparedness," *The Outlook* 113 (June 14, 1916): 333–34.

"The Business of Day-after-Tomorrow," *American Silk Journal* 37 (February 1918): 63–64.

"The Call for a War-Lord," *Literary Digest* 56 (January 26, 1918): 10–11.

"Clay Products Industry is Big Enough to Have a Separate Section on War Board," *Brick and Clay Record* 53 (August 13, 1918): 276–79.

"Climbing the High-Cost-High-Price-Hill," *American Machinist* 471 (August 23, 1917): 344–45.

"Concerning the Coming Year," *Hardware Age* 102 (December 12, 1918): 56.

"The Conduct of the War," *New Republic* 13 (December 8, 1917): 136–38.

"Congress and the Advisory Commission," *American Machinist* 47 (July 19, 1917): 125.

"The Conservation of Industries," *Shoe and Leather Reporter* 131 (September 12, 1918): 20.

"Contracts and Fixed Prices," *Iron Age* 100 (October 11, 1917), 888–89.

"The Controversy over Prices," *Engineering and Mining Journal* 104 (July 14, 1917): 100–101.

"Convince Washington or Be a Non-Essential," *Motor World* 53 (November 7, 1917): 36–37.

"Co-operation Redivivus," *Iron Age* 99 (May 31, 1917): 1324.

"The Copper Producers Gift to the Government," *Engineering and Mining Journal* 103 (March 31, 1917): 547.

"Council of National Defense," *American Machinist* 45 (September 21, 1916): 521.

"Defeat of War Cabinet Bill Predicted," *Iron Age* 101 (February 7, 1918): 423.

"Details of Retailers' Washington Conference," *Dry Goods Reporter* 47 (October 12, 1918): 7, 32, 46.

"Dr. Garfield's Action as Viewed in Washington," *Iron Age* 101 (January 24, 1918): 249.

"Drain Tile and Open Price," *Brick and Clay Record* 52 (March 26, 1918): 577.

"Eliminating the Unessentials," *Iron Age* 100 (November 8, 1917): 1130.

"Ending Government Regulation of Steel," *Iron Age* 102 (December 5, 1918): 1394–95.

"Essential and Non-Essential," *Pottery, Glass, and Brass Salesman*, 18 (June 27, 1918): 20.

"Federal Regulation of Steel," *Iron Age* 101 (January 3, 1918): 98–99.

"Fixing the Price for Platinum," *Engineering and Mining Journal* 105 (May 25, 1918): 976–77.

"For and against Quick Action," *Dry Goods Reporter* 47 (November 23, 1918): 7.

"A Free Market Jan. 1," *Iron Age* 102 (December 5, 1918): 1412.

"Fuel Agreement Big Benefit to Industry," *Motor World* 54 (March 13, 1918): 41.

"Future Government Buying of Steel," *Iron Age* 101 (January 31, 1918): 334.

"Go the Limit–NOW," *American Machinist* 48 (January 10, 1918): 78.

"Government Changes Attitude toward Car Industry," *Motor World* 53 (November 28, 1917): 39–40.

"Governmental Price Fixing Brings Cost Keeping into the Limelight," *Brick and Clay Record* 51 (September 11, 1917): 479.

"Hardwood Manufacturers Provide for Enlarged Association Effort," *American Lumberman*, No. 2275 (December 21, 1918), p. 30.

"How the Priority Board Works," *American Machinist* 48 (January 3, 1918): 7–8.

"Idealism Coming into Its Own," *American Paint and Oil Dealer* 11 (October 1918): 17.

"If Peace Came–" *Iron Age* 102 (October 31, 1918): 978–79.

"In Time of War Prepare for Peace," *American Industries* 19 (November 1918): 7.

"Incorporation of Men's Straw Hat Manufacturers' Association," *American Hatter* 49 (August 1918): 64, 92.

"Industrial Preparedness for Peace," *Scientific American* 114 (January 8, 1916): 54.

"Industrial Preparedness for War," *Scientific American* 114 (March 25, 1916): 320.

"Industry Will Be Organized for War Production," *Pottery, Glass, and Brass Salesman*, 17 (June 13, 1918): 20.

"Is This Industry Non-Essential?" *Motor World* 53 (November 7, 1917): 10.

"Linking Up American Industries for Defense," *New York Times Magazine*, February 6, 1916, pp. 11–12.

"Makers Fixing Prices," *Iron Age* 100 (November 1, 1917): 1076.

"The Matter of Prices," *Engineering and Mining Journal* 103 (April 14, 1917): 683; 103 (June 30, 1917): 1166–67; 104 (August 11, 1917): 271.

"Mobilizing American Industry," *Commercial America* 14 (October 1917): 11.

"More War-Time Eliminations," *The Implement Age* 51 (March 20, 1918): 11.

"National Defense," *Scientific American* 114 (January 1, 1916): 6.

"The Navy We Need," *Scientific American* 114 (January 8, 1916): 54.

"A New Era in the Trade," *Pottery, Glass, and Brass Salesman* 18 (August 29, 1918): 21.

"The New Government Shoe Regulations," *Shoe and Leather Reporter* 132 (October 10, 1918): 21–22.

"New Position for C. F. C. Stout," *Hide and Leather* 55 (March 30, 1918): 7.

"The New Shoe Conservation Agreement," *Shoe and Leather Reporter* 131 (September 19, 1918): 20.

"No Restriction of Passenger Car Output by Government Probable," *Automobile Trade Journal* 22 (December 1, 1917): 125–26.

"No Startling Effect from Order to Curtail," *Motor World* 54 (March 13, 1918): 36.

"Notes from Washington," *American Lumberman*, No. 2193 (May 26, 1917), p. 42.

"Nothing Will be Done to Upset the Motor Car Industry," *Automobile Trade Journal* 22 (December 1, 1917): 140.

"Now is the Time for Red-Blooded Policies," *Printers' Ink* 100 (August 9, 1917): 142-43.

"Now is the Time to Prepare for the After-War Period," *Brick and Clay Record* 53 (August 27, 1918): 364-65.

"Now What?" *Brick and Clay Record* 53 (November 19, 1918): 868-71.

"One Function of Scientific and Engineering Societies in Democracy," *Metallurgical and Chemical Engineering* 14 (April 15, 1916): 405-7.

"Passenger Car Dealers Adding Truck and Tractors to Their Lines," *Automobile Trade Journal* 22 (April 1, 1918): 142-142A.

"Peace and Impending Prosperity Usher in 1919," *Brick and Clay Record* 53 (December 13, 1919): 1128-31.

"Peace and Its Possibilities," *Hardware Age* 102 (November 21, 1918): 70-71.

"Peace and Prices–Pessimists and Panics," *Dry Goods Reporter* 47 (November 16, 1918): 8.

"Peace on Earth!" *American Hatter* 49 (November 1918): 43.

"A Plattsburg of the Sea," *The Outlook* 113 (May 10, 1916): 51.

"Politics and the War Industries Board," *Shoe and Leather Reporter* 132 (October 10, 1918): 20-21.

"Preliminary to Reconstruction," *New Republic* 16 (October 12, 1918): 304-5.

"President Wilson's Appeal to Business Men," *American Hatter* 47 (August 1917): 57.

"Price Fixing and Maximum Output," *Iron Age* 100 (July 12, 1917): 88-89.

"Price Fixing in Doubt," *Iron Age* 100 (October 25, 1917): 1108.

"Price Regulation at Hand," *Iron Age* 100 (July 19, 1917): 142-43.

"Prices for Government Steel," *Iron Age* 99 (May 17, 1917): 1208-9.

"Priority for Essential Industries," *Shoe and Leather Reporter* 131 (July 18, 1918): 21.

"Private Interest in Government Work," *American Industries* 18 (August 1917): 8-9.

"Progress of the Industrial Inventory," *American Machinist* 45 (August 17, 1916): 303.

"Raw Materials and the Cost of War," *American Machinist* 471 (July 26, 1917): 167.

"The Raw Materials Committee," *Engineering and Cement World* 12 (May 1, 1918): 6.

"The Raw Materials Situation," *Implement Age* 64 (June 16, 1917):6.

"Reformation of Trade Practices," *Shoe and Leather Reporter* 131 (July 18, 1918): 20-21.

"Refused to Consider Prices Emphasized," *Iron Age* 102 (December 19, 1918): 1514-15.

"The Regulation of Retail Prices," *Dry Goods Reporter* 47 (October 19, 1918): 7.

"Regulation that May Hamper Emergency Boards," *Hardware Age* 100 (July 19, 1917): 70-71.

"Relations between the Government and Our Industry," *Shoe and Leather Reporter* 131 (August 22, 1918): 20-21.

"Respecting Combinations," *Engineering and Mining Journal* 104 (July 7, 1917): 32.

"Restrict Passenger Car Manufacture 50 Per Cent for Remainder of Year," *Motor World* 56 (August 28, 1918): 5-6.

"Retaining Restrictions," *Dry Goods Reporter* 47 (December 21, 1918): 4.

"Shall the Conservation Program for Hardware Be Maintained?" *Hardware Age* 102 (November 28, 1918): 61-62.

"Standardizing Production," *Pottery, Glass, and Brass Salesman* 18 (September 12, 1918): 20.

"Status of Iron and Steel Advisers," *Iron Age* 100 (September 13, 1917): 631-32.

"The Status of the Engineer: A Symposium," *Proceedings of the American Institute of Electrical Engineers*, 341 (1915).

"Steel Control by Producers," *Iron Age* 102 (July 18, 1918): 161.

"Steel for the 'Unessentials'?" *Iron Age* 100 (November 29, 1917): 1304-5.

"Steel Price Fixing Is Close at Hand," *Iron Age* 100 (August 23, 1917): 500-501.

"Steel Prices Fixed–A New Era," *Hardware Age* 100 (October 4, 1917): 70-71.

"Steel Prices Fixed–A New Era," *Iron Age* 100 (September 27, 1917): 752-53.

"Steel Trade in Confusion," *Iron Age* 100 (September 27, 1917): 758.

"Tampering with the Machinery," *Engineering and Mining Journal* 104 (August 4, 1917): 225-26.

"Ten Munitions Districts Established," *American Machinist* 48 (March 28, 1918): 539-40.

"The Threatened Production Curtailment," *Automobile Trade Journal* 22 (June 1, 1918): 130.

"To Fix All Steel Prices," *Iron Age* 100 (October 4, 1917): 834.

"To Prevent a Shortage of Farm Implements," *Hardware Age* 100 (July 26, 1917): 50-51.

"Trade Associations Dominant in War Organization of Business," *American Lumberman*, No. 2230 (February 9, 1918), p. 28.

"Turning Over a New Leaf," *Engineering and Mining Journal* 105 (February 16, 1918): 345.

"Wanted–a Master Hand," *American Machinist* 47 (September 20, 1917): 518-19.

"Wanted–a National Drain Tile Association," *Brick and Clay Record* 51 (December 4, 1917): 1020.

"War Board May Control Trade," *Dry Goods Reporter* 47 (November 2, 1918): 5.

"War Industries Board and Iron and Steel," *Iron Age* 102 (December 12, 1918): 1450.

"The War Is Over–Now What?" *Dry Goods Reporter* 47 (November 16, 1918): 7.

"The War's Economic Changes," *Iron Age* 100 (November 22, 1917): 1248.

"Washington Aims Destructive Blow at Dealer Industry," *Motor World* 53 (November 7, 1917): 5-8.

"The Washington Situation," *Motor World* 54 (January 9, 1918): 560.

"The Week in Washington," *Motor World* 53 (November 28, 1917): 40-41; 53 (December 5, 1917): 53-54.

"What Commercial Economy Board Is Doing," *Dry Goods Reporter* 48 (November 17, 1917): 5.

"What Happened in Washington about Shutting off the Industry," *Motor World* 56 (August 14, 1918): 42-43.

"What Is the Matter with the War Industries Board?" *Shoe and Leather Reporter* 132 (October 3, 1918): 23-24.

"Widespread Closing Down of Industry," *Iron Age* 101 (January 24, 1918): 249.

"Will Machine Shops Decentralize after the War?" *American Machinist* 49 (October 31, 1918): 822.

"Working Out the Prices of Steel Products," *Iron Age* 100 (October 4, 1917): 832-33.

"Your Major Business," *Motor World* 56 (August 14, 1918): 28.

GOVERNMENT DOCUMENTS

U.S. *Statutes at Large.* Vol. 39, part 1.

U.S. Congress. *Congressional Record*, 65th Cong., 1st sess., 1917, Vol. 55; 2nd sess., 1918, Vol. 56.

U.S. Congress. *Hearings before the Commission Appointed under the Authority of Public Resolution No. 98*, 71st Cong., 2nd sess., 1931, 3 parts, Res. 251.

U.S. Congress, House, Committee on Naval Affairs. *Hearings on Estimates Submitted by the Secretary of the Navy, 1918*, 65th Cong., 2nd sess., 1918.

U.S. Congress, House, Select Committee on Expenditures in the War Department. *Hearings on Expenditures in the War Department*, 66th Cong., 1st-3rd sess., 1919-1921. 15 vols.

U.S. Congress, House, Select Committee on Expenditures in the War Department. *Report no. 1400*, 66th Cong., 3rd sess., 1921.

U.S. Congress, Senate. *Report Regarding Profiteering.* 65th Cong., 2nd sess., 1918, Vol. 20, doc. no. 248.

U.S. Congress, Senate, Committee on Military Affairs. *Hearings, Investigation of the War Department*, 65th Cong., 2d sess., 1918. 8 parts.

U.S. Congress, Senate, Committee on Military Affairs. *Hearings, Reorganization of the Army*, 66th Cong., 1st and 2d sess., 1919. 2 parts.

U.S. Congress, Senate, Special Committee to Investigate the Munitions Industry. *Hearings, Munitions Industry*, 73rd–74th Cong., 1934–1937. 40 parts.

U.S. Congress, Senate, Special Committee to Investigate the Munitions Industry. *Munitions Industry. Digest of the Proceedings of the Council of National Defense during the World War*, by Franklin H. Martin, 73rd Cong., 2d sess., 1934, doc. no. 193.

U.S. Congress, Senate, Special Committee to Investigate the Munitions Industry. *Munitions Industry. Final Report of the Chairman of the United States War Industries Board to the President of the United States, February 1919*, 74th Cong., 1st sess., 1935, Senate committee print no. 3.

U.S. Council of National Defense. *First Annual Report of the Council of National Defense, 1917.*

U.S. Council of National Defense. *Second Annual Report of the Council of National Defense, 1918.*

U.S. Council of National Defense. *Third Annual Report of the United States Council of National Defense, 1919.*

U.S. Department of Justice. *Annual Report of the Attorney General of the United States for the Year 1917; 1918; 1919.*

U.S. Department of the Navy. *Annual Report of the Paymaster General of The Navy for the Fiscal Year 1918.*

U.S. Federal Trade Commission. *Annual Report of the Federal Trade Commission for the Year 1917; 1918.*

U.S. Federal Trade Commission. *Memorandum on War Activities of Federal Trade Commission.* Mimeographed.

U.S. War Industries Board. *Directory. Members of the War Industries Board Organization*, 1919.

U.S. War Industries Board. *Directory of the War Industries Board*, 1918.

U.S. War Industries Board. *Government Control over Prices*, 1920.

MANUSCRIPT MATERIALS

Cleveland, Ohio. Western Reserve Historical Society. Robert J. Bulkley papers.

Columbia, Mo. University of Missouri. Western Historical Manuscript Collection. Enoch H. Crowder papers.

Columbia, Mo. University of Missouri. Western Historical Manuscript Collection. George N. Peek papers.

Ithaca, N.Y. Cornell University. Willard Straight papers.

Memphis, Tenn. Memphis Public Library. Kenneth D. McKellar papers.

New Haven. Yale University. Edward M. House papers.

New York. Columbia University. Henry E. Crampton papers.
New York. Columbia University. George W. Perkins papers.
New York. Columbia University. Frank Vanderlip papers.
New York. Columbia University. Oral History Collection. Eugene Meyer, Jr. Memoir.
New York. Columbia University. Oral History Collection. Gerard Swope. Memoir.
New York. Columbia University. Oral History Collection. Robert E. Wood. Memoir.
Philadelphia. Pennsylvania Historical Society. J. Hampton Moore papers.
Philadelphia. Pennsylvania Historical Society. Ernest T. Trigg papers.
Philadelphia. Pennsylvania Historical Society. Samuel M. Vauclain papers.
Philadelphia. Pennsylvania Historical Society. William B. Wilson papers.
Princeton, N.J. Princeton University. Bernard M. Baruch papers and diary.
Princeton, N.J. Princeton University. Frank A. Scott papers.
Stanford, Cal. Stanford University. Hoover Institute. Edwin F. Gay papers and diary.
Suitland, Md. Federal Records Center. Record Group 61. Records of the War Industries Board.
Suitland, Md. Federal Records Center. Record Group 62. Records of the Council of National Defense.
Washington, D.C. Library of Congress. Chandler P. Anderson papers and diary.
Washington, D.C. Library of Congress. Leonard P. Ayres papers.
Washington, D.C. Library of Congress. Newton D. Baker papers.
Washington, D.C. Library of Congress. Ray Stannard Baker papers.
Washington, D.C. Library of Congress. Albert S. Burleson papers.
Washington, D.C. Library of Congress. Josephus Daniels papers.
Washington, D.C. Library of Congress. Felix Frankfurter papers.
Washington, D.C. Library of Congress. George W. Goethals papers and desk diaries.
Washington, D.C. Library of Congress. Thomas Watt Gregory papers.
Washington, D.C. Library of Congress. James G. Harbord papers.
Washington, D.C. Library of Congress. William Gibbs McAdoo papers.
Washington, D.C. Library of Congress. William C. Redfield papers.
Washington, D.C. Library of Congress. Hugh L. Scott papers.
Washington, D.C. Library of Congress. Woodrow Wilson papers.
Washington, D.C. Library of Congress. Robert W. Woolley papers.
Washington, D.C. Library of Congress. Leonard Wood papers and diary.
Washington, D.C. National Archives. Federal Trade Commission General Records, 1914–1921.
Washington, D.C. National Archives. Record Group 1. General Records of the War Labor Policies Board.
Washington, D.C. National Archives. Record Group 40. General Records of the Department of Commerce.
Washington, D.C. National Archives. Record Group 60. General Records of the Department of Justice.
Washington, D.C. National Archives. Record Group 80. General Records of the Department of the Navy.
Washington, D.C. National Archives. Record Group 94. Records of the Office of the Adjutant General.
Washington, D.C. National Archives. Record Group 165. Records of the War College Division of the General Staff.
Washington, D.C. National Archives. Record Group 179. Records of the War Production Board.

NEWSPAPERS AND PERIODICALS

The American Hatter, 1917-1918.
American Industries, 1916-1919.
American Institute of Electrical Engineers, *Proceedings*, 1915.
American Iron and Steel Institute, *Yearbook*, 1915-1919.
American Lumberman, 1917-1918.
American Machinist, 1916-1918.
American Paint and Oil Dealer, 1917-1919.
The American Silk Journal, 1917-1918.
American Society of Mechanical Engineers, *Transactions*, 1914-1916.
The Annalist, 1915-1916.
Automobile Trade Journal, 1917-1918.
Brick and Clay Record, 1917-1918.
Cement World, 1917.
The Chemical Engineer, 1917-1918.
Commercial America, 1914-1917.
Dry Goods Reporter, 1917-1918.
Engineering and Cement World, 1918.
Engineering and Mining Journal, 1917-1918.
The Forum, 1917-1918.
Hardware Age, 1917-1918.
Hide and Leather, 1918.
The Implement Age, 1917-1918.
The Iron Age, 1917-1918.
The Literary Digest, 1917-1918.
Metallurgical and Chemical Engineering, 1914-1916.
Motor World, 1916-1918.
National Association of Manufacturers of the United States of America, *Proceedings*,
    1915-1919.
The Nation's Business, 1916-1918.
The New Republic, 1917-1918.
The New York Times, 1917-1918.
New York World, 1915-1916.
Paper Trade Journal, 1918.
The Pottery, Glass, & Brass Salesman, 1918-1919.
Printers' Ink, 1917-1918.
The Rubber Age and Tire News, 1917-1918.
Scientific American, 1916.
Shoe and Leather Reporter, 1918.
Society of Automobile Engineers, *S.A.E. Bulletin*, 1913-1916.
Wall Street Journal, 1917-1918.
Washington Post, 1917.

INDEX

Advisory Commission of the Council of National Defense, 12, 40, 41, 46, 56, 89, 103, 133, 193; immediate origins, 36-38; staffing of, 38-40; first meeting of, December 6, 1916, 43-45; weaknesses of, 44, 61; criticizes CND and military departments, 60-64, 268
Aircraft Production Board, 51, 76, 86
Aleshire, J. B., 91, 93
Allen, Frederick, 103
Allied Purchasing Commission, 1, 109, 114; McAdoo's plans for defeated, 99, 101, 102-3, 111
Aluminum Company of America, 199, 201
American Federation of Labor, 10
American Hatter, 127, 255
American Industries, 255
American Iron and Steel Institute, 56, 126, 199-200, 210, 212
American Machinist, 27, 40, 131*n*, 137, 200*n*
American Museum of Natural History, 30
American Paint and Oil Dealer, 255
American Sheet and Tin Plate Company, 200
Anaconda Copper Company, 49, 59
Armsby, George, 120, 200
Army, 10, 52, 62, 63, 64-66, 88, 91, 93, 136, 140, 155; early ideas of, on Council of National Defense, 35, 36-37; relations with Baruch's raw materials committee and cooperative committees, 69-73, 75, 76, 77-80, 82, 117, 152-53; relations with Rosenwald's supplies committee, 73, 160, 179-80; relationship with early War Industries Board, 115, 116, 121-22, 129, 193-94, 196; relationship with WIB after

March 1918, 146-47, 149, 162-69, 179, 182, 183, 184, 186, 187, 189, 190, 197, 199, 222, 224, 241, 249*n*-250*n*, 257-58, 263, 268
Army & Navy Journal, 31
Arnold, Thurman, 270
Associated Advertising Clubs of the World, 21
Authority: business advisers' ambiguity about source of, 4-5; implications of presidential delegation of, 112, 192-93, 227-28; conflict between hierarchial, and specialist, 168-69, 174; distribution of, in War Industries Board, 174, 182; distribution of, between commodity sections and industry, 177, 182; conflict between legal and traditional, 232
Automobile industry, 17, 133-34; as a case study in WIB's priorities program, 204-19
Automobile Trade Journal, 207, 211, 218
Ayres, W. A., 224

Babbitt, C. B., 52
Baker, Newton D., 24, 53, 58, 63, 64, 101-2, 105, 136, 137, 139, 140-41, 147, 150, 155, 160, 247, 255; role in formation of Council of National Defense, 34, 35, 36, 37, 43*n*-44*n*, 45; role in staffing Advisory Commission, 38-39; and General Munitions Board, 64-66, 93; and Baruch, 99, 101-2, 143-44, 145, 259-60; on price policy, 100; and War Industries Board, 101-2, 110, 111, 125, 258; testimony before Senate Military Affairs Committee, January 1918, described and analyzed, 140-41
Baker, Rhodes, 204

THE JOHNS HOPKINS UNIVERSITY PRESS

This book was composed in Press Roman text
by Jones Composition Company from a design by Victoria Dudley.
It was printed by Universal Lithographers, Inc. on S. D. Warren's
60-lb. Sebago paper in a text shade. The book was bound by
L. H. Jenkins, Inc. in Roxite linen finish cloth.

Library of Congress Cataloging in Publication Data

Cuff, Robert D   1941-
   The War Industries Board.

   Includes bibliographical references.
   1. United States. War Industries Board.
2. European War, 1914-1918–Economic aspects–United States. I. Title.
HC106.2.C8   338'.0973   72-4022
ISBN 0-8018-1360-3